BRANCH LINE
EMPIRES

RAILROADS PAST AND PRESENT

George M. Smerk and H. Roger Grant, editors

BRANCH LINE EMPIRES

The Pennsylvania
⟵ and the ⟶
New York Central Railroads

MICHAEL BEZILLA
with Luther Gette

INDIANA UNIVERSITY PRESS

This book is a publication of

Indiana University Press
Office of Scholarly Publishing
Herman B Wells Library 350
1320 East 10th Street
Bloomington, Indiana 47405 USA

iupress.indiana.edu

The paper used in this publication
meets the minimum requirements
of the American National Standard for
Information Sciences—Permanence of
Paper for Printed Library Materials,
ANSI Z39.48–1992.

Manufactured in the
United States of America

Library of Congress
Cataloging-in-Publication Data

Names: Bezilla, Michael, author.
Title: Branch line empires : the Pennsyl-
vania and the New York Central rail-
roads / Michael Bezilla.
Other titles: Railroads past and present.
Description: Bloomington, Indiana : In-
diana University Press, [2017] |
Series: Railroads past and present | In-
cludes index.
Identifiers: LCCN 2017035674 (print)
| LCCN 2017001784 (ebook) | ISBN
9780253029584 (cl : alk. paper) | ISBN
9780253029911 (eb)
Subjects: LCSH: Pennsylvania Railroad—
History. | New York Central Railroad
Company—History. | Railroads, Local
and light—Pennsylvania—History. |
Railroads—Pennsylvania—History.
Classification: LCC TF25.P4 B49 2017
(ebook) | LCC TF25.P4 (print) | DDC
385.06/5748—dc23
LC record available at https://lccn.loc.gov
/2017035674

1 2 3 4 5 22 21 20 19 18 17

In memory of

JEFFREY L. FELDMEIER (1965–2016),

*whose knowledge of the Beech Creek Railroad
and its territory was unsurpassed.*

Contents

Preface

PHILIPSBURG, PENNSYLVANIA, NOVEMBER 20, 1884. CORNELIUS Vanderbilt II, chairman of the New York Central and Hudson River Railroad and one of America's wealthiest men, arrives by special train in this community of some 1,800 residents high on the Allegheny Plateau. Accompanying him on this overcast, unseasonably cold afternoon are his brother William K. Vanderbilt and a host of coal company investors and local dignitaries. They have traveled over the newly constructed Beech Creek, Clearfield and South Western Railroad—a carrier within the New York Central's orbit—from the town of Jersey Shore, 74 miles to the east.

They intend to inspect a site proposed for the Beech Creek's station, to be built in a flat, treeless area called Beaver Meadow, off Presque Isle Street just across the Moshannon Creek from the downtown. The new station, with a supporting roundhouse nearby, represents the spearhead of the NYC's attempt to break the monopoly that the Pennsylvania Railroad has enjoyed in the coal-rich Moshannon Valley for more than twenty years. The monopoly fills the PRR's gondolas with nearly 4 million tons of coal annually and is the largest single source of bituminous riches in the railroad's eleven-state system. Many of the valley's coal operators, merchants, and mill owners see in the coming of the New York Central deliverance from what they regard as unwanted by-products of the monopoly: unreasonably high freight rates and poor car service.

The Vanderbilts' train is unable to reach the Meadow because the Pennsylvania has obtained a court order that prohibits the Beech Creek from crossing the PRR's existing Tyrone and Clearfield Branch at grade.

The Pennsylvania has insisted publicly that such a crossing would be unsafe, but there is speculation that the injunction is intended primarily to slow the advance of archrival New York Central. So the special must halt in the swamps north of town, a half-mile short of the proposed Beech Creek station. The tycoons continue their journey toward Philipsburg aboard carriages provided by local citizens. They go first to the Meadow, then to the Potter House at Front and Presque Isle Streets, where the chill of the day is replaced by a warm welcome from the town's dignitaries and capped by a sumptuous dinner.

By midnight, the Vanderbilts and their associates are on their way back to Jersey Shore, delighted with their enthusiastic reception and confident in their decision to confront the Philadelphia-based PRR in the heart of that road's own territory. The next day, the Philipsburg Journal reports ecstatically on the visit. "The days of grinding, unjust railroad monopolies are past in this section of the country," the editor proclaims. "The crown has been torn from the brow of the tyrant and placed on the head of one who would see justice done to our people."

That bit of theater on a long-ago autumnal day symbolized the beginning of earnest competition between the Pennsylvania and the New York Central railroads for the lucrative coal traffic of central Pennsylvania. It was the first time the two companies battled on a grand scale for the coal trade anywhere. In fact, it was the first time the two carriers went head to head to capture a variety of natural resources—not only coal, but clay, timber, limestone, and even iron ore, all of which were essential to powering America's industrialization. Those resources could be found to varying degrees along the Moshannon Creek, which forms the boundary between Clearfield and Centre Counties high on the Allegheny Plateau, and in the valleys of Centre County to the southeast. There were few if any other locations where the PRR and NYC competed so intensely with one another for such a broad array of nature's bounty.

Within this territory, roughly 40 miles square, the two corporate giants sometimes slugged it out head to head. Philipsburg was ground zero for that kind of rough-and-tumble sparring. At other times, they battled by proxy, positioning short lines as pawns. The New York Central, for example, used the tiny Altoona and Philipsburg Connecting Railroad as a stalking horse for developing coal traffic in the Moshannon Valley's

upper reaches, beyond Philipsburg. Elsewhere in Centre County, where
fertile valleys and forested ridges contrasted with the harsh terrain on
the plateau, other short line railroads carried the NYC's flag. There were
no coal deposits off the plateau. The primary trade in the Nittany Valley,
which encompassed the county seat of Bellefonte, was in limestone, lime,
and iron ore; and the Pennsylvania was the exclusive carrier of those resources to distant markets. Nittany Valley residents professed the same
eagerness as their Philipsburg brethren for a competing railroad. After
the PRR foiled an attempt by the Philadelphia and Reading Railroad
to penetrate the valley in the 1880s, the newly formed Central Railroad
of Pennsylvania linked Bellefonte with the Beech Creek Railroad in
1893. The CRR and its tiny affiliate, the Nittany Valley Railroad, were
creations of Vanderbilt allies. Another short line, the Bellefonte Central,
interchanged with both the Pennsylvania and the Central Railroad but
tried to steer an independent course.

The PRR owed its dominance to the fact that it was first on the scene
in central Pennsylvania. The PRR's acquisition in the 1860s of such fledgling railroads as the Lewisburg, Centre and Spruce Creek, the Tyrone
and Clearfield, and the Bald Eagle Valley rescued those lines from obliv-
ion at a time when local investors were unable to bring them to fruition.
Whether they resided in Bellefonte or Philipsburg, Philadelphia or New
York, investors realized that only rail transport could give economic
worth to central Pennsylvania's natural resources. Railroads offered the
only practical, low-cost way to ship raw materials to the far-away markets that demanded them. Roads were primitive; and while a system of
canals was attempted, it proved unequal to the task. Without railroads,
the minerals and the forests that were so abundant in the region had little
value. At no other place and no other time was Ralph Waldo Emerson's
famous declaration more applicable: "Railroad iron is a magician's rod,
in its power to evoke the sleeping energies of land and water."[1]

The competition between the PRR and the NYC in this small patch
of central Pennsylvania during the late nineteenth century evolved into
coexistence by the early twentieth century. The two lines worked side by
side—sometimes literally—to exploit coalfields, clay beds, and forests.
Still later, coexistence was transformed into cooperation as the two railroads confronted such common foes as stifling government regulation

and competition from trucks and automobiles. Rivalry between the two roads was not entirely absent in the twentieth century, however. As late as 1932, the PRR was maneuvering to neutralize a threat from a possible NYC incursion via the Bellefonte Central Railroad into the Broad Top coalfields of southern Pennsylvania, and beyond to a connection with another trunk line south of the Mason-Dixon Line.

This is the story of how and why the Pennsylvania and the New York Central as rivals came to establish branch line empires in Centre and Clearfield Counties—dense networks of trackage and supporting infrastructure that enabled the two carriers to exploit the area's enormous natural resources with remarkable efficiency. The narrative then moves beyond the competitive phase to show how the PRR and the NYC managed their respective empires deep into the twentieth century, climaxing with the ultimate form of cooperation: the Penn Central merger. And from the Penn Central debacle ultimately emerged revitalized parts of the empires that were emblematic of the revitalization of the American railroad industry as a whole.

Note

1. Ralph Waldo Emerson, "The Young American," 1844.

Acknowledgments

THIS BOOK BEGAN AS A RAILROAD HISTORY OF CENTRE COUNTY, Pennsylvania, intended primarily for a local audience. As the story unfolded, however, it became obvious that an important but largely unknown chapter in the history of both the Pennsylvania and the New York Central railroads played out in Centre and surrounding counties. It was a story that might appeal to readers far beyond the confines of central Pennsylvania.

Branch Line Empires could not have been written without the efforts of two good friends and fellow railroad historians who were involved in the project from the very start. Luther Gette has unstintingly shared the fruits of his many years of research and writing related to the early history of PRR-controlled lines. His drafts relating to those lines form a significant portion of the narrative for the first three chapters, and he contributed to several of the later chapters in important ways. For example, Luther discovered in an obscure archival file the report by PRR civil engineer C. S. d'Invilliers (see chapter 6) that proved crucial in explaining why the PRR did not initially resist the New York Central's encroachment on its bituminous coal territory. He also generously made available notes from his interviews with PRR Clearfield Branch retirees, thus adding detail and color to the narrative of that line's operations in the mid-twentieth century (see chapter 10).

I am equally indebted to the late Jeffrey Feldmeier, who had family roots in the territory served by the Beech Creek Railroad, the NYC affiliate that invaded the PRR's domain. Jeff possessed an awe-inspiring command of nearly every aspect of the Beech Creek. He put at my disposal his massive chronology of the railroad's history, a meticulously researched work that included Beech Creek district operations under successive owners New York Central, Penn Central, Conrail, and R. J. Corman Pennsylvania Lines. He also shared extensive notes, tabular data, maps, and photos that proved invaluable as I tried to make sense of the New York Central side of railroading on the Allegheny Plateau. His passing on the eve of this book's publication was a profound loss for me personally and for all those who are interested in the history of the New York Central System and in the history of Centre and Clearfield Counties.

Gette and Feldmeier read various iterations of the entire manuscript, made substantive suggestions for its improvement, and steered the author away from factual inaccuracies. John C. Spychalski, one of my former mentors at Penn State University and a board member of the SEDA-COG Joint Rail Authority, also read and commented on the manuscript in its entirety. Roger Mayhew, who began his railroad career with the New York Central at Clearfield, Pennsylvania, and retired from Norfolk Southern, provided a wealth of information about NYC, Penn Central, and Conrail operations. He read portions of the manuscript, as did Tim Potts of R. J. Corman Pennsylvania Lines and Douglas Macneal of the Centre County Historical Society.

Gette, Feldmeier, and Mayhew were companions for numerous field trips spanning more than two decades that took us to the most obscure sectors of the "branch line empires." Jim Davy, a native of Monument, Pennsylvania, and author of a delightful history of that community, shared his detailed knowledge of the "brickyard towns" along the New York Central in northern Centre County and led a field trip in that area. The late Bill Hall, who undertook preservation of the history of the Snow Shoe area as a labor of love, contributed to my knowledge of the Mountaintop's railroads and coal companies and shared historic photos. Pat McKinney shared PRR valuation data. Bob Hazleton involved me in exploring the industrial archaeology of Scotia and Tow Hill that added much to my knowledge of the PRR's handling of the iron ore trade in that vicinity. Jack Hicks of Phillipsburg contributed detail to the PRR's story in that locale, and Tom Phillips of Houtzdale was a source of information and photos relating to the area's coal-mining history. I am grateful to Jack Rudnicki and Rick Bates for their research in the archives of the

Pennsylvania Railroad and the Reading Company, respectively. While their findings were intended for earlier writing projects in which I was involved, that information has proven useful in this work as well.

Contributors of photographs are credited along with the photos they kindly made available for this book. Likewise, those people whom I interviewed, or who were interviewed by Gette or Feldmeier, are acknowledged in the notes. I also thank Bill Metzger for his excellent maps, drawn especially for this volume, and Carol Kennedy, for her expert editing of the manuscript. I am indebted to so many people at Indiana University Press in so many ways that I hope they will pardon me if I do not attempt to mention each by name and the capacity in which she or he assisted in making this book possible. While this work is the product of the people mentioned above—and many who go unmentioned but not unappreciated—any errors of fact or interpretation are my own.

BRANCH LINE EMPIRES

ONE

Switchbacks and Rattlesnakes

The Bellefonte and Snow Shoe Railroad

SETTING THE STAGE FOR COMPETITION BETWEEN THE PENN-
sylvania and the New York Central railroads for the natural riches of
Centre County and the Moshannon Valley began a half-century before the two railroads actually met head to head—in fact, before either
company was established. In the 1830s, men of affairs in the county and
the valley recognized commercial possibilities for the area's abundant
reserves of timber, coal, and iron ore. They also knew that these reserves
had no real value unless a practical way could be found to send them
to market. The area was far from any navigable waterway. For several
decades, small amounts of pig iron, smelted from local ore deposits,
were transported to distant cities via pack mule and wagon, but that
effort only underscored the gross inferiority of public roads and private
turnpikes.

A system of canals might resolve the problem of geographic isolation. "Canal fever" swept across Pennsylvania in the years following the
completion of the Erie Canal in 1825. The commercial benefits of that
waterway, which linked New York City with the West via the Great
Lakes, were immediate and abundant. Canal proponents in Pennsylvania eagerly sought a waterway linking Philadelphia with the Ohio River
at Pittsburgh. In 1826 they persuaded the state legislature to finance

construction of two segments: one extended from Columbia on the lower Susquehanna River 170 miles west to Hollidaysburg; the other went east from Pittsburgh 103 miles to Johnstown. The highest ridges of the Allegheny Mountains separated the two canal segments. The aptly named Allegheny Portage Railroad, using a series of inclined planes to scale the rugged slopes, was intended to close the 36-mile gap. East of the Susquehanna, the Philadelphia and Columbia Railroad linked the Delaware and the Susquehanna Rivers. The entire state owned and operated route was opened in 1834 and came to be known as the Main Line of Public Works.

Calls for feeder or branch canals were heard even before construction began on the Main Line. In the spring of 1827, dirt began to fly on the Main Line canal's Susquehanna Extension from a point near Harrisburg up the river to Northumberland, while surveyors laid out a further extension along the river's West Branch to Williamsport and beyond. Business and civic leaders of Bellefonte, county seat of Centre County in the geographic center of the state, watched this activity with great interest. In 1829 a group of Bellefonte promoters commissioned one of their own, James Dunlop Harris, to make a preliminary survey for a canal linking Bellefonte with the canal being built up the West Branch and determine how much traffic might use such a waterway. Harris had supervised construction of parts of the Main Line canal, and was the son and grandson, respectively, of the cofounders of Bellefonte, James Harris and his father-in-law, James Dunlop. Between the state-owned system on the east end and the village of Milesburg in the Bald Eagle Valley, the young engineer recommended a 25-mile combination of canal and slackwater navigation in Bald Eagle Creek. For the 2.5 miles between Milesburg and Bellefonte, the canal would parallel Spring Creek through the gap that stream had cut in Bald Eagle Ridge. Harris estimated annual revenues of $11,500 against a projected cost of $100,000.[1]

Harris's report found a forceful public advocate in Centre County judge Thomas Burnside. A native of Ireland, Burnside had read law in Philadelphia before moving to Centre County in 1804 to establish a practice. As a representative of central Pennsylvania in the state senate and then Congress, he had distinguished himself as a champion of internal improvements. Persuaded by Burnside and others, the legislature in 1833 underwrote an extension of the state-owned canal from the new town of Lock Haven on the West Branch 3.5 miles to a dam on Bald Eagle Creek. The Bald Eagle and Spring Creek Navigation Company was organized to build on to Bellefonte using James Dunlop Harris's survey. Legislators also guaranteed 5 percent annual interest over twenty-five years on Navigation company stock. With Burnside as president, the Navigation by the end of 1838 was able to reach Dowdy's Hole, a pool in the creek just below the village of Curtin, site of a large ironworks. But the company had exhausted its funds, thanks largely to the economic depression that descended on the nation following the Panic of 1837.[2] Dowdy's Hole remained the western terminus for another ten years as the canal eked out a meager existence hauling pig iron from Curtin.

As he tried to round up more investors, Burnside also sought additional traffic for his canal. On occasion, a boatload of coal or lumber was loaded at Dowdy's Hole. Usually such cargo came from Snow Shoe, a township high on the Allegheny Plateau in northern Centre County, a place known to be rich in natural resources yet so remote and sparsely settled that rattlesnakes were said to be the chief inhabitants. In 1839 Burnside and several members of his canal group received a charter for the Allegheny and Bald Eagle Railroad, Coal and Iron Company, authorizing them to build a railroad from Bald Eagle Creek up the mountains' eastern face—the Allegheny Front—to lands they had acquired on the plateau.[3] Included in the group was Philadelphian Jacob Gratz, who with his brother Joseph owned more than 40,000 acres in the area that would soon become popularly styled as the Mountaintop. Attracting investment to build a railroad through the unforgiving terrain of the Front was impossible in hard economic times, and the A&BE entered a period of dormancy.

Prosperity had returned by 1846, when the Philadelphia-headquartered Pennsylvania Railroad received a charter to build an all-rail line from Harrisburg to Pittsburgh, more or less paralleling the Main Line canal and the cumbersome inclined planes over the mountains. Under the leadership of chief engineer and later president J. Edgar Thomson, the PRR built its line between 1847 and 1854, surmounting the Allegheny Front by means of the Horseshoe Curve west of Altoona and a 3,600-foot tunnel under the summit near Gallitzin. Meanwhile, construction resumed on the Bald Eagle Navigation, which reached Bellefonte in 1848 and finally gave ironworks there a low-cost outlet for their products.

The Allegheny and Bald Eagle Railroad stirred to life in 1855, when the Gratz lands were purchased by William A. Thomas, who had been making iron in the Bellefonte area with members of the Valentine family—successors to founding ironmasters Dunlop and Harris—for thirty years.[4] By the 1850s, most of the Valentine family had retired from the iron business, leaving management of the firm to Thomas. The firm of Valentines and Thomas had been bringing small quantities of coal and timber down the mountain for their iron furnace and forge for decades. Using his firsthand knowledge of the Mountaintop resources, Thomas now opened the door to outside investors in exploiting those resources.[5] At least 50 percent of the Allegheny and Bald Eagle's stock was purchased by Philadelphians. With Thomas as president, the A&BE at last had sufficient cash to start construction. The board of directors was a close-knit mix of Bellefonte investors and Philadelphians who had connections with the Valentine or Thomas families.[6] (Thomas Burnside was out of the picture, having died in 1851.) Director Wistar Morris of Philadelphia, for example, married Mary Harris (cousin of canal engineer James Dunlop Harris) who, orphaned at a young age, came under the guardianship of William Thomas. Morris was also a director of the Pennsylvania Railroad.

One of the board's first actions was to retain William Harris, brother of canal engineer James Dunlop Harris, to lay out a 19-mile line from the floor of the Bald Eagle Valley up the mountain to Snow Shoe. William Harris was an experienced engineer; he had worked on the Bald Eagle Navigation survey of 1835 and was the canal company's chief engineer following his brother's death in 1842. Testament to his technical skill was the fact that the Allegheny and Bald Eagle Railroad was fully built and equipped for $269,000, far under the company's $600,000 capitalization, thus giving it great distinction among early area rail projects, which typically were dogged by large cost overruns. The total cost was even more remarkable because it included completion of an additional 4 miles not initially contemplated.

The extra mileage came about in complicated fashion. The Allegheny and Bald Eagle's terminus in the valley was to be at Snow Shoe Intersection. The "intersection" described a projected junction with the Lock Haven and Tyrone Railroad, which was to run the length of the valley with a 2-mile branch to Bellefonte. But the financially hard-pressed LH&T was only partially graded and had laid no track. In 1857 the company was reorganized as the Tyrone and Lock Haven Railroad. The following year the T&LH reached an accord with the A&BE whereby the latter road built 4 miles of line between Snow Shoe Intersection and Bellefonte on Tyrone and Lock Haven right-of-way, then leased it for one dollar for 999 years. The Allegheny and Bald Eagle used its remaining capital to establish mines and sawmills, erect company houses for employees, build the spacious Mountain House hotel at Snow Shoe, and purchase additional lands. The majority of the acreage was held by the railroad's owners in the name of the Snow Shoe Land Association.[7]

William Harris faced the problem of building a serviceable railroad up one of the steepest parts of the Allegheny Front, with a change in elevation of about 1,000 feet from the valley floor. His choice of a ladder of four switchbacks to accomplish the task was hardly a novel solution, even in central Pennsylvania—the Clinton Coal Company Railroad near Eagleton in adjacent Clinton County was then using a six-tail switchback.[8] Harris designed his railroad with great acuity, so that one locomotive could haul back from Snow Shoe the same number of loaded cars that it had previously brought empty up the switchbacks. This was an honored principle of coal-road engineering, dating back to England's Stockton and Darlington Railway of 1825 and imitated worldwide.

Grades against empty coal cars on the scenic ascent of the Allegheny Front were as steep as 2.84 percent (that is, a rise of 2.84 feet for every 100 feet of horizontal distance). Trains leaving Snow Shoe faced a 1.09 percent ruling grade leading to the 1,736-foot summit at a location soon named Rhoads before descending to the switchbacks. With their laborious back-and-forth train movements, switchbacks were practicable only on lightly traveled lines.[9]

Harris sliced construction of the line into two divisions with their boundary near the summit. Contracts for grading were let on March 31, 1858. Crossties were cut locally, while most of the iron rail—a total of 1,727 tons at 45 pounds to the yard—came from the Yardley Iron Works in Pottsville and arrived in Bellefonte by way of the canal. Bellefonte's

Central Press reported that the first shipment, consisting of six boats, each laden with 50 tons of iron, tied up at the Bellefonte canal basin on May 2, 1859. Freight houses were erected at Snow Shoe and Bellefonte. Thomas Burnside Jr.'s shoe store on the west bank of Spring Creek accommodated passengers in downtown Bellefonte until a wood-frame station could be erected north of High Street near the freight house. A short distance south of the station, railroad-owned trackage gave way to a short segment constructed by Valentines and Thomas to reach their iron-making operation. The area's other large iron manufacturer, McCoy and Linn, was conveniently located adjacent to the railroad in the gap between Bellefonte and Milesburg.[10] While grading was still underway, the railroad contracted with James I. Nutting of Pine Grove, Schuylkill County, for forty four-wheel coal cars, ten eight-wheel coal cars, and forty four-wheel lumber cars, all of which arrived in the county seat by canal.[11]

The railroad's board also directed Morris to contract with the Baldwin Locomotive Works of Philadelphia for a 25-ton, 0-8-0 locomotive.[12] Christened *Snow Shoe*, it was a flexible-beam design that was already outmoded when it was built. The flexible-beam truck, pioneered by company founder Mathias W. Baldwin in 1842, was a complicated affair that enabled a locomotive's two forward axles to move laterally but remain parallel. This arrangement eliminated the long, rigid frame typical of a locomotive having eight driving wheels. It permitted locomotives to negotiate sharp curves, undoubtedly a key attraction to B&SS management, but worked efficiently only at low speeds, hence its declining popularity as railroads ran faster trains.

Snow Shoe was a fitting name for the engine in more ways than one. Effective March 24, 1859, the Allegheny and Bald Eagle Railroad, Coal and Iron Company changed its name to the Bellefonte and Snow Shoe Railroad, which was more descriptive of the intent of the enterprise. *Snow Shoe* also caught the public's fancy, judging by the enthusiastic reception the engine received when it arrived partially assembled at the Thomas wharf in Bellefonte on Friday May 27, 1859. It had come by rail as far as Williamsport and was transported the remaining distance by canal boat. It was placed on a temporary track adjacent to the wharf amid general rejoicing. "Bonfires were kindled on the canal wharf, and throats

Figure 1.1. Bellefonte and Snow Shoe No. 3, one of four flexible-beam 0-8-0s on the roster. These Baldwin-built locomotives were well suited to the railroad's heavy grades and sharp curves. *Author's collection.*

were strained with huzzas of welcome to the iron horse," reported Bellefonte's *Central Press*. "His whistle will soon awaken the echoes of these old hills." The whistle surely awakened a good portion of the local population on June 18, when the locomotive made its first trial run. Three days later the railroad operated its first excursion. President Thomas and the board of directors had eleven freight cars outfitted with seats for about 300 invited guests and the Bellefonte Brass Band, who traveled from the county seat to the end of serviceable track at the first switchback, about 2 miles beyond the hamlet of Gum Stump. Passengers were reported to have been "delighted with their ride."[13]

Regular train service began on June 27, 1859, under the supervision of conductor R. J. Downing. He collected $0.25 for the roundtrip, though the train could not go through to Snow Shoe pending completion of a large wooden trestle over the South Fork of Beech Creek. Once the trestle was finished, service to Snow Shoe was still delayed, first by a walkout by track workers unhappy with wages, then by a disagreement with William Fearon in interpreting his contract for the eastern division. *Snow Shoe* finally pulled the first official train into Snow Shoe from Bellefonte on November 9, 1859. A new eight-wheel passenger car went into service in December. The car was simply attached to the freight train, which normally made a daily trip from Bellefonte to Snow Shoe and return.[14]

On a railroad with only one locomotive, isolated from the larger rail network, what to do when any of the rolling stock needed repairs posed an awkward problem. The board foresaw this predicament as early as June 1859, when it authorized the purchase of the necessary fixtures for a blacksmith shop to keep the locomotive and cars in running order. *Snow Shoe* soon needed extra attention, after derailing near Rhoads and chewing up a segment of track in the process. Smiths and mechanics kept the locomotive running more or less daily until April 1860, when the railroad ordered four new driving wheels from Baldwin. Until they arrived (by canal boat), *Snow Shoe* was restricted to running every other day. Baldwin shipped the wheels and also dispatched a traveling engineer to supervise repair work to the locomotive's tender. Such ready support from Baldwin, experienced by hundreds of other customers, helped to make the company America's largest locomotive builder and kept the B&SS safely in the Baldwin camp when the need for additional motive power arose.[15]

The railroad may have deleted "coal" from its corporate name, but it was very much in the business of mining coal. It opened its first mine—a drift, or lateral, tunnel into a hillside outcropping of the Mountaintop's prime coal seam, the 6-foot-thick Upper Kittanning—in April 1859, a little south of what was becoming the settlement of Snow Shoe. To reach the mine, workers built a short branch from the main line and laid it with strap-iron on wood rail. A similarly crude branch connected the company's steam-powered sawmill with the main line. Horses and mules served as motive power on both branches, which were cheaply constructed and sharply graded.[16]

Coal shipments surpassed 50,000 tons annually by the end of the Civil War in 1865. Much of the fuel was destined for Centre County markets, where one of the largest buyers was the Bellefonte gas works. (Inflammable gas released from the partial combustion of coal was piped throughout the town for street lighting and domestic use.) The gasworks was controlled by the Valentine family and attorney Edmund Blanchard, who had investments in numerous local enterprises. He was even a B&SS

director until getting into a dispute over rent owed him for the company offices in one of his buildings in Bellefonte.[17] (Any ill feeling did not last long; he was reelected to the board a few years later.) In 1866 the B&SS declared its first stock dividend: $1 per share for a total payout of $12,000, representing a 2 percent return on the original $600,000 capitalization. Similarly modest dividends were repeated annually for more than a decade.

Coal production increased significantly immediately after the war, with virtually all of it still coming from the railroad's own mines. The astute William Harris had located the railroad line close by additional outcroppings of the Upper Kittanning seam. He and his successor as chief engineer, James L. Somerville, sited at least nine separate drifts. Snow Shoe coals quickly gained a reputation for high quality and were eagerly sought by customers in eastern Pennsylvania, New Jersey, and New York City for domestic heating and to make steam in industrial applications, particularly as locomotive fuel.[18]

Increased coal traffic required additional motive power. *Moshannon*, another 0-8-0 type that was a slightly heavier version of *Snow Shoe*, went into service in the spring of 1863. Its namesake village lay at the very end of the rail line and was reached by the new Moshannon Railroad, in practice merely a 2-mile extension of the Bellefonte and Snow Shoe's line. The Moshannon Railroad, chartered and built by the Moshannon Coal and Lumber Company, offered traffic from several new mines and sawmills. The B&SS operated the railroad and paid the Moshannon company a half-cent for each ton coal hauled over its rails.[19]

The B&SS miscalculated on its next new locomotive, a small 0-4-0 tank engine, *Monitor*, delivered from Baldwin in September 1864. *Monitor*'s job was to make up trains and shift cars at the mines in Snow Shoe. Its 25 tons on four driving wheels proved too heavy for the 28-lb. rail laid on sidings and branches. *Monitor* immediately began to tear up track and was taken out of service. The Philadelphia and Reading Railroad acquired it in December and rechristened it *Ant*. The B&SS then reverted to the flexible-beam design, ordering two more 0-8-0s similar to *Moshannon*. These engines, 3 and 4, arrived in March 1865 without being named and were among the last flexible-beams built by Baldwin. The B&SS thus became a rolling museum of four obsolete locomotives, which were not joined by modern power until the purchase of a 4-6-0 type, No. 5, in 1869 and another, No. 6, in 1880.[20]

For its connection to the outside world, the Bellefonte and Snow Shoe relied on the canal until completion of the Bald Eagle Valley Railroad—successor to the Tyrone and Lock Haven Railroad—from Tyrone to Snow Shoe Intersection at the beginning of 1863. By then the Navigation was having difficulty turning a profit. The B&SS nonetheless engaged in serious efforts to retain the canal's viability, as might be expected since a large segment of ownership was common to both companies. There was also hope that competition between the canal and the Bald Eagle Valley Railroad might lead to more favorable rates for B&SS shipments.

In April 1860, when Navigation stock became worthless after expiration of the 25-year state guarantee (which cost taxpayers $207,000 in interest payments), William Thomas and canal company president Andrew G. Curtin (who would soon be elected Pennsylvania's governor), arranged to transfer one-third of the Navigation's shares to the B&SS in return for completion of a "shipping port" at Milesburg. The details of this pioneer intermodal transfer facility were not recorded, but it undoubtedly included a wharf where carloads of coal and lumber were transferred from the B&SS directly to canal boats or stored dockside and transloaded later. In January 1861 the railroad requested rebates of up to 33 percent on canal tolls, with the expectation that at least 5,000 tons of coal, mostly destined for Philadelphia, would be shipped during the season. Rebating apparently became customary, for in April 1864 the B&SS agreed to help repair and enlarge the Navigation to pass boats of the largest class then in use on the connecting West Branch and Susquehanna Canal. Private investors had organized the latter company in 1858 after a bargain sale of all state-owned canals, whose value had dwindled in the shadow of an expanding railroad system. But the great floods of early 1865 washed away the enlargement plans, along with much of the Navigation and that part of the Bald Eagle Valley Railroad still under construction between Milesburg and Lock Haven. Work quickly resumed on the unfinished railroad, but the Bald Eagle Navigation was abandoned above the mouth of Beech Creek and ceased operating altogether in 1874.[21] Absent the canal, the Bellefonte and Snow Shoe was captive to the BEV's freight rates.

Passenger service did not figure prominently in B&SS operations because the Mountaintop had so few inhabitants. Mining and lumbering encouraged decentralized settlement patterns. Snow Shoe Township had 432 residents according to the 1850 census, yet numbered only 1,410 by 1880 and still lacked an incorporated borough. Other than the hamlet of Snow Shoe itself, where the railroad encouraged growth by giving away town lots to anyone who built a house on one, most of the population was scattered among an array of coal patches.

The B&SS never rostered more than two passenger coaches at a time and had no baggage or express cars at all. It charged riders about $0.03 a mile—no surprise, then, that less than one dollar in every ten in total annual operating income came from passenger revenues. By the 1870s, the railroad was operating two Snow Shoe–Bellefonte round-trips Monday through Saturday, carrying upward of 10,000 passengers each year. Trains departed Snow Shoe Monday through Saturday at 9:10 AM and 2:25 PM, reached the county seat at 12:10 PM and 5:10 PM, respectively, and arrived back in Snow Shoe at 10:40 AM and 5:35 PM.[22] Trains worked at least eight stations en route, mostly flag stops, where the facilities were little more than primitive sheds or three-sided shelters. All scheduled trains ran as mixed trains; freight cars in the consists in effect subsidized passenger operations. The trains' leisurely schedules allowed plenty of time to pick up a flatcar or two of lumber while heading down the mountain or to set out a few empty cars at a mine tipple on the return trip. Cabooses were not used until 1877.[23] It is uncertain what kind of arrangement was made prior to that time to provide shelter for the conductor and rear brakemen on freight-only trains the railroad operated, although indications are that relatively few unscheduled "pure" freights were operated in the early years.

Overseeing operations was Daniel Rhoads, appointed superintendent in October 1860. The 39-year-old Philadelphia native was a devout Quaker and a Whig-turned-Republican, mirroring the preferences of Bellefonte's Thomas and Valentine families. He came to Centre County in 1853 as a partner in a Mountaintop sawmill operation that soon became Smith, Rhoads, and Smith, for many years one of the area's biggest lumber enterprises. Rhoads earned the respect and affection of B&SS employees, who affectionately called him "Dad," a nickname that was to cling to him long after he left the railroad.[24] Under his leadership, the Bellefonte and Snow Shoe strengthened its reputation as an efficiently operated, dividend-paying company that controlled production of most of the coal and lumber that it hauled. According to the railroad's annual reports to the Commonwealth, in 1874 it manufactured 1.5 million board feet of pine and hemlock lumber at its mill near Clarence, employing 25 men for four months as loggers and choppers and for four additional months as mill hands, with 10 men working during the slack season. In 1875, the B&SS worked two mines, employing 114 men and shipping 81,908 tons of coal. Railroad operations engaged another 50 or so employees. In 1878 the company began erecting beehive coke ovens near the mouths of several mines; sixty-five such ovens were in operation by 1880, with production geared mostly to smiths and iron forges in the Bellefonte area.[25]

Steady traffic enabled the company to make significant upgrades to the property. It enlarged the brick roundhouse it had built in 1859 in Bellefonte on a tract purchased from William Thomas, whose family's mansion overlooked the site. A spacious freight warehouse was built nearer the passenger station. The old four-wheel coal cars were supplanted by about fifty larger, eight-wheel cars. In 1866 a new coach was purchased from Philadelphia car builder Murphy & Allison, just then starting to make a name for themselves as manufacturers of fire-resistant rolling stock (an important advantage in the days when coaches were heated by potbellied stoves). The B&SS began replacing iron rail with steel around 1874, and by 1880 had installed about 8 track-miles of steel, including the 4 miles of leased line from Snow Shoe Intersection to Bellefonte. The enginehouse at Snow Shoe burned in May 1875, the result of a great fire that swept through surrounding forests. Engine No. 3 was trapped inside and severely damaged; but it was later overhauled and returned to service and the enginehouse rebuilt. The following year flooding destroyed the timber bridge over Bald Eagle Creek at Milesburg. It was replaced with a prefabricated Howe-truss type made of iron.[26]

A more serious incident occurred on June 11, 1878, when the timber trestle over Miller's Spring ravine, east of Snow Shoe, collapsed under the weight of the morning train to Bellefonte. The train, consisting of the locomotive, one car of shingles, two cars of coal, and a passenger coach,

Figure 1.2. This wooden trestle carried the B&SS over the South Fork of Beech Creek. The PRR replaced it with a steel span in the early 1900s. *Author's collection.*

had reached the middle of the 650-foot-long span when the structure gave way, collapsing downward and forward. The train plunged about 65 feet, the cars landing in line. Four trainmen were injured, along with chief engineer James Somerville and his 10-year-old son. The only paying passenger aboard was William F. Holt, prominent lumber and coal operator from Moshannon and a stockholder in the Moshannon Railroad. He suffered serious injuries and died a few hours later. The B&SS offered his widow $3,000; but she refused and initiated a lawsuit, retaining Bellefonte's most prominent lawyer, James A. Beaver, as counsel. In 1879 Beaver negotiated an $8,000 settlement for Mrs. Holt, who then moved to Philipsburg with her son, also William F. They retained their Mountain properties and eventually became important coal shippers.[27]

The Bellefonte and Snow Shoe's 1865 report to the state auditor general's office indicated eleven wooden bridges or trestles on the line. Miller's Spring was the second longest, being outranked only by the span across the South Fork of Beech Creek. Even before the accident, the railroad had begun filling in some of the trestles or realigning the right of way to make them redundant—possible evidence of concern about the safety of the structures that gave Beaver an advantage in the Holt settlement. Following the Miller's Spring collapse, a route was surveyed that passed around the head of the ravine instead of across it, and temporary trestlework was quickly erected until the new line was completed in June 1879. Freight cars damaged in the wreck were scrapped on site for their iron; the passenger car and the locomotive were repaired. Over the South Fork, where no rerouting was possible, the timbers were reinforced, and more than a hundred feet of trestlework was filled in on either end.

By the late 1870s the early mines, driven into the thickest, most easily recoverable coal deposits, were nearly played out. From an all-time high of about 95,000 tons carried in 1873, the B&SS reported that coal traffic fell to 68,000 tons in 1880. Lumber held strong. The 7,950 tons hauled in 1880 was the highest since 1871. Much of it came from the huge Hopkins and Weymouth sawmill at Clarence, the largest in the entire Snow Shoe district. (The hamlet that grew up around the mill took its name from co-owner George Weymouth's son.) But coal was the Bellefonte and Snow Shoe's lifeblood; as the number of carloads declined, so did revenues. The railroad posted operating deficits in 1878 and 1879 and eked out a modest $1,400 in net operating income in 1880.[28] The days when the rich Upper Kittanning seam outcropped from hillsides and stood as high as the miners who worked it were over, yet plenty of coal remained in the area. The deeper Lower Kittanning lay almost untouched, awaiting investors who had the hefty financial resources to go after it.

Enter the Pennsylvania Railroad. The PRR acquired the B&SS in March 1881 as part of a broader effort to secure long-term sources of bituminous coal traffic. It merged the smaller road into the Bald Eagle Valley Railroad in consideration of one share of BEV stock for two of the Bellefonte and Snow Shoe. The PRR designated its new property the Snow Shoe Branch and for operating and managerial purposes made it part of the Tyrone Division. The deal was ceremonially consummated by PRR and B&SS officials on March 17 over lunch at the Chinklacamoose House in Snow Shoe, a hotel that was operated by one-time B&SS conductor Ed Nolan under contract to the railroad. A special inspection train had journeyed up the switchbacks earlier that day, carrying general superintendent Charles E. Pugh (who would eventually rise to the rank of first vice president), superintendent of motive power Theodore Ely (whose talents as a mechanical engineer were legendary even then), and Tyrone Division superintendent Samuel S. Blair. The larger road's executives assured B&SS rank-and-file employees that they would be retained under the new ownership.[29] Superintendent "Dad" Rhoads voluntarily left the B&SS, however, to engage in the iron-ore mining business in the Nittany Valley. He later accepted a gubernatorial appointment as associate judge of Centre County.

The takeover was fair to both parties, hardly in keeping with the Pennsylvania's reputation for pillaging smaller companies coming under its control. It seems probable that the terms of the sale were influenced by the fact that a number of wealthy Philadelphians held stock in both roads. Wistar Morris was a director of both companies, while Philadelphian Richard Downing has served continuously as B&SS president since the 1861 retirement of William Thomas of Bellefonte. Philadelphians held all of the B&SS board seats save one retained by a member of the Valentine family.

In the 1881 acquisition, the PRR also purchased the Snow Shoe Land Association assets for $150,000, then immediately sold the association's 40,000 acres with accompanying mineral rights to the Snow Shoe Coal and Improvement Company, an affiliate of Berwind, White and Company, a Philadelphia-based coal mining and marketing enterprise. Berwind, White also purchased 3,000 acres directly from the B&SS and 5,000 acres from the Moshannon Coal and Lumber Company, whose Moshannon Railroad was also merged into the Bald Eagle Valley Railroad.[30] Berwind, White had embarked on an ambitious expansion strategy that was soon to make it one of the nation's largest bituminous coal producers. It quickly doubled output at the old B&SS mines to 12,000 tons per month, employing some 300 miners. In June 1882, nearly a hundred men were building the new 4-mile Sugar Camp Branch to reach Berwind, White Mines 1 and 2 in an area north of Snow Shoe settlement known as Old Side. The mines began shipping coal that fall. The railroad transported 235,000 tons of coal in 1882 and 265,000 tons in 1883, straining the capacity of the mountainous line and especially the switchbacks.

As an alternative to the tortuous route down the Allegheny Front, the PRR considered running a new line north from Snow Shoe in the direction of Pine Glen in Burnside Township, then down Miles Run to Sterling Run and ultimately reaching the West Branch of the Susquehanna River near Buttermilk Falls. After bridging the river, the line would meet the Pennsylvania's Susquehanna and Clearfield Railroad, which was building upriver from Keating to Karthaus. This route would have tapped additional coal deposits and eliminated the need for switchbacks.[31]

The need for an alternate route lost urgency when Berwind, White suddenly announced it was pulling out of the Snow Shoe area in order to concentrate on the upper Moshannon Valley around Houtzdale, where the company had opened its first mine in 1874. Coal deposits— particularly the Lower Freeport seam—were more plentiful and accessible there and would better position the company for future growth. Berwind, White consequently sold its Snow Shoe operations in 1884 to the Lehigh Valley Coal Company, an arm of the Lehigh Valley Railroad. Unlike Berwind, White, the Lehigh Valley company was to remain active in the Snow Shoe coal fields for many decades to come.

Notes

1. Harris's report is in the James Dunlop Harris Papers, Centre County Library and Historical Museum, Bellefonte.

2. Bald Eagle and Spring Creek Navigation Co., *First Report of the President and Managers to the Legislature of Pennsylvania, and the Stock Holders* (N.p., 1835).

3. A&BE act of incorporation: *Laws of the General Assembly of the Commonwealth of Pennsylvania Passed at the Session of 1838–1839* (Harrisburg: n.p., 1839), 285–290.

4. Gratz sale: James Gilliland, *Historical Sketches of the Snow Shoe Region* (Washington, DC: Thos. McGill, 1881).

5. *Centre Daily Times* (State College), 25 March 1959.

6. B&SS board of directors minute book, 22 July and 7 August 1857, in Penn Central Collection, Pennsylvania Railroad Subsidiary Lines, Manuscript Group 286.576, Pennsylvania State Archives.

7. B&SS minutes, 3 August and 30 December 1858. The B&SS and all other railroads in the state were required to submit brief annual reports to the state auditor general, which were subsequently published in book form in *Annual Report of the Auditor General on Railroads, Canals, and Telegraphs* (Harrisburg: Pennsylvania Auditor General). Terms of the 999-year lease are in the B&SS report in *Annual Report of the Auditor General for 1878*, 37–38.

8. Samuel H. Fredericks Jr., "Rails along Tangascootac Creek," *Keystone* (Winter 2003): 12. The *Keystone* is a publication of the Pennsylvania Railroad Technical and Historical Society.

9. B&SS minutes, 7 September 1859; Pennsylvania Railroad Snow Shoe Branch track chart, 1955.

10. B&SS minutes, various dates, 1858–59; *Centre Democrat* (Bellefonte), 5 January 1905; John Blair Linn, *History of Centre and Clinton Counties, Pennsylvania* (Philadelphia: Louis H. Everts, 1883), 99.

11. *Central Press* (Bellefonte), 14 April 1859.

12. Beginning around 1900, steam locomotives were classified according to the Whyte system, which counts the number of leading (unpowered) wheels, then the number of driving (powered) wheels, and finally the number of trailing (unpowered) wheels, with each group being separated by dashes. Thus a 0-8-0 had no leading or trailing wheels and eight driving wheels.

13. *Central Press*, 23 June 1859; *Democratic Watchman* (Bellefonte), 23 June 1859; B&SS minutes, 18 June 1859.

14. Linn, *Centre County*, 171; B&SS minutes, various dates, 1859–60; *Central Press*, 14 July 14, 1859; *Democratic Watchman*, 15 December 1859.

15. B&SS minutes, various dates, 1860–61; John K. Brown, *The Baldwin Locomotive Works, 1831–1915* (Baltimore: Johns Hopkins University Press, 1995), 174–175.

16. B&SS minutes, various dates, 1859–62; *Atlas of Centre County, Pennsylvania* (Philadelphia: A. Pomeroy, 1874), 73.

17. B&SS minutes, 13 March and 2 July 1860, and 23 February 1861.

18. Frederick E. Saward, *The Coal Trade* (New York: Coal Trade Journal, 1875), 10–11, and E. V. D'Invilliers, *Geology of Centre County* (Harrisburg: Board of Commissioners for the Second Geological Survey, 1884), 59, 63–76.

19. B&SS minutes, 27 October 1881. Moshannon Railroad board of directors minutes for 1881 are in Penn Central Collection, Pennsylvania Railroad Subsidiary Lines, MG 286.1094, PSA.

20. B&SS minutes, 7 September 1859, 26 March and 14 December 1864, 3 May 1865; Eugene Connelly and William Edson, comps., *PRR-FAX List*, "PRR Numerical Roster, Steam and Electric Locomotives," revision of 29 December 2011, accessed 25 October, 2012, https:/groups.yahoo.com/group/PRR/.

21. F. Charles Petrillo, "The Pennsylvania Canal Company, 1857–1926: The New Main Line Canal Nanticoke to Columbia," *Canal History and Technology Proceedings* 6 (1987): 83–89; William H. Shank, "Pennsylvania Canal Company 1857–926," *Canal Currents* 73 (Winter 1986): 3–4.

22. *Democratic Watchman*, 2 June 1875.

23. B&SS report in *Annual Report of the Auditor General for 1877*.

24. *Commemorative Biographical Record of Central Pennsylvania: Including the Counties of Centre, Clearfield, Jefferson and Clarion: Containing Biographical Sketches of Prominent and Representative Citizens, Etc.* (Chicago: J. H. Beers, 1898), 40–41.

25. B&SS reports in *Annual Report of the Auditor General*; B&SS minutes, 1877–1880.

26. Repairs and improvements: B&SS minutes.

27. Bellefonte newspapers reported extensively on the Miller's Spring trestle wreck. A retrospective is *Centre Democrat*, 14 January 1960.

28. Production and financial information is in B&SS reports in *Annual Report of the Auditor General* for the years under discussion.

29. BEV board of directors minute book, 16 May 1884, in Penn Central Collection, Pennsylvania Railroad Subsidiary Lines, MG 286.551, PSA; *Democratic Watchman*, 4 March, 18 March, and 1 April 1881.

30. B&SS minutes, 16 March 1881; *The Pennsylvania Railroad Company: Corporate, Financial and Construction History of Lines Owned, Operated and Controlled to December 31, 1945*, 4 vols. (New York: Coverdale and Colpitts Consulting Engineers, 1946), 1:366–369.

31. Coal tonnage: BEV board of directors minutes, 19 June and 20 October 1882, in Penn Central Collection, Pennsylvania Railroad Subsidiary Lines, MG 286.551, Pennsylvania State Archives; D'Invilliers, *Geology of Centre County*, 73–74; *Philipsburg Journal*, 5 January 1884. A corporate-sponsored work is *The History of Berwind, 1886–1993* (Philadelphia: Berwind Group, 1993).

TWO

Moshannon's Black Gold

The Tyrone and Clearfield Railroad

THE BELLEFONTE AND SNOW SHOE RAILROAD BUILT FROM THE
Bald Eagle Valley floor to the top of the Allegheny Front, then descended
200 feet or so to the Snow Shoe coal basin. The Tyrone and Clearfield
Railroad, by contrast, built from the valley over the Front and descended
about 600 feet into a much lower basin. Within the basin was Moshannon Creek, which formed the boundary between Centre and Clearfield
counties. On either side of the creek lay enormous reserves of coal and
other natural resources.

The Tyrone and Clearfield had its beginning in a proposal made by
Hardman Philips of Philipsburg at the height of "canal fever." Philips,
scion of a large family of English merchants and industrialists, had been
sole owner since 1811 of more than 100,000 acres of wilderness in the
Moshannon Valley and, to its west, along the upper reaches of Clearfield
Creek. He recognized that a state-owned canal system might provide
an outlet for the large amounts of coal and timber under his control,
yet building a branch canal to reach his holdings high in the mountains
was utterly impractical. So in 1826 he ordered preliminary surveys for a
railroad about 28 miles long to run between his proposed mines at the
crest of the Alleghenies near present-day Sandy Ridge to the proposed
Pennsylvania Main Line canal at Petersburg on the Juniata River. The

best route lay through Emigh's Gap in the Allegheny Front, at an elevation of 2,046 feet, then down the mountain to the Little Bald Eagle Creek
and the Little Juniata River and on south.[1]

By 1830, having obtained a charter for his Philipsburg and Juniata
Railroad, Philips secured the services of Richard Cowling Taylor, an
English geologist and surveyor whom he had induced to settle at Philips-
burg, then a rustic, unincorporated settlement of about hundred people.
Taylor, who had done pioneering work in mapping coal seams in the
Moshannon Valley, in 1831 produced a prospectus for the Philipsburg
and Juniata Railroad. He believed the entire line could be built for as
little as $60,000. After Philips's brother Francis expressed doubt that the
cost was realistic in light of the rough country to be traversed, Hardman
Philips resolved to get a more definitive survey.[2] He hired Moncure Robinson, the engineer most responsible for the final configuration of the Allegheny Portage Railroad with its series of inclined planes having grades
as high as 10.25 percent. Robinson assigned his cousin Wirt Robinson to
the Philipsburg and Juniata fieldwork, completed in 1833. Wirt Robinson
recommended a plan much like that of the Portage Railroad but with
even steeper planes—up to a jaw-dropping 30.3 percent—for lowering
coal cars a thousand feet from Emigh's Gap to the Bald Eagle Valley. The
system's total estimated cost: $277,000.[3]

Handicapped by the financial upheavals of President Andrew Jack-
son's administration, which culminated in the Panic of 1837 and a subsequent economic depression, the project failed to attract investors.
Inclined planes in any case were falling out of favor because of their
slow and dangerous mode of operation. The Allegheny Portage Railroad itself was morphing from engineering wonder to transportation
bottleneck. Philips eventually suffered a series of personal and financial
misfortunes that prompted him to sell his Moshannon Valley holdings
and return to England. Purchasers of his Pennsylvania estate soon failed
in their payments, however; the land reverted to Philips, who finally sold
its last acreage shortly before his death in 1854.[4]

Philips's departure brought a lull in efforts to reach the Moshannon
Valley by rail. That interlude was probably a positive thing in the long
run because it allowed the state's railroad network to mature until an
all-rail route from central Pennsylvania to large eastern markets was

feasible. Key to that development was the Pennsylvania Railroad, chartered in 1846 to build from Harrisburg to Pittsburgh. The PRR began building west from Harrisburg along the Juniata River, paralleling the Main Line in most places and spelling the canal's inevitable doom. The railroad soon came under the leadership of J. Edgar Thomson, a skilled engineer, who as president would also prove to be a brilliant business executive. The PRR track reached Tyrone on the Little Juniata River in September 1850, finally giving Centre County and Moshannon Valley promoters something better than canals as a connection for their own commercial enterprises.

Among those promoters were David I. Pruner, Joseph J. Lingle, and Andrew G. Curtin, all of Bellefonte. Pruner was a building contractor with an interest in securing a prime source of lumber. Lingle was a former Centre County sheriff who had a variety of business interests. Both owned land in the Moshannon Valley. So did Curtin, an attorney whose family was in the iron trade. He was driven mainly by aspirations for political office, but he knew a promising investment when he saw one, as evidenced by his involvement in the Bellefonte and Snow Shoe Railroad. The three men joined with John Mulhallan Hale to establish a steam-powered sawmill on Trout Run, a tributary to the Moshannon Creek in Rush Township. Hale, a native of Lewistown (an iron-making and railroad center in the Juniata River valley) and sometime Bellefonte resident, was at that time living in Philadelphia, engaged primarily in insurance underwriting, a line of business that acquainted him with many of that city's financial elite. The four partners were cutting virgin white pine and hemlock on 2,000 acres purchased from the Philips estate. They envisioned opening coal mines after making a quick profit in lumber. To ensure success, they needed a railroad. It cost as much to wagon lumber over the mountain to Tyrone—$4.50 per 1,000 board feet—as it did to ship it the rest of the way to Philadelphia on the railroad.[5]

The partners obtained a state charter on March 23, 1854, for the Tyrone and Clearfield Railroad. Favorable stories planted in the local press and in Philadelphia newspapers encouraged stock sales.[6] By June 1854, the Tyrone and Clearfield had sufficient funds to hire civil engineer James E. Montgomery of Philadelphia to make the preliminary surveys. The 27-year-old Montgomery, a Princeton graduate, had little practical engineering experience but he just happened to be an investor in the T&C and a grandson of Henry Philips, Hardman's older brother and the founder of Philipsburg. He got the job over the objections of David Pruner, who feared he might be too closely allied with the Philips interests.[7]

Before Montgomery left Philadelphia in July 1854, he got some advice from J. Edgar Thomson. Exactly how the two came to meet is lost to history, but Thomson told him to go up the mountain by the shortest route, even if it would make a heavy grade.[8] Thomson himself had used that prescription for the Alleghenies, running the PRR main line west of Altoona around Horseshoe Curve and up through Sugar Run Gap on a stiff 1.86 percent ruling grade. That line opened in February 1854.

Montgomery took to the field in July 1854. The Allegheny wilderness was formidable. "While in the mountains we had a pretty rough time," recounted Montgomery's assistant, Thomas McNair. "The second day, on returning to quarters, a storm came up, our guide got lost, and we were from 5 ½ to 9 PM reaching shelter. Rattlesnakes were quite plentiful—the first day we killed two and averaged one a day from that time forward."[9] Recalling Thomson's dictum, Montgomery ran at least three lines down the steep-sided slopes southwest of Emigh's Gap directly toward Tyrone, confidently predicting that he could secure an ascent not exceeding 1.5 percent.[10] On the strength of that forecast, meetings were held and more stock subscribed. On May 5, 1856, the T&C was formally organized at a gathering of investors in Philipsburg, the Moshannon Valley's largest population center. Bellefonte attorney and banker James Tracy Hale, the road's largest stockholder and a cousin of John Mulhallan Hale, was elected president. A Towanda native, James T. Hale had moved to Lewistown after his father died to live with relatives and read law. He became a familiar figure before the court throughout the central counties of the state and arguably was the most prominent of the Hale clan.[11]

In the meantime, David Pruner had purchased land on which the new town of Osceola would be platted. The town's name honored the great Seminole chief—it was not uncommon to recognize Native Americans with place names at that time—while the streets were named for the sawmill partners and their wives. Simultaneous with Pruner's activities,

John M. Hale organized a family-owned firm, Morgan, Hale & Company, to purchase the entire remainder of the Philips estate of 36,400 acres. Included in the firm were John's cousin James T. Hale, and brothers Reuben and Elias Hale. The "Morgan" in the firm belonged to John M. Hale's brother-in-law George Morgan of New York, and George's cousin, banker Edwin D. Morgan, who became New York's governor in 1859. The New York connection was aimed at developing additional investors and markets for the railroad in America's largest city.[12] Morgan, Hale & Company made an initial investment of $30,000 in T&C stock and thereby largely controlled the railroad's early fortunes.

By July 1856 Montgomery had located only 5 miles of line, and his projected grades were becoming steeper. J. Edgar Thomson followed events closely, eager to have his own PRR receive the considerable traffic that might come to it from the Moshannon Valley. In October he advised the T&C directors that even a 2.5 percent grade up the Allegheny Front would be acceptable, provided the line had only gentle curvature.[13] However, Montgomery proposed an incredibly tight 22-degree curve near the headwaters of Mount Pleasant Run, which had carved a cleft known as Emigh's Gap in the face of the Allegheny Front. His assistant, Thomas Westcott, calculated that moving the alignment further downstream would ease the curvature, though requiring more fill—a hundred feet high at its midpoint over the ravine—to maintain a practical grade. The directors approved Westcott's alternative, but it was still a fearsome curve: its bend of more than 17 degrees made it nearly twice as sharp as the Horseshoe Curve's 9 degrees in about half the latter's 2,375-foot length. Known early as the Deep Fill, the alignment over Mount Pleasant Run eventually gained legendary status among railroaders and locals alike as the Big Fill.[14]

The T&C's final line climbed 1,000 feet in its 10-mile ascent from Bald Eagle Valley to the summit (2,043 feet above sea level) of the Alleghenies, featuring grades as severe as 2.86 percent and nine curves sharper than 9 degrees.[15] From Vail on the valley floor, the T&C followed Vanscoyoc Run for several miles before it made a sweeping curve across the stream and headed for Emigh's Gap. The ascent through Taylor and then Rush Townships remained unforgiving. The country was heavily forested and nearly devoid of human habitation. Indeed, Rush

DEEP FILL NEAR TYRONE, PA.

Figure 2.1. The Tyrone and Clearfield's signature engineering work, the Big Fill, or Deep Fill as it was initially known. This postcard view looks upgrade. *Author's collection.*

was among Pennsylvania's largest townships by area yet had fewer than 600 residents, most of them clustered around Philipsburg. Black bears, timber rattlers, and even a few mountain lions roamed freely.

On the other side of the mountain, Montgomery had planned a 1.0 percent descent along Cold Stream directly to Philipsburg. Pruner, Curtin, Lingle, and John M. Hale vetoed this recommendation because it would miss their Trout Run sawmill by several miles and bypass the new townsite of Osceola, where they were selling lots. After much discussion, Montgomery agreed to a descent along Trout Run rather than Cold Stream, with Osceola at the bottom of a grade that exceeded 2 percent.[16] The decision resolved short-term issues, but by creating a daunting slope rising against heavily laden coal trains, it had unfortunate long-term consequences.

The general contract to grade the first 20 miles of the T&C, from Vail to Osceola and on to Philipsburg, went to the firm of Brady, Maurer, and Lingle (the same Joseph Lingle who was on the railroad's board) in November 1856 for $90,000. By mid-December shanties were being built all along the line; soon thereafter, about 300 Irish laborers were reported to be working for the various subcontractors hired by Brady. Campbell Brothers of Philipsburg built the Big Fill, their own force of Irishmen depending on picks and shovels and mules and wagons to do the job. The Fill went $15,000 over budget at a time when a laborer typically earned about a dollar a day. The overrun was thus equivalent to employing a force of fifty men full-time for a year.[17]

By the time the economic depression known as the Panic of 1857 swept over the land, about two-thirds of the grading had been completed. Early in 1858, the T&C board learned of a total cost overrun of $28,000 above the original projection of $90,000. Chief engineer James Montgomery lost his job in the wake of that revelation. In his place the board hired PRR civil engineer George W. Leuffer, who retained Thomas Westcott as the project's resident engineer. Hoping to save money and revitalize construction, Leuffer voided the contract with Brady, Maurer, and Lingle (who had already shut down, apparently because they had bid too low and were losing money) and gave the work directly to the subcontractors. Raising new money in the financial markets or by local stock sales proved impossible, so in 1859 the T&C directors went to the Pennsylvania Railroad for help. After considering several proposals, the PRR chose to take the majority of a $225,000 bond issue in exchange for a first mortgage. The infusion of new money enabled tracklaying to begin.[18]

More construction than originally contemplated was forced on the T&C by the failure of the Tyrone and Lock Haven Railroad, over whose track from Vail to Tyrone the T&C planned to obtain rights in order to reach a junction with the PRR main line. With that 3-mile segment not even graded, the T&C surveyed and built its own line into Tyrone. Track work all along the railroad nearly came to a halt after the onset of the Civil War in 1861 reduced the number of laborers to just a few dozen.

Subcontractor David Edmiston finally completed laying track over the 15 miles from Tyrone up to the summit and down the other side as far as the hamlet of Sandy Ridge in January 1862. For the next six months, Edmiston operated the line using his own battered rolling stock and a light 4-4-0 locomotive rented from the PRR for $5 a day, hauling the road's first shipments of lumber and coal, and its first passengers, who rode in a primitive accommodation car attached to short freight trains. At Sandy Ridge there was a stagecoach connection for Philipsburg and Clearfield.[19]

Adding to the complexity was a change in the T&C's leadership. In 1858 James T. Hale won election to Congress (he would be twice reelected) and stepped down from the company's presidency. Andrew Curtin succeeded him but soon vacated the post—he was elected governor in the fall of 1860. James T. Hale's cousin Reuben Hale then assumed the presidency; but with the outbreak of the Civil War Curtin tapped him to be Pennsylvania's quartermaster general. He remained the T&C's president but had little time to devote to company affairs. Early in 1862, he named William A. Purse his general factotum for the railroad. Purse had worked during the first year of the Civil War as a field agent for the quartermaster general's office. Hale must have figured that his experience in dealing with balky contractors and provisioners would come in handy on the new railroad. Purse arrived in early April, just in time to deal with two weeks of heavy rain that washed out much T&C trackage in the Tyrone area. He then began a walking tour of the unfinished 4-mile line from Osceola to Sandy Ridge, only to cut short his inspection and beat a hasty retreat after he encountered two large bears.[20] Bears proved to be the least of Purse's difficulties. Chief engineer George Leuffer was supervising numerous other PRR construction projects and made few appearances on the T&C. When Leuffer did show up, Purse complained to General Hale that he exaggerated the amount of work he examined and overcharged the T&C for materials supplied by PRR.[21]

The rail labor market was tight—the Bald Eagle Valley Railroad (successor to the T&LH) and the PRR itself were under construction and recruiting able-bodied men, as was the Union army. At the very time Purse and contractor David Edmiston were beating the bushes for workers, the Army of the Potomac was massing on the Virginia Peninsula, preparing for its first prolonged engagement with the Confederate Army. Purse and Edmiston between them could round up barely two dozen employees, who were constantly threatening to leave unless paid more. On May 16, 1862, after a short walkout, Purse finally raised wages in an attempt to compete with Edmiston, who was paying $1.12 a day, and the BEV, paying $1.28. In June 1862, Purse asked General Hale to see if there were any Irish track workers among Confederate prisoners being held at Harrisburg. The quartermaster general may have sent some prisoners, for by August Purse had some forty men. In October, he rejected Hale's suggestion that black laborers be hired, fearing all his white employees would quit.

In an attempt to raise revenues for his cash-strapped railroad, Purse in May 1862 suggested a fifty-cent surcharge on all cars handled between Vail and Tyrone. His accounts show that this traffic included rail and supplies the PRR was shipping via Tyrone for the Bald Eagle Valley Railroad and coal that the T&C was hauling from John Nuttall's mine north of Sandy Ridge, the first to be opened on the line. Nuttall had leased the mine just then to Robert Lemon, a Hollidaysburg coal merchant. Nuttall, who had mined coal in his native England, had emigrated to New York in 1849 to work in the textile industry while saving enough money to buy his own mine. He and several partners had purchased land around Sandy Ridge in 1856 on the assumption that the coming of the railroad would make their fortune. They opened a drift into a hillside coal seam and built Nuttallville, a collection of houses and other structures clustered around the mine. The lease to Lemon in 1861 seems to have been a short-term expedient to develop a cash flow while Nuttall was preoccupied elsewhere.[22]

Lemon was operating as early as January 1862 and shipping coal to the US Navy,[23] ravenous in its demand for black diamonds since its vast expansion to cover the blockade of Southern ports instituted under Lincoln's secretary of the navy, Gideon Welles—who just happened to be a brother-in-law of Reuben and John M. Hale, and an investor in Morgan, Hale & Company. Lemon shipped 7,239 tons of steam coal in 1862, the first and only coal tonnage the T&C carried that year.[24]

By the end of 1862 Philadelphian Robert Hare Powel had bought out Nuttall and his partners and ended Lemon's lease. Powel was descended from a family of impeccable social and financial credentials and had already used his wealth and connections to open the rich Broad Top coalfield about 50 miles to the south in Huntingdon County, where he also established a large iron-smelting works. Those enterprises demanded most of his attention for the moment, so John Nuttall agreed to manage operations at Nuttallville, or Powelton as the village was rechristened. Within two years, the Powelton mine was shipping as much as 4,000 tons of coal per month.[25]

Meanwhile, General Reuben Hale, desperate to save his shaky railroad, arranged to lease it to the Pennsylvania Railroad for operation, under terms that gave the PRR 75 percent of gross earnings—the earnings to be computed by the larger road.[26] On July 2, 1862, the day the lease took effect, PRR superintendent of branch lines James Lewis arrived in Tyrone and with William Purse toured the T&C aboard a special train. Apparently Lewis was appalled with the poor physical condition of the railroad—bridge abutments still consisted of temporary wood cribbing rather than stone, spindly wooden trestles carried the track where it should have rested on earthen fill, poor drainage guaranteed washouts after heavy rains, and on and on. Transfer of the T&C to PRR operational control was delayed until assistant to the president George Roberts could come from Philadelphia as J. Edgar Thomson's proxy and see the property for himself.

Roberts, one of the few professionally trained civil engineers who was involved with the T&C's construction, arrived in Tyrone on July 22 to go over the road with chief engineer Leuffer. At the end of the day, he dashed off a letter to his boss, declaring that "it was not claimed on the part of any person present that in its present condition it could be considered safe for transportation use." He noted that the T&C had not even built an enginehouse, water tank, or side tracks at Tyrone, which was to be the road's base of operations. At the Big Fill, "the embankment was barely wide enough to support the ties, which in many cases projected beyond and over the sides of the embankment when it was nearly one hundred feet high." He went on to give a detailed summation of unacceptably narrow cuts and embankments, weak trestling, inadequate provision for runoff, insufficient ballast, and all the other things that Lewis said were wrong with the T&C. To make things right, Roberts estimated, would cost about $23,000. Still, he decided that the Pennsylvania would take immediate possession of the road and begin making the needed improvements, "which would of course be charged to the T&C R. R. as construction expenses." He made no mention of how the T&C's poor condition had apparently escaped notice by George Leuffer. The T&C's executive committee was less forgiving and accepted Leuffer's resignation as chief engineer two days later.[27]

The PRR took over operations from contractor Edmiston on July 23, 1862, when superintendent Lewis finally put in service a regulation PRR passenger coach and a locomotive. By mid-August the engine was making two daily roundtrips up to Sandy Ridge and Powelton from Tyrone, hauling the coach and a maximum load of about seven 10-ton capacity coal or lumber cars each way.

Lewis told Purse that he had no need for a superintendent of transportation on the T&C but would approve his appointment as supervisor of track and construction for $60 per month. Purse accepted but grumbled about the salary to Reuben Hale, who gave him a supplement plus rent for his house in Tyrone. Hale believed Purse would be "first rate to watch & catch shingle thieves & to talk lumber & cost to speculators."[28] During the following year, Purse was constantly trying to light a fire under Edmiston, who he believed was proceeding with unwarranted deliberation in extending the line to Philipsburg. During his forays on the mountain, Purse discovered that the contractor—even after Roberts and Lewis had inspected the road—was skimping on labor and materials, using such time-honored shortcuts as substituting yellow clay from nearby ditches as ballast instead of the specified gravel. He also found that Edmiston's men had spiked only the joints and centers of the rail along one section of track near the Big Fill, inviting a serious derailment.

In spite of these obstacles, Purse had things in fair shape by the spring of 1863, with a new wood-frame freight station at Sandy Ridge and sturdy oak ties fully spiked under the rails around the Big Fill. The track between Powelton and Osceola was finished by late summer of 1862; but it did not open for service, as the T&C, Edmiston, and the PRR wrangled over the condition of the road's infrastructure. Purse experimented with a 30-ton engine on the Tyrone–Powelton run, but it tore up the 45-lb. iron rail and had to be withdrawn. He was sure the T&C would never become a paying proposition until heavier rail was laid all the way to Osceola, permitting the use of more powerful locomotives and heavier cars. In June 1863, before those improvements could be implemented, Purse suddenly left Tyrone for a navy paymaster's job secured through the influence of General Hale and Navy Secretary Welles.[29]

Reuben Hale's death on July 2, 1863, from complications of tuberculosis, opened the door to tighter control of the road by the PRR. George Roberts succeeded him as T&C president, and the Pennsylvania proceeded to pack the smaller road's board of directors with its own operatives. Roberts hastened a program of improvements that included passing sidings at Vail, Summit, and Powelton; wye tracks for turning engines at Summit and Powelton; water stations at Gardner and the Fill; 64-lb. iron rails on curves; and general upgrades of ballast and drainage as identified in his earlier inspection trip. Under construction at Tyrone were a fifteen-stall brick enginehouse, turntable, machine shop, and water station, and plans for a freight car repair shop were being drawn up—all in anticipation that Tyrone would be the operational hub for both the T&C and the Bald Eagle Valley line to Bellefonte and Lock Haven. Sidings for storing coal cars heading to and from the T&C were added on Tyrone's east side.

Roberts and the new board demanded that superintendent Lewis crack the whip over David Edmiston to finish the road to Philipsburg, which lay about 4 miles beyond Osceola. Following additional mortgages of $35,000 and $50,000 to finance construction, track was finally in place to Philipsburg by October 21, 1863, when the first visitor of note, Governor Andrew G. Curtin, arrived by special train. Curtin and his entourage were feted to a sumptuous dinner at the Conrad House. The governor (who had a sizable investment in the fledgling Osceola Coal Company) noted that Philipsburg was "looking up," with several new brick buildings in the downtown and an air of optimism among its residents. In fact, the following year both Philipsburg and Osceola were incorporated as boroughs—Philipsburg with roughly 800 residents and Osceola about half that.[30]

Work on the Philipsburg passenger station got under way in December on a lot at the northeast corner of Presquisle and Water Streets, and just down the track from the station construction began on a two-stall enginehouse and iron turntable. A published schedule effective December 17 showed a passenger train making a Monday through Saturday round-trip from Tyrone, in charge of the "accommodating and urbane" Dan Wood as conductor. The train departed Tyrone at 8:40 AM and arrived in Philipsburg at 11:10 AM. The return trip left at 2:00 PM with a 4:30 PM arrival back in Tyrone.[31] The passenger train superseded the twice-daily mixed passenger and freight trains that superintendent Lewis had inaugurated earlier that year.

Although Philipsburg had an enginehouse, Osceola was the strategically more important location. Situated on the Clearfield County side of the Moshannon Creek near its juncture with Trout Run, the town was growing rapidly, now that the coming of the railroad made possible the development of nearby natural resources. The T&C built passenger and freight stations on the Centre County side of the creek, and Tyrone-based engines and crews handled trains from Osceola heavily laden with coal and forest products. Osceola also was at the junction of the T&C main track and the Moshannon Branch, which over the next twenty years was extended deep into Clearfield County and became by far the largest originator of coal traffic on the T&C.

One of the first mines to be served by the Moshannon Branch was located about 2 miles beyond Osceola along Coal Run and was opened by the Decatur Coal Company in 1866. The company's investors included J. Edgar Thomson and other PRR executives; they hired John Nuttall away from the Powel organization as superintendent of mine operations. A short spur linked the Decatur mine with the Moshannon Branch proper at a point designated Coal Run Junction. The Decatur mine was short-lived. The coal bed turned out to be heavily faulted; the sudden rising or falling of the seam meant it could not be easily or cheaply mined by then-current methods. The mine closed in November 1868, and the spur was torn up soon thereafter (only to be reinstalled and extended to new mines in the 1870s as the Coal Run Branch). Meanwhile the PRR continued to push the main stem of the Moshannon Branch westward. In 1869 it reached Sterling, nearly 5 miles from Osceola, where the Powelton Coal and Iron Company opened two mines along Goss Run.[32]

After the Decatur mine's closure, the irrepressible Nuttall moved to Philipsburg and resumed mining independently. Northeast of the town, on the Clearfield County side of the Moshannon Creek, Nuttall opened Decatur mines Nos. 1 and 2 near Morrisdale, shipping his first carloads on the newly opened Philipsburg Branch, a spur about 2 miles long that ran mostly through marshland before joining the T&C in downtown Philipsburg. The Philipsburg Coal, Iron and Oil Company had built part of the branch to reach several of the company's coal mines on the east side of town. The coal proved to be dirty, however, and failed to find a market. In 1866 the PCI&O sold the branch to the T&C, which reoriented it in the direction of Morrisdale and a more promising coal bed tapped by Nuttall and the newly formed Morrisdale Coal Company.[33]

Forest products ranked second in value to coal as a revenue source for the T&C. Many of the logs that were to be cut into lumber ended up at the "Big Mill" in Osceola, where they were stored in a dam on the Moshannon Creek. In anticipation of the railroad's arrival, the mill had accumulated a large backlog of sawed and stacked lumber under two separate owners between 1860 and 1862, when it was acquired by John Lawshe and Allison White, both of Jersey Shore, Clinton County. Lawshe and White were eager to begin shipping their accumulated inventory right away, but the track into Osceola was not yet in service. Early in 1863, they convinced contractor Edmiston to bring down some flatcars from Sandy Ridge to be loaded by wagons from the mill for transport to the main line at Tyrone. When trains started running regularly to Osceola late in the year, rail was laid on top of a long, 18-foot-high wooden trestle that was built across the creek and adjacent lowlands to link the main track with the Big Mill. The T&C soon filled in this structure, using it as the beginning of the Moshannon Branch. While Lawshe and White's mill was the largest in the area, within a few years of the coming of the railroad there were at least a dozen other, smaller sawmills up and down the Moshannon Valley between Philipsburg and Sterling.[34]

The prosperity wrought by the exploitation of natural resources did not sweep evenly through the valley. With the Civil War driving demand steadily upward, shippers complained they could not obtain an adequate

Figure 2.2. "The Big Mill," a steam-powered sawmill on the Moshannon Creek at Osceola Mills, could produce 8 million board feet of lumber each week. It ceased operation by 1891 with the exhaustion of nearby white pine forests. *Osceola Mills Community Historical Foundation.*

number of empty cars from the PRR. Robert Hare Powel, the largest coal shipper, also was the most vociferous in expressing his frustration. He paid the Pennsylvania a premium of nearly $5,000 a year—in addition to the railroad's normal transportation rate—to guarantee an adequate car supply for his T&C and Broad Top mines. Yet, Powel asserted, coal still piled up at his mines because there were no cars to be had, as the railroad reported one delay after another in providing empties.[35] Other coal shippers voiced similar complaints, and also took issue with the PRR's practice of changing transportation rates virtually without warning. Mines that contracted to sell their coal at a fixed price could have their profits undercut—or wiped out—if the railroad suddenly jacked up the cost of transportation after the contracts were signed.

Shipper discontent led to hearings before the state senate's judiciary committee in 1867. Some witnesses charged that car shortages and rate fluctuations were part of the Pennsylvania's plan to take over the T&C completely by intentionally depressing the smaller road's earnings and inflating its costs. Other witnesses, after describing how shortages of empty cars disrupted their operations, noted that one producer, the Decatur mine, always seemed to receive an adequate number of cars to load. Decatur also had stable rates and over its relatively brief life sold much of its coal to the Pennsylvania for use as locomotive fuel. The PRR even installed side tracks at Decatur mine to facilitate loading, while refusing to complete loading tracks at Powelton, letting Powel shoulder that expense himself. Powel angrily denounced the PRR at the hearings as "a corporation whose iron bars have made almost a prison-house of the state of Pennsylvania." He noted that in the space of three years, the Pennsylvania had modified his rates a dozen times. Fluctuations between the new rate and the previous rate varied anywhere between $0.25 and $1.50 per ton.

The hearings were organized in part by state senator and Clearfield attorney William A. Wallace, who was forced out as a T&C director in 1866. Wallace—who had an interest in at least one Osceola-based coal company—agreed with Powel's declaration that the PRR took control of the T&C "at much less than half of its value . . . an almost entire loss to its shareholders." Wallace was ousted after the PRR foreclosed on the Tyrone and Clearfield Railroad's first mortgage bonds, whose interest the weakened company had failed to pay. The actual forecloser was J. Edgar Thomson, trustee for the mortgage. Some of the PRR's officers then arranged to sell the road to themselves for $50,000 and subsequently organized a new corporation, the Tyrone and Clearfield Railway, effective April 1, 1867.[36] This business strategy would be used again by the up-and-coming PRR, which saddled minority stockholders in some companies it took over with losses of as much as ninety cents on the dollar. The strategy also casts a different light on the events surrounding the PRR's assumption of T&C operations in mid-1862, when Lewis and

Roberts had claimed the smaller road was in such poor condition and charged it thousands of dollars for improvements. Perhaps their claims were accurate, or perhaps they were part of PRR's effort to deflate the value of the T&C and pave the way for an eventual takeover at a bargain price A verdict is impossible to render at this great historical distance.

That the Pennsylvania felt it could afford to alienate an influential politician like Wallace said something about the railroad's influence among state lawmakers in general. The hearings allowed disgruntled shippers to air their grievances but resulted in no legislative action. Coming away empty-handed, many Moshannon Valley coal operators continued to harbor bitter feelings toward the PRR—feelings that eventually opened the door to a competing railroad, a railroad in which Wallace himself would play a key role. In the short term, however, the coal trade was becoming so lucrative in spite of the PRR's seemingly arbitrary ways that the network of mines and their attendant railroad branch lines blossomed.

Even Powel made peace of sorts with the PRR when the circumstances made good economic sense. Indeed, he opened his testimony at the senate investigation by noting that "while I disapprove of the management of the Pennsylvania Railroad, I do not wish to be considered as an opponent of the institution itself, which under judicious guidance would, beyond a doubt, become the chief auxiliary to the wealth and greatness of Pennsylvania." As already noted, after excoriating the railroad in Harrisburg, Powel opened two new mines at Sterling on the Moshannon Branch.[37] The Powelton Coal and Iron Company also secured a fleet of 500 of its own cars for T&C coal service. It paid the same transportation rate as it did for coal shipped in PRR-owned cars, but the company was more confident that it would have a sufficient number of empties to handle the output of its mines. To make doubly sure, each car was marked with a black ball painted on a white square and had "Return to P.R.R. Tyrone" stenciled on its flanks.[38]

The Pennsylvania solidified its hold on the T&C at about the same time a group of Clearfielders led by Wallace (temporarily putting his aside his differences with the PRR) and former governor William Bigler agreed to pay part of the construction costs if the railroad would extend its line from Philipsburg to Clearfield, fulfilling the T&C's charter. The

Wallace and Bigler group raised $77,000 for grading, ties, and bridge-work on the 17-mile extension, contracting directly with Philadelphia-based Philip and Thomas Collins, partners in P & T Collins, one of the Northeast's largest and most well-known railroad-building firms. The PRR then agreed to bear the remaining $300,000 cost of the project. The first scheduled passenger train arrived in Clearfield on January 11, 1869.[39] The T&C thus had a single-track main line about 40 miles long, linking two towns having especially promising futures—one a railroad center and the other a hub for coal and timber enterprises.

As if to repair its tarnished image with the public, the Pennsylvania took the unusual step of operating a special train from Clearfield and the Moshannon Valley to Williamsport and return on June 23–25, 1870, to celebrate the opening of the Clearfield extension. The train of four "clean and bright" coaches plus a baggage car came under the watchful eye of trainmaster Dan Wood, who had first caught the public's fancy as the conductor on the first regular passenger trains between Tyrone and Philipsburg. The party of approximately a hundred invited guests left Clearfield at 8:30 A M and stopped at Wallaceton and Philipsburg to pick up additional celebrants. At midday the train reached Lock Haven, where the railroad treated its guests to lunch at the Fallon and Montour hotels and a tour of the city. The excursionists arrived in Williamsport at dusk and lodged at the Herdic House for two days of fun and frolic, including a grand ball on Friday evening. Host Peter Herdic, Williams-port mayor and millionaire lumber baron, set the crowd atwitter when he declared he would not rest until he had danced with every lady from Clearfield. The group returned home on June 25 after a stop in Bellefonte for lunch at the Bush and Brockerhoff hotels.[40]

A few years later the Pennsylvania garnered even more widespread goodwill. On May 20, 1875, a huge wildfire swept toward Osceola from the southwest, driven by high winds and feeding on underbrush left vulnerable by an unusually dry spring. Soon buildings throughout the town were ablaze, panicking the borough's 1,500 inhabitants. Dan Wood, in the Tyrone Division offices, received word of the impending disaster via telegraph and quickly summoned superintendent Samuel Blair. The two men mapped out a rescue strategy that sent four separate trains of about five boxcars and gondolas each over the mountain to Osceola under Wood's direction. In quick succession the trains embarked more than a thousand exhausted residents fleeing the flames and departed for Philipsburg. The last train to pull out sped right through fire from the burning Walker Brothers planing mill adjacent to the track. The blaze ultimately consumed 80 percent of Osceola's buildings and destroyed $1.5 million in property. In the catastrophe's aftermath, the T&C board donated $2,500 to the town's relief committee. Buoyed by a strong demand for coal, the town was quickly rebuilt.[41]

The great fire presented no obstacle to the Tyrone and Clearfield Railway. It was verging on a coal-powered economic take-off the likes of which neither the Pennsylvania Railroad nor the Commonwealth of Pennsylvania had ever witnessed. From 1862, when Robert Lemon shipped the first carload of coal, through 1869, the T&C had hauled 696,000 tons of bituminous from the Moshannon Valley—nearly 70,000 carloads in that era of 10-ton-capacity gondolas.[42] As astounding as that tonnage was, it merely hinted at the enormous flow of black diamonds yet to come.

Notes

1. S. B. Row and C.U. Hoffer, *Illustrated Souvenir History of Philipsburg* (Williamsport, PA: Grit Publishing, 1909), 7–23; Luther Gette, "Emigh's Gap: Focus of Railroad Longing, 1826–1932," *Keystone* 35 (Winter 2002): 23–42.

2. Richard C. Taylor, "Section of the Alleghany Mountain, and Moshannon Valley, in Centre County, Penn.," *Monthly American Journal of Geology* (April 1832): 433–38; Francis Philips to John C. Montgomery (father of James E. Montgomery), 27 February 1831, photocopy in Philips Papers, Philipsburg Historical Foundation.

3. *First Annual Report of the Philipsburg & Juniata Railroad* (New York: n.p., 1833).

4. Mahlon R. Hagerty, "Hardman Philips," in *Our Pioneer Heritage* (Philipsburg, PA: Philipsburg Historical Foundation, 1976), 17–20.

5. Details surrounding the T&C's founding and early finances are noted in correspondence between David I. Pruner and John Mulhallan Hale in the John Mulhallan Hale Papers, MS 66–1903, Historical Society of Pennsylvania, Philadelphia.

6. Charter information: inside front cover of Tyrone and Clearfield Railway board of directors minute book, in Penn Central Collection, Pennsylvania Railroad Subsidiary Lines, MG 286.1431, PSA. Stories favorable to the T&C appeared in the *Clearfield Republican* throughout December 1853 and January 1854, most likely the handiwork of J. M. Hale.

7. Pruner–J. M. Hale correspondence; Thomas H. Montgomery, *Genealogical History of the Family of Montgomery* (Philadelphia: Privately printed, 1863), 98–99.

A list of the T&C's initial stockholders is in the railroad folder of the William A. Wallace Papers, Clearfield County Historical Society, Clearfield, PA.

8. Pruner to J. M. Hale, 25 July 1854.

9. McNair to his sister, 13 August 1854, in James B. McNair, *With Rod and Transit: The Engineering Career of Thomas S. McNair* (Los Angeles: Privately printed, 1951), 100.

10. James E. Montgomery, *Report of Survey of the Tyrone, Clearfield and Erie Railroad* (Philadelphia: Brown's Printing, 1854), 2–3.

11. *Raftsman's Journal* (Clearfield), 15 August, 29 August, and 5 September 1855; Tyrone and Clearfield Railroad board of directors minutes, 5 May 1856, in Penn Central Collection, Pennsylvania Railroad Subsidiary Lines, MG 286.1426, PSA.

12. Jasper M. Fritz and Gerald R. Fritz, *Osceola Mills from the Beginning* (N.p.: 1991), 17–19, 27–28; John Blair Linn, *History of Centre and Clinton Counties, Pennsylvania* (Philadelphia: Louis H. Everts, 1883), 395–96. The town was incorporated as Osceola Mills in 1864, but popular usage has favored Osceola. This narrative adheres to Osceola.

13. Pruner to J. M. Hale, 13 October 1856; T&C minutes, 23 January 1857.

14. In American railroad practice, degree of curvature is found by connecting two points on an arc formed by the track with a 100-foot chord, drawing radii from the center of the arc to the chord endpoints, and then measuring the angle between the radii lines.

15. T&C grades, little changed over the years, are shown in the PRR Pittsburgh Region track chart of 1 January 1959.

16. Pruner–J. M. Hale correspondence, April–June 1854, September–October 1856; *Raftsman's Journal*, 30 August 1854.

17. *Raftsman's Journal*, 24 December 1856 and 17 June 1857; and T&C minutes, 23 January 1857. Workmen and wages are mentioned in Pruner to J. M. Hale, 29 January 1857, and William A. Purse to Reuben C. Hale, 2 May 1862, Hale-Mull Papers, microfilm roll 8.1, Box 1, Historical Collections and Labor Archives 1582, Pennsylvania State University Special Collections Library.

18. T&C minutes, 5 March, 18 June, and 20 August 1858; 9 January 1859.

19. T&C minutes, 18 January 1862; *Raftsman's Journal*, 29 April 1863.

20. Purse to R. Hale, 1 June 1861, and Purse to George Gibbons, 10 June 1863, in Quartermaster General's Dispatches Rec'd, RG 19.152, PSA.

21. Purse describes his T&C activities in his correspondence with Reuben Hale, May–August 1862, Hale-Mull Papers.

22. "The Life of John Nuttall, Written by His Grandson, John Nuttall," n.d., typescript, accessed 31 March 2016, http://nuttallfamilywv.com/research-materials.

23. T&C treasurer Henry Shillingford to James Tracy Hale, 17 January 1862. The letter is in the J. T. Hale Papers, microfilm roll 1.10, part of the Hale-Mull Papers.

24. Linn, *Centre County*, 401; Row and Hoffer, *History of Philipsburg*, 29; Lewis Cass Aldrich, *History of Clearfield County, Pennsylvania* (Syracuse, NY: D. Mason, 1887), chapter 14, "A Review of the Development of the Celebrated Coal Interests of the Houtzdale-Osceola-Philipsburg Region," 215–32.

25. J. Simpson Africa, *History of Huntingdon County, Pennsylvania* (Philadelphia: L. H. Everts, 1883), 232; Jon D. Baughman, *Men of Iron: A History of the Iron Industry in South-Central Pennsylvania* (Saxton, PA: Broad Top Bulletin, 1998), 72–87.

26. T&C minutes, 28 June and 8 July 1862, 12 January 1863, and 2 February 1864.

27. Roberts to J. Edgar Thomson, 22 July 1862. Roberts provides additional details in another letter to Thomson dated only "August 1862." Both letters are filed with the T&C minutes. See also T&C minutes, 24 July 1862.

28. R. Hale to J. T. Hale, 3 July 1862, in J. T. Hale Papers.

29. Purse noted his experiments in correspondence with Reuben Hale in the summer and fall of 1862. See also Pennsylvania Railroad Company, *Annual Report of the Board of Directors to the Stockholders* (Philadelphia: PRR) for 1863 and 1864; Aldrich, *Clearfield County*, 515–17.

30. *Raftsman's Journal*, 28 October 1863; PRR *Annual Reports* for 1863–65; and Row and Hoffer, *History of Philipsburg*, 41. Following Reuben Hale's death in 1863, his family moved to Philipsburg, occupying and expanding the manor house built by Hardman Philips in 1813 and renaming it Halehurst, as it is still known today.

31. *Raftsman's Journal*, 9 and 23 December 1863.

32. Aldrich, *Clearfield County*, 218–19; T&C minutes, 15 April 1868.

33. Aldrich, *Clearfield County*, 217–22; Row and Hoffer, *History of Philipsburg*, 29–30.

34. Fritz and Fritz, *Osceola Mills*, 40–41.

35. "Testimony . . . relative to the alleged extortionate charges . . . by the railroad corporations of the Commonwealth," *Legislative Documents, Comprising the Department and Other Reports Made to the Senate and House of Representatives of Pennsylvania during the Session of 1868* (Harrisburg: State Printer, 1868), 9–254. Powel's testimony, 216–37, includes his description of the state of affairs in both the Moshannon and the Broad Top regions.

36. T&C minutes, various, 28 June 1865–4 May 1867; *Clearfield Republican*, 21 February 1866.

37. Andrew Arnold, *Fueling the Gilded Age: Railroads, Miners, and Disorder in Pennsylvania Coal Country* (New York: New York University Press, 2014) has little to say about railroads but is a pioneer study of relations between miners and mine owners, centering on Clearfield County.

38. Richard Burg, "The Berwind-White Coal Mining Co.: When Empty Return to Windber P.R.R.," *Keystone* (Autumn 1986): 7–24.

39. Luther Gette, "The Clearfield Extension of the Tyrone and Clearfield Railway," *Keystone* (Spring 2012): 15–38; George A. Scott, *Clearfield Today and Tomorrow: Railroads of the Area* (Clearfield, PA: Progressive Publishing, 1968), 13–17.

40. *Raftsman's Journal*, 24 June 1870.

41. Fritz and Fritz, *Osceola Mills*, 47–57; *Raftsman's Journal*, 2 June and 9 1875; T&C minutes, 24 May 1875.

42. Frederick E. Saward, *The Coal Trade* (New York: Coal Trade Journal, 1875), 12. Aldrich, *Clearfield County*, 217–19, 232, gives annual tonnages over the T&C through 1886.

THREE

The PRR Tightens Its Grip

The Bald Eagle Valley Railroad

AT FIRST GLANCE, BUILDING A RAILROAD THE 54 MILES BETWEEN Tyrone and Lock Haven should have proven simpler than bringing either the Bellefonte and Snow Shoe or the Tyrone and Clearfield railroads into the world. The line, entirely through the Bald Eagle Valley, had no steep grades to overcome, and it was hardly a speculative venture, since it would link at each end with other PRR lines of sound value. Yet false starts, disappointing public subscriptions, shortages of materials and labor, floods, and even a bit of financial chicanery thwarted construction of what was to come the Bald Eagle Valley Railroad. The BEV did not become fully operational until after the B&SS and the T&C were earning steady revenues.

Backers of a rail line through the Bald Eagle Valley incorporated the Lock Haven and Tyrone Railroad Company on February 26, 1853, with Lock Haven lumber and coal entrepreneur David K. Jackman as president. As chief engineer John M. McMinn explained, "the great object of this road is to connect the main thoroughfares of Pennsylvania in the middle of the state."[1] The "thoroughfares" were the main line of the Pennsylvania Railroad at Tyrone and the projected main line of the Sunbury and Erie Railroad at Lock Haven. Connecting these two important routes by way of a line through the heart of Centre County seemed to make good economic sense. The new railroad would provide an outlet for traffic from the Allegheny Plateau, forwarding coal and timber east or west, as markets demanded. Passengers, too, would find the Bald Eagle line a convenient connection for travel to or from more distant points.

Centre County investors who jumped on the Lock Haven and Tyrone bandwagon soon found that not everyone shared their enthusiasm. Other promoters were beating the drum for a railroad that would run parallel to the LH&T through valleys on the county's southern edge, connecting Lewisburg on the Sunbury and Erie line with Spruce Creek on the PRR line. In the fall of 1853, the Lock Haven and Tyrone Railroad offered for public sale stock having a total par value of $350,000; but after two years, only $280,000 of it had been subscribed. Net proceeds were even less, because many buyers—primarily residents of Blair, Centre, and Clinton counties—bought the stock well below par, evidence of a lack of confidence in the venture. Expectations that English investors, who had shown a predilection for putting money into American railroads, would back the Lock Haven and Tyrone came to naught, as the possibility of a disruptive civil war between North and South loomed ever larger, scaring away foreign capital.

A renewed stock subscription drive in 1855 finally raised enough money to enable chief engineer McMinn to undertake a survey of the railroad's Western Division from Tyrone east to Milesburg, the jumping-off point for a 2-mile branch to Bellefonte, by far the largest population center between the railroad's namesake towns. The highest elevation on the line between Tyrone and Bellefonte was at Dix, near the Centre–Blair County border. At that point, the Bald Eagle Creek rose and flowed northeast to Lock Haven, while Little Bald Eagle Creek rose and flowed southwest to Tyrone.[2] McMinn estimated that building the 33-mile Western Division would cost $379,000, or approximately $11,500 per mile. Although this figure was less than half the average cost per mile of American railroads of that era, mostly because so little excavation was necessary, it soon became apparent the money could not be raised through stock sales alone. Since the Lock Haven and Tyrone's charter gave the company no borrowing power, promoters decided to incorporate a new entity with authority to sell bonds and to mortgage the line itself as security. Thus was born on February 21, 1857, the Tyrone and Lock Haven Railroad, with 46-year-old William H. Underwood as president.[3]

Underwood was the founder of Unionville, a village built around his sawmill and gristmill, at the point in the Bald Eagle Valley where the Philadelphia and Erie Turnpike began a steep, serpentine climb up the Allegheny Front on its way to Philipsburg. Underwood knew something about the transportation business, having accumulated moderate wealth as a carriage maker in Bellefonte. He also built a 25-mile plank road from Unionville to Tyrone to give his mills a commercial outlet. A tributary of that road climbed the Front from Julian to reach Underwood's extensive timber holdings around Beaver Mills on the upper reaches of Black Moshannon Creek.[4]

Underwood's involvement in the Tyrone and Lock Haven Railroad signaled increased influence in the enterprise by some of the Bellefonte area's wealthiest citizens. Investors included Edmund Blanchard and James T. Hale, both of whom, as already noted, had invested in other area railroads; Edward C. Humes, a founding partner of what would become the First National Bank of Bellefonte; and ironmasters James Irvin, Moses Thompson, William A. Thomas, and Roland Curtin (father of Andrew G. Curtin). All of them recognized that building a railroad through the Bald Eagle Valley could only add value to their shares in other business undertakings.

Contracts totaling $66,000 to grade the Western Division between Tyrone and Bellefonte were awarded to Samuel Brady and Company of Lock Haven on May 7, 1857. Because Brady was "an experienced contractor, a good judge of work, and an energetic and thorough man, and will no doubt drive this work to completion," according to the *Democratic Watchman* (Bellefonte) of May 20, "the Tyrone and Lock Haven Railroad may now be looked upon as a fixed fact." The *Watchman* reported that Underwood and McMinn presided over a May 16 groundbreaking ceremony near Milesburg. They took turns reading from the company's new charter before doffing coats and hats and wielding picks and shovels for a few minutes alongside Brady's workmen.

Brady's crews had just set to work when the T&LH ran headlong into the Panic of 1857. The nationwide economic downturn began that summer with a string of bank failures. Stronger banks then began calling in their loans, vastly reducing the supply of money available for investment. The Tyrone and Lock Haven Railroad was no longer "a fixed fact" as funds needed to sustain Brady's efforts dwindled. At a public meeting in Bellefonte in April 1858, a desperate Edmund Blanchard pleaded with ordinary citizens to buy stock in the road. In lieu of cash, he told the crowd, the railroad would gladly accept payments in grain, meat, lumber, or anything else that would satisfy the contractor. Similar appeals continued throughout the summer, and were successful enough to allow McMinn to survey the Eastern Division from Milesburg to Lock Haven.[5]

At the stockholders' annual meeting in Bellefonte in January 1859, chief engineer McMinn admitted that "the severe financial depression under which this whole country has labored was seriously felt by all connected with the road during this past year." He had already estimated that $17,000 would be needed to finish grading and bridgework on the Western Division and prepare it for ties and rails. Total cost to complete the railroad from end to end, including work already done, was pegged at $820,000, including the acquisition of locomotives and rolling stock. McMinn had been an assistant engineer on the Sunbury and Erie Railroad, and there was little reason for stockholders to doubt his word. They authorized the sale of up to $500,000 in twenty-year bonds, surely enough to finish both divisions.

McMinn also reported that grading the branch from Milesburg to Bellefonte, which would be used by the Bellefonte and Snow Shoe Railroad, was underway. "This branch will probably be continued up the [Nittany] valley to the Farmers' High School, a distance of eight miles," the chief engineer told the stockholders.[6] The "high school" was actually a college—destined to become the Pennsylvania State University (and the air-line distance was actually 10 miles.) The Pennsylvania legislature had chartered the Farmers' High School in 1855 at the behest of the state agricultural society, which intended to launch one of the nation's first baccalaureate-level institutions dedicated to agricultural science. The society chose to call it a high school to allay farmers' suspicions of colleges as centers of effete book learning and moral debauchery. The school was preparing to admit its first class in February 1859.

How seriously the T&LH's directors contemplated extending a track to the campus is impossible to say. The railroad would benefit modestly from agricultural traffic along the way, but the prospects for other freight were speculative. There was certain to be passenger business, since the founding trustees—in another nod to farmers who might send their sons to the institution—had deliberately chosen an isolated locale far from the supposed temptations of city living. One of those trustees was prominent Bellefonte civic booster and attorney Hugh N. McAllister, who supervised laying out the Farmers' High School grounds and constructing its main building. McAllister also held stock in the Tyrone and Lock Haven Railroad. It is not hard to believe that Underwood and McMinn dangled the possibility of a railroad line to the college to appeal to this influential investor, as well as to Moses Thompson, who owned thousands of acres of ore- and timber-rich land surrounding the college. In any case, the idea of extending the Bellefonte branch further through the Nittany Valley never resurfaced.

At a June 1859 public gathering at the Centre County courthouse, officials of the Catawissa, Williamsport and Erie Railroad discussed their proposal to fund completion of part of the Tyrone and Lock Haven and take it under lease. The Catawissa, starting from a junction with the Philadelphia and Reading Railroad at Tamaqua in the state's anthracite coal region, had built as far as Milton on the West Branch of the Susquehanna River and from that point obtained trackage rights over the Sunbury and Erie to Williamsport. Its leaders viewed the T&LH mainly as a link to Snow Shoe–area coal reserves, although they did not make clear how or if the two roads would physically connect. Negotiations halted almost before they began. The Catawissa was on shaky financial ground and ill-positioned to acquire the T&LH. In 1860 the company was reorganized as the Catawissa Rail Road to sidestep its indebtedness. The proposed lease is noteworthy only because the Catawissa in 1872 became part of the Philadelphia and Reading.[7] Had the Catawissa taken over the Tyrone and Lock Haven Railroad prior to itself being swallowed up, the P&R would have had a competitive foothold in central Pennsylvania. The area's railroad history would surely have evolved in a fundamentally different way. As it was, the P&R periodically cast longing glances at the coal and other natural riches of Centre County but was forever shut out.

Negotiations with the Catawissa only intensified Centre Countians' impatience with the fitful pace of T&LH construction. The railroad's pause to reorganize and its inability to sell most of its bonds contrasted with the energy that propelled the Bellefonte and Snow Shoe Railroad, in full operation by November 1859. "We must have a railroad!" shouted the *Democratic Watchman* of June 9. "Our coal, iron, grain, and lumber will be worth much more if we have a rail outlet." Under public and stockholder pressure to save his railroad from collapse, William Underwood went to New York in the summer of 1859 to peddle its bonds. There was nothing extraordinary about his plan. More than half the nation's negotiable securities consisted of railroad stocks and bonds, and New York's Wall Street even then was the largest exchange.

The details of what happened there remain sketchy. Working through an intermediary, Underwood exchanged as much as $200,000 in bonds for bank notes underwritten by the Southern Bank of Georgia, intending to use the notes to pay contractor Brady and other creditors in what ostensibly would be a legitimate transaction. Since the nation had no central bank, bank notes served as currency. Government oversight of this system was almost nonexistent, however, and fully one-third of all bank notes in that era were fraudulent or otherwise worthless—including those issued by the Southern Bank, which had just failed. Its paper had no value, and Underwood reportedly knew it. If he did, he obviously was gambling that the Tyrone and Lock Haven's creditors as recipients of the worthless notes would not suspect anything was amiss until it was too late. Underwood later claimed he traded the bonds for bank notes in good faith, and it was not his fault that the T&LH got stuck with valueless paper. Through what he vaguely termed the "fraud and treachery" of unscrupulous third parties in New York, the bonds passed from the Southern Bank into the hands of speculators who threatened to take possession of the railroad if the bonds' 6 percent interest payments were not met.[8]

Samuel Brady saw the transaction as an attempt to defraud him and went searching for a lawyer. The stockholders meanwhile persuaded Edmund Blanchard to chair a committee charged with sorting out the company's affairs. The committee presented its report at the annual meeting on January 9, 1860, revealing an almost hopeless financial tangle, made worse when President Underwood disclosed that speculators and "bona fide holders" of T&LH bonds were willing to return most of them for cash payments totaling $17,000. The outraged stockholders, regarding the offer as extortion, booted Underwood (who immediately left the state) and elected Blanchard president.

The 35-year-old Bellefonte lawyer was fast emerging as a key figure in the county's railroad development. A Dartmouth College graduate, he learned both law and politics from his father, John Blanchard, a US congressman and for more than thirty years a fixture of the Centre County bar. After the elder Blanchard's death in 1849, Edmund became a law partner with Andrew Curtin, a collaboration that continued until Curtin was elected governor in 1860. Shortly thereafter he formed a partnership with his brother Evan Blanchard, the two restricting their practice to corporate law and counting among their clients the Valentines and Thomas iron company and the Bellefonte and Snow Shoe Railroad. Commerce fascinated Edmund Blanchard even more than law. His involvement with the Tyrone and Lock Haven Railroad marked the beginning of his liberal investments in local enterprises ranging from railroads to glassmaking to coal mining. The *Democratic Watchman* put aside its normal partisanship when it described Blanchard, a staunch Republican, as "a leading spirit in all public enterprises designed to advance the interests of the town or county."[9]

Even a leader of Blanchard's considerable skills and connections had trouble saving the Tyrone and Lock Haven. With no source of operating revenue, the company failed to meet its interest payments and was legally declared in default on July 6, 1860. At a court-ordered auction of the property in January 1861, a consortium led by Philip M. Price, a leading citizen of Lock Haven who also served on the Sunbury and Erie's board of directors, successfully bid a mere $21,000 for the railroad. On April 1, Price transferred the T&LH's rights and franchises to the newly incorporated Bald Eagle Valley Railroad in exchange for 8,000 shares of BEV stock, which he then parceled out to major T&LH investors.[10] Price was the Bald Eagle's president; the board of directors included prominent business leaders from various communities between Bellefonte and Williamsport, among them Edmund Blanchard, who also served as secretary and legal counsel.

An outsider on the board was Thomas A. Scott, a Pennsylvania Railroad vice president and second in command to President J. Edgar Thomson. Scott was in the process of wrapping up a delicate political task for his boss, which indirectly led to his presence as a BEV director. When the Pennsylvania was incorporated in 1846 to build a railroad between Harrisburg and Pittsburgh, the state legislature levied a $0.20 per ton tax on freight moving more than 20 miles on that line. Lawmakers wanted this "tonnage tax" to offset economic losses that the PRR was expected to inflict on the less efficient, state-owned canal that paralleled much of the railroad. The PRR bought the canal in 1857 with the understanding that the tonnage tax would be annulled, only to have that provision of the sale struck down by the Pennsylvania Supreme Court on appeal from the canal commissioners, who saw all too clearly that the railroad was aiming to put them out of business.

Thomson was furious. His company found itself in the absurd position of having to pay a tax to protect dwindling traffic on an outmoded carrier that it had just purchased with intent to dismantle. He refused further payments to the state and directed Scott, a masterful diplomat, to work with political leaders to get the tonnage tax repealed. The canal commissioners enjoyed grassroots support in central and western Pennsylvania, where citizens benefited most from the canal system's bloated political patronage. Some of the region's shippers also feared the PRR would increase transportation costs if it had no competition—ignoring the fact that the Pennsylvania owned the competition.

A compromise was reached in March 1861 whereby the legislature "commuted" the tonnage tax to an investment by the Pennsylvania Railroad of $850,000—the amount of tax it owed—in the bonds of up to eleven smaller, unfinished railroads. All were located in the central or western part of the state. The Pennsylvania chose to buy into seven of the railroads, including the Bald Eagle Valley and the Tyrone and Clearfield. Critics charged that the Commutation Act simply gave the PRR an opportunity to gain control of feeder railroads at bargain prices, as in the case of both the BEV and the T&C. Defenders of the legislation countered that the roads selected for assistance held great promise for the state's economic development but probably would not be finished without some form of external succor. Moreover, the PRR's 1846 charter prohibited it from building branch lines except in those counties traversed by its main line, putting Centre and Clearfield Counties out of bounds. The Commutation Act in effect lifted that restriction.

There was no question that the Pennsylvania Railroad benefited handsomely from the Commutation Act. For $200,000 the PRR bought BEV bonds paying 6 percent annually and having a $400,000 face value upon their maturation in 1881. The transaction represented the Pennsylvania's largest single investment in any of the commutation roads and evidenced the importance Thomson and Scott attached to the line. The PRR also obtained a minority interest in the Bald Eagle's common stock and took out a three-year lease of the line. Under PRR control, the Bald Eagle Valley Railroad was not an operating entity: it had no locomotives, cars, or train crews. The Pennsylvania handled construction, operations, and maintenance, provided all motive power and rolling stock, and met payroll.[11]

In mid-1861, PRR civil engineer George Leuffer took over supervision of grading and tracklaying carried out by a new general contractor. Tom Scott had arranged to bring in Porter, Glasgow, and Company to replace the troublesome Samuel Brady.[12] Two segments of the BEV were already in service: between Snow Shoe Intersection and Bellefonte, built and operated by the Bellefonte and Snow Shoe, and between Vail and Tyrone, built and operated by the Tyrone and Clearfield.[13] Leuffer drove the contractor hard to connect those two segments. Pushing east from Vail, the track was finally opened to Snow Shoe Intersection late in 1862. The first passenger train from Tyrone arrived in Bellefonte on the evening of January 2, 1863. Scheduled service between the two communities began the next day in the form of one freight and one passenger train each making a daily roundtrip. "The passenger cars are always filled, both going and coming, and there is a large amount of freight carried both ways," reported Bellefonte's *Central Press*.[14] The following year witnessed another milestone of sorts. On June 22, 1864, brakeman William Geary of Unionville was crushed to death while coupling cars as the freight train worked a sidetrack at Port Matilda. It was the first operational fatality in the county's railroad history.[15] There would be many more.

At the valley's eastern end, Lock Haven was now being served by the Pennsylvania Railroad, which in 1862 had taken a 999-year lease of the

Figure 3.1. The Bald Eagle Valley Railroad's western terminus was the Tyrone passenger station, at right, with the freight station in the background. This 1860s view looks west on the PRR main line. *Tyrone Area Historical Society.*

Philadelphia and Erie Railroad, successor to the Sunbury and Erie. The PRR began to see value in the Bald Eagle Valley Railroad as the Confederate army came north into Pennsylvania in June 1863. Rebel raiders threatened to make a shambles of the Pennsylvania's Middle Division, between Harrisburg and Altoona, in the same manner that they wrecked the Baltimore and Ohio Railroad's main line in Maryland and West Virginia during the Antietam campaign of 1862, putting it out of service for six months. State militia in Huntingdon County turned back a Confederate advance party that intended to cut the PRR at Mount Union; the main Southern invasion force was halted at the Battle of

Gettysburg, just as the railroad was sending patterns, blueprints, and other engineering materials from its Altoona shops up to Snow Shoe to keep them out of harm's way.[16] Tom Scott was serving temporarily as assistant secretary of war in charge of the federal government's military railroads. He recognized that the Bald Eagle line would give the PRR an alternate east–west route in the event of a Middle Division catastrophe. So far as Scott was concerned, the Confederates' defeat at Gettysburg did not end the chance that they might come north again to harm the Pennsylvania Railroad's main line.

Scott sent word to chief engineer Leuffer to make sure the road's contractors finished their work by the end of 1864. However, as on the T&C, a shortage of men and materials hindered progress. Leuffer hoped to see 500 men engaged all along the line that fall; but even at the premium wage of $1.28 per day, the railroad could not attract enough help.[17] Exactly where his small force did come from is unknown. The PRR relied heavily on Irish immigrants to build its main line, and likewise contractors on the Tyrone and Clearfield used Irish workmen. But the wartime market for labor was catch-as-catch-can; the BEV likely made do with anyone willing and able to wield a pick and shovel.

The railroad was completed to the ironworks at Howard in August 1864. Rails and ties were installed over the remaining 14 miles to Lock Haven by December. However, the work was done so hurriedly that the track proved unfit for service. The contractors had to wait until spring to complete the job, only to encounter a series of late-winter snows followed by record floods. The line was officially opened on May 1, 1865, when regularly scheduled passenger service began over the entire 54 miles between Tyrone and Lock Haven.[18] Trains going in either direction made a stop at Bellefonte. There was no wye at Milesburg; westbounds backed from that point to the county seat, and eastbounds backed out. A wye at Milesburg would have been of little value without another one in downtown Bellefonte. But cost and a lack of a suitable tract in town expansive enough for a wye that could accommodate an entire train worked against such an option. The PRR did opt to build a new combination passenger-and-freight station for Bellefonte rather than use the small Bellefonte and Snow Shoe depot. In 1864, a more spacious wood-frame station was erected on a donated lot just beyond the High Street crossing. The B&SS

paid one-third of the station's construction costs in return for rights to use the facility.[19]

Effective July 1, 1864, the Bald Eagle Valley Railroad negotiated a new 99-year lease with the Pennsylvania that gave the larger company 40 percent of annual gross receipts, compared with the 75 percent of gross stipulated the PRR when it leased the Tyrone and Clearfield. The division favorable to the BEV helped to keep the carrier's ledgers free of red ink. In 1871 it posted a net operating income of about $21,100 from gross revenues of $81,500. The following year, it brought approximately $25,000 down to net after grossing a little over $90,000 and remained a dependable moneymaker thereafter. There is no evidence that Edmund Blanchard, Moses Thompson, or any other BEV investor ever regretted turning the company over to the PRR.

The Bald Eagle Valley Railroad had cost $1,050,000 to build and equip —just about on target with McMinn's original $820,000 estimate of 1859, allowing for war-induced inflation. Original plans called for eighteen depots or stations of varying size and sophistication to be spread along the route, although it is not clear if all were in service by May 1, 1865. Water, wood, and coaling stations were located at Port Matilda and Julian when end-to-end service began; wood stocks were discontinued by the end of the decade as the PRR fully converted its motive power to burning coal. Considering all the time it took to build the road, there were no great engineering features to mark its passage through the valley. The ruling grade eastward was 1.1 percent, located between Vail and Dix as the line climbed a low extrusion of Bald Eagle Ridge to avoid the flood plain of Little Bald Eagle Creek. From Dix, the line mimicked the gradual descent of Bald Eagle Creek to Lock Haven, except for a short 0.9 percent ascent of another ridge extrusion through Howard. Westbound trains encountered a 0.7 percent ruling grade in the 5 miles from Martha Furnace to Port Matilda. There were no extreme cuts, fills, or curves; and while the railroad counted sixty-seven wooden bridges, including several crossings of Bald Eagle Creek, most of the spans were hardly more than culverts.[20]

Coal from the mines around Snow Shoe and in the Moshannon Valley dominated the BEV's freight haulage. Coal cars from the T&C were weighed and made into trains in the yard at East Tyrone for dispatching east over the BEV or the PRR Middle Division main line. Snow Shoe trains set out most of their carloads of coal at the Intersection for forwarding east to the Lehigh Valley Railroad. The Pennsylvania's annual report to the stockholders for 1873 shows the T&C and the B&SS combined originated 667,000 tons of coal; 166,000 tons, or 24 percent, went east over BEV rails to Lock Haven. The remainder, except for local consumption, was routed east over Middle Division.

Lumber was the top commodity originated by the Bald Eagle Valley Railroad. By 1870, sawmills were shipping more than 12 million board feet of lumber over the BEV, having a market value of nearly $200,000. Oak, pine, and hemlock were the favored species. In his 1875 history of the Pennsylvania Railroad, William B. Sipes noted that a variety of enterprises throughout the valley were rail-dependent: "At Bald Eagle, five miles from Tyrone, iron ore is mined for shipment. . . . A saw mill and a grist mill are located at Martha. . . . Charcoal for use in iron manufacture is burned at Julian. . . . Two iron establishments are in operation [at Curtin.] Grist and saw mills also exist. . . . An iron furnace and rolling mill are located at Howard, employing about 125 hands. The surrounding country is rich in agricultural productions. . . . Lumbering is the principal business at Eagleville, some 300 men being employed."[21]

Bellefonte originated and terminated more freight than any other station, in fact "more than any four [other] stations," crowed the *Democratic Watchman* in 1870. Outbound traffic dominated: pig iron and semifinished iron products came from the two largest iron shippers, Valentines and Thomas, and McCoy and Linn; and lumber came from Bellefonte sawmills. Significant quantities of grain and fruit also were shipped in season from Nittany Valley farms.

Little noted was the occasional outbound car of lime shipped by William Shortlidge. It could not be foretold then, but lime and the limestone from which it was made would eventually distinguish Bellefonte from the hundreds of other small towns served by the PRR throughout Pennsylvania. Shortlidge was the office manager for the Valentines and Thomas ironworks and supervisor of its limekilns, which made lime for use as a purifier in iron manufacture. Shortlidge had prior knowledge of lime making, dating from his youth in Chester County. Sometime

Figure 3.2. A westbound work train on the Bald Eagle Valley line pauses at Milesburg, site of the junction with the branch to Bellefonte. *Author's collection.*

around 1861, he consulted with his cousin, Farmers' High School president Evan Pugh, a German-trained chemist, about the commercial value of the valley's limestone deposits. Pugh said the deposits along the flank of Bald Eagle Ridge were exceptionally high in calcium carbonate— ideal for lime making—and would likely have commercial value beyond merely supplying local iron furnaces as a purifying agent. Thus encouraged, Shortlidge bought a tract of land on the east side of Spring Creek just north of Bellefonte. He began quarrying and making lime there in 1862. As Pugh had foretold, his product found eager buyers in distant markets. Shortlidge became the first to "export" lime beyond Centre County using the new railroad. The first large-scale shipment went to

Pittsburgh in 1864, where the PRR used it in mortar for building a new passenger station for that city.[22]

On the passenger side, the Bald Eagle Valley Railroad initially offered two daytime passenger trains—one designated "mail" and the other "express"—in each direction between Tyrone and Lock Haven, a level of service that would prevail for many years. Both mail and express trains typically consisted of one or two coaches and a combination baggage-express-mail car and required about three hours to transit the valley, stopping at virtually every settlement.[23] Schedules varied slightly over the years but were designed to allow local travelers to make convenient connections with long-distance trains at Tyrone and Lock Haven. Trains of the Bellefonte and Snow Railroad were timed to allow connections with BEV trains at Snow Shoe Intersection, Milesburg, or Bellefonte. There was no Sunday or overnight passenger service.

The Bald Eagle Valley Railroad had no chance to compete head to head with the Bald Eagle and Spring Creek Navigation Company. The severe flooding that delayed completion of the railroad early in 1865 made a mess of the canal, damaging or destroying all twenty-eight locks, breaching embankments, and swamping boats. There was little pointing in rebuilding. The PRR's experience after purchasing the Main Line of Public Works in 1857 showed that most former canal shippers preferred the faster, more dependable all-season transportation offered by the railroad, even if it meant higher costs. After the floods in the Bald Eagle Valley, the Bald Eagle and Spring Creek Navigation canal terminated above the mouth of Beech Creek, where it served several large sawmills. The waterway came under the Pennsylvania's control in 1869 and was abandoned within five years. The Navigation was formally dissolved upon petition to the Clinton County court in 1877.[24]

The completion of the Bald Eagle Valley Railroad cemented the Pennsylvania Railroad's grip on Centre County and the Moshannon Valley and for the first time brought to the region the might of big business. Barely twenty years old in 1867, the PRR was by nearly every measure America's largest railroad; indeed, within a few years it would become America's largest privately owned business corporation. It operated directly and through leases nearly 1,000 route-miles of principal track in Pennsylvania—more than three times as much as its nearest competitors, and about one-third of the state's entire main line mileage. Boasting a fleet of 6,000 freight cars, it hauled roughly one-third (1.4 million tons) of all bituminous coal transported by rail in the state, one-third of all lumber, and one-third of all agricultural products. It owned or leased one of every three locomotives in the state, and carried one of every three passengers who rode by rail. The $18.5 million in gross operating income the PRR reported in 1867 was more than double that of the state's second largest railroad, the Philadelphia and Reading. Operating expenses that year totaled $14.8 million, allowing the Pennsylvania to service its $13.9 million debt and still reward its stockholders with 5 percent dividends.[25]

Although many of those stockholders lived in the railroad's headquarters city of Philadelphia, and by law the members of its board of directors were Pennsylvanians, the PRR was rapidly evolving into a company of national identity and influence. Its control of the Philadelphia and Erie Railroad and the Northern Central Railway, reaching Lake Erie and upstate New York on one end and Baltimore and the Chesapeake Bay on the other, added a north–south dimension to its service territory. To the west, the railroad had obtained an extension from Pittsburgh to Chicago in 1858 over allied roads, and in 1869 it secured this route with a 999-year lease. A year later, similar long-term agreements gave it control of lines from Pittsburgh to Cincinnati and St. Louis. To the east, it gained access to the New York harbor area and to Washington, D.C. The PRR thus transformed itself from a narrow rail corridor linking Philadelphia and Pittsburgh into a transportation empire, a steel network binding hundreds of communities in Pennsylvania and other states. This transformation was evident in Centre County and the Moshannon Valley. As the nineteenth century wore on, that region would continue to mirror the evolution of this great railroad system.

Notes

1. Quoted in *Democratic Watchman* (Bellefonte), 20 January 1859. See also "An Act to Incorporate the Lock Haven and Tyrone Railroad Company," in *Laws of the General Assembly of the State of Pennsylvania of the Session of 1853* (Harrisburg: Finn and Co., 1853), 737; and John Blair Linn, *History of Centre and Clinton Counties, Pennsylvania* (Philadelphia: Louis H. Everts, 1883), 92–93.

2. *Democratic Watchman*, 17 December 1856, and Linn, *Centre County*, 172. A digitized version of J. M. McMinn's "Map of the Proposed Lock Haven and Tyrone Rail Road" is available from the Library of Congress: accessed 15 June 2015, http://hdl.loc.gov./loc.gmd/g3821p.rr004450.

3. "An Act to Incorporate the Tyrone and Lock Haven Railroad Company," in *Laws of the General Assembly of the State of Pennsylvania of the Session of 1857* (Harrisburg: A. Boyd Hamilton, 1857), 122–23; Coverdale & Colpitts, *The Pennsylvania Railroad Company: Corporate, Financial and Construction History of Lines Owned, Operated and Controlled to December 31, 1945*, 4 vols. (New York: Coverdale and Colpitts Consulting Engineers, 1946), 1:364–66; and D. S. Maynard, *Industries and Institutions of Centre County* (Bellefonte, PA: Richie and Maynard, 1877), 125–27.

4. Linn, *Centre County*, 451–52. Black Moshannon Creek is a tributary of the Moshannon Creek, which is sometimes called the Red Moshannon.

5. The *Democratic Watchman* reported regularly on T&LH activities. See 28 April 1858 and later issues through 1858 and early 1859.

6. B&SS board of directors minute book, 3 August and 30 December 1858, Penn Central Collection, Pennsylvania State Archives; *Democratic Watchman*, 20 and 27 January 1859. The *Watchman* reprinted the T&LH's annual report to stockholders in full each year.

7. *Democratic Watchman*, 7 June 1859; Stephen C. Troy, "Early History of the Catawissa Railroad," *Beeline* 23, no. 4 (2001): 8–16. The *Beeline* is a publication of the Reading Co. Technical and Historical Society.

8. *Central Press* (Bellefonte), 9 June 1859 and 18 October 1860, and *Democratic Watchman*, 19 January 1860. For the national financial context, see John Steel Gordon, *An Empire of Wealth* (New York: HarperCollins, 2004), 183–86.

9. *Democratic Watchman*, 7 January 1887; *Commemorative Biographical Record of Central Pennsylvania, Including Centre, Clinton, Union and Snyder Counties* (Chicago: J. H. Beers, 1898), 49, 185; Linn, *Centre County*, 97, 149, 155.

10. BEV board of directors minutes, 1 April 1861 and 29 April 1879, Penn Central Collection, Pennsylvania Railroad Subsidiary Lines, MG 286.551, Pennsylvania State Archives.

11. The complexities of the tonnage tax and commutation roads is explained by George H. Burgess and Miles C. Kennedy, *Centennial History of the Pennsylvania Railroad Company* (Philadelphia: PRR, 1949), 93–99, 106–13. See also James A. Ward, *J. Edgar Thomson, Master of the Pennsylvania* (Westport, CT: Greenwood Press, 1980), 113–16.

12. Brady filed suit against the T&LH and BEV but lost his case in common pleas court in 1863 and died soon thereafter. His estate appealed to the Pennsylvania Supreme Court, which ruled on 8 September 1865 that the T&LH had discharged all of its obligations to him. The case summary in Lewis Walker, *Reports of Cases Decided by the Supreme Court of Pennsylvania* (Pottsville, PA: Standard Publishing, 1889), 472–509, details the intricate finances underpinning the two railroads.

13. BEV minutes, 2 August 1861 to 12 January 1863.

14. *Central Press*, 17 April 1863.

15. *Democratic Watchman*, 24 June 1864.

16. Christopher Baer, "1863," in *A General Chronology of the Pennsylvania Railroad Company, Predecessors and Successors, and Its Historical Context*, accessed 8 April 2016, http://www.prrths.com/newprr_files/Hagley/PRR1860.pdf.

17. BEV minutes, 23 December 1862, 13 January 1863; William A. Purse to Reuben C. Hale, 17 May 1862, Hale- Mull Papers, microfilm roll 8.1, Box 1, Historical Collections and Labor Archives 1582, Pennsylvania State University Special Collections Library.

18. Pennsylvania Railroad Company, *Annual Report of the Board of Directors to the Stockholders* (Philadelphia: PRR, 1864 and 1865); BEV minutes, 8 January 1872; *Central Press*, 12 May 1865.

19. B&SS minutes, 14 December 1864.

20. Bald Eagle Valley Railroad report in *Annual Report of the Auditor General on Railroads, Canals, and Telegraphs* (Harrisburg: Pennsylvania Auditor General, 1867), 16–18; PRR *Annual Report* for various years through the 1860s.

21. William B. Sipes, *The Pennsylvania Railroad* (Philadelphia: PRR, 1875), 207–9.

22. *Commemorative Biographical Record of Central Pennsylvania: Including the Counties of Centre, Clearfield, Jefferson and Clarion: Containing Biographical Sketches of Prominent and Representative Citizens, Etc.* (Chicago: J. H. Beers, 1898), 80; *Democratic Watchman*, 14 June 1895.

23. The PRR *Annual Report* for 1876 notes the average length of a Tyrone Division passenger train was 2.6 cars.

24. West Branch and Susquehanna Canal Company journal, 9–10, in Penn Central Collection, Pennsylvania Railroad Subsidiary Lines, MG 286.1447, PSA; Ernest H. Coleman, "Bald Eagle and Spring Creek Navigation," *Canal Currents* 19 (Winter 1972): 5–7.

25. Pennsylvania Railroad Company report in *Annual Report of the Auditor for 1867*, xi–xxi, 237–43, 261–67, 278–81; Burgess and Kennedy, *Centennial History*, 176–335; Albert Churella, *The Pennsylvania Railroad: Building an Empire, 1846–1917* (Philadelphia: University of Pennsylvania Press, 2012), ix.

FOUR

Forever Divided

The Lewisburg and Tyrone Railroad

THE PENNSYLVANIA RAILROAD AGGRESSIVELY PURSUED CONTROL
and operation of the Tyrone and Clearfield and the Bald Eagle Valley
lines. It showed less enthusiasm for bringing what would become the
Lewisburg and Tyrone Railroad into the fold. The PRR used the L&T to
block attempts by other roads to enter its territory. Otherwise, the L&T
offered the Pennsylvania neither long-term traffic in natural resources
nor a route of strategic value.

The Lewisburg and Tyrone Railroad began as the Lewisburg, Centre
and Spruce Creek Railroad. Construction began at the eastern and western ends and worked sporadically toward the middle, but the two segments never met. A disconnected rail line was not what the road's found-
ers envisioned when they gathered on February 11, 1853, at Potter's Fort
tavern in Penns Valley to incorporate the LC&SC. The meeting capped
a series of public gatherings held in Centre and Union Counties to discuss building a railroad between Montandon, on the Sunbury and Erie
Railroad, and Spruce Creek on the PRR's Middle Division. The projected
route stretched nearly a hundred miles through forest and farmland that
the road's promoters hoped would be rich in iron ore and possibly even
coal. The company was formally organized on August 5, 1856, with Lewisburg banker, politician, and canal-boat builder Eli Slifer as president.[1]

A survey of the route was commissioned, led by A. B. Warford, an experienced civil engineer who had just finished laying out a route for a railroad (eventually part of the PRR) between Sunbury and Harrisburg. Warford's eighteen-member team spent six months in the field between Lewisburg and Spruce Creek beginning in October 1856. Its report gave the LC&SC directors a choice of two parallel routes west from Lewisburg. The northerly route followed Rapid Run to its headwaters in western Union County, then crossed a series of ridges to descend into Brush Valley in Centre County. It included an average westbound ascent of 1.3 percent over a 19-mile distance. The southerly route ran through Mifflinburg to reach the low ground along Penns Creek, then followed that stream as it threaded a gap through Paddy Mountain into Centre County's Penns Valley. It was a few miles longer than the northern route, but Warford said it offered a maximum average grade of 0.6 percent over 8 miles. The two projected routes merged at the confluence of Brush and Penns Valleys and followed a common line for the rest of the way through the Nittany Valley to Spruce Creek.

The Rapid Run line, requiring considerable excavation to keep the grade within reason, carried an estimated cost of $4,900 per mile, while the Penns Creek line could be built for about $3,600, Warford advised.[2] These figures were unrealistically low, even though they excluded the cost of laying track. At about the same time Warford was crunching his numbers, John McMinn was calculating a far more accurate cost of $11,500 per mile (with track) to build a railroad through the mostly flat terrain of the Bald Eagle Valley. But Warford's estimates appealed to the LC&SC's board of directors, who approved the Penns Creek line and moved ahead with raising money to begin construction. The onset of the Civil War in 1861 kept most potential investors away. Slifer himself served as wartime assistant to Governor Andrew Curtin and had little time for railroad affairs.

Lurking in the background while the LC&SC bided its time was the Atlantic and Great Western Railway, then operating in western Pennsylvania and Ohio. The Lewisburg, Centre and Spruce Creek might prove useful as a link in the A&GW's projections for a trunk line from New York and Philadelphia to the Midwest, running more or less parallel to and competing with the Pennsylvania Railroad. The A&GW was especially interested in shipping crude oil from newly developed fields in western Pennsylvania to seaboard refineries. Even if the trunk line failed to materialize, the LC&SC could still serve as the central link in an oil route, if its western terminus was changed from Spruce Creek to Bellefonte. East of the river the LC&SC could connect with the Catawissa Rail Road, which had a friendly connection on its eastern end with the Philadelphia and Reading Railroad. West of Bellefonte, the A&GW's backers figured to build a new line through Clearfield County to the parent company's rails near Franklin. It was a complicated, flimsy scheme, supported more by wishful thinking than anything else. Yet the A&GW did manage to lease both the LC&SC and the Catawissa in 1866.

The Atlantic and Great Western's actions alerted the Pennsylvania to the strategic value that the Lewisburg, Centre and Spruce Creek might have to a rival railroad. As the PRR prepared to take legal steps to thwart the A&GW, the latter road declared bankruptcy, dashing its owners' hopes for a great east–west trunk line. It relinquished its lease of the LS&SC, and the initiative for making that railroad a reality reverted to its stockholders.[3] (The A&GW, meanwhile, disappeared into the Erie Railroad.)

When the nation returned to a peacetime economy in 1865, enough investors came forward to enable the Lewisburg, Centre and Spruce Creek to begin construction. Between Montandon and Lewisburg, the railroad crossed the West Branch of the Susquehanna River on a privately owned iron bridge and paid tolls for its use. The first train arrived in Lewisburg on July 23, 1869, prompting one of that town's newspapers to exclaim that the LC&SC "will wake us up from our Rip Van Winkle slumber and place us right on the thoroughfare to prosperity!"[4] Local enthusiasm for the new railroad did not yield the cash necessary to sustain construction. The company's stock, having a $1.5 million par value, after several years on the market netted only $265,000 in sales. The only recourse was to offer a share of the road to the Pennsylvania. A $1.9 million bond issue was prepared, with the PRR taking most of those securities as well as a lease of the property. Lewisburg attorney and former congressman George F. Miller succeeded Slifer as president, answering to a board that included both local investors and PRR representatives.

The Pennsylvania's engineer of branch lines, George Leuffer, was named the LC&SC's chief engineer.

Only modest grading was required as crews pushed the single-track railroad through the Buffalo Valley of western Union County. Upon reaching Mifflinburg in 1871, the railroad went no further, much to the dismay of Centre Countians. Circumstantial evidence indicates that the Pennsylvania turned off the financial spigot because it was unhappy with the LC&SC's principal stockholders. Miller seemed unable to focus their energies on common objectives. Some wanted the railroad to continue west as a narrow-gauge line in order to reduce construction costs. Others wanted to build east to Danville and a connection with the Catawissa Rail Road, or southwest to the Broad Top coalfields. At the urging of Moses Thompson, a local iron master and proprietor of Centre Furnace, the board did approve an amendment allowing the LC&SC to circle around the base of Nittany Mountain and head for Bellefonte and a junction with the Bellefonte and Snow Shoe Railroad, in which Thompson held shares. Another amendment, passed at the behest of the PRR, changed the LS&SC's projected western terminus from Spruce Creek to Tyrone, which offered more potential for industrial traffic and thus greater possibilities to lure investors.[5]

The Pennsylvania also had problems of its own. As it gained control of other railroads beyond the Harrisburg–Pittsburgh corridor stipulated in its charter, the PRR accumulated a large bonded debt that worried many stockholders. At the same time, vice president and de facto chief financial officer Tom Scott had gotten the company involved in one grand proposal to secure a route to New Orleans and another to form an alliance with Union Pacific to create a transcontinental railroad. Scott's plans presaged the great railroad combinations of the late twentieth century but outstripped the practicalities of his own time. Had Thomson not been ailing by then, he likely would have reigned in his subordinate. When the Panic of 1873 sparked a nationwide economic recession, stockholders worried that the Pennsylvania was overextended. They formed an investigating committee to look into the company's finances. Scott still enjoyed sufficient popularity to assume the road's presidency upon J. Edgar Thomson's death in 1874, but he was under strict orders to stabilize mileage and bring down indebtedness.[6] Scott reduced dividends and then, for only the second time in the road's history, forbade paying them altogether for a year and a half as the company retrenched.

The parent company's financial woes pushed completion of the LC&SC, a low priority to begin with, even further into the future. The hiatus did give chief engineer Leuffer a chance to modify Warford's original survey. To save excavation costs, he allowed a 1 percent ascent along Penns Creek as the railroad climbed the flank of Paddy Mountain. Construction in that area finally resumed in 1875. "Nearly two hundred men are engaged in work on the railroad in the mountains," the *Centre Reporter* (Centre Hall) noted on November 11 of that year.[7] Of the various contractors responsible for building separate segments of the road, Bridgens, Noyes and Company of Lock Haven undertook perhaps the most daunting task: boring the curving, 320-foot Paddy Mountain tunnel, which saved the railroad mileage where Penns Creek made a hairpin bend at the Centre County line. Using only hand labor and nitroglycerine, a highly volatile explosive, crews successfully clawed their way through solid rock. Three miles further west, employees of L. J. and H. H. Vandyke and Company of Lewistown were boring the 260-foot Beaver Dam tunnel through less resistant material at another hairpin bend.

Beyond Beaver Dam was the Forks—the juncture of Penns Creek and Pine Creek, and the head of navigation during seasonal high water. From that location, rafts of timber and arks of grain took advantage of springtime freshets to make their way down Penns Creek to the Susquehanna and eventually Eastern markets. The village that grew up near the Forks was named Coburn, honoring banker and LC&SC director James P. Coburn of nearby Aaronsburg. From the Forks, the railroad might have followed Pine Creek and its tributary, Elk Creek, 2 miles north to Millheim, Penns Valley's largest population center, with about 500 residents. Millheim was an important point on the old turnpike that led from Lewisburg to Potter's Fort. But to obtain an easy grade paralleling the turnpike from Millheim west to Spring Mills would have required much cutting and filling. Such earthmoving expenses were to be avoided for a railroad that had cash-flow problems; LC&SC contactors were known to pull their men off the job when payrolls could not be met. So Leuffer stayed with Warford's original line that steered clear of Millheim and followed Penns Creek to Spring Mills.

On May 26, 1876, Tom Scott arrived on the property leading an inspection party that included PRR vice president George Roberts; George Leuffer; PRR board of directors finance committee chairman Wistar Morris of Philadelphia, who was also a director of LC&SC and the Bellefonte and Snow Shoe Railroad; and LC&SC president George Miller. The party journeyed by rail to the end of track near Laurelton, then boarded horse-drawn carriages for the ride out to Paddy Mountain tunnel. Since the bore had not yet been holed through, the executives "footed it" over the mountain, according to the *Centre Reporter*, to another set of carriages, which took them to a lunch of fresh-caught trout at the hamlet of Ingleby (then named Fowler) hosted by LS&SC directors Coburn and Robert H. Duncan, a Spring Mills merchant. Then it was on to Centre Hall, where, according to the *Reporter*, they "were escorted by some of our local citizens to the top of Nittany Mountain and shown the magnificence of its valley which they had for so long permitted to suffer for want of a railroad. [The view] filled Mr. Scott and his party with incredible delight." The gathering darkness forced the visitors back to their carriages, which took them to a late supper at Moses Thompson's house at Centre Furnace, near the village of Lemont at the end of Nittany Mountain. It was almost midnight by the time the group returned to Bellefonte and a waiting train that sped them overnight to Philadelphia. "We think the visit had a good effect," declared the *Reporter*, "and that these gentlemen returned more favorably impressed with the necessity and obligation of completing the work than before."

Scott and his associates were sufficiently impressed to have the Pennsylvania end its series of annual leases and sign a new 99-year lease of the LC&SC, effective August 1, 1876. Residents along the line regarded the long-term lease as a sign that the railroad would be finished. When rails reached Spring Mills in the summer of 1877, a Fourth of July excursion train arrived from Lewisburg, carrying 1,200 Union County citizens for a day of picnics, band music, games, and the customary speech making. A similar celebratory train ran from Spring Mills and Coburn to Lewisburg the next month. The mood would not have been so merry had the locals known the Pennsylvania had no immediate plans to extend the line beyond Spring Mills. Additional miles of right-of-way west of the village "are graded and ready for superstructure," Scott noted in his annual report to PRR stockholders for 1877. "The unfinished portion will be completed, from time to time, if the business of the region it traverses will justify it."

At the same time, internal turmoil plagued the LC&SC as stockholders had yet to see any payback on their investment. George Miller was forced out as president in favor of the venerable Eli Slifer. Moses Thompson was elected a director but had to step down when other directors raised conflict-of-interest objections, because he held a contract to grade the right-of-way approaching Lemont.[8] "Our total expenditure has been $2,347,975," Slifer told the stockholders in 1878, against gross earnings of just $30,881 for the previous year. "If we had means to rapidly complete the work, we might hope for some reasonable return from the investment. As it is, the unpaid interest on the cost of our work is accumulating and the delay in completion is destructive."[9] So destructive, in fact, that PRR executives feared the road was becoming a money pit. Using the same technique that had won them absolute control of the Tyrone and Clearfield Railroad a few years earlier, they foreclosed on the LC&SC's bonds in 1879, forcing the road into default. Pennsylvania officials then bought the company at a sheriff's sale, transferred its assets to the newly incorporated Lewisburg and Tyrone Railroad to get it out from under the LC&SC's debt, and leased the L&T back to the PRR for 99 years, effective January 1, 1880. The company's president—now more a figurehead than ever—was Philadelphia civil engineer Strickland Kneass, assistant to President Scott and president in his own right of nearly a dozen other PRR leased lines, testifying to his intimate knowledge of how the game was played. The moribund LC&SC was dissolved in 1893.

By the time the LC&SC was reorganized, it had already graded 17 miles of right-of-way on the west end. From Tyrone, the route ran east through the Nittany Valley to Pennsylvania Furnace, where ore had been dug and iron made since 1813. This section included a formidable 1.6 percent grade as the railroad climbed away from the bottomlands along the Little Juniata River and headed east toward the village of Warriors Mark. Chief engineer Leuffer did not consider the climb a significant liability, because most of the tonnage—in the form of iron ore—would be moving west, downgrade.

It was the quest for ore that prompted the Pennsylvania to shift its focus from Spring Mills to Tyrone. Famed industrialist Andrew Carnegie
and his partners were gearing up for large-scale production of steel in
the Pittsburgh area, opening in 1875 the massive Edgar Thomson Works.
(Carnegie personally selected the name.) The Works pioneered on a
grand scale the Bessemer process of making steel and required huge
quantities of iron. In their search for long-term sources of iron ore, the
Carnegie interests sent geologist William Prousser to examine deposits
known to lie along the Centre–Huntingdon County line. "He sent us a
report of analyses of ore remarkable for the absence of phosphorous,"
Andrew Carnegie later recalled.

> It was really an ore suitable for making Bessemer steel. Such a discovery attracted
> our attention at once. The owner of the property was Moses Thompson, a rich
> farmer, proprietor of seven thousand acres of the most beautiful agricultural land
> in Center [sic] County, Pennsylvania. An appointment was made to meet him
> upon the ground from which the ore samples had been obtained. We found the
> mine had been worked for a charcoal blast furnace fifty or sixty years before, but it
> had not borne a good reputation then, the reason no doubt being that its product
> was so much purer than other ores that the same amount of flux used caused
> trouble in smelting. It was so good it was good for nothing in those days of old.[10]

Carnegie had eighty exploratory shafts sunk on the land "and the ore
was analyzed at every few feet of depth, so that before we paid over the
hundred thousand dollars asked, we knew exactly what there was of ore."
In all, the Carnegie interests purchased or leased land or mineral rights
encompassing about 500 acres. But before production could begin, a
railroad had to be built to haul the ore to the main line at Tyrone for
shipment to Pittsburgh.

The Pennsylvania was eager to comply, even if it meant starting the
west end of the L&T while the east end languished. Eli Slifer wanted to
build all the way east to State College—the town adjacent to the steadily
growing campus of the Pennsylvania State College (formerly the Farmers' High School.) Interested mostly in accommodating Carnegie, however, the PRR vetoed that idea and completed the L&T only as far as
Fairbrook, 20 miles from Tyrone. It then built a 5-mile branch north to
the new community of Scotia, where the Carnegie company was preparing to mine iron ore. The Scotia Branch officially opened for service on
November 10, 1881.

Within a few years, Scotia—Latin for Carnegie's homeland of Scot-
land—was home to about 200 employees plus their families. It boasted a
post office (officially named Benore, or "mountain of iron"), a school, two
churches, and numerous single- and double-family dwellings. Two Bos-
ton Excavators scooped open pits 20–25 feet deep and were the among
the first steam shovels to be used in Pennsylvania for iron ore mining.
They loaded the ore into small wooden "bank cars," which were then
transported over a narrow-gauge railway system powered by two steam
locomotives. The trains carried the ore a half-mile or so to a preparation
plant, where it was crushed, washed, and loaded into standard-gauge
rail cars for the trip to Tyrone. Scotia and the other two agency stations,
Warriors Mark and Pennsylvania Furnace, were served by two-daily-
except-Sunday mixed trains that carried passengers, mail and express,
and miscellaneous freight in addition to ore. Wye tracks were constructed at Scotia and Fairbrook in order to turn the locomotives.[11]

Scotia was the largest but not the sole source of ore traffic for the L&T.
A 2-mile spur, the Juniata Branch, left the Scotia Branch to reach mines at
Tow Hill, a kind of small-scale version of Scotia, from which associates
of Carnegie shipped ore to Pittsburgh and to Robert Hare Powel's iron
furnaces in Huntingdon County. Powel also opened his own ore pit at
Dry Hollow, along the L&T a mile or so east of the village of Warriors
Mark, shortly before his death in 1883. His coal and iron enterprises en-
dured for another decade. Scotia, Tow Hill, and Dry Hollow accounted
for nearly all the approximately 6,000 carloads that came off the west end
of the L&T each year in the late 1880s. In its peak year of 1890, the line
also accommodated some 22,000 passengers.[12]

Pennsylvania Furnace was in its twilight as an iron center by the time
the railroad came through. It had once made 2,000 tons of pig iron annually, impressive in its day but Lilliputian when hundred-ton-per-day
furnaces became common in the state after the Civil War. With its ore
reserves nearing exhaustion and its production techniques antiquated,
the furnace permanently ceased operations in 1888.[13]

Development of the west end of the L&T made Penns Valley citizens
all the more frustrated with the lack of progress on their end. They were
indignant when the Pennsylvania demanded $25,000 in local contribu-
tions to complete the railroad from Spring Mills to Lemont. A citizens'

Figure 4.1. Iron ore mining at Scotia was so extensive that this narrow-gauge railroad was constructed to carry the raw ore from the pit to the site where it was crushed, washed, and loaded into Pittsburgh-bound PRR trains. *Centre County Historical Society Koch Collection.*

committee, organized to persuade the PRR to resume construction, called the $25,000 requirement "exceedingly unfair and too oppressive to be complied with," even though it amounted to less than 10 percent of the 15-mile segment's total estimated cost of $318,000. On December 11, 1883, the committee made a counterproposal: instead of cash, the right-of-way and lots for station buildings would be donated. Andrew Curtin, then in his second term as a congressman and still a political force to be reckoned with, learned of the offer while he was in Washington. He rushed to Philadelphia to meet with George Roberts, who had succeeded to the PRR's top job on Scott's retirement. Roberts had a reputation for being cautious and deliberate, unlikely to act upon impulse. Whether the passion and eloquence with which Curtin argued the L&T's case made an impression on him is open to speculation; but the offer of free land surely captured Roberts's attention. On December 26, at the president's recommendation, the Pennsylvania's board agreed to the citizens' terms.[14] The residents of Penns Valley "are kicking up their heels with pure joy" at the PRR's change of heart, proclaimed the *Democratic Watchman*. The first carload of construction materials arrived at Spring Mills in mid-March 1884.

In his meeting with Roberts, Curtin also pitched the idea of revisiting Moses Thompson's recommendation to turn the L&T toward Bellefonte instead of pushing it west toward State College and Fairbrook—unaware that the Pennsylvania was already poised to do just that in order to block attempts by a rival to reach the Nittany Valley from the east. The Philadelphia and Reading Railroad was contemplating a variety of construction and trackage-rights schemes from the Susquehanna Valley to gain entry to the Bellefonte market with its pig iron, limestone, grain, glass, and other commodities. Bellefonte also might serve as the launching point for a thrust into the coalfields of the Moshannon Valley and Clearfield County. The P&R even bought real estate in the town, although it tried to keep that transaction and its general yearning for Bellefonte under wraps. Nonetheless, the Pennsylvania soon got wind of its competitor's intentions. Roberts had decided to resume construction of the L&T and aim for the county seat before Curtin ever set foot in his office. However, there was no harm in allowing the aging politico to play the role of local hero.[15]

The business of extending the L&T to Lemont was in full swing by the summer of 1884. Contractors L. J. and H. H. Vandyke returned with a large force of Italian laborers, equipped with picks, shovels, and horse carts, to build the segment from Spring Mills to Centre Hall. Part of that route included a 1.16 percent climb—the ruling westbound grade over the L&T's entire length. In June the Vandykes reached Centre Hall, near the Potters Fort tavern that had birthed the railroad. The new station there opened for service in January 1885, and the village would be incorporated as a borough a few months later with a population of about 400. Work continued on toward Lemont.[16]

The Pennsylvania organized another subsidiary, the Bellefonte, Nittany and Lemont Railroad, to construct a 9.5-mile line north from Lemont around the base of Nittany Mountain to Bellefonte. Legally speaking, the L&T ended a few hundred feet east of the Lemont station, and the BN&L began. The need to create a subsidiary stemmed from an absence in the L&T's charter of any provision to build branch lines. Ironically, the LC&SC's charter did contain such a clause. Why the PRR did not incorporate it into the L&T's legal foundation is unknown.

On July 22, 1885, the entire 67.4 miles of track between Montandon and Bellefonte were opened for service without ceremony. The first car through the connection at Lemont that day carried a load of coal from Philipsburg consigned to a new steam-powered flour mill at Centre Hall. The first passenger train operated on July 29, a nine-car excursion that embarked 450 riders at Bellefonte and Lemont for a picnic and band concert at Spring Mills.[17] (Because the PRR already had a Spring Mills station in southeastern Pennsylvania, in the fall of 1885 it re-named the place Rising Springs, a designation that for railroad purposes lasted into the twentieth century.) A second excursion on September 3 originated at Coburn and headed for Snow Shoe, picking up passengers all along the route. "The scenery from Bellefonte to Snow Shoe is the grandest in the state, rivaling that of the Alleghenies from Altoona to the summit," declared the *Centre Reporter*. "The picnic ground near the [Snow Shoe] station will be thrown open to excursionists, and opportunity also given to visit numerous and interesting coal mines."

Scheduled passenger service began around October 1. Two round trips were made over the line Monday through Saturday. At Montandon, L&T trains connected with those running between Harrisburg, Buffalo, and Erie. Passenger service on the L&T proved to be a great boon to the students and faculty at the Pennsylvania State College. President George W. Atherton's announcements to the college community for the fall semester in 1885 included a declaration that "since trains are now running regularly between Montandon and Bellefonte, this makes Lemont our nearest station [3 miles from campus], and conveyances will hereafter be provided for students to and from that place."[18] The college would furnish the "conveyances" primarily at vacation times and also would transport trunks and other luggage at no charge, provided students secured tickets in advance from the college business office. Such arrangements remained in effect for many years.

To simplify the corporate structure, the PRR merged the Bellefonte, Nittany and Lemont Railroad into the Bald Eagle Valley Railroad in 1889, but local residents spoke (incorrectly) of the L&T "branch" as if it came all the way into Bellefonte. Popular usage varied from PRR terminology in that the Pennsylvania did not refer to any of the L&T as a branch at all. Instead, it was designated in public and employee timetables as the Lewisburg and Tyrone Railroad. "Bellefonte is now a great railroad center," proclaimed the October 9, 1885, edition of the *Democratic Watchman*, "and trains are arriving and departing continually, connections being made in all directions."

Penns Valley residents now had much more convenient access to the county seat, whether for shopping, courthouse business, or any number of other matters. Despite their impatience with the PRR for taking so long to complete the railroad, citizens of the valley seemed to harbor no ill will toward the company. The *Centre Reporter* chronicled an incident that, while modest in its newsworthiness, had much to say about the community's attitude. In March 1884, a locomotive was placing cars on the siding at a Spring Mills granary. "The venerable John Sweetwood of Potter Township ... did not notice the moving cars and attempted to drive across [the tracks] with his horse and buggy." The cars plowed into the rig, reducing it to splinters, killing the horse, and leaving Sweetwood with two broken ribs. The horrified station agent telegraphed details of the accident to division headquarters in Williamsport. By return wire, "the agent was authorized to offer Mr. Sweetwood $200 for damages sustained, but the latter refused, saying it was too much. . . . He asked only $75."[19]

The eastern half of the L&T originated more traffic than it received; the bulk of the carloads came from shippers from Glen Iron—site of a large iron furnace—eastward to Lewisburg. A miscellany of outbound freight included livestock, wood furniture, nails, whiskey, fruit and grain in season, and lumber. In 1886, the L&T's first full year of operation between Montandon and Bellefonte, the railroad shipped 7,646 cars to the P&E at the Montandon gateway and received about 4,656. Through

Figure 4.2. The L&T main line, looking timetable east, near the Mifflin–Centre County border. Logs were floated to sawmills via spring freshets on Penns Creek, right, until the railroad provided a year-round means of transport. *Author's collection.*

the Bellefonte gateway went 347 carloads outbound from L&T shippers and 449 inbound.[20]

The numbers skewed more heavily toward outbound traffic when the lumber industry hit full stride in the 1890s. Piercing a remote, mountainous area, the railroad gave loggers ready access to vast stands of white pine and hemlock. At least six large sawmills operated between Mifflinburg and Linden Hall, producing materials essential to Pennsylvania's growing economy: construction lumber, mine props, bark (for tanneries), ship timbers, and pulpwood (for paper). All created networks of narrow-gauge railroads to haul timber to the railroad. In 1893 the Linden Hall Lumber Company's sawmill, located in the village that gave the enterprise its name, shipped 2.4 million board feet of lumber and 10 million feet of mine props, cut from the rugged slopes of Tussey Mountain and adjoining rides south of the railroad. For a few years Linden Hall accounted for more freight than any other station on the L&T. Reichley Brothers timbered to the east of the Linden Hall company and hauled some of their logs to Poe Mills, which the L&T reached by a half-mile spur that left the main track just west of Paddy Mountain tunnel. Poe Mills owed its creation in the late 1880s to lumberman Adam Gotshall, who built a steam-powered sawmill there. A few years later Gotshall sold his interests to the Reichleys and moved his timbering activities out of the area. Poe Mills had more than 300 residents in the early 1890s, a larger population than State College in the 1890 census. The place generated so much traffic, together with John Duncan's logging operation east of Paddy Mountain tunnel, that the railroad built a station at the bore's east portal. The agent there handled billing and other paperwork and controlled the passing siding east of the portal. A number of smaller logging operations had sawmills or loaded forest products onto the L&T at Ingleby, Coburn, Spring Mills, and elsewhere. In addition, former schoolteacher Evan M. Huyett cut timber for barrel staves and shipped as many as ten boxcars of staves each week from his mills at Centre Hall and Coburn.[21]

Timber was a resource not quickly renewed, especially given the wasteful practices of the lumber barons of that era. By 1900, the Poe forests were exhausted and the Paddy Mountain agency withdrawn. "Ingleby, a once-lively lumber settlement with perhaps a dozen families, has dried up and now has two families left," observed the *Centre Democrat* on July 10, 1902. "Poe Mills, two miles from Ingleby, is in the same predicament." Reichley Brothers continued to work in the Seven Mountains area and load on the Poe Mills spur track; but by 1910 its reserves, too, were depleted. The lumber companies sold tens of thousands of despoiled acres to the state for reforestation.

The disappearance of its largest single source of revenue left the L&T in Centre County largely dependent on farm products for income. For example, creameries in Coburn, Spring Mills, and Centre Hall shipped milk, cream, and butter by rail. The high quality of the local herds soon became widely known among dairymen throughout the mid-Atlantic states. In 1900, the Centre Hall station dispatched more than a hundred carloads of dairy cattle for breeding purposes. Flour mills generated traffic for the railroad at Coburn and Centre Hall, and Coburn also boasted a cannery. Several towns had feed, grain, and coal dealers; fresh fruits and berries were shipped in season from various points along the line. One dedicated freight train operating daily in each direction was usually adequate to serve the needs of shippers, although the railroad did run extra trains as seasonal demand warranted.

The more perishable goods, such as milk, were transported on the two passenger trains that traveled each way over the L&T six days a week. One of those trains also carried a railway post office, picking up and dropping off at stations along the line while sorting and canceling mail en route. Private contract carriers handled the mail between railroad stations and rural residents. In Spring Mills in 1903, for example, four carriers fanned out after the arrival of the mail on the 8:45 AM train, making deliveries along 97 route-miles before returning with outgoing mail in time for the late afternoon train. It was an efficient system that, combined with telephone lines being introduced at that time, did much to break down the isolation of rural life.[22]

The combined net income of the L&T's east and west segments peaked early in the company's history—about $34,000 in 1888. The decline of lumbering and iron ore mining around Scotia the west end brought a corresponding reduction in income. The railroad netted only $5,600 in 1906, the last year it would operate in the black. By 1911, the PRR's books showed that L&T operations were losing more than $20,000 a year.[23]

Financial losses might have been even greater had the Pennsylvania closed the gap in the L&T between Lemont and Fairbrook and run the line through State College, incorporated as a borough in 1896 with about 500 residents, exclusive of students. Since 1892, the town had been served by the Bellefonte Central Railroad, an independently owned short line that interchanged with the PRR at the county seat. But the quality of the BFC's passenger service did not meet everyone's expectations. The short line operated only mixed trains, which made a circuitous 19-mile journey between terminals that were less than 12 air-line miles apart. Riders complained of frequent equipment breakdowns, minor derailments, and other disruptions typical of rural, short line railroading. Much of the college population hailed from urban areas and were accustomed to a level of sophistication in travel that the rustic Bellefonte Central simply could not furnish. Travelers heading from State College to Pittsburgh and points west disliked having to go east on the BFC to Bellefonte, change trains, and then go west to Tyrone over the Bald Eagle Valley Railroad. A direct link to Tyrone that the L&T could provide would save several hours for passengers and a day's transit time for freight. The Pennsylvania's corporate identity and standard of service were known worldwide, and could help put the college on the map, literally and figuratively.

Beginning in the 1890s, Penn State president George Atherton lobbied PRR officials to finish the L&T. Atherton died in office in 1906, but his successor, Edwin E. Sparks, kept up the pressure. It was Sparks who reportedly first uttered the oft-repeated phrase that "Penn State is in the exact center of the state—equally inaccessible from every point." He enlisted support from the state Grange and the state Board of Agriculture, historically two of the college's closest allies. In the face of pressure from these bodies, the Pennsylvania conducted a feasibility study that found no significant potential for freight revenue between Fairbrook and Lemont beyond miscellaneous farm products and a bit of pulpwood. On the passenger side, after years of sluggish growth Penn State enrollment was exploding, surpassing 600 undergraduates in 1905 and growing by a hundred or so each year after that. The population of State College borough had increased to about 3,000 residents by 1910, steadily closing in on Bellefonte, which had 4,100. Nevertheless, the PRR believed local passenger trains to be money-losers, a conclusion affirmed in the immediate area by the L&T's experience. Hoping to put an end to the matter, PRR president James McCrea explained in a February 7, 1910, letter to the head of the state Grange that "the construction of this line has heretofore been looked into with the result that additional revenues to be derived therefrom would not justify the expenditure involved."[24]

Bellefonte resident James A. Beaver—chairman of the college's board of trustees and a former Pennsylvania governor—took up the cause. He asked his friend Samuel Rea, PRR second vice president, to have McCrea reconsider the matter. "I do not know that the increase of trade upon this road would pay a return on the money invested in the completion of it," Beaver confessed to Rea. "[But] I will be glad if you could take a broader view than that of securing a return for the money invested." The state's entire population would greatly benefit from an improved means of travel to and from Pennsylvania's only land-grant college, maintained Beaver. He also reminded Rea that Penn State was providing technical training for PRR employees at Altoona and Williamsport and supplying the railroad with graduate civil and mechanical engineers.[25]

Rea was sympathetic. He had grown up in Hollidaysburg, in adjacent Blair County, and appreciated the problems associated with a rural location. He sent a note to McCrea suggesting factors beyond bottom-line financial statements should be examined in deciding whether to build the L&T into State College.

> You are aware that this matter has already been carefully considered by our operating department. But due weight also should be given to the work the college is doing for the state and its citizens, and unless the Pennsylvania R.R. Co., which has a monopoly of the railroad business in that section, is willing to thus indirectly contribute to the common good, and to its own good—perhaps remotely —no better railroad facilities are likely to be secured for many years. I think we should consider the matter in this light. . . . I think the cost of this proposed extension should be ascertained and the probable additional loss incurred in its operation, and full consideration be given to all sides of the subject.[26]

Such pleas had no effect on James McCrea, who was arguably the most financially conservative executive ever to head the PRR. Possessing a well-known dislike for branch line passenger operations, the president refused to change his mind. "While I recognize that it would no doubt be a convenience to State College," McCrea told Rea, "we both know it would not pay, and I cannot say that State College is isolated in such a manner as to make it incumbent upon us, from the standpoint of public policy, to build such a branch. [It] would simply be for local accommodation and have no other importance whatever."[27]

Despite his blunt words, McCrea could not put the issue to rest. In May 1912, newspapers reported that the New York Central wanted to acquire the Bellefonte Central and the Central Railroad of Pennsylvania, a relatively new short line that ran between Bellefonte and a connection with the New York Central at Mill Hall, Clinton County. It was widely rumored that the NYC planned the acquisition as the first step in a larger effort to reach the Broad Top coalfields and then establish a connection with the Western Maryland Railway near Cumberland, Maryland.[28] Worried about those intentions, Rea asked George Creighton, general superintendent of the railroad's Eastern Pennsylvania Grand Division, to run a survey for the proposed line that would run through State College. He also asked Creighton if completing the L&T could attract enough State College business away from the Bellefonte Central so as to bankrupt the short line. The PRR could then step in and buy the little railroad at a bargain price, thus denying the property to the NYC. Creighton reported that the missing link would cost about $330,000 to build and $14,000 a year to operate and maintain. The added revenue would just about cover the Pennsylvania's increased operations and maintenance costs, and yes, said the superintendent, the PRR would probably suck the BFC dry of both passenger and freight business.[29]

On November 12, 1912, Samuel Rea visited Penn State and met with Edwin Sparks. The PRR executive said he would recommend to the board of directors that the L&T be completed on condition that local property owners donate land for the right-of-way. But months passed and the Pennsylvania failed to move ahead with the project. Sparks was baffled. He wrote to Rea's assistant, Albert J. County, on December 29, 1913: "We have been hoping that Santa Claus in the form of the Pennsylvania Railroad would have a Christmas present for us, but thus far he has not come down our chimney." County's reply was cryptic: "We have had so many unproductive propositions during the past few years that we do not wish to undertake any more for some time."[30] He did not mention that his company had concluded that the New York Central lost interest—if it ever had any—in expanding into the Nittany Valley. As a result, building a line of dubious profitability to ward off a competitor lost urgency for the PRR.

In 1913, in an effort to simplify the L&T's labyrinthine corporate and financial structure, the Pennsylvania foreclosed on its bonds. It reorganized the company as the Lewisburg & Tyrone Railway and purchased all of its stock. Then on April 30, 1915, the "new" L&T was absorbed into the PRR. The eastern half became the Bellefonte Branch, which extended from Milesburg through Bellefonte to Montandon. The western half became the Fairbrook Branch. The two segments were forever divided.

Notes

1. John Blair Linn, *Annals of Buffalo Valley, Pennsylvania, 1755–1855* (Harrisburg: L. S. Hart, 1877; reprint, Bowie, MD: Heritage Books, 1989), 554. The board of directors minute books for the LC&SC and successor companies are in the Penn Central Collection, Pennsylvania Railroad Subsidiary Lines, MG 286.986, 286.989, and 286.996, Pennsylvania State Archives. An overview of the railroad's history is Michael Bezilla, "The PRR's Lewisburg & Tyrone Railroad: When Two Halves Didn't Make a Whole," *Keystone* 39 (Spring 2006):18–40.

2. A. B. Warford, *Report of the Survey for the Lewisburg, Centre and Spruce Creek Railroad* (Harrisburg: Keystone Printers, 1857).

3. *New York Times*, 3 December 1865; *Report of the President and Managers of the Philadelphia and Reading Railroad to the Stockholders* (Philadelphia: Leisenring's Steam Printing House, 1866), 63–77; Stephen C. Troy, "Early History of the Catawissa Railroad." *Beeline* 23, no. 4 (2001): 8–16.

4. Mary Belle Lontz, *Early Railroads of Union County, Pennsylvania* (Lewisburg, PA: M. B. Lontz, 2002), 14–15. This work reprints local newspaper articles about the LC&SC from the 1860s and early 1870s. Union County also is the focus of Tony Shively's three-part history, "The Arrival of the Lewisburg & Tyrone Railroad," *Millmont Times*, February, March, and April 2012.

5. *Lewisburg Chronicle* articles 1870–71, reprinted in Lontz, *Early Railroads of Union County*, 12–49.

6. *Report of the Investigating Committee of the Pennsylvania Railroad Co.* (Philadelphia: Allen, Lane & Scott, 1874); Albert Churella, *The Pennsylvania Railroad: Building an Empire, 1846–1917* (Philadelphia: University of Pennsylvania Press, 2012), 446–47, 538–39.

7. The *Centre Reporter* was published at Centre Hall by LC&SC stockholder Fred Kurtz.

8. *Centre Reporter*, 21 June 1877.

9. The *Tyrone Herald*, 27 June 1878, reprinted Slifer's report.

10. Andrew Carnegie, *Autobiography of Andrew Carnegie* (New York: Houghton, Mifflin, 1920), 212–14.

11. H. H. Stoek, "The Mining and Washing of Iron Ores at Scotia, Pennsylvania," *Colliery Engineer and Metal Miner* 16 (December 1895): 101–3; Charles H. Ness, "Andrew Carnegie in Centre County: The Scotia Venture," *Journal of the Alleghenies* 10 (1974): 25–29; *Philipsburg Journal*, 4 June 1886; *Keystone Gazette* (Bellefonte), 15 June 1888.

12. W. R. White, "Early Iron Production in Central Pennsylvania," 22-page typescript, 1924, Pennsylvania State University Special Collections Library; E. V. D'Inviliers, "The Brown Hematite (Limonite) Ores of Siluro-Cambrian Limestone, No. II, of Centre County, Pennsylvania," *Proceedings of the Engineers' Club of Philadelphia* (November 1884): 209–22; Elizabeth Nearhoof, *Echoes from Warriors Mark and Surrounding Areas* (State College, PA: Self-published, 1968), 62–64, 113–20.

13. White, "Early Iron Production," 6–8.

14. *Centre Reporter*, 2 January 1884.

78 BRANCH LINE EMPIRES

15. Ibid.; Michael Bezilla, "P&R in the Nittany Valley," *Bee Line* 23, no. 2 (2001): 19–23.

16. Pennsylvania Railroad Bellefonte Branch track chart, office of the Susquehanna District engineer, 31 December 1964. John Szwarc, "The Centre Hall, Pa., Depot," *Railroad Model Craftsman* 63 (April 1995): 61–64, includes building elevations and details for modelers.

17. Nearly every edition of the weekly *Centre Reporter* from summer through fall 1885 contained information about the start-up of service over the L&T.

18. "Announcements to the students of the Pennsylvania State College concerning conveyances for Lemont trains," 25 August 1885 and 29 March 1897, George W. Atherton Papers, Subseries B, Box 6, Pennsylvania State University Special Collections Library.

19. *Centre Reporter*, 2 April 1884.

20. Pennsylvania Railroad Company, *Annual Report of the Board of Directors to the Stockholders* (Philadelphia: PRR, 1886).

21. Benjamin F. G. Kline Jr.'s two self-published works (at Lancaster, PA), *Pitch Pine and Prop Timber* (1971) and *Wildcatting on the Mountain* (1970), chronicle logging operations along the L&T.

22. L&T passenger and freight traffic data: *Centre Reporter*, various dates. Shippers are identified in PRR Form C. T. 1000, "List of Stations and Sidings," various dates. A secondary source is Bruce Teeple, ed., *Glimpses of the Past: A Selected History of Penn Township, Centre County, Pennsylvania, 1844–1994* (Aaronsburg, PA: Aaronsburg Historical Museum, 1994), 11–28.

23. PRR *Annual Report*, various dates 1888–1913.

24. McCrea to W. T. Creasy, 7 February 1910, Pennsylvania Railroad Co., Executive Department, Record Group 5, Subgroup B, Office of Vice President Samuel Rea, Hagley Museum and Library, Wilmington, DE.

25. Beaver to Rea, 27 May 1910, Rea file.

26. Rea to McCrea, 31 May 1910, Rea file.

27. McCrea to Rea, 3 June 1910, Rea file.

28. *Philipsburg Daily Journal*, 23 May 1912; *Centre Democrat* (Bellefonte), 14 November 1912.

29. Creighton to Rea, 7 June 1912 and 4 November 1912, Rea file.

30. Sparks to County, 29 December 1913, and County to Sparks, 30 December 1913, Rea file.

FIVE

Uniting the Branch Lines

The PRR's Tyrone Division

ON THE PENNSYLVANIA, AS ON MOST RAILROADS, DIVISIONS WERE
the core units of the operating department—that part of the company
charged with actually moving trains. The PRR consisted of nine divisions by 1872; each was semiautonomous, headed by a superintendent whose absolute power and sweeping responsibilities resembled
those of a general commanding a large military force—a division.
His "troops" were the train crews, maintenance-of-way gangs, station
agents, car inspectors, coach cleaners, and countless others who had a
hand in making sure that trains ran safely, efficiently, and on time. By
overlaying a divisional organization on the lines it controlled in Centre
County and the Moshannon Valley, the PRR was able to centralize
managerial oversight of those lines and achieve efficiencies typically
associated with such centralization. In addition, uniting a group of rural
branch lines that were off the beaten path of the railroad's main lines
testified to the great economic value of the territory those branches
served.

The Tyrone Division's formal origins are murky. The Pennsylvania's
annual report to stockholders for 1863 notes that the Tyrone and Clearfield and the Bald Eagle Valley railroads were detached from the Middle Division "and organized as a separate division under the charge of a

resident engineer," but it fails to specify the name of the new division. The resident engineer's post had evolved into a "superintendent of branch lines" by 1867, and the 1869 report is the first to reference a "Tyrone Division." As of that date, the division included 118 miles of "first track," that is, the principal stems of the T&C and BEV, plus many more miles of sidings and spurs.

In 1869 Tyrone had about 1,800 residents, with the Pennsylvania Railroad easily ranking as the town's largest employer. In 1880, soon after the original passenger station burned, the railroad built a three-story red-brick station that doubled as an office building for the superintendent and his assistants, train dispatchers, crew callers, clerks, and various lower-level supervisors. Across town on Tyrone's east side, there was constant activity in the freight yard, car and machine shops, car scales, and new thirty-stall enginehouse. Trains arrived from, or departed for, Altoona, Osceola, Clearfield, Bellefonte, Lock Haven, and other points at all hours of the day and night.[1]

Two additions to the Tyrone Division occurred in the early 1880s with the PRR's acquisition of the Bellefonte and Snow Shoe Railroad and the construction of the west end of the Lewisburg and Tyrone Railroad. Of the two, the Snow Shoe line was much longer-lived and originated far more tonnage. It deserves a closer look, along with the Tyrone and Clearfield and the Bald Eagle Valley lines.

When the Pennsylvania leased the T&C in 1862, James Lewis was placed in charge of operations, and Samuel Black was superintendent of the BEV. Both men were headquartered in Tyrone and oversaw railroads that were extremely primitive by later standards. Stations were not linked by telegraph, although the PRR had been using the telegraph to dispatch trains over the main line since the mid-1850s. Trains dispatched from Tyrone over the T&C and the BEV operated by authority of a written timetable, a system that worked fairly well when only one or two trains ran over the line each day. Thus, an evening train of empty coal cars bound for Osceola might be held at Tyrone until the arrival of the passenger train from Philipsburg. If the passenger train were delayed, the reason would not necessarily be apparent to the Tyrone dispatcher. He might opt to start the coal empties in the opposite direction; but its crew would have to "run curves," which meant stopping their train at every curve and sending a man ahead to flag anything that might be coming the other way.

Veteran conductor Bill Irvin of Philipsburg recollected the closest call he ever had in his career came while running curves in a snowstorm east of Julian on the Bald Eagle Valley Railroad.[2] A drunken engineer, forgetting that Irvin was proceeding on foot ahead of him, suddenly opened the throttle. "I ran into a cattle guard that was drifted full of snow and I got stuck there," Irvin wrote. "I tried to signal but the snow was flying and [the engineer] was in no condition to see the signal." The desperate conductor managed to fling himself off the track at the last second. Once the train stopped and he was back in the locomotive cab, Irvin thawed himself out by having a "warm conversation" with the man who almost "put me out of the railroad business."

Irvin related an equally harrowing tale from the Tyrone and Clearfield between Vail and Osceola, a segment that T&C men referred to simply as "the mountain." He was working the passenger train from Osceola when it derailed in a snowstorm just after dark near Powelton. "That left us in a fix," Irvin recounted. "Tyrone was 15 miles away and there was no communication. All the engines from Osceola had already gone down the mountain, so there was nothing to do but go to Tyrone and get another engine.... We intended to walk on up to Summit, where empty cars were frequently left, get a flat car, and start it down the hill." Pending rescue, the potbellied coal stove in the coach would keep the passengers warm.

Unfortunately there were no cars at Summit except for a section man's hand truck. Irvin and the train's brakeman, Sam Hood, no sooner set the little car in motion than it stuck fast in a snowdrift. The two then trudged down to the Big Fill, where section foreman Paddy Murphy lived in a shanty provided by the railroad. The beleaguered pair gratefully accepted a hot meal and some whiskey from Murphy and his wife, then set out again down the hill. At Gardner, they left the track to take a shortcut but lost their bearings in the darkness and falling snow. A farmer, awakened in the wee hours, pointed them in the direction of Vail, which they knew had a newly established telegraph office for trains running the Bald Eagle Valley line. The pair at length reached the Vail station and had the agent wire Tyrone for assistance. "That was the first information

Jimmy Lewis had of the whereabouts of our train, and there had been a good deal of excitement around division headquarters," Irvin recalled, no doubt with some understatement. Lewis saw to it that Irvin and Hood got some hot whiskey and a warm bed at the nearby Ward House, then sent a rescue train back up the mountain to assist the stalled train.

Irvin was fortunate in finding a telegraph at Vail. The railroad used wire strung along its line through the Bald Eagle Valley in 1865 by the Atlantic and Ohio Telegraph Company, part of the Western Union system. Telegraphic communication came to the T&C soon thereafter.[3] The telegraph allowed the Tyrone dispatcher to send running orders to stations along the railroad. Operators located at those wayside posts then copied the orders and handed them up to the train crews.

George C. Wilkins became the first official to actually hold the title of superintendent when the Tyrone Division was officially organized. Wilkins had begun his railroad career in 1853, serving mostly in civil engineering posts until being named to a division superintendency in 1866 on the PRR's Philadelphia and Erie line.[4] At Tyrone, he drew on his engineering experience to expand the yard and shop complex and realign the bed of Little Bald Eagle Creek to make room for more tracks, mostly to hold coal cars going to or from the T&C.

Wilkins arrived on the division about the same time that locomotive fuel was transitioning from wood to bituminous coal. The archetypal wood-burner was the 4-4-0, usually called the American type because of its widespread use on the nation's railroads. A 24-ton version could handle about seven cars of 10 gross tons each up the grade from Osceola. Within a few years, the heaviest engines on the mountain were newer, coal-burning 4-6-0 Ten-wheeler and 2-6-0 Mogul types, each weighing 30–33 tons. The Pennsylvania began experimenting with the even larger 2-8-0 Consolidation type, purchasing fourteen for freight service between 1868 and 1873. The second of this group, No. 1111, underwent three days of testing on the Tyrone and Clearfield in May 1870. The results showed the new engine could pull a 300-ton train from Osceola to Summit without assistance, compared with a maximum of 190 tons (ten cars of 19 gross tons each) typically assigned a single 4-6-0.[5]

The most unusual locomotives to grace T&C rails during Wilkins's reign were Baltimore builder Ross Winans's 0-8-0 "Camels," featuring

Figure 5.1. The train-order and telegraph office at Vail. The locomotive at left is likely in service on the T&C, as indicated by its spark arrestor–equipped diamond-shaped stack. *Tyrone Area Historical Society.*

slanted fireboxes and a huge cab atop the boiler. The PRR ordered eleven of these monsters in the mid-1850s for service on the main line over the Alleghenies. Between 1863 and 1867, the Altoona shops rebuilt them as conventional, rear-cab 2-6-0 types. They earned a reputation as good pullers but were also notorious for poor combustion and endless billows of cinder-filled black smoke as they ravenously consumed their fuel; they could be operated economically only on a line that had an abundant supply of cheap coal. Whether they could negotiate the curve at the Big Fill as 0-8-0s is a matter of conjecture, but they certainly visited the line after being rebuilt.[6]

The Winans machines turned out to be the first in a long line of aging power sent to the T&C, mostly for helper service. The PRR preferred newer locomotives for main line duties; anything that had trouble steaming or was approaching either major repairs or the scrap heap often ended up pushing coal. This strategy added its own risks to the dangers inherent in mountain railroading. When rebuilt Camel No. 91 exploded near Sandy Ridge on the morning of March 31, 1876, at the rear of a coal train, it had been in service for twenty-two years, a long time by the standards of the era. Three crewmen were killed, and the engine was demolished.[7]

In 1873 George Wilkins was named superintendent of the Baltimore Division. According to PRR historian William B. Wilson, "he left the Tyrone Division, which he had received in the usual poor condition of a lateral branch line, fully up to Pennsylvania Railroad standards."[8] In Baltimore, Wilkins replaced Samuel S. Blair, who came to Tyrone. Blair, a stout man whose round face and walrus mustache made him resemble the cartoonish tycoon figure in the Monopoly game, had started with the PRR as a freight conductor in 1854. Seven years later he was a station agent in Baltimore, heroically defending company property as Southern sympathizers rioted in an effort to stop Union troops from moving through the city. Blair was to remain in Tyrone for thirty years—an extraordinarily long time for a superintendent to stay in one place in an era when the Pennsylvania moved its managers as if pieces in a chess game.[9]

Samuel Blair took over just as coal traffic on the T&C began a period of incredible growth. The railroad carried 432,000 tons of coal in 1872 and topped a million tons four years later. Beginning in 1878, when shipments totaled nearly 1.3 million tons, the Tyrone and Clearfield became the PRR's largest single source of bituminous coal, a distinction it held until surpassed by the Westmoreland district in 1897. Annual shipments topped 3.2 million tons in 1884, a year that saw Pennsylvania coal mines statewide ship 28 million tons of bituminous. In 1884 the T&C also reported the second-highest gross operating income of any of the PRR's twenty-one leased railroad companies (east of Pittsburgh): $688,000, of which it brought about $241,000 down to net.[10]

To keep pace with the burgeoning coal industry, the T&C's main stem was extended from Clearfield 7 miles to Curwensville in 1874 and another 5 miles to reach mines around Grampian in 1892. That same year the Moshannon Branch, which accounted for more than half of the T&C's annual coal tonnage, reached what would become its ultimate terminus at McCartney in the highlands of southern Clearfield County, 21 miles from Osceola. It begat a multitude of lesser lines, which in turn begat their own branches, most named for the mines they served or a local geographic feature—Ednie, Forsyth, Burley, Banian, Betz, Vulcan, Trout Run, Muddy Run, Coal Run, Big Run, and on and on. As if weary of finding names for all these splinters, often the PRR simply numbered them, as in Amesville Branches 1, 2 and 3. Traffic funneling over the Moshannon Branch grew to such an extraordinary level that the railroad double-tracked the 5 miles between Osceola and Goss Run Junction, jumping-off point for Goss Run Branches 1, 2, and 3.[11]

Two factors propelled this tremendous growth: the exploitation of a coal seam known to geologists as the Lower Freeport, and the rise of Berwind, White as a mining and marketing powerhouse. In some parts of the upper Moshannon Valley, the Lower Freeport seam could be found in beds as thick as 7 feet. It possessed high heating values, was relatively low in sulfur and other impurities, ignited quickly yet was long-burning, and made little smoke and ash. Marketed as Moshannon Coal, it commanded premium prices. The editors of *Saward's Journal*, the bible of the coal trade, described it as "one of Nature's best gifts to man." So renowned was Moshannon Coal that a 7-foot section taken from a mine near Houtzdale received the Order of Specific Merit from the World's Columbian Commission at the Chicago Exposition in 1893.[12]

Moshannon Coal owed its unique brand to brothers Charles and Edward Berwind, sons of a German cabinetmaker who had settled in Philadelphia in the 1840s. Charles started as an office boy for coal and iron magnate Robert Hare Powel and rose to become a Powel vice president at the age of 23. "One of Charles's great strengths," wrote the official Berwind corporate historian, "was his ability to reconcile conflict through personal intervention." It was Charles Berwind who poured oil on troubled waters when relations between the Powel organization and the Pennsylvania Railroad had deteriorated to an uncomfortable level during the legislative hearings of the 1860s. That experience convinced Charles that an alliance between the larger coal producers and the coal carriers was essential to their mutual prosperity.

In 1874, he left Powel to join Allison White, a former congressman from Lock Haven who had moved to Philadelphia and invested heavily in coal and timber, including the Big Mill in Osceola. White was a principal in mines near Osceola and Houtzdale and wanted Berwind's expertise to help market the coal. Edward Berwind soon came on board as a partner. Berwind, White and Company's first mine, located at Houtzdale, was named Eureka—a Greek word meaning "I have found it!" The description applied perfectly, because it was first time the Berwinds peddled fuel under the Moshannon Coal label. The result far exceeded their expectations. By 1886, nearly half of the 500 or so coal cars weighed at the Tyrone scales every day came from as many as twenty Berwind, White mines, whose names would echo across generations of miners and their descendants: Eureka, Excelsior, Ocean, Atlantic, Pacific, Mapleton, and many more.

Until the Berwinds pointed the way, the Pennsylvania Railroad shipped little or no coal to the New York market. Edward Berwind, a former naval officer, made the rounds of the steamship company offices there, touting the superiority of Moshannon Coal. Within a few years, Berwind, White became the primary coal provisioner to virtually every large steamship line sailing from New York. The company also set up bunkering depots in the Caribbean and in coal-poor South America, supplying not only commercial vessels but the US Navy. Berwind, White grew so large and complex that the partnership became unwieldy; in 1886 it was incorporated as the Berwind-White Coal Mining Company. Allison White died soon after, but the name remained unchanged, although the firm was now controlled by the Berwind family—Charles and Edward, and their younger brothers Harry and John.[13]

Because entering the coal mining business was relatively easy and inexpensive, the Moshannon Valley counted numerous small-scale producers, many of whom felt threatened by Berwind-White. In the fall of 1883, the *Osceola Reveille* was reporting growing dissatisfaction among local coal operators with the PRR's car-supply methods. Owners

renewed their claims, first voiced in the 1860s, that an adequate number
of empty cars from the general freight pool came over the T&C from
Tyrone, but that upon the cars' arrival in Osceola, the Pennsylvania designated many of them for "special assignment," in effect reserving them
for Berwind-White. Coal mining was a highly cyclical enterprise, depending on the season of the year and the state of the economy. Smaller
mines tended to produce for the commercial market only in boom
times. It simply was not practical for the PRR to roster enough cars to
meet peak demand, because many of them would sit idle in less prosperous times. The Pennsylvania tried to steer a middle course, making sure
its largest customers always had enough cars while accepting the risk
that smaller shippers might sometimes be overlooked—and would be
highly vocal in their complaints. This compromise course meant that
in some years during the 1880s, car shortages prevented the railroad
from carrying as much as 200,000 tons of coal from the Moshannon
Valley.[14]

That policy suited Berwind-White; shutting out some would-be mine
operators would help to prevent a glut in the coal market that could cut
short a period of rising prices. To insulate itself from the vagaries of car
supply and to help control costs, Berwind-White acquired its own cars,
a relatively common practice among large coal shippers on many roads.
The core of the Berwind-White fleet once belonged to the Robert Hare
Powel organization. Responding to the shortages of the 1860s, Powel
had purchased about 500 20-ton-capacity hopper-bottom gondolas built
to PRR standard designs. When the Powelton Coal and Iron Company
started to fail after Powel's death in 1883, Berwind-White bought the
entire lot, then went on to order new cars until it rostered more than a
thousand. The cars were stenciled "Return to Tyrone, Pa., Penna. R.R."
and carried as the corporate logo a black ball within a white square—the
symbol that Powel had used and that Berwind-White cars would carry
well into the next century. To maintain its fleet, the coal company built
a large car shop in Osceola adjacent to the Moshannon Branch.[15]

Local coal operators also were disgruntled over what they correctly
perceived to be the PRR's discriminatory rates. State or federal oversight of freight rates was virtually nonexistent; Pennsylvania's constitution prohibited discriminatory rates but left it to the courts to define

Figure 5.2. "Return to Tyrone, Pa., Penna. R.R." is stenciled on the side of this wooden-bodied Berwind-White Coal Mining Company car. The company used hundreds of such cars to serve its mines in the Moshannon Valley, maintaining them at its Osceola shop. *Richard Burg collection.*

"discriminatory," and courts were reluctant to intervene in the relationship between shipper and carrier. Large companies such as Berwind-White often paid less per ton-mile than their smaller counterparts by receiving covert drawbacks or rebates from the railroad. Mine owners worked in an extremely competitive environment, with the thinnest of profit margins. Shaving off a few cents per ton in transportation costs could make a big difference in how much coal an owner could sell and a railroad could handle.

Even among large coal shippers, Berwind-White was exceptional in the influence it had on the Pennsylvania's executive officers. Where local coal operators might send a complaint or a request to superintendent Blair, the Berwinds discussed matters directly with PRR president George Roberts or his senior associates. The two companies' corporate headquarters were only a few blocks apart in Philadelphia, and their executives pretty much belonged to the same social circles and corporate boards. In July 1893, for instance, after Berwind-White leased rights to 120 acres of Lower Freeport coal in Rush Township on the high ground overlooking Osceola, vice president Harry Berwind asked Samuel Rea, then Roberts's assistant, if the PRR would build nearly a mile of track from Osceola yard to reach the proposed Eureka No. 21 colliery. A year later the Osceola Branch was completed—the railroad even built side tracks at the mine at no cost to Berwind-White.[16]

National recognition of the importance of the Moshannon Valley's coal and allied industries came in 1890 when US president Benjamin Harrison visited the area. Harrison and his wife, Carrie, were spending a late-summer vacation at Cresson Springs, a popular resort atop the Alleghenies, adjacent to the PRR main line. The president received many invitations to visit communities throughout the region. One such came from banker and former congressman John Patton of Curwensville to tour the Clearfield-area coalfields. Another came from a miners' organization in Houtzdale in the Moshannon Valley.

The president accepted both, deciding to combine them in a single trip. On Saturday, September 20, he arrived in Osceola at noon aboard a special two-car train draped in red, white, and blue bunting. Among the small party accompanying the Harrisons were PRR general superintendent Frank Sheppard, who was in charge of the overall move, and Samuel Blair, who boarded at Tyrone. More than 5,000 people turned out for the train's arrival, nearly three times as many as the town's resident population. The president gave a five-minute address in which he noted how pleased he was with the "welcome in this home of profit and industry." Osceola had favored the Republican Harrison over the Democrat Grover Cleveland in the 1888 election, but the crowd was warmly nonpartisan. "It was not a time when politics draws a line of demarcation," observed the *Philipsburg Journal*. The president and his wife toured the community by carriage before returning to their train for the 5-mile trip up the Moshannon Branch to Houtzdale, where an even bigger throng waited. Mines and stores were closed for the occasion, allowing an exceptionally large turnout to hear the chief executive make his only formal speech of the day.

The presidential special steamed back down the branch and went on to Philipsburg, arriving there at 2:40 PM. "You must excuse my not addressing you at any length because of the very limited time at our disposal," he explained to Mayor Warfel and the reception committee, before boarding yet another carriage for a fifteen-minute tour of the town amid cheers from the thousands who lined the streets. Harrison's party made additional stops at Clearfield and Curwensville before returning after dark to Tyrone and eventually Cresson Springs.[17]

The Moshannon Valley's "prosperity and industry" was most closely identified with coal, but fortunes were made in the exploitation of other natural resources, too. Lumbering flourished into the 1870s, as evidenced by the area's numerous sawmills. By the 1880s, as forest reserves thinned, the clay mines and brickyards of the refractories industry were just getting started. All along the T&C from Sandy Ridge north to Clearfield lay large deposits of flint clay, an extremely hard type of clay relatively free of iron and alkalies. Its ability to withstand high temperatures made it an ideal refractory or firebrick for lining industrial furnaces. In the Sandy Ridge area, the flint clay beds averaged 5 feet in thickness, although in some places it was as thick as 12 feet. The clay contained an unusually high concentration of alumina, as much as 35 percent by weight. Alumina brick had an even higher melting point than brick made from ordinary flint clay and was much in demand by steelmakers for lining Bessemer converters.

John Miller of Blair County started the very first brickyard along the T&C in 1866 at Sandy Ridge. He was soon joined in the fledgling enterprise by his son William. The Millers used a simple, centuries-old process for making brick. Raw flint clay was ground with a small amount of bonding clay (usually found in the same area as the harder clay) to give the material some stickiness or plasticity as it was carefully mixed with water. The material was then molded into the desired shapes, dried, and baked in coal-fired kilns.

Within twenty years the Sandy Ridge brickyard ranked among the largest in the state; it was also the PRR's leading source of refractory brick for lining steam locomotive fireboxes. The works boasted a 300-horsepower steam engine in the powerhouse, a smokestack 80 feet tall, and nearly a hundred employees. In operation around the clock, seven days a week, the plant could make nearly 15 million bricks a year. In 1908 it was acquired by local entrepreneurs D. Ross Wynn and James H. France, whose brickyard at West Decatur, north of Philipsburg, had more orders than it could fill. They sold the Sandy Ridge works two years later to a West Virginia–based brick maker in which Wynn had a financial interest. That company reorganized in 1911 as General Refractories and was destined to become a giant in the industry, with more than twenty plants in the Mid-Atlantic states. After fire destroyed the works in 1912, General Refractories quickly rebuilt the facility and increased its capacity.

Robert Hare Powel was a partner in a brickyard started at Retort—a settlement between Sandy Ridge and Powelton—in 1878. After Powel's death, a western Pennsylvania refractories firm, Isaac Reese and Sons, bought the plant. In 1908 Reese sold to Harbison-Walker, a Pittsburgh-based company that was an even larger force in the industry than General Refractories. Harbison-Walker had already purchased a Philipsburg brickyard established by Richard Benson Wigton, a Philadelphia entrepreneur and cofounder of the Morrisdale Coal Company, and continued buying out its smaller competitors at a pace that matched General Refractories' acquisitions. By 1912, the two giants owned nearly all of the brickyards between Philipsburg and Clearfield.[18]

Heavily tilted toward coal and brick, the Tyrone and Clearfield likely had the busiest main track of all the PRR's branch railroads, as measured by tonnage and the number of train movements. The railroad's standard coal car of the 1880s was the class GB hopper-bottom gondola of 20–25 tons capacity. The car had two four-wheel trucks and a wooden body, and discharged its load through a single chute or hopper in the bottom of the floor.[19] Twenty-five or so of these coal cars, together with three locomotives (two ahead and one pushing), comprised a typical train departing Osceola for Tyrone. On their first two trips up the hill, the locomotives set out their cars at Summit and returned to Osceola for more loads. On the third trip, they picked up the two cuts previously set out and headed down to Tyrone with a train of around seventy-five cars. Under that operating scenario, moving 3 million tons of coal and lesser amounts of brick, lumber, and other freight in a year's time required dispatching nearly 6,000 trains from Osceola to Summit, with about one-third that number continuing down the Allegheny Front. Trains returning from Tyrone, consisting largely of empties, could range up to a hundred cars powered by several locomotives fore and aft. The railroad also had to run two or three daily passenger trains each way amid the avalanche of freight traffic.[20]

Scant documentation has survived to reveal how the T&C handled all these trains. Philipsburg was the initial hub. It had a four-stall wood-frame enginehouse, completed in 1868, and an iron turntable.[21] The enginehouse hosted locomotives used for passenger locals on the Moshannon and the Philipsburg branches, and perhaps for a local freight that worked nearby mines and brickyards. Shifter engines to gather coal and set out empties at mines also were based at one time or another at Clearfield, Curwensville, or Grampian. Coal cars were marshaled at Osceola and taken over the mountain by crews and motive power based in Tyrone.

Osceola had an enginehouse as early as 1874, but details about its size and construction are sketchy. Located across the Moshannon Creek from Osceola borough, it seems to have been home to locomotives that worked the mine runs up and down the Moshannon Branch.[22] By 1884 the PRR established a train dispatcher's office at "Osceola Junction," denoting the connection between the Moshannon Branch and the T&C main track. The dispatcher there in all likelihood controlled traffic on the branch and its tributaries, but how responsibilities were divided between the dispatchers at Osceola and Tyrone is unclear. Throughout the 1880s, newspapers commonly referenced "Osceola yard," indicating the tracks where trains were made up for Tyrone crews. Clearfield County historian Lewis Cass Aldrich wrote in 1887 that "all the freight, coal, lumber, etc., shipped to Tyrone, are made up and dispatched from [Osceola's] suburbs."[23] By the end of the decade, the PRR had purchased more land to expand Osceola yard.[24] A larger enginehouse was erected at the north end of the yard in 1905, and the Philipsburg enginehouse was closed.[25] It is logical to conclude that around this time the railroad ended the practice of using Tyrone crews and power for the trains over the mountain in favor of basing them at Osceola. From then on, Osceola had the Tyrone Division's second-largest yard (after Tyrone), which stretched nearly a mile along the Moshannon Creek and was eight or more tracks wide. It featured offices for a trainmaster, yardmaster, and assorted supervisors; a scale for weighing cars; and facilities at the enginehouse for coaling, watering, sanding, and performing light maintenance on locomotives.

Track and equipment on the mountain took a beating from the endless parade of trains. In 1875, as the PRR was replacing iron rails with heavier, more durable steel rails, the Tyrone and Clearfield line was the only route other than the Philadelphia–Harrisburg–Pittsburgh main line to receive a significant quantity of steel replacement rails—521 tons. The Pennsylvania also reported in 1875 that Tyrone Division freight locomotives consumed an average of $7.65 worth of coal per 100 miles—the highest rate of fuel consumption on any PRR division, well above the $5.96 reported by the second-place Pittsburgh Division. Freight locomotive repair costs were elevated, too: $7.29 per engine per 100 miles on the Tyrone Division, second only to the Pittsburgh Division's $7.86.[26]

The Pennsylvania sought to increase the capacity of the T&C's line over the mountain without incurring a huge expense. One option was to use more powerful locomotives that could haul heavier trains. After experimenting with Consolidation-type 2-8-os on the T&C and elsewhere, the PRR adopted this type in a big way for heavy freight service system-wide. It built or bought 545 H1 class 2-8-os between 1875 and 1886. The H1 was an impressive puller, but its small firebox limited its steaming capabilities. By 1885 the H1 was being supplemented on the main line by the improved H3, the first class on the Pennsylvania to use a rectangular Belpaire firebox (as differentiated to the more common radial-stay design) for superior steam production and added strength. The railroad adopted the Belpaire design for nearly every other class of steam locomotive it developed. The first H3 appeared on the T&C in April 1891.[27]

Another capacity option was to add more track. A second main track was installed from Osceola Mills to Summit, and from Vail to Tyrone, between 1883 and 1885. The PRR considered adding another track between Summit and Vail but discarded the idea because of the high cost of excavation along the steep-sloped mountains.[28]

In the early days of railroading, trains descending severe grades relied on trainmen to mount nearly every car and turn a wheel that was connected by a chain to brakes on the wheels beneath the car. The Pennsylvania Railroad was the first to adopt an air-brake system patented by George Westinghouse in 1869, which allowed the locomotive engineer to use compressed air (produced by one or more locomotive-mounted air pumps) forced through a system of pipes and hoses to set brakes automatically throughout the train. Within a few years, the PRR embraced air brakes as standard on new rolling stock, starting with passenger cars.

However, the innovation removed only part of the uncertainty from the work of T&C brakemen. Air brakes were applied serially, beginning with the car immediately behind the locomotive. Several minutes could pass before all cars were fully braked. During that interval, slack between the cars could run in, making the train difficult to control and threatening to rupture air lines between cars. Into the early 1900s, trains still comprised a mix of air- and hand-braked cars. Since air braking stopped with the first hand-braked car, rules stated that all air-brake-equipped cars were to be placed together, immediately behind the locomotive. But in the rush to make up trains, this stipulation was sometimes ignored, making the brakemen's role even more critical, and putting a premium on the engineer's train-handling skills.[29]

The sharp curve around the Big Fill complicated matters still further. When laying out the line in the 1850s, James Montgomery had nearly flattened the grade on the Fill so as not to present an insurmountable obstacle to ascending trains, which already were forced to overcome the friction of the wheel flanges against the outside rail. Montgomery had not foreseen a time when trains descending the grade were so ponderous that they, too, might stall while rounding the Fill. The PRR's solution was almost counterintuitive: downhill pushers. At least one of the engines on the rear of the train from Osceola to Summit stayed on the rear to give the train a gentle, prolonged shove as it made its way through the curve at the Fill. Trainmen had to set brakes at Summit, the number of cars depending on train length, tonnage, and the number and location of air-braked cars. Next they had to jump from one car to the next to release brakes as the train approached the Fill, then reset them as soon as the cars started downhill again. Even in daylight and fair weather, the task was one of the most dangerous jobs imaginable in a nineteenth-century world full of high-risk jobs. Moreover, with mountain curves blocking visibility of brakemen's hand signals, engineers on the downhill pushers had to rely on their own judgment. They simply started pushing when they estimated the head end had reached the Fill.[30] If something went wrong, it was every man for himself—and far too often, things went terribly wrong, as on the night of October 9, 1875. A train started down from Summit with seventy cars of coal and lumber, one engine in the lead and two on the rear. On the Fill, the train broke in two, then slammed together again with great force as the pusher engineers, unaware the train had come apart, kept their throttles open. Twenty-two cars toppled off the track and down the steep embankment. When the wreck began, conductor James C. Miller of Tyrone was about mid-train, crossing from one car to another in his effort to release hand brakes. He was caught between the cars and rolled about halfway down the fill, suffering fatal injuries. With customary PRR efficiency, a large force was put to work clearing the wreckage, and the track was opened by the afternoon of the next day.[31]

A train could pass safely around the Fill and yet run into serious trouble. This fact was illustrated in spectacular fashion on May 30, 1893, when the seventeen-car Walter L. Main Circus train careened out of control and jumped the track while rounding the last curve before the straight line approaching Vail. Testimony about what happened is contradictory; the best evidence indicates that engineer Steve "Red" Cresswell began having trouble holding back his train about halfway down the mountain. His locomotive was H3 No. 1500. Its single pump supplied compressed air only to the first seven cars; why the crew was unable or unwilling to connect air lines beyond the seventh car was never fully explained. In any case, it was decided that all seventeen cars were to be braked by hand as a precaution. The four brakemen on the seven-man crew, aware that it might be a wild ride, had drawn lots at Summit to see who would take the most dangerous position near the lead car. William Heverly of Tyrone drew the short straw. He was killed in the derailment, along with three circus people and a stowaway. Many circus animals died, and only the fact that the three sleeping cars on the rear of the train miraculously held the rail forestalled greater carnage. Walter Main himself occupied a berth in one of the sleepers and escaped unharmed.

The story's many retellings usually portray superintendent Samuel Blair as the villain for allegedly refusing to add a second locomotive at Summit to increase braking capacity. Far more likely, it was a Tyrone dispatcher or other subordinate who withheld the second locomotive. The circus train had departed Houtzdale around midnight, bound for Lewistown. It ran from Osceola up to Summit in three sections, then was reassembled into one on the mountain top shortly after 4 AM for the trip down to Tyrone. Cresswell expressed misgivings about his locomotive's ability to control the train, so conductor Bill Snyder had the operator at Summit wire the Tyrone dispatcher for a second engine. Whether the dispatcher responded on his own or consulted other operating personnel is unknown, but he almost certainly did not wake Blair for a response. In any case, the answer to Snyder's request was no. Whoever responded from Tyrone apparently forgot (or did not know in the first place) that the first ten cars on the train were not standard 40-foot circus flats but much newer and heavier 60-footers that Main had added to the circus only the year before. Each of the three stock cars behind them also was 60 feet long, making the train equivalent to thirty cars of the old style (facts that Blair surely would have known). At Summit, Snyder was eager to get going. He inspected the train one final time, checked the air lines, and assured Cresswell that everything would be fine.

The crew admitted that the train approached the curve at McCann's at 25–30 miles per hour, far in excess of the 12 miles per hour limit. There was speculation that Cresswell reversed the locomotive—a risky, old-time method of slowing a runaway train—and that maneuver resulted in an abrupt shudder that caused the first car behind the tender to derail. The engineer and fireman denied trying a reversing maneuver. They blamed the accident on a broken or burned-through wheel or axle, but no evidence of such was ever found. The coroner's jury decided the cause was "fast running of the train down the mountain" but chose not to assign a specific reason for the fast running. The PRR indemnified the circus for its loss, and Main continued touring with as many as forty-one rail cars until selling the business after the 1904 season.[32]

Operations on the Osceola side of the mountain grade were not immune to horrific accidents. One of the worst happened on June 9, 1903, in the middle of a thunderstorm. A Tyrone-bound coal train had stopped to pick up a few cars at the Orient mine near Powelton. When the train started uphill again, the two engines pulling and one pushing gained uneven traction on the slippery rail, and slack action broke the train apart near the head end. The rear of the train began to drift backward, in spite of frantic efforts to stop it. The loaded cars were soon shoving the pusher engine rearward at about 20 miles per hour. Engineer Ogle Burley sent his fireman over the car tops to help the lone brakeman tie down the cars by hand, and he applied sand under the engine to halt the spinning driving wheels. But it was no use. Burley desperately yanked the whistle cord to signal that a runaway was in progress. He reminded himself that if the afternoon local had departed Osceola on time, it would be coming up the mountain on the same track his train occupied.

A mile or so below Powelton, on a 2.65 percent slope through a narrow excavation known as the Slate Cut, the runaway and the local collided at a combined speed of about 35 miles per hour. "Engineer Burley with most heroic courage remained at his post until the tender of his engine had almost come into contact with the local's engine, when he jumped," reported the Tyrone *Herald*. His fireman and brakeman "also proved themselves heroes by remaining at their posts. They were thrown heavily on the cars and partly covered by coal" but survived their injuries. The local's engineer and two head brakemen, who could not hear Burley's shrieking whistle and had no visual warning because of a sharp curve in the Slate Cut, were killed, as were most of a carload of mules that was coupled behind the local's engine. Amazingly, fireman Earl Waite, although "considerably squeezed," crawled out from the wreckage and lived to tell the tale.[33]

In the same year as the Slate Cut disaster, the PRR merged the T&C with five other coal-hauling subsidiaries to form the Cambria and Clearfield Railway Company. The reorganization represented a step toward simplification of the Pennsylvania's corporate structure, which over time had accumulated a mass of paper railroads akin to barnacles clinging to a ship's hull. For that same reason, the C&C itself was merged into parent PRR in 1913. These maneuverings were mostly out of the public eye and wrought few if any operational changes to the former T&C, whose main stem was renamed the Clearfield Branch.

The Tyrone Division's other coal-hauling line, the Snow Shoe Branch, entered a decade of prosperity at the start of PRR control in 1881, although not on the grand scale of the Tyrone and Clearfield Railway. Annual coal shipments over the branch increased from 56,000 tons in 1880 to about 175,000 tons in 1890—not even one-tenth of the tonnage sent over the T&C.[34] Centre County's Mountaintop region was not blessed with an abundant Lower Freeport seam; where the bed did exist, it was usually thin and uneconomical to mine. The Lehigh Valley Coal Company, successor to Berwind-White on the Mountaintop, sought the

Lower Kittanning seam, deeper than Moshannon Coal and containing more impurities, but still 4–5 feet thick and high in heat value. The Lower Kittanning was suitable as both a steam coal and a metallurgical coal that could be coked for iron and steel production.

Consequently the LVCC ramped up coke production at Snow Shoe until it reached nearly 60,000 tons annually in 1890. Some coke was shipped to ironworks around Reading, Bethlehem, and other locations in eastern Pennsylvania for about $4 per ton. The Lehigh Valley's coke sold in Bellefonte for only $0.90 per ton, giving it a decided price advantage over the famed Connellsville coke from southwest Pennsylvania.[35] The availability of less expensive Snow Shoe coke was influential in the establishment in the late 1880s of two large ironworks in the Bellefonte area: Centre Furnace (later named Nittany Furnace) and Bellefonte Furnace.

At its zenith, the Snow Shoe–area railroad map resembled a diminutive version of the spidery web woven by the Tyrone and Clearfield Railway. In 1890, state mine inspectors' reports showed the T&C serving fifty-one active mines, and the Snow Shoe Branch serving six with several more in development. With a much smaller reserve in play, the Lehigh Valley Coal Company had far fewer local competitors compared to Berwind-White in the Moshannon Valley. The Lehigh Valley Railroad, one of the nation's famed anthracite carriers, had formed the coal company as a wholly owned subsidiary in 1875 to consolidate the railroad's anthracite mining interests and make sure as much coal as possible stayed on LV rails. However, a growing number of customers required bituminous coal and coke. In acquiring bituminous reserves, the railroad also would have the option of burning this much cheaper fuel in place of anthracite in its own locomotives. Since no major bituminous deposits lay closer than 100 miles to the Lehigh Valley Railroad's tracks, in 1884 the Lehigh Valley Coal Company acquired the 48,000-acre Berwind, White properties on the Centre County Mountaintop, the LVCC's first and only bituminous mining division.[36]

The coal company arranged with the PRR to extend its Sugar Camp Branch. The first 4 miles of that track, which left the former B&SS main track just north of Snow Shoe, then curled back south and east, were laid down in 1881–82 to reach two new Berwind, White mines. Lehigh Valley

acquired those mines and opened two more drifts nearby, necessitat-
ing an extension of the branch. Those four mines accounted for about
90 percent of the coal shipped from the Snow Shoe district in 1890.[37]

William Grauer's Centre Coal Company entered the picture that year
with plans to build a new mine north of Snow Shoe village. To serve that
opening, the PRR in October 1890 completed at its own expense the 1.8-
mile Grauer Branch as a spur off the Sugar Camp Branch.[38] Most of the
coal deposits in the area of Grauer's mine were controlled by John and
William Holt, brother and son, respectively, of the William Holt who
perished in the 1878 Miller's Spring trestle collapse. By 1893, William
Holt's Snow Shoe Mining Company had taken over Grauer's mine. Holt
asked the PRR to extend the Grauer Branch another half-mile to reach
a new opening. This time the Pennsylvania balked. Its subsequent actions give insight into the process by which the railroad built a network
of feeder lines in coal territory. Rail lines that might appear helter-skelter
on a map in fact resulted from careful analysis by managers at a variety
of levels and locations, including senior executives at the Pennsylvania's
corporate headquarters on the upper floors of Philadelphia's brand new
Broad Street station.

Holt's request first went to Philadelphia-based engineer of branch
lines Joseph Crawford, who asked C. S. D'Invilliers, Tyrone Division
chief engineer, "to examine the condition of the Holt property, reporting . . . as to whether the extension would furnish sufficient additional
traffic to repay the expense" of building it.[39] D'Invilliers conducted his
field work in the fall of 1893 and turned in a report favoring the extension, which he said would cost about $3,500. He noted that Holt's "coal
is good and territory ample," and the new mine could load up to twenty
cars daily. The problem was, the bottom had fallen out of the coal market.
Failures of several large banks early in 1893 had led to a shortage of investment capital, which in turn caused a downturn in industrial production and weakened the demand for coal. The PRR shipped only 68,000
tons of Snow Shoe coal that year, which also saw the Lehigh Valley Coal
Company permanently cease all coking operations.

"The only parties besides [the Snow Shoe Mining Company] now
shipping from the Snow Shoe region are the Lehigh Valley . . . and Kel-
ley Bros., who are working odds and ends on the old Valentine lands,"

D'Invilliers told Crawford.[40] Division superintendent Samuel Blair, desperate for traffic, wholeheartedly endorsed Holt's request. "The proper thing to do is make the extension of the Grauer Branch," he wrote to Crawford. "Otherwise our trade on the Snow Shoe branch will be limited to such an extent as to scarcely justify operating it."[41] Holt himself emphasized that "the extension would more than double our facilities for shipping coal."[42] His pleading came just as economic conditions worsened. More banks toppled, and industrial and commercial activity sagged further. The PRR was wary of making financial commitments that might not have a quick payback and put off consideration of Holt's proposal until the spring of 1894. By then the financial panic had mushroomed into a full-blown depression, the worst in sixty years.

"The Snow Shoe Branch is without any traffic," D'Invilliers glumly admitted. The matter of extending the Grauer Branch now rested with PRR vice president Charles Pugh, who had led his company's purchase of the B&SS thirteen years earlier. He recommended a conservative course. "We have more coal on our lines than there are customers to purchase it," he pointed out. The amount of coal Holt expected to mine also was in doubt, since a large fault was known to run near the opening, which might make some of the seam unreachable. There would be no extension, not even a mere half-mile segment, declared Pugh. He also turned down another coal company's request for a 1.5-mile extension of the Snow Shoe Branch main line north of the village of Moshannon. The railroad would serve the producers only if they underwrote all construction costs.[43]

Holt did just that, putting his men to work grading the Grauer Branch extension in 1895 and contracting to have the track installed. Contrary to the skepticism in the PRR's executive offices, the line turned out to be a sound investment. State mine reports show Holt shipped some 52,000 tons of coal in the depression year of 1896, more than double his pre-extension production.

Ironically, Holt owed his good fortune in part to contracts he had secured to supply locomotive coal at Williamsport to none other than a Pennsylvania Railroad subsidiary, the Northern Central Railway. Overall, the coal trade remained lackluster until late in the decade, when the economy finally came roaring back, led by new investments in steel and other heavy manufacturing. Lehigh Valley Coal Company Snow Shoe

Division superintendent James Marsteller in April 1899 asked the PRR to extend the Sugar Camp Branch, then serving two Lehigh Valley mines, about 2.5 miles to a proposed third mine having an estimated lifetime yield of 600,000 tons. Marsteller was in a hurry. Even before getting a response from the railroad, he warned that if the Pennsylvania refused, the coal company would build its own extension—to the nearby Beech Creek Railroad,[44] an affiliate of the PRR's archrival, the New York Central and Hudson River Railroad, which had entered Centre County from the east just a few years earlier. The PRR was in a vulnerable position and could ill afford to lose traffic to a competitor. The Pennsylvania quickly approved the Sugar Camp extension for a cost of $16,000, and turned to one of its largest and most reliable contractors, the H. S. Kerbaugh Company of Philadelphia, to build it. By the end of the year the extension was ready for service.[45]

The Pennsylvania transported 543,000 tons of coal over the Snow Shoe Branch in the peak year of 1900. Lehigh Valley's nine active openings accounted for 413,000 tons. Snow Shoe–headquartered Kelly Brothers was coming on strong as the number-two producer, sending 103,000 tons to market from two mines. Brothers Harry and Michael Kelly, Centre County natives, would soon take control of the third-ranked producer, Holt's Snow Shoe Mining Company and its Cherry Run mine on the Grauer Branch, which shipped 27,000 tons by rail in 1900.[46]

As the coal trade regained strength on the Mountaintop, timber harvesting declined. The largest timbering operation was begun by Lock Haven residents Albert Hopkins and George Weymouth, who in 1885 established a sawmill at Clarence, a site named for Weymouth's son. It was one of the earliest band mills in the region; that is, it used an endless ribbon or band saw rather than the slower, less productive circular saw. George Weymouth dropped out of the partnership two years later, Nelson Byers of Williamsport bought into it, and the firm became Byers-Hopkins. Nearly all the big loggers used their own narrow-gauge railroads to bring timber to their mills, but Byers-Hopkins was again exceptional in that it built a standard-gauge line. Although it was not a common carrier, the road did have its own name—the Snow Shoe and Little Sandy Railroad (from the Little Sandy Run area it served). Byers-Hopkins harvested hemlock, pine, and oak, much of it finished by

Bellefonte-based P. B. Crider and Son, who had planing mills in several central Pennsylvania counties. The Criders' Snow Shoe mill alone could produce up to 60,000 board feet of graded lumber daily. Byers-Hopkins ceased operations in 1894–95 when they exhausted their final reserve of 5,000 acres, and dismantled their mill. The Criders then secured their timber elsewhere and continued in business into the next century.

A few smaller logging operations likewise survived, mostly living on the economic edge. The only one to significantly impact the Snow Shoe Branch was the Wallace Run Lumber Company, headed by veteran Centre County lumberman E. S. "Erv" Bennett. He and his partners leased or purchased 4,100 acres from the Lehigh Valley Coal Company in rugged terrain just below the Allegheny Front, contracting to supply pulpwood to the large paper mill in Tyrone. That mill, started in 1880 by Morrison, Bare, Cass and Company, had become one of the Tyrone Division's largest customers by the time the West Virginia Pulp and Paper Company merged with it in 1899. The mill consumed more than 20,000 cords of wood and 75,000 tons of coal each year, most of it sourced locally and brought in by rail.

In 1906, Bennett and his associates built a 9-mile, 42-inch-gauge railroad to haul logs to their sawmill and lumber from the mill down Wallace Run to the base of the Snow Shoe Branch switchbacks near Gum Stump. How much business the loggers gave the PRR is unknown; but in 1907, the lumber company's railroad was reported to be bringing logs to the mill on a daily basis. Clinton County interests bought the company in 1908, and two years later, when pulpwood contracts expired, relocated most of the equipment in order to supply a paper mill at Lock Haven.[47]

Mixed freight and passenger trains continued to be the norm on the Snow Shoe Branch, a way for the railroad to avoid financial losses that would inevitably result from running dedicated passenger service. The fact was that few people rode the trains. Snow Shoe and adjoining Burnside townships were thinly settled, having a combined population according to the 1890 census of only 2,926 residents. (Centre County then had a total population of 43,269.) The depression of the 1890s affected the Mountaintop economy so profoundly that even with a rekindled economy late in the decade, the 1900 census showed 85 fewer residents than ten years earlier. Snow Shoe did not even incorporate as a borough until 1907.

To bolster passenger revenues, the PRR tried to revive the Mountaintop's reputation as a destination for excursionists. Centre County historian John Blair Linn wrote in 1883 that "Snow Shoe has for many years been a popular summer resort, where mountain air and mountain scenery invites and charms hundreds of visitors yearly. The village occupies an elevation of eight hundred and fifty feet above Bellefonte and about two thousand feet above tide-water. The water is excellent, the roads superb, and hotel accommodations ample as well as agreeable." The Pennsylvania soon discovered Linn's description exceeded fact by a wide margin. The reality was that the town and environs had no first-class accommodations, certainly nothing like the Cresson Springs resort that the PRR owned and operated at the summit of the Alleghenies west of Altoona. The Mountaintop area also lacked the kind of infrastructure—expansive picnic areas, water recreation, athletic fields—that characterized Hecla and Hunters parks (both railroad-served) down in the Nittany Valley, where thousands of people could be comfortably entertained in a single day. The best it could offer were fishponds and John G. Uzzle's deer park, with its menagerie of wild game animals.[48] As a result, only an occasional excursion train came inching its way up the switchbacks, mostly for church picnics and similar social events that attracted people from other parts of the county. Not to be overlooked was the train sponsored each summer by Centre County judge Austin O. Furst for family and friends. The 1892 trip consisted of a locomotive and a single coach, carrying the judge "and about 50 of his friends, the majority of them young ladies," for a daylong visit to Uzzle's deer park and refreshments at the Mountain House.[49]

One impetus for incorporating Snow Shoe, which had about 600 residents, was the expectation that betterments in such areas as streets and sidewalks, policing, street lighting, and water supply would soften the community's rough coal-town exterior and encourage tourism. "With all these improvements, it is hoped that Snow Shoe will regain its lost prestige as a summer resort," observed the Keystone Gazette upon the occasion of the town's incorporation. "To those who have never journeyed there by rail, the switchbacks and steady and untiring efforts of the locomotive in climbing the mountain affords a pleasant and beautiful scenic trip." But the excursion trade remained elusive.

Snow Shoe borough was the hub for railroad operations, playing much the same role that Osceola did on the T&C, although on a much smaller scale. The Snow Shoe station housed a yardmaster, passenger and freight agent, telegrapher, and several clerks. It was the only telegraph station on the branch (call sign WS). The operator coordinated train movements with his counterpart at Snow Shoe Intersection (NO) and the Tyrone dispatcher, and handled Western Union wires for the community. After fire destroyed the original B&SS station in 1891, the PRR replaced it with a single-story wood-frame structure of standard design. For a short distance in either direction from the station, the main track was paralleled by several sidings, where individual coal cars could be weighed and stored and trains made up for the trip down the mountain. Locomotives were turned and watered on the wye track, which jutted from the main track where it made a horseshoe bend through the town. They usually took coal for their tenders at local mine tipples. In prosperous times, shifter engines working the mine runs brought back as many as sixty or seventy cars daily to be weighed and classified— enough to justify dispatching a couple of solid coal trains to the Bald Eagle Valley each day in addition to the scheduled mixed consists.[50] In order to fit on the tail tracks of the switchbacks, the trains had to be much shorter than the seventy-five-car consists that came down the T&C. The tail of the lower-most switch was the most restrictive, measuring only 1,295 feet.[51]

In operating up and down the Allegheny Front, trains faced the same risks as those on the T&C and often with the same fatal results. In February 1886, for example, engine No. 16, a 4-6-0 type, was bringing a cut of empty coal cars up the mountain from Snow Shoe Intersection. A broken rail caused the engine to jump the track near Fountain station and plunge down a 20-foot embankment. The engineer of the helper engine on the rear at first knew nothing of the wreck and kept his throttle open, pushing eleven cars down the bank behind No. 16. The train's conductor and the lead engine's fireman were killed.[52] Lead engineer Jerry Nolan, badly injured, had his fill of mountain railroading and left the Snow Shoe Branch for an engineer's job in the Nittany Valley on the new Buffalo

Run, Bellefonte and Bald Eagle Railroad. (He was fatally crushed by his own locomotive at State College in 1904.[53])

On a summer night in 1904, a coal train was descending the mountain on the approach to the uppermost switchback when a car wheel broke, sending six hopper cars careening down the slope adjacent to the track. Brakeman Bud Lucas, atop one of the cars, jumped 30 feet to get in the clear and suffered serious injuries. Fellow brakeman Scott Walker rode the derailed cars a hundred feet down the embankment and was completely buried in coal at the base. Other crewmen quickly came to his rescue and dug him out unscathed. In December 1908, that same location saw the derailment of an entire downbound train: a class H3 locomotive, eleven coal cars, and caboose. Engineer Alonza Baughman and fireman Clyde Woomer remained in the cab as their engine slid to bottom of the fill. The badly scalded Baughman was taken to the Bellefonte hospital aboard a locomotive especially called for that purpose, but he died soon after being admitted. Meanwhile, the PRR dispatched wreck trains from Tyrone and Altoona, each having a derrick to haul the derailed H3 back up the slope. The weight of the damaged hulk pulled the Altoona crane off the track and yanked the superstructure of the Tyrone crane off its base, sending it tumbling part way down the fill. Several men were seriously hurt, and the Huntingdon wreck train had to be called to help finish the cleanup. The branch was out of service nearly a week.[54]

Despite the operational dangers and the cumbersome switchbacks, the Snow Shoe Branch could move impressive amounts of coal when the economy demanded it. Most years in the early 1900s saw it carrying between a quarter- and a half-million tons, still less than 20 percent of the T&C's total and a tiny part of the Pennsylvania railroad's total bituminous haulage (39.7 million tons in 1907, a typical year), yet enough to sustain the livelihoods of hundreds of families in the Mountaintop communities.

The Tyrone Division's third major component was the Bald Eagle Valley Railroad. The Pennsylvania was slow to take advantage of the strategic value of this rail line as a link between two great PRR thoroughfares. The PRR's *Annual Reports* indicate that during the 1880s, more than half the coal tonnage off the T&C went east over the Middle

Division main line rather than east over the BEV. In 1886, for example, Tyrone received 113,545 carloads from the T&C but dispatched only 41,199 carloads east over the BEV. Most of the coal originating on the Snow Shoe Branch went east from Snow Shoe Intersection, as might be expected, since nearly all of it came from Lehigh Valley Coal Company mines. Such coal stayed on PRR rails as far as Mount Carmel in eastern Pennsylvania, where it was handed off to the Lehigh Valley Railroad.

Passenger operations on the Bald Eagle Valley Railroad also had a local focus. Riders (and mail and express) destined beyond Tyrone or Lock Haven had to change trains at those points, since the BEV operated neither through trains nor through cars in conjunction with the rest of the Pennsylvania's system. In fact, operation of through trains (passenger or freight) between the Bald Eagle Valley line at Tyrone and Altoona and other points west on the main line would have been extremely cumbersome, since the T&C's alignment (which the BEV used) curved eastward as it approached the Tyrone station and junction with the main line. There was no westward-facing junction. In sum, so far as the PRR was concerned, the Bald Eagle Valley Railroad served primarily as another link in a chain of branch lines that gave its parent access to the natural resources of the central part of the state.

Forward-thinking engineer John McMinn in the 1850s had identified the Bald Eagle's strategic value as connection for through traffic between the PRR's main line and the P&E line, but the Pennsylvania already possessed such a connector in its 44-mile Sunbury and Lewistown Railroad subsidiary, which linked its namesake towns and opened in 1871. The S&L enabled traffic moving between northeastern Pennsylvania and points west of Altoona to bypass the congested Harrisburg area. Anthracite coal, the principal westbound tonnage, moved from the Wilkes-Barre and Hazleton areas to Sunbury, then over the S&L to Lewistown and west on the Middle Division main line. Bituminous coal and coke from western Pennsylvania and bound for New England consignees took the opposite route: east over the Middle Division to Lewistown, then over the S&L, and finally on to Wilkes-Barre for interchange to other railroads. By the mid-1890s, the Sunbury and Lewistown was hosting twenty or more freight trains daily in each direction—far more than the Bald Eagle Valley Railroad.[55]

The busiest location along the BEV was Bellefonte, which originated more carloads than any other point between Tyrone and Lock Haven, as might be expected of Centre County's largest population center. (Bellefonte borough and surrounding Spring Township had about 7,000 residents according to the 1890 census.) The coming of the railroad enabled Bellefonte to develop a variety of small-scale manufacturing and extractive industries that shipped such materials as limestone and lime; iron ore, pig and bar iron; nails, wire, and chain; flour, corn meal, and animal feed; window glass; radiators and boilers; axes and other hand tools; and lumber. Not all of these enterprises operated concurrently, and many shipped sporadically if at all during the economic depression that began in 1893.

When the national economy revived, Bellefonte's also reawakened. In June 1899 the PRR based its first shifter or switch engine in the town. Heretofore, customers were served by locomotives and crews based in Tyrone or Lock Haven. A typical weekday saw locomotives from the PRR, from short lines Bellefonte Central, Central Railroad of Pennsylvania, and Nittany Valley, and from the town's two iron furnaces shuttling about the community.[56] (See chapter 7.) Activity slowed at night and on weekends but did not cease. The lime plants and ironworks operated around the clock, requiring rail service to do the same.

In 1901 the PRR added a few sidings along Spring Creek to accommodate incoming and outgoing cars. The railroad there had previously consisted only of the main track and one or two "make-up tracks" used to build outbound trains.[57] The location, near the nail factory in Spring Township's Sunnyside neighborhood, was soon known by railroaders as Sunnyside yard, although to the PRR officially it was Bellefonte yard. The Pennsylvania kept its Bellefonte shifter and one or two Snow Shoe Branch engines at the old brick roundhouse erected by Bellefonte and Snow Shoe Railroad near the mouth of Buffalo Run until razing that crumbling structure in 1904. "Engines repeatedly plunged through its walls until it became an eyesore," explained the *Keystone Gazette*. "It has outlived its usefulness." A single-stall brick enginehouse replaced the roundhouse to allow some protection from the weather during routine locomotive maintenance; nearby were facilities for taking on coal, water, and sand.[58]

One industry that held great promise as a railroad customer but never quite took off was the Bellefonte Car Manufacturing Company, established to make wooden superstructures for rail cars. In 1873 the company erected a paint shop, machine shop, erecting hall, and office on 11 acres sandwiched between South Potter Street and Spring Creek. Power came from a 75-horsepower steam engine and a 100-horsepower water wheel. The site was formerly occupied by a planing works owned by Bush House hotel proprietor Daniel Bush, who was among the car company's chief backers. Little is known about the firm's president, William McClellan of Chambersburg, but most of the other principals were local, including former governor Andrew Curtin, who served as vice president, and the ubiquitous Edmund Blanchard, treasurer.[59] The company got caught in the Panic of 1873 and closed before turning out a single car. The national economy remained sluggish for the remainder of the decade; the car shop stood idle.

Work finally resumed in the spring of 1881 under new owners led by Andrew Curtin, who had just been elected to Congress. They soon discovered the car manufacturing business had changed: buyers preferred cars ready for service, complete with wheel assemblies and brakes. New technologies such as air brakes and automatic couplers made car building more complex. The Bellefonte company lacked a foundry to make such components and was facing permanent closure. In December 1881 it received a 300-car order from the Erie Railroad, enough to breathe life into the enterprise. By that time the shop may have added a foundry. The cars, manufactured at the rate of six each day by a workforce of more than a hundred employees, were simple open-top gondolas for hauling coal and other bulk materials. The shop also built 500 gondolas for the Pennsylvania Railroad, but overall the demand was spasmodic and unable to sustain the company. A consortium headed by attorney James Beaver and two other investors—law partner J. Wesley Gephart and banking associate J. Dunlop Shugert—bought the car works in 1884 and began marketing it for other uses. It turned out to be something of a white elephant, too large for use by any single endeavor. A sawmill and a machine shop were among the non-railroad enterprises that later occupied part of the shop complex.[60]

The failure of the car shop disappointed a community that took increasing pride in its railroads. By 1885, with the completion of a connection to the west end of the Lewisburg and Tyrone Railroad, Bellefonte had become a hub for local PRR passenger service. The station saw at least seven trains arrive and depart Monday through Saturday from all points of the compass. Agitation had already begun to have the Pennsylvania replace the 1864 station with a more modern and spacious structure that befitted the town's economic and political importance. The *Centre Democrat* on October 18, 1883, dryly noted that "it has not yet been determined when the new Bald Eagle Valley depot at Bellefonte will be commenced, but we are assured by Mr. Roberts, president of the Pennsylvania Railroad, that it will be completed in time for the tri-centennial of the landing of the Pilgrims, which will occur in 1920." The newspaper spoke for many citizens when it decried the existing building as "a miserable old shed of a depot that would be a disgrace to a way-station on a coal road." Pressure for a finer station grew even more intense when the Buffalo Run, Bellefonte, and Bald Eagle Railroad (soon to become the Bellefonte Central) initiated thrice-daily passenger service between Bellefonte and the Pennsylvania State College. Beginning August 1, 1887, the BRB&BE also used that "miserable old shed," which many townsfolk feared would present an image of ugliness to sophisticates traveling to or from the college.

In truth, the PRR had determined the county seat needed a new passenger station even before the *Centre Democrat* relieved itself of its sarcasm. "We have estimated $5,000 for a passenger station at Bellefonte," General Superintendent S. M. Prevost wrote to Charles Pugh on May 11, 1883. "It is necessary to take the passenger business out of the warehouse [the 1864 station] in order to give increased room for freight business."[61] The railroad approached the project with its customary deliberation and exhaustive consultations between Tyrone Division officials and their Broad Street superiors. The new brick structure finally opened without fanfare on February 11, 1889. It contained a ticket and telegrapher's office (call sign BF), baggage and express rooms, and separate waiting rooms for men and women. President Roberts personally reviewed the blueprints and asked for a modification. "Mr. Roberts is anxious to have the plan revised," one of his subordinates told the architect, "so as to reduce the size of the gentlemen's water closet and put additional room into the ladies' water closet."[62]

The railroad moved the old station directly across the tracks from the new one, where it functioned as a freight depot. Within a few years, it was moved again, still as the town's freight station, to a roomier tract several hundred yards north along the right-of-way. Activity at the new passenger station was mostly a daylight affair. According to published timetables, the first arrival, an express from Lock Haven to Tyrone, was carded for 5:35 A M. As the day wore on, trains arrived from and departed for Snow Shoe, Sunbury, State College, and of course Tyrone and Lock Haven. The day drew to a close with the scheduled 8:45 PM departure of the final eastbound Bald Eagle Valley train.

Notes

1. Ralph T. Wolfgang, *A Short History of Tyrone Borough* (Tyrone, PA: Tyrone High School, 1950; reissued by Tyrone Area Historical Society, 2002), 24–27; and William B. Wilson, *History of the Pennsylvania Railroad*, 2 vols. (Philadelphia: H. T. Coates, 1899), 1:205–8.

2. Irvin recollections in the *Centre Democrat* (Bellefonte), 30 March 1899; reprinted in *Centre Democrat*, 28 September 1939.

3. D. S. Maynard, *Industries and Institutions of Centre County* (Bellefonte, PA: Republican Job Printing House, 1877), 127; *Telegrapher*, 29 July 1871; *Raftsman's Journal* (Clearfield), 25 November 1868.

4. Wilson, *History of the Pennsylvania Railroad*, 1:124–28.

5. Charles E. Fisher, "Steam Locomotives of the PRR System," *Railroad and Locomotive Historical Society Bulletin* 89 (Winter 1953): 139–58; Wilkins's report to Baldwin Locomotive Works, 5 June 1870, published as a testimonial in BLW, *Illustrated Catalogue* (Philadelphia: J. B. Lippincott, 1881; reprinted: Berkeley, CA: Howell-North, 1960), 110.

6. White, *American Locomotives*, 347–57. John H. White, *American Locomotives: An Engineering History, 1830–1880* (Baltimore: Johns Hopkins University Press, 1968), 347–57.

7. *Democratic Watchman* (Bellefonte), 7 April 1876.

8. Wilson, *History of the Pennsylvania Railroad*, 1:126.

9. Ibid., 1:114–15; "S. S. Blair," in Jesse C. Sell, *Twentieth Century History of Altoona and Blair County, Pennsylvania, and Representative Citizens* (Chicago: Richmond-Arnold, 1911): 965–66.

10. Frederick E. Saward, *The Coal Trade*, published annually by Saward's *Coal Trade Journal*, is the best single source for coal production and transportation statistics.

11. *Philipsburg Journal*, 10 August 1884; Lewis Cass Aldrich, *History of Clearfield County, Pennsylvania* (Syracuse, NY: D. Mason, 1887), 215–32.

12. "Famous Old Moshannon," *Saward's Journal*, 3 December 1927.

13. *The History of Berwind, 1886–1993* (Philadelphia: Berwind Group, 1993), 2–10; *Philipsburg Journal*, 16 January 1885; *Tyrone Herald*, 3 November 1887; PRR Form C. R. 76 "Stations and Sidings," 1884.

14. Aldrich, *Clearfield County*, 215; Albert Churella, *The Pennsylvania Railroad: Building an Empire, 1846–1917* (Philadelphia: University of Pennsylvania Press, 2012), 460, 633–47, 668–79.

15. Richard Burg, "The Berwind-White Coal Mining Co.: When Empty Return to Windber P.R.R," *Keystone* (Autumn 1986): 7–8; *History of Berwind*, 14.

16. Osceola Branch correspondence, Pennsylvania Railroad Co., Executive Department, Record Group 5, Subgroup B, Office of Vice President Samuel Rea, Hagley Museum and Library (hereafter Rea File).

17. *Philipsburg Journal*, 12 September and 26 September 1890; *Tyrone Herald*, 20 September 1890; Charles Hedges, comp., *Speeches of Benjamin Harrison, Twenty-Third President of the United States* (New York: United States Book Company, 1892), 231–34; Homer Socolofsky and Allan Spetter, *The Presidency of Benjamin Harrison* (Lawrence: University of Kansas Press, 1987), 169.

18. John Blair Linn, *History of Centre and Clinton Counties, Pennsylvania* (Philadelphia: Louis H. Everts, 1883), 418; *Philipsburg Journal*, 7 March 1884 and 27 November 1885; *Clearfield Progress*, 9 January 1940, 8 August 1947, 10 May 1954. The *Clearfield Progress* later restyled itself *The Progress* but continued to be published in Clearfield. George H. Ashley, "The Fire Brick Materials of Pennsylvania," *Journal of the American Ceramic Society* No. 6 (1923): 837–48; Corinne Azen Krause, *Refractories: The Hidden Industry* (Westerville, OH: American Ceramic Society, 1987), 12–13, 19–20; E. S. Moore and T. G. Taylor, *The Silica Refractories of Pennsylvania* (Harrisburg: Department of Forests and Waters, 1924), 39–48; James E. MacCloskey, *History of Harbison-Walker Refractories Company* (Pittsburgh: Davis & Wards, 1952), 51.

19. Ian S. Fischer, "Wooden Gondolas of the Pennsylvania System," *Keystone* (Spring 1986): 9–37; Al Buchan and Elden Gatwood, *Pennsylvania Railroad Gondolas* (Kutztown, PA: Pennsylvania Railroad Technical and Historical Society, 2011), 22–28.

20. James Dredge, *The Pennsylvania Railroad: Its Organization, Construction, and Management* (London: Engineering, 1879), 154–55.

21. Richard D. Adams, *Locomotives of the Pennsylvania Railroad: The Early Years, 1848–1874* (Kutztown: Pennsylvania Railroad Technical and Historical Society, 2010), 85–86.

22. Ibid., 85–86; *Philipsburg Journal*, 11 September 1891.

23. Aldrich, *Clearfield County*, 515.

24. *Philipsburg Journal*, 20 July 1884, 16 May 1888, 23 December 1891.

25. The closing of the Philipsburg enginehouse is referenced on the back of a photo at the Philipsburg Historical Foundation of locomotive No. 1130, captioned as the last locomotive to leave the enginehouse in 1905. Opening the Osceola enginehouse:

Cambria and Clearfield Railway minute book, 29 December 1905, in Penn Central Collection, Pennsylvania Railroad Subsidiary Lines, Manuscript Group 286.610, Pennsylvania State Archives.

26. Dredge, *Pennsylvania Railroad*, 148, 208, 215.

27. Richard D. Adams, "The Introduction of the Belpaire Firebox on PRR," *Keystone* (Winter 1985): 54–58; Richard D. Adams, "Class R Locomotives," *Keystone* (Summer 1987): 12–24; Paul T. Warner, "Motive Power Development on the Pennsylvania Railroad System, 1831–1924," *Baldwin Locomotives* (July 1924): 36–40, 45–47; and *Philipsburg Journal*, 1 May 1891. Before the PRR reorganized locomotive classes in the 1890s, the H1 was class I, and the H3 was class R.

28. *Philipsburg Journal*, 8 January 1881 and 9 November 1883; Tyrone and Clearfield Railway board of directors minutes, 14 February 1876, in Penn Central Collection, Pennsylvania Railroad Subsidiary Lines, Manuscript Group 286.1426, Pennsylvania State Archives.

29. Churella, *The Pennsylvania Railroad*, 575–77; Martin R. Karig, *Coal Cars: The First Three Hundred Years* (Scranton, PA: University of Scranton Press, 2007), 123–34.

30. Luther Gette interviews in 1999 with PRR Clearfield Branch retirees Paul Frank, engineman (31 August), and John Hughes (16 August) and Jack Renwick (19 October), conductors.

31. *Centre Democrat*, 14 October 1875.

32. The wreck received widespread newspaper coverage. Some retrospectives: Paula Zitzler with Susie O'Brien, *Unscheduled Stop: The Town of Tyrone and the Wreck of the Walter L. Main Circus Train* (Tyrone, PA: America's Stories Inc. and the Tyrone Area Historical Society, 2008); "Memoirs of Conductor Gordon Walk of Vail," *Tyrone PastTimes* 7 (Winter 1997): 10; Fred E. Long, "The Great Circus Train Wreck of 1893," *Pennsylvania Heritage* (Fall 1984), 10–17; *Tyrone Herald*, 21 and 30 May 1974.

33. *Tyrone Herald*, 11 June 1903; *Keystone Gazette*, 12 June 1903.

34. Frederick E. Saward, *The Coal Trade* (New York: Coal Trade Journal, 1893), 111; Michael Bezilla and Luther Gette, "The PRR's Snow Shoe Branch: Switchbacks, Coal, and Rattlesnakes," *Keystone* 44 (Summer 2011): 69–81.

35. Robert F. Archer, *History of the Lehigh Valley Railroad* (Berkeley, CA: Howell-North Books, 1977), 81, 99; D. G. Baird, comp., "A Statement of Some of the Important Matters that Have Entered into the History of the Lehigh Valley Coal Company, from Its Inception to and Including the Fiscal Year Ending June 30, 1906," 122–23, 338–44, typescript in Lehigh Valley Railroad Co. Records, Manuscript Group 274.439, Pennsylvania State Archives.

36. *Democratic Watchman*, 2 October 1885.

37. *Report of the Inspectors of Mines for the Year 1890* (Harrisburg: Bureau of Mines, 1891), 361, 472–73.

38. PRR general manager Charles Pugh to chief engineer William H. Brown, 30 October 1890, and PRR second vice president J. N. DuBarry to Brown, 5 July 1890. This correspondence and that referenced immediately below is in Rea File.

39. Crawford to D'Invilliers, 26 October 1893.

40. D'Invilliers to Crawford, 30 October 1893.

41. Blair to Crawford, 31 October 1893.

42. Holt to Brown, 12 March 1894.

43. Pugh to Brown, 25 April 1894.

44. Blair to PRR General Superintendent J. M. Wallis, 21 April 1899.

45. H. S. Kerbaugh to D'Invilliers, 3 July 1899, and Kerbaugh to Brown, 24 July 1899.

46. *Report of the Department of Mines for 1900* (Harrisburg: Pennsylvania Department of Mines, 1901). These reports continue the annual *Report of the Inspectors of Mines* after the state Bureau of Mines was given departmental status independent of the Department of Internal Affairs.

47. Benjamin F. G. Kline Jr. *Pitch Pine and Prop Timber* (Lancaster, PA: Self-published, 1971), 175–77, 180–81; *Philipsburg Journal*, 10 April 1891; *Centre Democrat* (Bellefonte), 25 July 1907.

48. *Centre Democrat*, 10 August 1905.

49. *Keystone Gazette*, 1 July 1892.

50. *Centre Democrat*, 11 January 1900.

51. Switchback lengths are noted in the PRR's valuation maps for 1918 and subsequent years.

52. *Philipsburg Journal*, 5 February 1886.

53. *Keystone Gazette*, 22 April 1904.

54. *Centre Democrat*, 24 July 1904 and 17 December 1908.

55. Pennsylvania Railroad Technical and Historical Society, *Lewistown and the Pennsylvania Railroad* (Altoona: PRRT&HS, 2000), 104–15; Wilson, *History of the Pennsylvania Railroad*, 1:204; David W. Messer, *Triumph IV: Harrisburg to Altoona, 1846–2001* (Baltimore: Barnard, Roberts and Co., 2001), 83.

56. *Keystone Gazette*, 16 June 1899; *Centre Democrat*, 24 August 1899.

57. PRR Tyrone Division map, "Railroad Connections Near Bellefonte," 7 July 1899, photocopy in author's collection.

58. *Keystone Gazette*, 9 December 1904.

59. Linn, *Centre County*, 149, 244; *Democratic Watchman*, 16 May and 30 May 1873.

60. *Democratic Watchman*, 27 May, 7 October, and 16 December 1881; 3 March 1882; 4 January 1884; *Bellefonte Industries: Bellefonte Car Manufacturing*, Pennsylvania Historic Resources Series (Bellefonte, PA: Bellefonte Borough, 2006), 1–2.

61. Prevost to Pugh, 11 May 1883, Rea File.

62. PRR third vice president J. N. DuBarry to William H. Brown, 9 April 1884, Rea File.

SIX

Breaking the Monopoly

Beech Creek Railroad/New York Central

IN THE SAME WAY THAT THE PENNSYLVANIA RAILROAD USED subsidiary lines to plant its corporate flag in Centre County and the Moshannon Valley, so too did archrival New York Central. The incorporation in 1882 of the Susquehanna and Southwestern Railroad was the NYC's first step toward staking a claim for some of the region's natural resources.

The Beech Creek Railroad—a successor to the Susquehanna and Southwestern—served a large number of mines and brickyards in the lower Moshannon Valley. Taking its name from a stream originating on the high ground around Snow Shoe and carving a path down the Allegheny Front, the Beech Creek built from an eastern terminus in Lycoming County into northern Centre County and the lower Moshannon Valley. Even as the BCR's main line sprouted dozens of branches to serve the area's coal mines, the invader's rails continued their westward thrust, pushing deeper into PRR territory toward the coalfields of northern Cambria and Indiana counties.

Parent New York Central was organized in 1853 as a consolidation of several short line railroads between Buffalo and Albany. The Hudson River Railroad connected the NYC at Albany with New York City. By 1869, Cornelius "Commodore" Vanderbilt, a former ferryboat captain, had gained control of both routes, uniting them as the New York Central and Hudson River Railroad between New York City and Buffalo. From the latter city, Vanderbilt secured control of rail lines west to Chicago and other Midwestern points, setting the stage for a storied rivalry with the Pennsylvania Railroad. Although the Commodore's descendants broadened the company's ownership, the Vanderbilt family continued to exert a powerful influence on NYC affairs for decades.

The New York Central's initial interest in central Pennsylvania in the 1880s stemmed from the carrier's escalating concern over the cost and supply of coal for locomotives and other company uses. It had virtually no coal reserves of its own, and coal for locomotive fuel alone accounted for about 13 percent of the company's operating expenses in 1880. When a core group of coal suppliers advised New York Central vice president Charles Clarke—who was in charge of the railroad's fuel purchases—that there would be a significant price increase, concern spread through the company's executive offices on the upper floors of Grand Central Depot in Manhattan. Clarke discussed strategic options with William H. Vanderbilt, the railroad's president and son of the Commodore. They decided to expand the NYC's reach into the bituminous coalfields of central and western Pennsylvania, confident that they could break the PRR's monopoly in that region.

In what corporate America would later term "in-sourcing," the railroad established a coal-company subsidiary as part of its strategy. The Vanderbilt family bought an interest in the McIntyre Coal Company, whose mines at McIntyre, near the border of Lycoming and Tioga Counties along Pennsylvania's northern tier, were nearly played out. Other Tioga County coal operators were facing a similar dilemma. The quality of their coal was high and production robust, peaking at 1.8 million tons in 1883. But known reserves in the Northern District, as it was termed, were fast being mined out. Output would decline to only 800,000 tons by 1892.[1]

The McIntyre Coal Company was reorganized as the Clearfield Bituminous Coal Company on December 27, 1882. The Vanderbilts agreed to finance purchase of new coal lands and construction of new rail lines in central and western Pennsylvania—an area that in the context of coal production was designated the Clearfield District. The CBC agreed to ship via the New York Central and its affiliates, whether or not those roads were the actual buyers of the coal. Holding nearly all of the Clearfield Bituminous Coal Company's stock was a small cadre of investors: William H. Vanderbilt, Vanderbilt associates George Magee of Watkins Glen and Charles J. Langdon of Elmira, New York; Joseph Gazzam and John Reading of Philadelphia; Samuel R. Peale of Lock Haven; and William A. Wallace of Clearfield.[2] Peale and Wallace were the only investors who had no strong ties to existing northern-tier coal and railroad enterprises, but they stood to gain immensely should the CBC succeed in developing the proposed bituminous fields of central Pennsylvania.

S. R. Peale (he preferred the initials) began his career as an attorney before being elected to the state senate in 1876 as a Democrat, representing portions of Clinton, Centre, and Clearfield Counties. He served only one term, then declined renomination in favor of pursuing business interests full time. Peale was an expert in real estate law, particularly as it applied to helping clients identify and acquire coal lands. He held some of those lands himself. "From certain railroad movements that I have learned about, the property owned by Mr. [John G.] Reading and myself is going to turn out unusually profitable," he wrote to his wife in January 1881. "The way to make the most out of it is to get railroads into it and then lease it out by the ton."[3]

William Wallace also was an attorney, formerly in partnership with Joseph Gazzam. At the time of the CBC's formation, he had just completed a six-year term as a US senator from Pennsylvania. As noted earlier, Wallace had helped bring the Pennsylvania Railroad into his home community of Clearfield, but he had no qualms about switching allegiance from the Pennsylvania to the New York Central, especially after George Roberts had booted him out of the Tyrone and Clearfield Railway in the reorganization of 1866–67. "Our idea in building the Beech Creek road," he later said, "was to get an outlet into Northern markets for Clearfield coal," markets in which the PRR had little interest.[4]

The Susquehanna and Southwestern Railroad was incorporated on August 12, 1882, with the understanding that it would become the principal carrier for the Clearfield Bituminous Coal Company. Its charter called for the road to be built from the Williamsport area to the southern

line "from Snow Shoe Summit east by Beech Creek to the Bald Eagle Valley canal and from Moshannon Creek west to a point near Woodland,"
a few miles from the town of Clearfield. The board approved the route
in September 1882.[5]

Brugger completed his survey quickly because he had previously located the eastern segment of this line for the Pennsylvania and Western
Railroad. The P&W had been organized in the 1870s by a small group
of speculators who owed no allegiance to the major trunk lines. Their
avowed goal was to build a railroad from New York City by way of central
Pennsylvania to Cleveland, by patching together a collection of small,
existing roads with a minimum of new construction. They failed to
attract like-minded investors, and the Pennsylvania and Western remained little more than a paper railroad. Even so, it attempted to deny
the Susquehanna and Southwestern the right to build through land that
the P&W had already surveyed. Legal skirmishing ensued. The S&SW
obtained a temporary restraining order against its rival that allowed
construction to proceed; then a court determined that the P&W had not
fulfilled the terms of its charter within the allowed timeframe and thus
lost exclusive rights to its projected right-of-way.[6] The ruling effectively
put the Pennsylvania and Western out of business.

The Pennsylvania Railroad made only a feeble attempt to block the
P&W. It organized the Lock Haven and Clearfield Railroad in 1879,
when the P&W was the sole threat to its coal and timberlands. Following its custom with such subsidiaries, the Pennsylvania filled the new
company's leadership positions with its own upper-level managers. The
LH&C was to extend from the Bald Eagle Valley Railroad near the
mouth of Beech Creek to the Tyrone and Clearfield Railroad at Philipsburg. The intent was to make it a less daunting alternative to the T&C's
precipitous descent of the Allegheny Front. However, the Pennsylvania
incorporated another railroad in 1879, the Susquehanna and Clearfield,
that was to start at Keating on the Philadelphia and Erie Railroad main
line and work its way up the West Branch of the Susquehanna. Judging
the water-level S&C route to be superior to that of the Lock Haven and

Clearfield, the Pennsylvania lost interest in the latter road, which it quietly dissolved in 1884.

Construction of the Susquehanna and Clearfield started early in 1882 —just about the time that PRR operatives would likely have gotten wind of the Vanderbilts' interest in central Pennsylvania coal lands. The S&C blazed a path through some of the most sparsely populated territory in the state until it reached the tiny village of Karthaus, site of a long-defunct iron furnace, 23 miles from Keating. The West Branch was the dividing line between Centre and Clearfield Counties in that locale, and the railroad remained on the Clearfield side for its entire length. The right-of-way "keeps close to the shore all the way," noted the *Renovo Record*. "The river is very crooked and winds through the mountains like a ram's horn. No farmland worth speaking of is seen on the way as the mountains come down almost to the water's edge. In some places they rise boldly to a height of 500 feet."[7]

It was on the Clearfield side that an outcropping of the Lower Freeport seam had been discovered. By mid-1884, the S&C began shipping as many as twenty carloads daily from a mine near the new settlement of Cataract, which boasted a population of about 200. The Berwind, White firm, impressed with the location's prospects, bought out the operation. Because the coal seam ran near the ridge top, the mine's portal was so high in elevation that the coal was brought down to the railroad by way of an inclined plane 1,050 feet long with a rise of 445 feet. Berwind, White also operated a smaller mine at nearby Karthaus.[8]

For the PRR, the easy grade of the Susquehanna and Clearfield offered a "back door" entry to the Moshannon Valley. Two miles upstream from Karthaus was Miller's Landing, where the Moshannon Creek flowed into the West Branch. The *Clearfield Republican* recognized the importance of this route as early as 1874. The newspaper asserted that it would be a sensible alternative to the arduous route around the Big Fill. Build a railroad from Keating up the West Branch "to the mouth of the Moshannon Creek and build up that stream to Philipsburg," exhorted the *Republican*. "We predict . . . all the coal mined in the Moshannon [Valley] will go to market via Karthaus and Lock Haven instead of over the mountain to Tyrone. This movement will do more to develop our

county and dig up our hidden treasures of coal and fire clay than anything contemplated in this section of the state."[9]

The PRR agreed—that's why it organized the S&C and gave up on
the Pennsylvania and Western. A line up the Moshannon Creek would
eliminate the punishing grades of the Tyrone and Clearfield. It also
would enable the PRR to tap Snow Shoe coal from the north and do away
with the clumsy zigzags down the Allegheny Front. Millions of dollars
in operating costs and probably many lives could be saved in the long
term. Just to make things official, the S&C directors, led by president Joseph N. DuBarry (a PRR vice president), voted in August 1883 to extend
their railroad "to a connection with the line of the Tyrone and Clearfield
Railway at or near Philipsburg."[10] If carried out, the plan would have
repainted the entire rail transportation picture in central Pennsylvania.
But the Susquehanna and Clearfield never reached Miller's Landing, let
alone Philipsburg. Exactly why has remained a mystery, but a study made
by PRR engineer Camille S. D'Invilliers sheds some light.

D'Invilliers, a college-educated civil engineer and geologist, started
his railroad career with the PRR in 1874, then briefly left the company to
work for the P & T Collins contracting firm in an ill-fated railroad-build-
ing venture in the Amazon jungle. Returning to the Pennsylvania, he
eventually was named head of the branch line construction department,
with headquarters in Philipsburg. As the company's resident expert on
bituminous coal beds, D'Invilliers was tasked with assessing the value
of the Moshannon Valley's coal reserves and proposing new rail lines to
reach them. In December 1883, he submitted a report to DuBarry that
questioned the wisdom of the S&C board's action. D'Invilliers reminded
DuBarry that

> our efforts so far have been entirely towards developing the Moshannon seam,
> which is right, since the great reputation of this coal will prevent the lower coals
> from coming into market in competition with it except in flush times. This seam,
> once so plentiful in the Houtzdale and Philipsburg basin, is now becoming com-
> paratively scarce, and I am informed by some of the larger operations that the col-
> lieries they are now working will not hold out longer than from 3 to 5 years.... It
> would seem therefore that the parties working the older collieries will seek other
> fields where the Moshannon is known to exist in good quality and thickness, and
> leave the lower seams for the distant future.[11]

D'Invilliers went on to note that those "other fields" lay primarily in the upper Moshannon Valley and further west, not downstream from Philipsburg. He recommended that the "lower seams" of the less desirable Kittanning coal below Philipsburg be conceded to the New York Central. "It would seem to me that our attention should be drawn to localities where the Moshannon exists in good shape," he wrote.

D'Invilliers' report is crucial to understanding the strategy that guided the Pennsylvania's subsequent construction of branch lines, and why the PRR did not vigorously oppose the New York Central's incursion into its domain. The Pennsylvania continued to extend its Moshannon Branch and tributary lines upstream from Osceola rather than downstream; and it pushed other branches northward from Cresson, on the main line near the summit of the Alleghenies, into the coalfields of northern Cambria, southwest Clearfield, and Indiana and Jefferson Counties, all in pursuit of what it considered to be what a later generation might call the "low-hanging fruit" of the Lower Freeport seam. D'Invilliers saw no compelling reason to parry the thrust made by the Vanderbilt interests.

Whether or not PRR and NYC leaders came to an informal understanding on this issue is unknown. It is worth noting, however, that the only known copy of D'Invilliers' 1,500-word report is to be found deep in the corporate archive of the New York Central–affiliated Fall Brook Coal and Railway Company. The railway was an outgrowth of the Fall Brook Coal Company, led by George Magee of Watkins, New York. The Fall Brook Coal Company included a number of Northern District mining enterprises and the short line railroads that served them. With the Vanderbilt family's backing, in 1883 the Fall Brook acquired the just-completed Pine Creek Railroad line that ran between Williamsport and a connection with Magee's existing rail properties near Wellsboro. Acquisition of the Pine Creek Railroad gave Magee control of a continuous route between Williamsport on the south, where a connection was made with the Philadelphia and Reading, and Lyons, New York, on the north, where the Fall Brook Railway joined the New York Central main line. The component railroads along that 257-mile route would eventually be consolidated into the Fall Brook Railway with Magee as president.[12]

The Fall Brook was crucial to the success of the Susquehanna and Southwestern Railroad and the Clearfield Bituminous Coal Company. A connection between the two rail lines at Jersey Shore gave CBC-mined coal a relatively short and secure path to the New York Central. Without the Fall Brook Railway, the most the S&SW could have hoped for was a connection with the Reading and a roundabout way of reaching not only the NYC but the "Northern markets" that had attracted William Wallace's attention.

Prior to construction, the Susquehanna and Southwestern issued $4 million in stock—80,000 shares, each having a $50 par value. Wallace, Peale, and Reading acted as front men, purchasing nearly all the shares, then quietly transferring most of them to William H. Vanderbilt, his son Cornelius Vanderbilt II, and Magee, a process begun as early as January 1883.[13] The railroad increased its stock offering to $5 million two months later, at which time its directors also approved a $5 million bond issue, payable in fifty years with 4 percent annual interest. The Clearfield Bituminous Coal Company agreed to open mines capable of collectively producing 500,000 tons of coal annually, build 200 coke ovens, and move all its traffic over the S&SW and affiliated lines. Soon thereafter, George Magee became the road's general contractor.[14] This was a commonly used procedure of the era to jumpstart construction. Since the railroad was generating no income, the contractor was paid in stock. The contractor usually farmed out actual grading, bridge building, tracklaying, and the like to subcontractors, at his own expense. In theory he would recoup his expenses and more after the railroad began operations.

Grading the right-of-way began toward the end of 1882. It was soon discovered that another entity of that same name existed, so the S&SW changed its name to the Beech Creek, Clearfield and South Western Railroad Company on March 20, 1883. On May 2 the *Clearfield Republican* reported the Beech Creek, as the new road was commonly known, was under construction for approximately 26 miles between the town of Beech Creek in the Bald Eagle Valley and the Mountaintop area near Snow Shoe. Tracklaying began in September.[15] The alignment along the rushing waters of Beech Creek afforded a ruling grade of only about 1 percent on the climb from the valley floor to a high point west of Snow Shoe known as Hurxthal's Summit, 1,617 feet above sea level. The grade was less than half as severe as the Tyrone and Clearfield Railway's assault on the Alleghenies, and the crest was 500 feet lower. But the more gentle ascent came at a price. The line included multiple bridges and numerous curves as the stream looped through the rugged terrain. A correspondent for Bellefonte's *Democratic Watchman* who observed the work noted that "all mountain streams are crooked, but few can show a more tortuous course than Beech Creek. In and out of the mountains the little river flows, and the railroad follows its winding course. In some places the road is one continuous series of curves."[16] One 10-mile stretch included thirteen bridges; even more spans would have been required if Brugger's survey had not called for realigning the creek bed in several places.

Construction standards were high in anticipation of heavy tonnage. Sandstone taken from earthen cuts for the right-of-way was crushed and used for ballast, and the track structure was composed of oak ties and 78-lb. steel rail, in contrast to the cinder ballast, hemlock ties, and lighter rail used on some PRR coal-region branches. Midway up the mountain, the 347-foot-long Hogback tunnel eliminated the need for the railroad to make a hairpin turn as it paralleled Beech Creek.

In 1883, work began on a much larger bore 8 miles west of Hurxthal's Summit. The job of excavating the 1,277-foot Peale tunnel went to P & T Collins, the same Philadelphia-based contractors who had graded the T&C from Philipsburg to Clearfield fourteen years earlier. Brothers Philip and Tom Collins had grown up in the Ebensburg area of Cambria County and had built sections of the PRR main line, the Huntingdon and Broad Top Mountain Railroad, Philadelphia and Reading Railroad, and other lines throughout Pennsylvania. They also held contracts to build other mountainous sections of the Beech Creek road. Construction began at the east portal of Peale tunnel on June 24 and on the west end on July 27. At about midnight on October 30, the two gangs of workers broke through to each other. Thanks to their previous experience, the Collins brothers were able to make quick work of the tunnel job, despite a heavy reliance on manual labor, black powder, and animals to cut through and haul away the bedrock, although they did use a new steam-powered drill on the east end. The tunnel was ready for traffic by mid-1884. Two miles farther west, construction of a bridge 771 feet long and 112 feet high over the valley of the Moshannon Creek overcame another natural barrier. The span, described by the *Democratic Watchman* as the "Great Moshannon Viaduct . . . built entirely of iron with the exception of the ties," was opened for service on November 11, 1884.[17]

As work on the railroad progressed, the Clearfield Bituminous Coal Company was opening its first mines near Peale tunnel and building a town—also christened Peale—to house miners and their families. The town of Peale was located along Moravian Run on the Clearfield County side of Moshannon Creek; but its passenger and freight station stood on the hillside above the creek in Centre County, about a quarter-mile west of Peale tunnel's west portal.[18] The *Clearfield Republican* in May 1883 carried a CBC solicitation for contractors to build "five blocks of six tenements each, 25 blocks of two tenements each and 20 single tenements" at Peale. By December 5, the *Clearfield Raftsman's Journal* reported that a hundred houses had been completed. Many of the miners and their families had migrated from McIntyre, where mines would close permanently by 1886.

The coal company had acquired more than 22,000 acres in Rush and Snow Shoe Townships in Centre County and Cooper Township in Clearfield County. It positioned Peale about midway between the settlement of Tunnel Mines (site of four separate mines) near the railroad in Centre County, and three mines near what would become the community of Grassflat in Clearfield County. Most if not all of the openings were in the Lower Kittanning seam. By the end of 1884, the railroad had transported 235,000 tons of coal. The CBC also built coke ovens near Gorton Heights (later shortened to Gorton), a village east of Tunnel Mines named for Alonzo H. Gorton, superintendent of the Fall Brook Railway. A hundred ovens were fired up in 1887, and 39,000 tons of coke were shipped that year. By 1900, 150 ovens were in operation.[19]

After the Beech Creek's track crossed the viaduct, it paralleled the Moshannon as far as Munson, then began climbing away from the creek toward a coalfield in the highlands of south-central Clearfield County. At Munson, a branch line left the main track and followed the creek another 7 miles to Philipsburg, prompting the opening of several mines along the way. The Beech Creek's Philipsburg Branch crossed the PRR's own Philipsburg Branch at grade at Loch Lomond Junction and terminated in Beaver Meadow, directly across the Moshannon from the

PRR's Philipsburg passenger station. (Beaver Meadow was incorporated as part of the new borough of Chester Hill in 1883.)

As elsewhere on the Beech Creek, Clearfield and South Western, contractors relied heavily on immigrant laborers to build the Philipsburg Branch. "A large number of Hungarians and Italians have commenced work on the new road at Munson's [sic]," reported the *Philipsburg Journal*. "The Hungarians are quartered in the Parker House barn here [Philipsburg], and the Italians are quartered on Second Street near Spruce." The workers, many of whom had been previously employed building branch lines for the PRR's Tyrone and Clearfield Railway, were "a lively set of chaps and seem to enjoy the life they lead."[20]

Philipsburg-area residents, who had donated much of the right of way for the branch line to their community, eagerly awaited the Beech Creek's arrival. Many believed a second railroad in town would lead to better service and lower rates than the community was receiving from the Pennsylvania. S. R. Peale was only too glad to encourage this feeling. "Every [coal] operator, little or big, shall have fair play," he told a newspaper reporter. Then, in a more obvious a jab at Berwind-White, he claimed that the Beech Creek "had originated from the necessities of the little operator, and Senator Wallace and other men of pluck have set their hearts on furnishing to every shipper in the Clearfield region equal and adequate facilities."[21]

"The Vanderbilt 'iron horse' will soon be among us," proclaimed the *Philipsburg Journal* on September 26, 1884, "and we hail its coming with feelings of indescribable delight, for . . . it means the opening of new markets for coal and lumber products, more work for our laborers, cheaper rates, cheaper prices for the necessaries of life, etc., and a general revival of business throughout the whole region."

Excitement grew to a fever pitch with the arrival of the first train on November 18, 1884. It stopped short of Philipsburg proper, at a makeshift station at the temporary end of track about midway between Loch Lomond Junction and Beaver Meadow. The train, originating in Williamsport and powered by locomotive No. 42, the *Wallaceton*, had two coaches carrying about thirty railroad officials and investors, led by Peale and Magee. According to the *Journal*, a large crowd had gathered in "bitter cold weather and in the face of a gathering storm" to greet the train. But the townspeople quickly forgot their discomfort when the train appeared near 3 PM, and "a shout of joy and gladness bursted forth." A celebratory dinner for the passengers was held that evening at Philipsburg's Potter House hotel.

Two days later, a second train arrived in Philipsburg over the BCC &SW, "loaded down with directors, stockholders and others," about forty passengers in all. Among the visitors this time were members of the corporate royalty—William K. Vanderbilt and Cornelius Vanderbilt II, sons of the ailing William H. Vanderbilt. Their presence was resounding evidence of the importance the New York Central attached to its affiliate road. Locals again hosted a Potter House banquet for their distinguished guests. "It was a beautiful repast," the *Journal* said, after which "the register was eagerly and carefully scanned to discover who the visitors were."

In reporting on the arrival of both trains, the *Journal* became even more outspoken in its criticism of the Pennsylvania Railroad. "The days of grinding, unjust railroad monopolies are past in this section of the country," the paper declared, "and the crown has been torn from the brow of the tyrant and placed on the head of one who would see justice done to our people." The overheated rhetoric obscured the fact that no major Philipsburg business or political leader had emerged as a champion of, or significant investor in, the BCC&SW. The town offered no one comparable to a Wallace, Peale, or Magee.

The first Beech Creek freight train came to Philipsburg on December 16, 1884, and regular service began soon thereafter. The *Journal* on March 27, 1885, noted with satisfaction that the new railroad had delivered goods to a Front Street grocer two days after the freight was shipped from Philadelphia: "This is as quick as it could possibly be done and speaks highly for the new road." Some goods arrived even more quickly. Watsontown wholesaler E. B. Hogue shipped a "market and general delivery car" from Philadelphia every Wednesday night; it was scheduled to arrive in Philipsburg on the express train the following evening. Hogue's specialty was produce, but he filled the car with a wide array of consumer goods ordered by local retailers for resale. Carloads of livestock were soon being dispatched in the afternoon from Philadelphia and arriving in Philipsburg twenty-four hours later.[22]

Figure 6.1. A short Beech Creek Railroad freight train is powered by 2-8-0 No. 5, an 1884 product of the Schenectady Locomotive Works, builder of the BCR's entire fifty-five-engine fleet. *Author's collection.*

In attempting to extend its line to the Beaver Meadows, site of the projected passenger and freight stations, the Beech Creek's Philipsburg Branch had to cross the main line of the Tyrone and Clearfield at grade. The PRR resolutely opposed such a crossing and demanded that the newcomer bridge the T&C instead. The Pennsylvania had not tried to block an at-grade crossing of its own Philipsburg Branch at Loch Lomond

Junction; that location saw far fewer trains, in particular fewer passenger trains. When the PRR sought an injunction against its rival in Clearfield County court, its attorneys claimed before Judge David L. Krebs that a busy at-grade crossing was unsafe and therefore the BCC&SW should be elevated. Beech Creek general counsel S. R. Peale personally argued his company's case in favor of crossing at grade. The issue dragged on through the winter of 1884–85, as Krebs gathered more information from both parties. In April, he ruled in favor of the BCC&SW. Its trains began using the new wood-frame passenger and freight stations in Chester Hill by September 1885.[23]

Over the next eight years, two serious but nonfatal collisions between PRR and Beech Creek trains occurred at the disputed crossing location, both times demolishing the "watch tower" that had been erected to guard against such accidents, though without serious injury to the signalman, who leaped from the window to safety on one of those occasions.[24] The incidents did not prompt the Pennsylvania to revive its case for grade separation, however, and after each accident the tower—assigned the telegraph call sign RG—was rebuilt.

The Beech Creek paused at Philipsburg amid popular speculation that it would resume building up the Moshannon Creek and that the Vanderbilts intended to drive it all the way to Pittsburgh. The railroad's board of directors requested Samuel Brugger to locate a right-of-way that would extend the Philipsburg Branch 20 miles to the coal-rich hills surrounding Madera, a village on the upper reaches of Clearfield Creek. The Pennsylvania's Moshannon Branch, too, was heading for Madera on an alignment roughly parallel to Brugger's survey. The PRR reached Madera in 1887, while the Beech Creek did not lay even one rail on Brugger's line.[25]

Any need for the Beech Creek to push on to Madera ended with the coming of the Altoona and Philipsburg Connecting Railroad, incorporated in July 1892. The A&PC was corporate child of United Collieries, which owned a number of mines in the upper Moshannon Valley. United's investors, led by Samuel P. Langdon of Philadelphia (unrelated to Clearfield Bituminous Coal Company president Charles J. Langdon), were unhappy with the PRR's monopoly in the area and welcomed the Beech Creek's arrival in Philipsburg. Construction of the A&PC began soon after the company was chartered, and the line reached Houtzdale in the summer of 1894, its route being no more than a mile from the PRR's Moshannon Branch at any given point. It used timber trestles to cross that branch or its tributaries four times. Initially Clearfield County's Judge Krebs had ruled that at-grade intersections would be satisfactory; but the PRR appealed all the way to the Pennsylvania Supreme Court, which overruled Krebs and left the A&PC with no choice but to build the elevated crossings. Soon after the Altoona and Philipsburg Connecting Railroad opened for service, President Langdon hosted the obligatory investors' reception and dinner at the Potter House, complete with welcoming speeches by Philipsburg Board of Trade members, music by a brass band, and carriage rides out to a few coal mines.

According to Richard Adams, the railroad's foremost historian,

> about this time the A&PC acquired a nickname which stuck with it for the rest of its life, and is the only name some of the residents of the Moshannon Valley know the line by today. No one is quite sure where the name originated, some say it grew out of the railroad's title, others claim it came about because the A&PC was built right down the middle of Hannah Street in Houtzdale. The A&PC became known as the "Alley Popper" and the name stuck. As time went on, it became easier to use the nickname than keep up with all the corporate name changes the line went through.[26]

The Alley Popper began where the Beech Creek's Philipsburg Branch ended: at Wigton Junction, so named for its proximity to the R. B. Wigton and Son brickyard and coal mine. The short line obtained trackage rights for the short distance between the junction and the Beech Creek's Philipsburg freight and passenger stations.

Other than the United Collieries mines, the Alley Popper served small mines working deposits that the PRR considered second rate— that is, mines that were not in the Lower Freeport seam. Nevertheless, the short line in some years handed off an impressive number of carloads to the Beech Creek. The Alley Popper originated nearly 111,000 tons of coal in fiscal 1895–96, equivalent to more than 4,400 25-ton capacity cars. Tonnage declined through the remainder of the decade as the nation struggled with prolonged economic depression. Coal going through the Wigton Junction interchange stabilized at roughly 50,000 tons annually in the early 1900s. The Alley Popper typically gave only a small fraction of its coal tonnage to the PRR, mostly when it was destined for customers served exclusively by that road in western Pennsylvania.[27]

Whether the Vanderbilts and their allies played a covert role in birthing the Altoona and Philipsburg Connecting Railroad is hard to say. It is plain to see, however, that the Alley Popper functioned as a proxy for the Beech Creek. The New York Central's Beech Creek District mine map showed the short line's trackage and the mines it served almost as if they were part of the NYC's own network. The Beech Creek stood to get nearly all the coal from the Alley Popper without investing in its construction and assuming any risk. Also, the alliance between the Pennsylvania and Berwind-White made it unlikely that the Beech Creek could win over any of the coal company's Eureka mines. Under those circumstances, expansion-by-proxy made sense.

After spinning off the Philipsburg Branch at Munson, the Beech Creek main line ran 38 miles to Gazzam, another mining community founded by the Clearfield Bituminous Coal Company. The CBC acquired about 11,000 acres of potential coal lands in the new town's vicinity. From Gazzam on the west to the Fall Brook Railway at Jersey Shore on the east, the Beech Creek operated 104 route-miles of main track. In spite of Philipsburgers' pleas (and an offer of $10,000) to locate car and locomotive shops in their town, the Beech Creek made Jersey Shore its headquarters and shop town. There the railroad established offices for the superintendent, general freight and passenger agents, auditor, cashier and paymaster, purchasing agent, master mechanic, train dispatcher, car accountant, and other supervisory and clerical personnel. Smaller enginehouses were erected at Viaduct (at the west end of the bridge) and Philipsburg.

As of January 29, 1886, the BCC&SW had 16 locomotives and 10 cabooses on its roster, while its freight rolling stock included 500 25-ton-capacity coal cars, 50 flat cars, and 28 boxcars. Passenger equipment included two passenger-baggage combines and five coaches. Motive power consisted of seven 2-8-0 Consolidation types, three each of the 2-6-0 Mogul and 4-4-0 American types, two 4-6-0 Ten-wheelers and one 0-6-0 switcher. All were purchased new from the Schenectady (New York) Locomotive Works, a forerunner of the famed American Locomotive Company, between 1883 and 1886. The Schenectady works was situated in the heart of New York Central territory, a likely factor in the Beech

Creek's choice of builder, just as the PRR favored Philadelphia-based Baldwin.[28]

The Beech Creek, like the PRR's Tyrone and Clearfield Railway, was primarily a coal hauler. Carrying people was a distinctly secondary business. Passenger Time Table No. 1 took effect on July 1, 1884, between Jersey Shore and Peale. One train running Monday through Saturday required about three and a half hours to make the 58-mile, one-way journey.[29] A new schedule effective February 2, 1885, showed two trains departing and arriving Philipsburg six days a week. Eastbound passengers had a choice between the *Philadelphia & New York Express* that ran to the Philadelphia and Reading's depot in Williamsport and an unnamed mixed train that terminated at Jersey Shore. Westbound counterparts were the *Philipsburg Express* originating at Williamsport and the mixed coming from Jersey Shore. The two express trains carried a baggage car and a smoker, along with coaches and a sleeping car.[30]

The Reading's cooperation enabled the sleeping car to operate in through service between Philadelphia and Philipsburg, eliminating the need for eastbound passengers to make a change at Williamsport in the middle of the night. The trip required approximately twelve hours. Within a few years, the western terminus was changed from Philipsburg to Clearfield; and by 1894, the famed Pullman Company had taken charge of the car. It was the first and only instance of regular sleeping car operation to and from the coalfields of Centre County and the Moshannon Valley. But the service did not last. By 1897 the sleeper from Philadelphia was being turned at Williamsport.[31]

If the market was insufficient to support a sleeper, it did sustain other kinds of passenger traffic. The railroad reported carrying a system-wide average of nearly 168,000 passengers annually in the early 1890s. Passenger-train revenues were enhanced when in April 1886 the Beech Creek contracted to carry the US mail on its Philipsburg and Gazzam routes.[32] Beech Creek riders could reach a wealth of destinations. As noted, Williamsport was the gateway via the Reading to Philadelphia, New York, and other eastern Pennsylvania and East Coast cities. At Jersey Shore, travelers could continue north over the Fall Brook Railway for upstate New York points. Those bound for distant points north and west of Munson continued on to Clearfield, where they changed to trains of the

Buffalo, Rochester & Pittsburgh Railway to reach any of that road's namesake cities. The Alley Popper, which shared the Beech Creek's Philipsburg station, offered local service to upper Moshannon Valley communities.

Beyond scheduled passenger service, the BCC&SW ran numerous excursions. In July 1885 alone, a special train from Lock Haven brought 300 people to Philipsburg's Fourth of July festivities; another ran from Philipsburg to a religious revival at Peale; and a third took baseball fans from the Moshannon Valley to watch the Philipsburg nine play Jersey Shore at the latter's home field. Meanwhile, the railroad added extra cars to its regular trains to accommodate persons who, for a $10 roundtrip ticket, wanted to see President Grover Cleveland dedicate the new international park at Niagara Falls on July 14. (Travelers changed trains at Jersey Shore for the journey northward to the Falls via Rochester, New York.) A popular Sunday excursion destination was the camp meeting grounds near Bigler in Clearfield County. The Beech Creek also sold "thousand-mile tickets" for $20 ($0.02 a mile), good for travel anywhere on the railroad by not only the purchaser but his or her family members or employees. The *Philipsburg Journal*, in contrast to the harsh words it often hurled at the Pennsylvania Railroad, gushed praise for the competing road's passenger efforts: "When you can find a more courteous, accommodating, obliging class of people than the Beech Creek railroad and its employees, just let us know and we will publish it to the world. It can't be done."[33]

When PRR engineer C. S. D'Invilliers had recommended that his road expand into the upper Moshannon Valley and leave the lower valley to the Vanderbilts, he was conceding only a small bit of territory to the rival railroad. The Beech Creek began an intense exploitation of that area's coal deposits and other natural resources; and rumors swirled that it planned to push westward beyond Gazzam, deeper into Clearfield County and beyond to Indiana and northern Cambria Counties. The Pennsylvania soon came to resent and fear what its official historians labeled "this invasion of its soft coal territory."[34]

The PRR's concern was well founded. William Wallace pointed out in October 1885 that "as a result of competition the Beech Creek's traffic has increased while that on the Tyrone and Clearfield has fallen off.

Coal rates are much lower today than they were three years ago—a result brought about by competition."[35] Austin King, state mine inspector for Centre and Clearfield Counties and presumably a neutral observer, reported that "the coal business is rapidly increasing in the district but mines on the Tyrone and Clearfield are falling behind in the percentage of total output." He added that the Beech Creek's "car service is better, and individual shippers claim to receive better service than is given by the Pennsylvania Railroad."[36]

There was plenty of evidence that many coal operators agreed with King. As soon as the BCC&SW reached Hawk Run, between Munson and Philipsburg, owners of the Acme, Empire, and Pardee mines gave to the Beech Creek the segment of the Pennsylvania's Pardee Branch they had paid for a few years earlier in order to obtain PRR service. (The Pardee Branch was an offshoot of the Pennsylvania's Philipsburg Branch.) It became the Beech Creek's Hawk Run Branch, and over its rails went thousands of tons of coal that had formerly gone via the Pennsylvania.[37] Not far away, the Beech Creek built its Decatur Branch into the Nuttall mines, previously the Pennsylvania's exclusive preserve. Closer to Philipsburg, the Beech Creek laid down a track parallel to the PRR's Derby Branch on the north edge of Beaver Meadow, and named it the Derby Branch, as if taunting its rival. Owners of the mines in that vicinity—Derby, Cuba, Victor No. 1, Colorado, Lancashire No. 1, and others—demanded a connection between the Derby Branches of both railroads; they soon got it at a swampy, nondescript location called Spring Hill Junction. The interchange enabled the mines to ship via either PRR or Beech Creek, depending on which railroad offered better rates, service, and car supply. In the three-year period beginning in 1887, the Pennsylvania turned over 14,800 carloads to the Beech Creek at the junction, and received only 11 carloads.[38] Based on an average of 25 tons of coal per car, the total originated on the PRR and sent out over Beech Creek rails was slightly less than 4 percent of all coal tonnage shipped on the Tyrone and Clearfield for those years. Still, it was a notable triumph for the New York Central and a galling defeat for the Pennsylvania.

If George Roberts and his associates had gotten their way, there would have been no Spring Hill Junction, and the Beech Creek, Clearfield and South Western itself would have been short-lived. Initially inclined to

Figure 6.2. Postcard view of a Beech Creek 0-6-0 shifting hopper-gondolas at a Morrisdale Coal Company tipple. The coal company was among the BCR's largest shippers. *Author's collection.*

follow D'Invilliers's 1883 view that the Vanderbilts should be allowed to seek the lesser coals of Centre County and the Moshannon Valley, PRR executives had changed their minds by 1885. They were alive to the threat posed by the Vanderbilts' thrust into central Pennsylvania and sought to parry the Beech Creek venture. For several years prior, a syndicate of industrialists that included William H. Vanderbilt, George Magee, Andrew Carnegie, and Philadelphia and Reading Railroad president Franklin B. Gowen had been backing an effort to build a railroad across southern Pennsylvania that could break the PRR's near-monopoly on shipping between Harrisburg and Pittsburgh. Just as this South Pennsylvania Railroad project got under way, construction began on the New York, West Shore and Buffalo Railroad, which aimed to build a line parallel to the New York Central's main route up the Hudson Valley and across New York state. The Vanderbilts accused Roberts and the PRR of encouraging the West Shore scheme, Roberts saw the Vanderbilt hand behind the South Penn, and a savage railroad war seemed certain.

Financier J. Pierpont Morgan intervened. Well along on his path to becoming the nation's preeminent investment banker, he viewed cutthroat competition between two of the nation's largest carriers as ruinous to the entire railroad industry. In what became a legendary business summit, he convened Roberts, NYC president Chauncey M. Depew, and William H. Vanderbilt's son-in-law and executive surrogate Hamilton Twombly for private talks aboard his yacht, the *Corsair*, in New York harbor in July 1885. (The ailing William H. Vanderbilt by then had withdrawn from active management of his railroad and would die before the year was out.) Morgan facilitated an agreement whereby the PRR would assume control of—and kill—the South Penn, partially reimburse its principals, and keep hands off the West Shore. The settlement also called for the Vanderbilts, Magee, Peale, and their associates to sell a controlling interest in the Beech Creek, Clearfield and South Western to the Pennsylvania.[39]

Why Depew and Twombly were willing to offer up the BCC&SW is open for debate. The Vanderbilts were eager to avoid the ruinous rate war with the Pennsylvania that would occur if the South Penn became reality. Plus, they desperately wanted control of the West Shore in order to block a possible PRR invasion of the New York Central's home territory. Selling a controlling interest in the Beech Creek would still have allowed the NYC to source locomotive coal from CBC mines, even if this coal did have to travel some distance over PRR-controlled rails. The Reading was the biggest loser in the deal Morgan had brokered. President Gowen saw in the Beech Creek a long-term source of lucrative bituminous traffic that the Reading could forward to East Coast destinations. Such traffic would be routed over the PRR under Morgan's scheme.

In light of William H. Vanderbilt's declining health, there is some question as to who was really making the corporate decisions that controlled the Beech Creek's destiny. The *Wall Street Journal* on December 15, 1885, reported that "it is said on good authority that Mr. Vanderbilt was personally opposed to the sale of the Beech Creek, and only con-

sented to it because his son-in-law, Mr. Twombly, had made the arrangements, and he felt compelled to sustain him."

Vanderbilt allies Magee and Peale had to be discreet in venting their
anger over the agreement. Magee presented it without enthusiasm to
the Beech Creek's stockholders; he told insiders that so long as his Fall
Brook Railway remained untouched by the PRR, he supposed he could
live without the Beech Creek. Peale threw down hard facts, though he
was careful not to cross the line into outright hostility. "Business in that
section of [the] country has been stimulated by the competition by our
road," he told the press when asked about the sale of his railroad. "Industries have improved right along. Freight rates are 20 to 50 percent less
than a year ago, owing to Beech Creek competition."[40]

Voices from Centre and Clearfield counties were more direct. The
Philipsburg Journal predicted the sale of the Beech Creek "is a thing that
will be very much regretted, and should be prevented if possible." Mine
owner A. V. Hoyt estimated the Beech Creek's lower rates had enabled
it to capture 200,000 tons of coal in a single year from the Pennsylvania.
Even the *New York Times* chimed in, predicting that "the transfer of the
Beech Creek Road to the Pennsylvania Company will check the development of coal deposits on the line of that road in which millions have
been invested."[41]

Coal companies and individuals who held small blocks of BCC&SW
stock vociferously opposed the sale. Representatives from these groups
along with other citizens met in Bellefonte in September 1885 and elected
James A. Beaver to head a committee charged with drafting a petition
to Governor Robert E. Pattison protesting the PRR's acquisition of the
road. Beaver did so without reluctance, even though he was a Republican
and had lost to Pattison in the 1882 gubernatorial election. Beaver had
shares in coal properties that could benefit from Beech Creek service. He
also was contemplating another run for governor in 1886 and had to be
sensitive to the rising tide of popular sentiment against the monopolistic
practices of the Pennsylvania Railroad.

The Democratic Pattison had no love for the PRR, whose officials
were staunchly Republican and had campaigned against him in the 1882
election. With the governor's blessing, state attorney general Lewis Cas-
sidy sought an injunction against the Beech Creek sale, citing a section

of the state constitution that prohibited a railroad taking over a parallel line. The Dauphin County court agreed in its January 1886 decision, which was upheld by the state Supreme Court later that year. The
high court noted that "it is clear that a violation of this section would be
threatened if the Pennsylvania Railroad Company, which leases certain
roads directly and substantially competing with the Beech Creek road,
were about to buy and hold in its own name a majority of the stock of the
latter company; for in that case the Pennsylvania Railroad Company, as
such lessee, would certainly 'control another railroad corporation owning or having under its control a parallel or competing line.'"[42]

The ruling also applied to the PRR's South Penn acquisition, but few
seemed to care, as construction of that road had ceased; it was so incomplete that there was some question whether it actually constituted
a parallel line. (Portions of its alignment became rights-of-way for the
Pennsylvania Turnpike in the 1930s.) In New York state, some segments
of the West Shore were integrated into the NYC system, while others
were left to decline as unwanted duplicate routes. Most importantly for
central Pennsylvania, the Beech Creek stayed in the New York Central
camp.

By the time of the Dauphin County court ruling, the Beech Creek,
Clearfield and South Western Railroad had been reorganized as the
Beech Creek Railroad. Early sales of BCC&SW stock had raised $5 mil-
lion, yet $6.3 million had been invested in constructing and equipping
the road. The BCC&SW borrowed $1.3 million from New York banks to
cover the shortfall, pledging some of its bonds as collateral. Repayment
of the loan was coming due, while prospects for finding the necessary
cash were slim, since the revenue-generating coal trade was still in its
infancy. A default would put the company's bonds at risk—the lenders
could sell these securities to another party, even another railroad, in
order to obtain the money owed them. The BCC&SW's principal investors then executed a stratagem not uncommon among railroads at that
time. They had a court declare their company insolvent and put up for
public sale—in this case, by the Clearfield County sheriff on June 4,
1886.[43] The principals then bought it back for the $1.3 million shortfall
and reincorporated it as the Beech Creek Railroad on June 30. The BCR
issued enough new securities to pay most, if not all, of the predecessor

company's old debt without having to wait for the railroad to develop sufficient earnings to pay it. In a parallel reorganization, the affiliated Clearfield Bituminous Coal Company became the Clearfield Bituminous Coal Corporation on October 7, 1886.

Membership of the committee that guided the railroad's reorganization reveals the various threads in the Beech Creek's fabric: William K. Vanderbilt and C. C. Clarke, representing the New York Central and the Vanderbilt family; George F. Baer, president of the Philadelphia and Reading Railroad; CBC president Charles J. Langdon; and Joseph Gazzam, who represented Pennsylvania-based investors who were independent of the Reading.[44] Although he was not a member of the reorganization committee, George Magee was named the Beech Creek Railroad's general manager and held a significant amount of the company's securities. (Magee also continued in his duties as head of the Fall Brook coal and railroad enterprises.) A noteworthy name among the reorganized railroad's lesser investors was Samuel L. Clemens (Mark Twain), then nearing the height of his popularity as a uniquely American writer and humorist. Clemens had married Charles Langdon's sister, Olivia, in 1870, and spent his summers writing on the Langdon family farm in Elmira. He held nearly $20,000 in Beech Creek Railroad stocks and bonds, and also was an investor in the Clearfield Bituminous Coal Corporation.[45]

Absent from the circle that reorganized the Beech Creek Railroad were any central Pennsylvania investors. S. R. Peale was a member of the reorganized company's board of directors, and he continued to serve as legal counsel, working primarily to secure land and leases; but he was no longer in a position to guide the company's destiny. Even so, he left a lasting imprint on the railroad and the area it served. "My principal achievement for the public good was the conception and execution [of] the scheme for building the Beech Creek Railroad, and the introduction of the NYC&HR RR into the soft coal regions of central Pennsylvania," he proudly recalled years later. "Great results have followed, and now cars marked NYC RR may be seen west of the Allegheny Mountains bearing coal to the Eastern Seaboard. Towns have sprung up, thousands of working men have found employment, and the hundreds of thousands of idle acres have become sources of prosperity."[46] At his death in 1910 at age 80, he was one of central Pennsylvania's wealthiest and most highly esteemed citizens.

William A. Wallace resigned from the presidency of the reorganized Beech Creek Railroad in 1889 at the age of 62. It appeared to be a friendly separation, judging by a letter he sent to the board of directors at the time. "My connection with your company for the entire time since its organization has been pleasant and agreeable to me," he wrote, "and I leave your association with regret."[47] His departure left more time for political and other business pursuits. Unfortunately, he did not fare well in either. He tried but failed to obtain the Democratic nomination for governor in mid-1890, his second such unsuccessful attempt. Also, some bad investments soon ruined him financially; he had not recovered by the time he died in 1896.

Wallace's resignation coincided with a move by the Vanderbilts to strengthen their control of the Beech Creek Railroad, increasing their stock ownership beyond the 55 percent that various family members already held. They even acquired shares held by such BCR stalwarts as Magee and Langdon.[48] The Vanderbilts were mum on the reasons for their purchase, which was followed by the New York Central's lease of the Beech Creek for 999 years, effective October 1, 1890. The lease allowed the BCR to maintain its corporate organization and operational independence: it would continue to have its own managers and directors, its cars and locomotives would continue to carry Beech Creek lettering and livery, and general offices remained in Jersey Shore.[49]

Circumstantial evidence points to several reasons why the Vanderbilts may have desired to tighten their grip on the BCR. As the PRR demonstrated, a large road leasing a smaller line gave the smaller one access to the parent's resources. In the Beech Creek's case, more resources from the New York Central could help end a car shortage that had developed in the face of rapidly increasing traffic. Coal shipments had catapulted from 235,000 tons in 1884 to 1.3 million tons in 1887 to 2.1 million tons in 1890.[50] "A regular howl has gone up from the coal shippers who send their coal to customers in eastern Pennsylvania and New Jersey over a scarcity of cars," reported the *Philipsburg Journal* in August 1889. "One coal operator . . . said yesterday he has orders on his books for two months' production and is getting more orders every day, but the [Beech Creek] Railroad will not furnish him enough cars to fill even the most pressing orders. All along the line, the same complaint is heard."[51]

An especially embarrassing incident occurred the next month, when BCR general manager George Magee turned down a request from James Beaver—who was then Pennsylvania's governor—to extend a siding to his coal property near what would become Winburne. "Early this season the managers of this road decided that it was inexpedient for us to extend more sidings or construct laterals or encourage other parties so to do, on account of our want of equipment," Magee explained delicately. "We are very limited in our supply of cars, and our locomotives are unable to take all the business now offered us from present openings. The present collieries are able to work hardly two thirds of the time as it is, and our position is that it would be unfair to them if we encouraged any new business which would demand more cars."[52] Surely the Vanderbilts cringed at having to turn away business from an influential politico.

Another factor behind the lease of the Beech Creek may well have been the New York Central's desire to use the road as a link in a Chicago–Philadelphia trunk line. From Ashtabula, Ohio, on the main line, the NYC had a branch extending to Franklin in northwest Pennsylvania, about 80 miles from the Beech Creek's west end in Clearfield County. On the BCR's east end was the friendly Reading. In December 1889, the *Philipsburg Journal* reported surveyors were in the field staking out possible alignments for a railroad that would close the 80-mile gap.[53] Using the Beech Creek as part of the Chicago–Philadelphia route would save about 150 miles compared with running trains via the Fall Brook Railway and upstate New York. Lending credence to the notion of reshaping the Beech Creek into a link in a grand east–west through-route was the relocation of the BCR's general passenger and freight agents from Jersey Shore Junction to Philadelphia in mid-1893.

Months passed with no public comment from railroad officials. Meanwhile, the BCR extended its western terminus to Mahaffey in Clearfield County and reached into northern Cambria County to serve newly developed mines around Patton. In 1895, the New York Central formed another subsidiary to build west from Mahaffey into coal-rich Indiana County. This growth increased tonnage over the BCR's main line and reinforced the original vision of the railroad as a regional coal hauler rather than as part of a through-route.

As new mines opened in Indiana and Cambria Counties, there was retrenchment in Centre County. Despite optimistic early reports, the Tunnel mines, Gorton coke ovens, and associated community of Peale were all short-lived. The Clearfield Bituminous Coal Corporation closed the Tunnel mines in 1892, admitting that the quality and quantity of coal there did not meet expectations. At the same time, the CBC opened three more drifts around Grassflat to make up for the production short-fall. Those mines were served by the Grassflat Branch, which began at Viaduct. Some of Peale's residents moved to Grassflat, while others de-parted for nearby coal patches or jobs outside the region. The coal com-pany began dismantling houses to be re-erected elsewhere; by 1910, the once-lively community was a ghost town.[54]

In spite of Peale's disappointing fate and the economic malaise that followed the Panic of 1893, the Beech Creek regularly reported annual net earnings in excess of a half-million dollars. Coal shipments fluctu-ated only slightly from year to year, thanks at least in part to the New York Central's steady demand for locomotive fuel. In the depression year of 1894, the Beech Creek actually surpassed the slumping T&C in coal tonnage, 2.4 million tons versus 2.0 million tons. The T&C shipped coal from a relatively concentrated area in the Moshannon Valley, of course, while the BCR's mines were strung over four counties and also included coal originated by the Alley Popper. The Beech Creek pulled ahead for good in 1897, 3.8 million tons to 2.3 million tons, although in tonnage per mile of road, the T&C was still on top.[55]

The BCR's locomotive and car fleets grew to keep pace with increased traffic. As of July 1, 1899, fifty-four locomotives were on the roster. Thirty-two 4-8-0s, variously designated Twelve Wheeler or Mastodon types, were used in heavy road service. (The only other 4-8-0s rostered by New York Central–affiliated lines were eleven belonging to the Bos-ton & Albany Railroad, which used them primarily in the Berkshires of western Massachusetts.) Less demanding road duties and pusher as-signments normally went to 2-8-0 Consolidations. Four 4-4-0 American types and two 4-6-0 Ten-wheelers handled passenger trains. Rounding out the fleet were a handful of 0-6-0 shifters for yard work and 2-6-0

Moguls for service on lightly built mine spurs. The BCR rostered 4,733 coal cars (mostly hopper gondolas ranging in capacity from 25 to 32 tons), 50 flatcars, and 27 boxcars. For passenger operations, the railroad had nine "general" passenger cars (probably coaches), and two cars for baggage, mail, and express service. All equipment was lettered "Beech Creek Railroad" and/or "B. C. R." The railroad had only a small car shop at Jersey Shore, so most or all rolling stock came from such traditional NYC suppliers as the Buffalo Car Manufacturing Company, Union Car Company, and Michigan Car Company.[56]

Having so much traffic course over the its single-track main stem strained the Beech Creek's capacity. Until 1893 one Jersey Shore–based dispatcher controlled all train operations. In that year, the territory was halved: one dispatcher's authority extended from Jersey Shore to Munson, including the Philipsburg Branch and its spurs; a second dispatcher had authority over everything west of Munson. Dispatchers were linked by telegraph to station agents/operators up and down the railroad.[57] Also in 1893, passing sidings were installed or lengthened at five locations on the 41 miles between Munson and the town of Beech Creek. Even with these additional measures, accidents happened. In March 1895, for example, a westbound locomotive "became unmanageable" as it headed west downgrade from Hurxthal's Summit. The engineer and fireman jumped, and the engine hit an oncoming train near Peale. Both locomotives were badly damaged. In May, on a curve between Peale and Viaduct, a westbound light helper engine ran headlong into an eastbound passenger train. The ramming must have occurred at low speed because the only injury was to a passenger, who lost several teeth when she slammed face first into the coach's coal stove. In November, on a bridge just above Hayes Run on the climb to Snow Shoe, two coal trains collided. Both locomotives were destroyed, and some fifty cars derailed and were declared a total loss. One of the conductors was killed, an engineer was badly injured, and one of the fireman saved himself by jumping from the cab directly into Beech Creek as the trains approached one another on the bridge.[58] Such were the dangers of railroading in the late nineteenth century.

The Beech Creek Railroad remained an independent operating entity until May 1, 1899, when it became the Beech Creek District of the

New York Central's newly created Pennsylvania Division. The BCR then became a non-operating company, primarily to own real estate on behalf of its parent.[59] The division's other component was the Fall Brook District—the former Fall Brook Railway—which was also operating under NYC lease. The formation of the Pennsylvania Division, headquartered in Corning, New York, and consisting of 412 route-miles, resulted from NYC's desire to achieve the efficiencies that common management over the affiliated roads would bring. The BCR still possessed its own officers and board of directors, but—in the manner of so many of the PRR's leased lines—they were mostly executives of the parent company or selected with the approval of the parent. Despite the change, generations of central Pennsylvanians would often use the familiar "Beech Creek" when referring to the railroad that finally brought competition to the area's coalfields.

Notes

1. James MacFarlane, *The Coal-Regions of America* (New York: D. Appleton, 1875), 124–69; A. J. Musser, "Coal and the New York Central Railroad Company," *Explosives Engineer* (March/April 1944): 68–75.

2. *New York Times*, 28 December 1882.

3. S. R. Peale to Harriet Frances Peale, 11 January 1881, S. R. Peale Papers, Clinton County Historical Society, Lock Haven, PA.

4. Quoted in the *Philipsburg Journal*, 16 October 1885.

5. Beech Creek Railroad board of directors minute book, 22 September 1882, Box 533, HCLA 1710, Pennsylvania Railroad and New York Central Railroad Collection, Pennsylvania State University Special Collections Library. The PRR material encompasses the carrier's Central Region of western Pennsylvania and eastern Ohio lines and excludes central Pennsylvania. The NYC material consists primarily of the administrative records of the Beech Creek Railroad and predecessors and the Clearfield Bituminous Coal Corp.

6. *Commonwealth of Pennsylvania v. Pennsylvania and Western Railroad Company*, Common Pleas Court of Dauphin County, Pa., filed 18 July 1883, with ruling on or about 29 September 1884. See also *Centre Democrat* (Bellefonte), 18 October 1883.

7. *Renovo Record*, 4 December 1884.

8. S&C board of directors minute book, 1 December 1879, 25 July and 1 August 1882, in Box 537, PRR NYC Collection; *Renovo Record*, 4 December 1884; Aldrich, *Clearfield County*, 231.

9. Quoted in George A. Scott, *Clearfield Today and Tomorrow: Railroads of the Area* (Clearfield, PA: Progressive Publishing, 1968), 61.

10. S&C minutes, 24 August 1883.

11. D'Invilliers to DuBarry, 23 December 1883, in Fall Brook Coal and Railway Co. Records, Manuscript Group 48.21, Pennsylvania State Archives.

12. An online overview of the Fall Brook Railway is www.fallbrookrailway.com.

13. BCR minutes, 11 January 1883.

14. *Clearfield Raftsman's Journal,* 22 November 1882; *New York Times,* 10 December 1885.

15. *Centre Democrat* (Bellefonte), 27 September 1883.

16. *Democratic Watchman* (Bellefonte), 11 September 1885.

17. *Democratic Watchman,* 14 November 1884.

18. *Philipsburg Journal,* 30 May and 29 August 1884. *Peale, Pennsylvania, 1883–1912,* "Historical Information about Peale Pennsylvania and the Tunnel Mines," 26 May 2000, accessed 21 July 2016, http://krygier.owu.edu/krygier_html/peale/peale _pabia.html.

19. Frederick E. Saward, *The Coal Trade* (New York: *Coal Trade Journal,* 1884), 16; 1888, 27; CBC minutes, 31 May 1888 and 28 May 1890, Box 4, PRR NYC Collection; Jeffrey Feldmeier, "The Gorton Coke Ovens," *Snow Shoe Rails to Trails Association Newsletter,* December 2014, 2; H. B. Douglas (CBC manager), "Odds and Ends and Things," *New York Central Lines,* 16 August 1922.

20. The *Philipsburg Journal* throughout May and June 1884 commented at length on the BCR's immigrant labor force.

21. *Lock Haven Express,* 24 January 1883.

22. *Philipsburg Journal,* 12 June 1885 and 19 June 1891.

23. The *Philipsburg Journal* covered the crossing dispute extensively but, curiously, did not report on the opening of the new station.

24. *Philipsburg Journal,* 17 June 1892 and 13 October 1893.

25. *Philipsburg Journal,* 17 June 1892.

26. Richard D. Adams, *The Alley Popper* (Victor, NY: R. D. Adams, 1980), 18.

27. Alley Popper tonnage data: *Annual Report of the Secretary of Internal Affairs on Railroads, Canals, Telegraphs, and Telephones* (Harrisburg: Pennsylvania Department of Internal Affairs) for the years under discussion.

28. BCR minutes, 29 January 1886.

29. *Clearfield Republican,* 2 July 1884; *Clinton Democrat,* 13 November 1884.

30. *Philipsburg Journal,* 6 February 1885.

31. The *Philipsburg Journal* published passenger train schedules weekly.

32. "Report of the Beech Creek Railroad Company" for the years ending 30 June 1891 through 30 June 30 1895, Box 509, HCLA 1710, PRR and NYC Collection. These are annual reports to the stockholders. US mail: *Philipsburg Journal,* 16 April 1886.

33. *Philipsburg Journal,* 27 August 1886.

34. George H. Burgess and Miles C. Kennedy, *Centennial History of the Pennsylvania Railroad Company* (Philadelphia: PRR, 1949), 408.

35. Quoted in *Philipsburg Journal,* 16 October 1885.

36. Eighth Bituminous District report in *Report of the Inspectors of Mines for the Year 1890* (Harrisburg: Pennsylvania Bureau of Mines, 1891), 456.

37. S. B. Row and C. U. Hoffer, *Illustrated Souvenir History of Philipsburg* (Williamsport, PA: Grit Publishing, 1909), 29–30; *Philipsburg Journal*, 19 August 1887 and 28 September 1888.

38. Pennsylvania Railroad Company, *Annual Report of the Board of Directors to the Stockholders* (Philadelphia: PRR, 1887 through 1889).

39. Herbert Harwood, *The Railroad That Never Was: Vanderbilt, Morgan, and the South Pennsylvania Railroad* (Bloomington: Indiana University Press, 2010), 90–100; Marvin W. Schlegel, *Ruler of the Reading: The Life of Franklin B. Gowen* (Harrisburg: Archives Publishing Co. of Pennsylvania, 1947), 244–65.

40. Albert Churella, *The Pennsylvania Railroad: Building an Empire, 1846–1917* (Philadelphia: University of Pennsylvania Press, 2012), 521–23; *New York Times*, 29 July 1885.

41. *Philipsburg Journal*, 21 August 1885 and 16 October 1885; *New York Times*, 10 August 1885.

42. *Pennsylvania R. Co. v. Commonwealth*, Supreme Court of Pennsylvania, 4 October 1886, in *Atlantic Reporter* 5 (St. Paul: West Publishing Co., 1886), 374–77. Dauphin County court decision: *Commonwealth v. Beech Creek, Clearfield and Southwestern Railroad Co. et al., Pennsylvania County Court Reports* 1 (Philadelphia: T. and J. W. Johnson, 1886), 223–28.

43. *Commercial and Financial Chronicle*, 12 June 1886.

44. *Wall Street Journal*, 15 December 1885; BCR minutes, 29 June 1886.

45. A list of shareholders is in BCR minutes, 29 June 1886.

46. Peale to "Mrs. Barrows," 24 September 1907, Peale Papers. Barrows, whose first name was not mentioned, may have been a reporter for the *Lock Haven Express*.

47. Wallace to the BCR directors, 12 September 1889, in BCR minutes, 25 September 1889.

48. *Philipsburg Journal*, 8 August 1889.

49. BCR minutes, 3 December 1890.

50. Frederick E. Saward, *The Coal Trade* (New York: Coal Trade Journal, 1893), 15.

51. *Philipsburg Journal*, 9 August 1889.

52. Magee to Beaver, 13 September 1889, James A. Beaver Papers, Series 7, HCLA 1433, Historical Collections and Labor Archives, Pennsylvania State University Special Collections Library.

53. *Philipsburg Journal*, 13 December 1889; *New York Times*, 29 November 1889.

54. CBC minutes, 28 May 1890, 26 October 1892; Andy Petkac, "Peale—A Ghost Coal Mine Town That Still Exists," *The Progress* (Clearfield), 21 July 1975.

55. Saward, *Coal Trade*, various years. The BCR minutes report slightly different tonnages from Saward year to year. Saward is used here for consistency when comparing to other rail lines' tonnages.

56. *Poor's Manual of Railroads* (New York: H. V. and H. W. Poor, 1900), 134; and William D. Edson and H. L. Vail Jr., *Steam Locomotives of the New York Central Lines*, vol. 1 (Cleveland: New York Central System Historical Society, 1997), 82, 84.

57. *Philipsburg Journal*, 9 June 1893, 15 and 22 September 1893.

58. *Democratic Watchman*, 22 March and 31 May 1895; *Centre Democrat*, 14 November 1895.

59. *New York Times*, 2 May 1899. Penn Central became the Beech Creek Railroad's parent in 1968. Eight years later, newly formed Conrail took ownership of BCR lines in active use. In 1981 PC consolidated the inactive remnants of the Beech Creek with several other "paper" railroads under its control and began selling off its assets, consisting mostly of abandoned rights-of-way.

SEVEN

Nittany Valley Short Lines

Bellefonte Central Railroad/Central Railroad of Pennsylvania/Nittany Valley Railroad

IN THE UPPER MOSHANNON VALLEY, THE ALTOONA AND Philipsburg Connecting Railroad acted as a surrogate for the New York Central. To the southwest, in the Nittany Valley, the Central Railroad of Pennsylvania played that role. From an interchange with the Beech Creek/NYC at Mill Hall, the Central Railroad ran southwest 27 miles through the valley to Bellefonte, giving shippers and passengers an alternative to the Pennsylvania Railroad. At Bellefonte, the CRR connected with two other short lines, the Nittany Valley Railroad and the Bellefonte Central Railroad. Although the NVRR was a common carrier, it operated only 4.75 route-miles and was captive to a large ironworks, feeding it ore and limestone and hauling out pig iron to a connection with the CRR. The Bellefonte Central, through a predecessor road, was the first of the three Nittany Valley short lines to begin operations. Its 19-mile main line linked the Centre County seat with the academic community of State College and passed through territory rich in limestone and iron ore.

Commercial-grade deposits of brown hematite ore were scattered throughout the Nittany Valley, giving rise in the early 1800s to a smelting industry whose pig iron was highly prized by foundries in the Mid-Atlantic states. Some of the largest and purest ore deposits lay on an uplift in the valley floor along the Centre–Huntingdon County line, some 15 miles southwest of Bellefonte. That was where Andrew Carnegie had acquired several hundred acres from Moses Thompson and begun the town of Scotia. Years earlier, Thompson himself had drawn ore from that area to supply his iron-making operation at Centre Furnace. However, new technology and failure to adopt economies of scale led to high production costs, made even higher by the difficulty of transporting the iron to distant markets. Centre Furnace went of out blast permanently in 1858. By the time the Civil War erupted three years later, Centre County's iron-making industry was nearly extinct. A dozen or more stone furnace stacks that once dotted the Nittany Valley in testament to a vibrant enterprise sat cold and crumbling.

Thompson and a few other locals retained control of hundreds of additional ore-rich acres in the general vicinity of Scotia. Making iron in the postwar era required large, brick-lined steel furnaces, fed by steam-driven blasts of superheated air instead of cold air from manually operated bellows. Modern furnaces burned coke rather than charcoal. Demand for iron by structural fabricators—bridge builders, for example—and by the nation's emerging steel industry, which relied on pig iron as a key ingredient, was growing steadily by the 1880s. Along with iron ore, the Nittany Valley still had plenty of limestone, while the Mountaintop area had coking coal, all vital to the iron-making process. The coming of the railroad meant lower transportation costs. If the appropriate technological advances could be adopted, the county might again become a source of quality iron.

So reasoned a group of Bellefonte-area promoters that included Thompson, Edmund Blanchard, James Beaver, and Frank McCoy. The last-named was a principal in McCoy and Linn, one of the area's few remaining cold-blast charcoal ironworks. In 1881 they petitioned George Roberts to have the Pennsylvania Railroad build a line from the county seat to known reserves of hematite on the Conrad Struble farm, located about a mile beyond the Pennsylvania State College campus. They commissioned Samuel Brugger to survey a preliminary line. "Our iron manufacturers and those connected with them confidently believe that the ores along the route of said road could be developed to such an extent... that from 3,000 to 5,000 tons per day of traffic may be relied upon," the group noted in its formal proposal.[1]

Roberts declined, based on a negative recommendation from Tyrone Division superintendent Samuel Blair. The PRR had just completed building the Lewisburg and Tyrone Railroad to Scotia and had little to gain by approaching the same ore field from a different direction. The local boosters then decided to go it alone. On September 16, 1882, they met in Bellefonte's Bush House—proprietor Daniel Bush also was a member of the group—and formed the Bellefonte and Buffalo Run Railroad with Blanchard as president.[2]

None of the shareholders was able or willing to make a large financial commitment to the new company, so they searched for a wealthy partner. They found him in 54-year-old Frank McLaughlin, publisher of the *Philadelphia Times*, one of that city's largest newspapers. Exactly how and why McLaughlin became interested is a matter of speculation; but he was joined by two close friends, railroad contractors Philip and Thomas Collins. The Collins brothers had built the Tyrone and Clearfield Railway's extension from Philipsburg to Clearfield and would soon win contracts to construct part of the Beech Creek Railroad. The brothers and McLaughlin were united by a common Irish Catholic heritage and allegiance to the state Democratic Party. Philip Collins had a financial stake in the *Times*, which carried the banner for their party's progressive wing.

McLaughlin became general contractor for building the B&BR, fulfilling the same role that George Magee had filled for the Beech Creek, Clearfield and South Western Railroad. McLaughlin received the bulk of the B&BR's common stock. In return he put up the money to finance construction and subcontracted grading and tracklaying to the Collins brothers. Work got under way early in 1883. The following year the graded line reached its projected terminus, the 195-acre Struble farm. The Collinses stopped short of putting down track because McLaughlin had exhausted his own money and was unable to secure more local investors. "The half dozen wealthiest people in Bellefonte will not give or promise a dollar," lamented the *Centre Democrat* (Bellefonte). "This absolutely prohibits building of the road."[3] Tom Collins left to build the Beech Creek in northern Centre County, while Philip continued to beat the financial bushes in Bellefonte.

McLaughlin decided to promote the Bellefonte and Buffalo Run Railroad as part of a larger plan to bring competition to the Bellefonte market. In 1885, he merged the B&BR with another company he controlled, the Nittany Valley and Southwestern Railroad, to create the Buffalo Run, Bellefonte and Bald Eagle Railroad. The Nittany Valley and Southwestern existed only on paper, chartered to build a line between Bellefonte and a connection with the Beech Creek Railroad. McLaughlin next turned to General Beaver to serve as president of the new road. McLaughlin also recruited to the board of directors two additional central Pennsylvania luminaries: Robert Valentine, who presided over the family ironworks in Bellefonte, and fellow Democratic Party influential William Wallace of Clearfield, who had been a principal in the Nittany Valley and Southwestern.[4] Largely on the strength of his new recruits, McLaughlin was able to sell $364,000 in bonds. Tom Collins rounded up a crew to begin laying 56-lb. steel rail, and in August 1886 the road opened for service between a PRR connection at Sunnyside yard and the Struble ore bank. Shops and an enginehouse were erected on the banks of Buffalo Run in the village of Coleville, a half-mile west of the PRR interchange.

The Collins brothers calculated that the iron business could be as remunerative as the railroad. Tom formed a company to mine ore at Red Bank, about a mile from Carnegie's diggings at Scotia, and brought in a steam shovel for most of the excavation work.[5] The BRB&BE reached Red Bank over a 5-mile branch that began where the main line made a big horseshoe bend at the hamlet of Waddle. Philip meanwhile organized the Bellefonte Furnace Company, whose 12-acre plant across Buffalo Run from the BRB&BE's enginehouse would use ore from brother Tom's mine, along with ore from the Struble property and several smaller ore banks that were independent of the Collins companies.

The Buffalo Run, Bellefonte and Bald Eagle had only one locomotive, a 4-6-0 type bought new from the Baldwin Locomotive Works. Its principal duty was pulling ore trains. The BRB&BE operated passenger service, initiated in January 1887, almost as an afterthought. Coaches, modified from boxcars, were attached to the ore trains,[6] and the station stop for State College was a nondescript wood-frame building near the

Struble farm. Travelers to and from the college had to make the 1-mile connecting journey by carriage or wagon, or on foot.

Yet another shortage of funds forced McLaughlin to delay his plans to extend the BRB&BE eastward to the Beech Creek Railroad. *Democratic Watchman* editor Peter Gray Meek—a shareholder in the furnace company—scolded his fellow townsmen for not coming to the rescue. "The road to the Beech Creek ought to have been finished this summer," he wrote in the December 12, 1886, edition of the *Watchman*, "and it would have been if our local capitalists were as wise as they are stingy." Discouraged by the inability of his railroad to link up with the Beech Creek, McLaughlin abruptly sold his stock to Philip Collins and washed his hands of any further involvement in Centre County's railroads. General Beaver departed, too, preferring to devote his energies to mounting a second campaign for governor. His successor as BRB&BE president was John Reilly, a Collins political crony who had represented Blair County in Congress and served as president of the Bell's Gap Railroad, a narrow-gauge coal hauler. Reilly also was president of the Bellefonte Furnace Company, but he had moved to Philadelphia after failing to be reelected to the House of Representatives. For practical purposes, Philip Collins was now in charge of both the railroad and the furnace.[7]

On January 31, 1888, Bellefonte Furnace roared to life, lit with a ceremonial torch heaved by Peter Gray Meek's daughter, Winifred Meek Morris. The furnace was the first in Centre County to use the coke-fed, hot-blast method of making pig iron, technology that other furnaces around the state also were beginning to adopt. The ironworks more closely resembled a steel mill than the stone stacks that symbolized the charcoal-iron era. The furnace chamber was a brick-lined steel cylinder 70 feet tall, with ore, coke, and limestone being fed continuously into the top. Because coke burned at much higher temperatures than charcoal, it reduced the ore to molten iron more quickly. Steam-driven pumps blasted preheated air at high pressure into the mix to speed up the reduction process. The ore's impurities were driven off and combined with limestone to form slag, which floated to the top and was drawn off by hand. Workers periodically opened the bottom of the furnace to discharge molten iron into "pigs" or molds. The furnace could produce 110 tons of pig iron every twenty-four hours—ten times as much as most old-fashioned charcoal furnaces. To sustain that output, the furnace each day required 225 tons of ore (ten to fifteen railcar loads), 150 tons of coke, and 100 tons of limestone.[8]

To the Collins brothers' surprise and dismay, local mines could not provide enough high-quality hematite to keep the furnace running at capacity, the level at which it operated most efficiently. Operating below capacity pushed up the per-ton production cost. At the same time, enormous reserves of easily accessible high-grade iron ore were discovered in the Lake Superior regions of Minnesota, Wisconsin, and Michigan. The amount of ore mined nationwide climbed from 7.1 million tons in 1880 to 16.1 million tons in 1890; pig iron production rose correspondingly. Pennsylvania alone accounted for 4.9 million tons of pig iron in 1890, more than double the 1880 amount. The supply of iron soon outpaced demand, sending market prices tumbling. Bellefonte Furnace, already struggling with higher than expected costs, shut down early in 1891.[9]

Deprived of its chief source of traffic, the BRB&BE failed to meet interest payments on its bonds, which McLaughlin had peddled to a handful of individual investors in Philadelphia. The bondholders took possession of the bankrupt company, reorganizing it as the Bellefonte Central Railroad on January 12, 1892. The 71-year-old Philip Collins, in poor health, retired to his hometown of Ebensburg. Brother Tom went back to the contracting business for a few years before he, too, retired.

The destiny of the Bellefonte Central was largely in the hands of its new president, Robert Frazer. Unlike his fellow bondholders, most of whom were attorneys or bankers, Frazer was an engineer and knew Centre County firsthand. A University of Pennsylvania graduate, he had supervised the development of mines in the Snow Shoe area for the Lehigh Valley Coal Company. Although the railroad's executive offices were relocated to Philadelphia, where Frazer resided, he visited the BFC regularly. Using those visits and the daily written reports he required of his Bellefonte-based superintendent, Thomas Shoemaker—nephew of the Collins brothers and former superintendent of the BRB&BE—Frazer closely managed the Bellefonte Central's affairs.

With Bellefonte Furnace facing an uncertain future, Frazer sought to broaden his railroad's customer base. To better accommodate the Pennsylvania State College community, the BFC built a 1-mile line from

Struble's to the campus and erected a wood-frame station along College Avenue, the boundary between town and gown. The college gave the BFC property rights for the right-of-way and station, provided the land was used for railroad purposes. The track terminated just east of the station, where a campus power and steam plant then under construction would receive bituminous coal by the carload. Passenger service over the new line began on April 4, 1892. A mixed train made three round-trips daily from Bellefonte, where the BFC used the PRR station in exchange for a small monthly rental fee. The short line purchased several new coaches and a combination baggage and express car for the service, although it seldom used more than one coach and the combine on any given day. The BFC also partnered with several State College merchants and faculty members to open the University Inn, a hotel and dormitory situated near the station. "This enterprise is primarily intended for the accommodation of professors and students during the college year, but it also well adapted for summer visitors," Frazer explained to the railroad's stockholders.[10] The three-story brick edifice contained fifty rooms and opened in April 1894.

Following the lead of many railroads of that era, the BFC created its own destination for passengers when it bought 18 acres along Buffalo Run 5 miles west of Bellefonte and developed the site for outdoor recreation. Hunters Park—named for the family that formerly owned the tract—featured a baseball field, a lake for swimming and boating, a grandstand and band shell, and similar amenities.[11]

The passenger business was challenging: the University Inn never met expectations (it burned in 1903), the borough of State College had fewer than 600 residents including students, and the Hunters Park business was seasonal. Nevertheless, passenger fares gave the BFC a financial shot in the arm at a time it when the company scratched for every penny just to stay afloat. In some years during the economically troubled 1890s, passenger income accounted for nearly 40 percent of the Bellefonte Central's gross revenues.

On the freight side, Bellefonte Furnace resumed making iron early in 1893, and ore once again flowed over BFC rails—only to halt abruptly later in the year as the financial panic took hold and the furnace closed. It remained idle for most of the remainder of the decade, forcing the railroad to fall back on a miscellany of revenue sources. The BFC delivered coal to State College for the power plant and local wholesalers, building materials for a steadily growing campus and town, merchandise for the town's retailers, and animal feed for the college and area farmers. Outbound traffic was scarce and consisted mostly of farm products (fruit and grain in season) and timber from a couple of sawmills. The BFC also did a modest express business and obtained a contract to carry the mail between Bellefonte and State College. Intermediate postal stops were made at Fillmore and Waddle, reducing delivery times to those points by a day. Remarkably, the BFC operated profitably throughout the depression of the 1890s, although in most years only marginally so. It paid no stockholder dividends; Frazer and the board of directors preferred to invest surplus income in upgrading motive power and improving Hunters Park and the fixed plant.

The Bellefonte Central had a salubrious effect on the State College community. President Sparks's comment about the location's inaccessibility notwithstanding, the railroad greatly mitigated the geographic isolation of the college, one of the biggest obstacles to the institution's growth. Undergraduate enrollment increased from 209 in 1890 to 504 in 1900, and by a hundred or so every year during the following decade. The majority of students pursued engineering studies, making Penn State one the nation's ten largest engineering schools by the turn of the century.[12] The BFC obliged the college's request to give undergraduates in the new (1904) railway mechanical engineering program a chance to gain practical experience. Under the supervision of program head A. J. Wood, students operated a BFC locomotive and a few freight cars between State College and Bellefonte, as often as once a semester. They learned to calculate the rate of coal and water consumption, and determine other measures of a locomotive's efficiency. A few years later, the Pennsylvania Railroad donated an obsolete 4-4-0 locomotive and dynamometer car to Penn State, allowing Wood's classes to make more sophisticated calculations and run the rails more often, with the BFC's permission.[13]

The BFC's arrival spurred growth on the town side of College Avenue, too. State College incorporated as a borough with about 600 residents in 1896. Two years later, a weekly newspaper was established, the *State*

College Times (predecessor of the *Centre Daily Times*), which received newsprint by rail. Nittany Light, Heat and Power Company, formed in 1906, received carloads of anthracite coal for its producer-gas plant. A bank, two telephone companies, a water company, a hardware store, churches, and schools also were established around the turn of the century—not all railroad customers, perhaps, but certainly hallmarks of an aspiring community.[14]

As previously noted, when the L&T approached the area, some State College residents maintained their community was worthy of being a station stop along the Pennsylvania PRR, and were dissatisfied with the rustic Bellefonte Central and its mixed trains that stopped to set out and pick up freight cars along the way. Penn State students in particular found in the BFC an endless source of humor and practical jokes. Robert Frazer did not take kindly to pranksters who greased the rails as his locomotives attempted to depart the campus station, or stole handcars for joy rides to Bellefonte. He reacted even more negatively to the way the college administration always seemed to be in arrears in paying its freight bills. On more than one occasion he threatened to halt service to Penn State until a bill was paid. "The college people are very irritating," he told a subordinate charged with bill collecting. "I believe [they] look upon us as a lot of no account people not worth troubling themselves about."[15]

Frazer's ambitions for the Bellefonte Central went far beyond State College. He envisioned the BFC as a bridge line between the coal-hauling Huntingdon and Broad Top Mountain Railroad to the southwest and the Beech Creek Railroad to the northeast. Anticipating a connection with the H&BTM, Frazer persuaded his board of directors to approve extending the main line track 4 miles across the Nittany Valley to Pine Grove Mills at the foot of Tussey Mountain. As the extension, completed in 1896, began to generate a modest volume of freight business—mostly lumber and farm products—the railroad's chief engineer, Robert Boal, undertook surveys to find the best route to Huntingdon County and a junction with the H&BTM. At first he advocated tunneling through Tussey Mountain about halfway up its flank; he soon dropped that horrifically expensive idea in favor of running an easy-grade line from Pine Grove Mills down the Nittany Valley to Spruce Creek, then using the gap formed in Tussey Mountain by the Little Juniata River to head for Huntingdon—alongside the Pennsylvania Railroad's main line. At the opposite end of the BFC, Boal dusted off a survey done in the McLaughlin years to build through the Bald Eagle Valley to connect with the Beech Creek Railroad in the town of Beech Creek.

Frazer apprised New York vice president Walter Webb of his railroad's intentions, although there seems to be no record of Webb's response. The Broad Top people likewise were keenly aware of Frazer's desire to link up with their road. In fact, the H&BTM commissioned its own survey of a line into the Nittany Valley. To Frazer's chagrin, however, the BFC's board nixed any new construction because it would mean borrowing a large sum of money at a time when the company could ill-afford to be burdened with debt. The PRR had made it clear to the board that it would under no circumstances grant a right-of-way through the water gap in Tussey Mountain. The big road was not about to share its corridor with a competitor—even a pint-sized short line such as the BFC.[16] Left unstated but understood was the Pennsylvania's unwavering opposition to any BFC attempt to link up with the Beech Creek Railroad.

The national economic picture finally brightened as the nineteenth century came to a close. Investor confidence returned, and American industry prepared to meet years of pent-up demand. The need for pig iron by suddenly booming steel mills sent prices soaring. Bellefonte entrepreneur J. Wesley Gephart, backed by New York and Philadelphia investors, bought Bellefonte Furnace in May 1899 and prepared to resume production. The Carnegie interests by then were looking almost exclusively to the Mesabi Range and other areas around Lake Superior for ore and gladly sold their Scotia holdings to Gephart's group. Chief engineer Boal hurriedly laid out a new 1.5-mile line from existing BFC trackage to Scotia, and ore shipments began in October 1899.

Hauling ore accounted for nearly 40 percent of the BFC's gross freight revenues and in 1901 nudged the company's total operating income above $50,000 for the first time. To power the heavy ore trains, the short line in 1902 purchased a former PRR class H1 2-8-0, a type that had proven highly successful in coal service on the Tyrone and Clearfield Railway. The H1 was to be the first of fifteen 2-8-0s that graced the Bellefonte Central's roster over the next half-century—all obtained

Figure 7.1. Bellefonte Central No. 4, a former PRR class H1 2-8-0 purchased secondhand, is coupled to one of the short line's 25-ton-capacity flat-bottomed ore cars. *Author's collection.*

secondhand and rarely more than two or three fit for service at any given time. The railroad's freight car fleet in 1902 consisted of twenty-eight wooden gondola and hopper-gondola cars ranging in capacity between 25 and 30 tons. Some the railroad had purchased from the used equipment market; others the company built in its own Coleville shops. Sixteen of the cars were dedicated exclusively to ore service, since they featured old-style link-and-pin couplers and under federal regulations could not be interchanged with other railroads.[17]

Steady returns from the iron ore trade compensated for a passenger business that, according to Robert Frazer, had become barely profitable despite an increasing number of riders—from about 30,000 in 1900 to

57,000 in 1910. Frazer blamed part of the problem on the newly created (in 1907) Pennsylvania State Railroad Commission and its refusal to allow railroads to raise fares above $0.02 per passenger-mile, despite increased operating costs.[18]

The BFC occasionally operated special trains for Penn State football games, church picnics at Hunters Park, evening performances as Bellefonte's opera house, and the like. None compared to the special train it ran in 1904 for two of the world's richest men. Multimillionaire steel magnates Andrew Carnegie and Charles Schwab and their wives journeyed over Bellefonte Central rails aboard Schwab's private car, *Loretto*, on November 17 to attend the dedication of Penn State's Carnegie Library, built with a $150,000 donation from the building's namesake. Schwab, a longtime Carnegie lieutenant, made the trip because he had given an identical sum for the new Schwab Auditorium but had been unable to attend its 1903 dedication. Now, partly at Carnegie's urging, he had accepted President George Atherton's invitation to be honored in person for his generosity.[19] Despite their decision to travel together, by the time the two men came to the college, a rift was developing between them. Schwab had recently resigned the presidency of the U.S. Steel Corporation, whose core had been Carnegie Steel until its founder sold the company to the J. P. Morgan interests in 1901. Schwab got the top job at the new company but was soon complaining that U.S. Steel was too large to manage efficiently; his attempts to reorganize it were rebuffed. Carnegie felt Schwab's comments demeaned his own business acumen in crafting the deal with Morgan. As he chatted with Carnegie aboard *Loretto*, Schwab was only weeks away from announcing the formation of his own company, Bethlehem Steel, destined to become U.S. Steel's chief rival. Whether or not the two captains of industry talked business while they made the trip to and from Penn State is not a matter of record.

Coincidentally, the same centralization of America's steel industry that caused ill feeling between Carnegie and Schwab also led to the ore trade's demise on the Bellefonte Central. By 1910, the component companies of "Big Steel" had found it more economical to integrate blast furnaces into their overall mill operations instead of buying and transporting pig iron from small, distant producers such as Bellefonte Furnace. In addition, they preferred to source their iron ore from the Lake Superior region because it was better suited than Pennsylvania's native ores for use in the open-hearth furnaces that were replacing Bessemer converters at most mills. Even when small-scale iron producers substituted Lake Superior ore for native ore, they still could not overcome the disadvantages inherent in their obsolete, low-capacity plants and the cost of shipping pig iron to Pittsburgh, Youngstown, and other steel centers. Bellefonte Furnace shut down in December 1910, and its near twin across town, Nittany Furnace, went out of blast a month later. Mining at Scotia came to an end, replaced briefly by a whirlwind of logging activity when the McNitt-Huyett Lumber Company went after stands of second-growth timber.

The Bellefonte Central's bottom line gave no hint that the demise of iron-making marked the conclusion of an important era in the area's economic and social history. In 1910, as the furnaces were nearing their end, the BFC hauled 160,000 tons of limestone and lime. The stone came from the Valentine Formation, a vein of limestone up to 90 feet thick that ran along the southern flank of Bald Eagle Ridge. Limestone found a ready market as a fluxing agent in making steel, and lime was essential to the manufacture of such diverse products as steel, paper, leather, glass, and household and industrial chemicals. In its simplest form, lime was made by crushing limestone (which was primarily calcium carbonate, or $CaCO_3$), then calcining it—that is, heating it in kilns to temperatures of more than 1,000 degrees F. in order to drive off carbon dioxide (CO_2) and other impurities. The resulting quicklime (calcium oxide, or CaO) could be further crushed, pulverized, or hydrated, depending on its intended use. The higher the percentage of calcium carbonate the limestone contained, the cheaper and more efficient the lime-making process was because there were fewer impurities to eliminate. The Valentine Formation was extraordinarily pure—as much as 98 percent calcium carbonate.[20]

After William Shortlidge commercialized lime making in the Bellefonte area in the 1860s, the industry began steady growth. Shortlidge married Rose McCalmont of Bellefonte, then partnered with the McCalmont family in enlarging the business, which took the name McCalmont and Company. In 1873, a second producer entered the picture. Alexander G. Morris, who was making lime in the Tyrone area, began purchasing land around Bellefonte and opened several quarries into the Valentine Formation. By the mid-1890s, despite the weak economy, the Pennsylvania Railroad was shipping about a dozen carloads of lime and limestone a day from the two companies.[21] In 1907, a small lime company headed by John Walker joined with several other small producers to form the Chemical Lime Company. Chemical bought the Charles Whitmer farm, about a mile upstream from Coleville, opened a large pit directly into the formation, and a erected a battery of shaft kilns. The enterprise thrived from the start. The *Centre Democrat* reported on December 24, 1909, that Chemical Lime "was considering the advisability of accepting several orders which would necessitate running their stone crusher day and night. Orders have been coming in so fast that it is probable they will build a new kiln."

Chemical became the largest of ten lime and limestone operations that the BFC was serving in 1910. The railroad derived more than one-third of its freight revenues from hauling quarry products, a proportion that would soon grow to a much higher level. Concentration of the steel industry to achieve economies of scale doomed small iron producers such as Bellefonte Furnace. It simultaneously created an enormous demand for limestone and lime that would sustain the Bellefonte Central for many decades to come.

Robert Frazer was forty-two years old when he assumed the presidency of the Bellefonte Central Railroad in 1892. John Wesley Gephart was thirty-nine when he organized the Central Railroad of Pennsylvania in 1893. Both men were college graduates. There the similarities ended. Differences between the two railroaders were profound and could be seen in the imprints they made on their respective companies.

Frazer was an outsider among Bellefonters—whom he once labeled "a queer lot"—and had little affinity for the community.[22] He preferred to immerse himself in the minutiae of railroad operations from his Philadelphia office, engaging in daily correspondence with his superintendent in Bellefonte and sending him detailed instructions on topics ranging from where to buy locomotive coal to how much to charge for a carload shipment of apples. He was careful and methodical in his approach as befitted a trained engineer, and he abhorred waste and inefficiency. He did not view the BFC as a pathway to great wealth, but rather as a reliable performer that would produce a steady if unspectacular rate of return over the long term. Reserved and stiff in his public demeanor, Frazer did not enjoy the spotlight; few if any Centre Countians really knew him.

"Wes" Gephart, on the other hand, was a natural promoter—community-minded, a skillful orator, known and admired by all—and he liked to dream big. He was born in Millheim in 1853, son of a Penns Valley merchant and farmer who was sufficiently prosperous to send Wes to Princeton. After graduating in 1874, the younger Gephart read law in the office of James A. Beaver and within three years went into partnership with his mentor. Their firm won much distinction, and both partners earned comfortable incomes; but the law did not satisfy Gephart's entrepreneurial aspirations. After Beaver was elected governor in 1888, Gephart assumed stewardship over many of his partner's business interests and also began making investments of his own. He also became more deeply rooted in Bellefonte's social and cultural fabric—heading the town's Young Men's Christian Association, for example, and serving as superintendent of the Presbyterian Sunday school.[23]

Gephart succeeded another attorney turned entrepreneur, Edmund Blanchard, who had died of heart failure in 1886, as the town's chief drumbeater. A venture that Blanchard helped put in motion eventually led to Gephart's involvement with the Central Railroad of Pennsylvania. The CRR was the outgrowth of some exceedingly complex maneuvering aimed at bringing railroad competition to the Bellefonte market. In the early 1880s, some members of the Bellefonte business community voiced displeasure with what they perceived to be the Pennsylvania's unreasonably high freight rates. The *Democratic Watchman* of October 2, 1885, summed up their discontent when it declared, "The policy of the Pennsylvania Railroad toward this locality has kept its industries in a state of subjugation." According to the *Watchman*, the PRR charged Nittany Valley farmers more to move their grain to seaboard cities for export than it charged farmers in Illinois and Indiana for the same service. The cost to transport Bellefonte pig iron to Baltimore via the PRR was about the same as ironmasters had paid a half-century earlier when they shipped iron to that city via pack mule.

Frank McLaughlin had tried to exploit this dissatisfaction when he bought into the Bellefonte and Buffalo Run and the Nittany Valley and

Southern railroads. In 1883, he offered to sell both properties to the Philadelphia and Reading Railroad.[24] McLaughlin knew the P&R would be
interested. Its president, Franklin B. Gowen, made no secret of his desire
to wean his company from dependence on anthracite traffic and recast
it as a great east-west trunk line in partnership with the New York Central. Gowen and McLaughlin were longtime friends and political allies.
McLaughlin often used his Philadelphia *Times* to boost P&R interests,
especially when he could tweak the nose of that road's most fearsome
competitor, the mighty Pennsylvania.[25]

Gowen quickly warmed to McLaughlin's proposal. In the spring of
1884, through the affiliated Philadelphia and Reading Coal and Iron
Company, the P&R bought several lots in downtown Bellefonte as a site
for a terminal. Bellefonte banker J. Dunlop Shugert acted as the company's front man so as not to arouse the PRR's suspicions. (As indicated in
chapter 4, the Pennsylvania was already suspicious, deciding to turn the
Lewisburg and Tyrone Railway in the direction of Bellefonte to counter
the P&R's attempted invasion.) Shugert also quietly secured 2.5 miles
of right-of-way leading eastward out of town. The P&R then experienced
a series of financial reverses, widely blamed on Gowen's free-spending
ways, and he was forced out. The railroad entered receivership on June
2, 1884, and the cash-strapped new management shunned westward expansion. The P&R's withdrawal prompted McLaughlin to merge the
Bellefonte and Buffalo Run with the Nittany Valley and Southwestern
to form the Buffalo Run, Bellefonte and Bald Eagle Railroad, and link it
to the Beech Creek Railroad—next best thing to the P&R—somewhere
in the Bald Eagle Valley.

Unable to capitalize on the locals' dissatisfaction with the PRR, the
frustrated McLaughlin was gone from the central Pennsylvania railroad
scene by the time Archibald A. McLeod was named president of the Philadelphia and Reading in June 1890. McLeod turned out to be as much
of an expansionist as Gowen and revisited the possibility of extending
his road west. Various groups of promoters tried to interest the P&R in
their respective proposals for building a railroad through central Pennsylvania. One group, led by business leaders from the mid-Susquehanna
Valley, incorporated the Bellefonte and Eastern Railroad with an eye
toward building west from the Susquehanna River at White Deer, which

the P&R served via its main line to Williamsport. The Bellefonte and Eastern was to run through Sugar Valley and Loganton to Lamar in the Nittany Valley. There it would fork, one prong going to a connection with the Beech Creek Railroad at Mill Hall, and the other going west through the Nittany Valley to Bellefonte and a likely connection with the BRB&BE. The Bellefonte and Eastern failed to catch fire with investors, however. A second group of promoters, a mix of regional and Philadelphia investors, repackaged the B&E idea as two companies to lessen the financial risk. The Central Pennsylvania Railroad would construct a line from Bellefonte to Mill Hall via Lamar. The Central Pennsylvania Railroad Eastern Extension would build a line from Lamar east to White Deer, where it would join the P&R.

A prospectus for the Central Pennsylvania Railroad claimed that "numerous saw mills, flour and feed mills, fire-brick kilns, coal yards, ore mines, and stores" would develop along the line "as soon as the road is built."[26] The Pennsylvania Railroad was shipping 990,000 tons of freight annually in and out of Bellefonte, the prospectus claimed, and the town boasted at least twenty-seven industries that produced such diverse materials as iron, flour, glass, nails, lime and limestone, brick, lumber, and manufactured goods ranging from steam radiators to coal-washing machinery to axes. The PRR was reportedly grossing $75,000 a month in passenger and freight revenue. Surely the community was ripe for rail competition.

The Central Pennsylvania Railroad got President McLeod's attention for two reasons: the Bellefonte market's intrinsic value as a source of traffic, and the town's strategic value as a jumping-off point for a thrust to the bituminous coalfields. A westward reach was tempting for the P&R executive, but he placed an even higher priority on expanding his railroad on other fronts. The P&R leased the Lehigh Valley and the Central of New Jersey railroads, and even acquired a controlling interest in railroads stretching from the Hudson River to Boston. Deeply in debt, the company did not have the financial means to build a line into Bellefonte. Backers of the Central Pennsylvania Railroad subsequently shelved their idea of a White Deer connection with the Reading and decided to hitch their star exclusively to the Beech Creek Railroad and its New York Central parent. They reincorporated their company as the

Central Railroad of Pennsylvania on September 11, 1891, aiming to build a line between Bellefonte and Mill Hall. Grading began the following year but soon halted for lack of funds. Saplings and wild flowers might have soon reclaimed the unfinished right-of-way had not John Wesley Gephart intervened.

Gephart just then was president of the newly formed Valentine Iron Company, successor to an ill-fated venture called the Centre Iron Works. Centre Iron was organized in 1886, about the same time as Philip Collins was launching the Bellefonte Furnace Company on the other side of town, and for the same reasons: abundant native ore and limestone, and a strong demand for iron by the emerging steel industry and other industrial consumers. The two furnaces used the same hot-blast, coke-fed technology and were nearly identical, even down to their respective 125 tons of daily output. Combined, they could produce more iron in a day than all of the Nittany Valley's early nineteenth-century charcoal furnaces had made in a week.

Centre Iron Works was founded by Edmund Blanchard (only weeks before he died), Robert Valentine, and other members of the Valentine family but was financed largely by a group of Philadelphia investors led by banker B. K. Jamison, who had coal and iron interests in several other areas of Pennsylvania. Centre Iron Works was located south of Bellefonte along Logan Branch, on the site where the venerable firm of Valentines and Thomas had been making iron since 1815. For generations, iron ore was delivered by horse-drawn wagons from mines a few miles east of Bellefonte on what was known locally as the Valentine ore lands. The new furnace would consume far too much ore to be delivered by wagons. In their place, the Nittany Valley Railroad was chartered on March 15, 1887. Thomas Shoemaker, who had been overseeing completion of the BRB&BE on behalf of his uncle Tom Collins, supervised the NVRR's construction. The railroad cost $141,000 and had nearly 5 miles of main line track between the ironworks and Taylor bank, the largest of the ore pits, and about 2 miles of track in and around the ironworks. The line used a switchback on the hillside above Logan Branch to make the steep descent to the works feasible. The NVRR owned two locomotives and leased twelve 25-ton capacity ore cars from the PRR. Although legally it was a common carrier, the Nittany Valley carried little or no freight that was unrelated to the ironworks' operation and no passengers at all. The railroad's president was Jones Wister of Philadelphia, a veteran of the iron industry in eastern Pennsylvania and one of the principal investors in the Centre Iron Works.[27]

The same slump in iron prices that forced the closure of Bellefonte Furnace caused Centre Iron Works to declare bankruptcy in 1890. However, Wesley Gephart believed that a revitalized ironworks was key to his community's future. Centre Iron's creditors were only too glad to allow him to reorganize the company in 1891. Gephart led Robert Valentine and several other local and Philadelphia-based partners in reopening the works under the historic Valentine name, which had decades-old cachet in the iron industry.[28]

Under Gephart's watch, the Valentine Iron Works became the Pennsylvania Railroad's largest Bellefonte-area customer, bestowing as much as $200,000 in annual gross revenues on the carrier. The NVRR also prospered, hauling on average more than 100,000 tons of ore and limestone each year. The problem was, the furnace ran sporadically, going full tilt for a few months, then sitting idle for an extended time. Gephart claimed that the unevenness of the business stemmed mostly from the Pennsylvania's high freight rates, which put the ironworks at a disadvantage when trying to engage customers in long-term contracts. He condemned the PRR's Bellefonte rate-making policy as "arbitrary extortion" and called for railroad competition in the area.[29]

Freight rates were an ongoing point of contention between the Pennsylvania and many of its shippers system-wide. Partly because the national economy in the late nineteenth century experienced a sustained period of deflation—declining wages and prices—and partly because of the PRR's extraordinary efficiency, the railroad's rates on average fell from $0.03 to $0.007 per ton-mile between 1855 and 1884, bottoming out at about $0.005 in 1899. Thanks to the enormous volume of traffic the PRR handled, it steadily increased its profit per ton-mile during that same period.[30] Rates declined most in those markets where the Pennsylvania competed with other railroads for long-haul business. For moving grain from Chicago to ports along the eastern seaboard, for example, the PRR had to keep its rates low to protect its traffic from the likes of the New York Central, Baltimore and Ohio, and Erie railroads. Pooling agreements, in which the railroads decided among themselves how much to charge and how to allot traffic, were generally unsuccessful. Thus competition among railroads was cutthroat. The PRR (and other railroads in similar situations) made up for slim or no profits in fiercely competitive markets by charging higher rates in captive markets such as Bellefonte, and to a lesser extent, the Moshannon Valley. In the absence of any other mechanism to determine fair and equitable rates, such a practice seemed reasonable to the carriers.

Shippers, of course, had a different perspective, as Wes Gephart amply demonstrated. To bring a competing road to Bellefonte, he put together a complex deal involving a variety of investors that enabled the Central Railroad of Pennsylvania to resume construction in May 1893. To his chagrin, Bellefonte-area citizens took less than $75,000 in subscriptions in the new road. Many of the wealthier residents held stock in the PRR and its local affiliates and had little to gain from backing a new railroad. Observed the *Keystone Gazette*: "We have a class of citizens . . . who are comfortably fixed and drawing a big interest on government bonds and Bald Eagle Valley Railroad stock, and naturally do not have any desire to see a competing line enter our borough."[31] The *Gazette* might have added that not one Centre Countian had backed the stillborn Bellefonte and Eastern or the Central Pennsylvania railroads as an officer, director, or principal investor.

Gephart convinced thirteen individuals from outside the county to buy into the CRR, yet he still came up short. The railroad ultimately issued $600,000 worth of fifteen-year, 6 percent bonds, all of which were purchased by the Philadelphia banking house of Drexel and Company, financier to the Reading and the New York Central railroads and an ally of the house of Morgan. As part of the deal, Gephart was named superintendent of the Central Railroad, a post he held concurrently with the presidency of the Valentine Iron Works. Walter L. Ross, a Drexel operative, served as the CRR's president. The composition of the board of directors reflected the road's ownership: joining Bellefonte's Robert Valentine were five directors from Philadelphia and three from Susquehanna valley communities.[32] (One of the latter directors was Charles M.

Clement of Sunbury, who also served as the road's legal counsel and, in an ironic twist, was the father of future Pennsylvania Railroad president Martin W. Clement.)

The Central Railroad's main line, which had been partially laid out and graded in 1891—before Gephart's involvement—extended 27.3 miles through the heart of the Nittany Valley. H. E. Richter, a civil engineer and retired army officer from Selinsgrove, finished locating the line, and a construction company headed by J. I. Higbee of Watsontown completed the grading and track laying. The road began at the Beech Creek Railroad's Mill Hall station; the BCR's agent there also served the CRR. Eight stations were established along the line west of Mill Hall, each overseen by an agent who collected passenger fares, quoted freight rates, and handed up operating orders to passing trains. The Phoenix Planing Mill of Bellefonte received a contract to build combination passenger and freight agency stations at Zion, Hecla, Kriders, and Clintondale. P. B. Crider and Son, also of Bellefonte, contracted to erect stations at Nittany, Hublersburg, and Lamar. A railroad-owned telephone and telegraph line linked all station agents.[33]

Near Zion, the CRR built a siding and tipple to facilitate the development of Nigh bank, which soon rivaled the NVRR-served Taylor bank as the largest pit on the Valentine ore lands. Approaching Bellefonte, the CRR crossed a ravine on a low wooden trestle 500 feet long before passing beneath the Nittany Valley Railroad's own trestle-and-earthen fill carrying that road's line out to Taylor bank. A connection was made between the two roads by means of an earthen ramp. The Central Railroad leased the Nittany Valley and used the connection to reach the Valentine Iron Works without having to construct its own track.

The CRR then descended a 1.5 percent grade through Armor Gap to the bottomlands around Spring Creek, midway between Bellefonte and Milesburg. On the creek's east side, the railroad built a car shop, brick enginehouse, and small freight yard. A spur led north from the yard to serve the McCoy and Linn Iron Works near Milesburg. Later, a siding was added opposite the ironworks to accommodate a tipple where a Bellefonte partnership headed by Frank Clemson—formerly Carnegie's superintendent at Scotia—loaded ganister quarried from the top of Bald Eagle Ridge.[34] Another short spur served the Alexander Morris limestone quarries and limekilns in Armor Gap. The PRR also served the Morris kilns via its Morris Branch; an interchange between the two roads was established near the kilns. From the freight yard, the main track headed south on the old canal tow path that paralleled Spring Creek, terminating at a temporary wood-frame passenger and freight station at the foot of Lamb Street in Bellefonte. (The structure was soon replaced by a more stately two-story brick edifice.[35]) A turntable adjacent to the station enabled locomotives to swing round for the trip out of town. Most of the right-of-way between Armor Gap and the Bellefonte station consisted of the land purchased years earlier by J. D. Shugert, who had carefully protected it for the day his community might get a competing railroad.[36]

The Central Railroad cost slightly more than $1 million to build and equip. It was opened for service its entire length on December 6, 1893, when the first freight train ran through from Mill Hall to Bellefonte. Passenger service began twelve days later. Company-owned rolling stock consisted of thirty-eight freight cars and six passenger cars. The largest of the road's five locomotives were two 4-8-0s delivered new from the Schenectady Locomotive Works. Those engines were heavier and more powerful than anything the PRR or the Bellefonte Central operated in the Bellefonte area at that time and would be the mainstays of freight and later passenger service for the next twenty-five years.[37]

To mark the railroad's opening, the Bellefonte Board of Trade hosted a grand banquet at the Bush House on December 21. Guests included senior executives from the Philadelphia and Reading, New York Central, Beech Creek, and Buffalo, Rochester & Pittsburgh railroads. The BR&P maintained a friendly connection with the NYC at Clearfield to points in western New York. All of these larger roads stood to gain from traffic developed by the CRR.

Even as the railroad men were toasting one another and the CRR amid the splendor of the Bush House ball room, Gephart was thinking ahead to his next move. He soon became the chief promoter of the Bellefonte and Clearfield Railroad, projected as an extension of the CRR into the coalfields of northern Centre County and beyond to Clearfield County. The Central Railroad's charter authorized it to build to Unionville, at the foot of the old Philadelphia and Erie turnpike across the mountains, so that location was the planned starting point of the B&C.[38]

Building a railroad up and over the Allegheny Front posed a formidable challenge. In addition, the Pennsylvania and the Beech Creek railroads had already constructed an extensive network of branch lines to serve the coal mines of Clearfield and Centre counties. Potential investors decided there was no compelling need for the Bellefonte and Clearfield Railroad and stayed away. The venture disappeared from the public consciousness by 1900.

Pennsylvania Railroad executives correctly saw the Central Railroad of Pennsylvania, even without an extension to the coalfields, as a New York Central–backed intrusion into their road's exclusive domain. They moved quickly to thwart their rival. The final spike had not yet been driven on the Central Railroad when the PRR filed suit in Centre County court to prevent the Nittany Valley Railroad from interchanging any traffic to the CRR that originated at the Valentine Iron Works. The PRR's case rested on the original contract between the Nittany Valley and the Centre Iron Works. When Centre Iron was formed in 1887, the PRR had agreed to buy $75,000 worth of its bonds on condition that the NVRR, which the iron company controlled, would deliver all outbound tonnage to the Pennsylvania. When Gephart and his associates formed the Valentine Iron Works in 1891, the PRR's bonds were converted to Valentine stock. Therefore, argued the Pennsylvania's lawyers, the 1887 agreement was still in effect. The Nittany Valley Railroad had no right to give Valentine traffic to the Central Railroad.

The PRR's stance infuriated Gephart. "This litigation," he told the Centre County court, "is part of a scheme by the Pennsylvania company to intimidate and brow-beat the stockholders of the Nittany Valley [Railroad] company."[39] The court agreed and ruled against the PRR. However, the Pennsylvania appealed the decision to the state supreme court, which ruled in the plaintiff's favor, saying the 1887 agreement was part of the sale of Centre Iron Works to Valentine ownership and its terms were still in effect. Beginning November 1, 1895, all of Valentine's output had to be shipped via the Pennsylvania Railroad. The CRR ended its lease of the NVRR on that same date.

"To say that our company and our legal advisers were dumb-founded by this summary disposition by the supreme court is to put it mildly," Gephart later wrote.[40] The high court's ruling devastated the Central

Railroad; providing a competing service to the Valentine works was the prime reason it had been created. For the year ending June 30, 1895, the road grossed nearly $88,000 hauling 185,900 tons of freight, much of it consisting of pig and bar iron coming from the ironworks. Hampered by the lack of furnace traffic and the ongoing national economic depression, the CRR averaged only 65,000 tons and $16,000 in gross revenues for each of the next few years. Traffic mainstays included iron chain from McCoy and Linn's ironworks and limestone and lime from A. G. Morris at Bellefonte. Those two customers also shipped via the PRR, so the Central Railroad for the most part received carloads that were destined for NYC or P&R consignees. The CRR also received carloads of lumber and agricultural products from various points in the Nittany Valley; axes from the Mann Edge Tool Company near Mill Hall; and coal from the Beech Creek Railroad destined for the Bellefonte gas works and electric light plant. The Central Railroad launched overnight less-than-carload service between Bellefonte and Philadelphia routed via the New York Central and the Reading. A boxcar left each terminal late in the afternoon with guaranteed delivery at the other end by late afternoon of the following day. The service quickly gained ample patronage. Nevertheless, all of those revenue sources combined could not make up for the loss of the Valentine furnace business.

As a result, the Central Railroad of Pennsylvania depended more heavily on passenger revenue than it originally anticipated. Three passenger trains from Bellefonte to Mill Hall and return were scheduled Monday through Saturday. The one-way fare between the two points was $0.50.[41] The CRR trumpeted its New York Central connection as the travelers' gateway to Philadelphia and New York via the Reading, and to Buffalo and Niagara Falls via the Buffalo, Rochester and Pittsburgh Railway.

Hecla Park, established in 1894 9 miles east of Bellefonte as a destination for excursion trains, turned out to be a godsend. The park—the CRR's answer to the Bellefonte Central's Hunters Park—featured athletic fields, a bicycle track, picnic areas, and a three-story brick edifice that enclosed a dance pavilion. A lake was built for swimming and boating (which in winter provided ice that was shipped by the carload to big-city icehouses). On a typical summer Sunday, the CRR sold more than a thousand excursion tickets to Hecla Park; through coaches arrived from as far away as Clearfield and Williamsport. Special events at the park attracted even more visitors. One of the largest was the annual Centre and Clinton Counties businessmen's picnic, drawing upward of 12,000 participants for food, games, a parade, and fireworks.[42] Thanks in part to Hecla's popularity, more than 70,000 people were riding the CRR each year, and annual passenger revenues nearly equaled freight income. Mail and express carried by passenger trains brought it in additional dollars for the railroad.

Still, the company's finances were shaky. In the years immediately following the loss of Valentine Iron Works traffic, the CRR typically posted annual net operating deficits of about $8,000. It furloughed twenty of its seventy employees, sold two locomotives and most of its freight cars, and otherwise tightened its belt. The only significant improvement project it undertook came from necessity. The hemlock timbers in the long trestle east of Bellefonte began rotting, so in the winter of 1896–97 the railroad filled in the structure with waste rock from the Morris quarries, leaving only a short steel span where a roadway passed beneath. Otherwise the Central Railroad avoided big expenditures, limping along while Gephart—who had severed his ties with the furnace and abandoned his law practice—searched for ways to save the company.[43]

The Nittany Valley Railroad fared much worse. Surviving tonnage records are incomplete, but its annual reports to the state's Department of Internal Affairs indicate the short line went into eclipse immediately upon termination of the CRR's lease. It posted a net deficit totaling nearly $15,000 from fiscal 1895 through 1897, the year that the sputtering Valentine Iron Company finally ceased operations. The railroad was inactive in 1898 and 1899.

Then, at the end of the decade, salvation for both the Central and the Nittany Valley roads suddenly seemed at hand. Bankrolled by New York and Philadelphia investors, Gephart acquired the Bellefonte Furnace Company in April 1899. Bellefonte Furnace—the fruit of Philip Collins's labors—had been idle for six years. But now the economy was reviving, and the demand for iron seemed insatiable. Along with the ironworks, Gephart's Bellefonte Furnace Company acquired quarries and limekilns at Salona (near Mill Hall) from Alexander Morris and the Scotia ore lands from the Carnegie interests. The Bellefonte Central was contracted to haul the ore from Scotia to the Bellefonte Furnace, but Gephart decided to end the previous arrangement whereby the BFC picked up outbound cars of pig and bar iron at the furnace and took them to the PRR interchange. In contrast to contractual restrictions at the Valentine works, the Pennsylvania did not have exclusive rights to Bellefonte Furnace traffic. The iron company was free to deal with the Central Railroad; all the CRR had to do was build a track to reach the facility. Gephart decided to do just that.

In May 1899, the CRR began construction of its Furnace Branch, nearly a mile in length. The railroad again retained H. E. Richter to lay out the track and supervise construction. The branch left the main line south of the enginehouse, climbed a short 3 percent grade, then soared above Spring Creek and the PRR's tracks on a 707-foot steel viaduct of Richter's own design.[44] It entered the Bellefonte Furnace property from the east (whereas the BFC entered from the west). The Central Railroad had received permission to span the PRR; but apparently word did not filter down from Philadelphia headquarters to Tyrone Division managers, who were alarmed at the prospect of losing furnace traffic to the CRR and NYC. As reported in the May 26 *Keystone Gazette*, employees of a CRR contractor had just begun excavating foundations for the viaduct's stone piers on either side of the Pennsylvania's tracks when the Tyrone Division's assistant superintendent appeared and ordered a halt to the digging. The contractor's men ignored him, and he departed. Later in the day, he returned with a locomotive and two carloads of gravel, and a gang of men who quickly shoveled the gravel into the foundation. The contractor's men promptly shoveled the gravel back out and dumped it into the creek. The Pennsylvania official then backed his train to the old Bellefonte and Snow Shoe Railroad enginehouse nearby and loaded a steel pivot, weighing several tons, that had been removed from an old turntable. The train returned to the construction site, PRR employees heaved the pivot into the foundation, and smothered it with a few tons of coal. "There!" barked the assistant superintendent, "Shovel that out!"

Gephart got the matter straightened out with senior PRR executives a few days later, and work on the viaduct resumed. (It was not reported who removed the pivot.) The big bridge was opened for service on July 17,

1899, after the Central's two heavy 4-8-os traveled slowly back and forth over the structure to make sure it was sound. So good was Richter's engineering that the viaduct settled less than a half-inch. Bellefonte Furnace traffic made a huge difference in the CRR's fortunes. The *Keystone Gazette* of November 10, 1899, noted that "the Central Railroad of Pennsylvania is now doing a big business in freight traffic. On Monday, nearly 200 cars were exchanged by this railroad and the New York Central. The [Bellefonte] yard is full of cars and new sidings are being built as quickly as possible." Ten-car drags of pig and bar iron became a familiar sight, crossing the great viaduct and climbing upgrade through Armor Gap, a snorting 4-8-0 at each end. Frequently seen moving in the opposite direction across the viaduct were carloads of limestone from Gephart's quarries at Salona and coke from the ovens at Gorton on the Beech Creek Railroad.

Gephart's ventures in railroads, iron, and quarries had a common headquarters that occupied the entire third floor of Bellefonte's Temple Court building. The three companies that he managed gave direct or indirect employment to more than a thousand people. The *Keystone Gazette* labeled the 1899 purchase of Bellefonte Furnace and the Scotia ore lands "one of the biggest deals ever made in Centre County," but sourly noted that outside investment had made it possible. Gephart first had "made a proposition to the moneyed men of Bellefonte, but found they had no backbone."[45]

Gephart put together another deal in 1902 when he arranged for a syndicate of New York and Philadelphia financiers to buy the Valentine Iron Company, whose furnace stood idle since a brief spurt of operation in 1899–1900. He promised the facility—now shorn of its restrictive PRR covenant—would resume operation under the name Nittany Iron Works and create 400 new jobs for furnace men, miners, and railroaders. He was still in New York City putting finishing touches on the deal when word of the furnace's reopening filtered back to Bellefonte. When Gephart's train arrived in the county seat on the evening of April 5, it was met by a brass band, hundreds of cheering citizens, and "a barouche to which four sprightly steeds were attached." Conveyed in splendor to his Linn Street residence, Gephart declared in an impromptu front-porch speech that his life's greatest pleasure came when he sat down to sign the payroll checks for his employees. The crowd cheered heartily.[46]

Figure 7.2. Nittany Furnace in Bellefonte could produce about 125 tons of pig and bar iron daily, which it could opt to ship over the PRR or the Central Railroad of Pennsylvania. *Author's collection.*

Bellefonte had never before witnessed such a swirl of industrial activity. The ironworks, commonly known as Nittany Furnace, mixed native ore from Scotia and Nigh and Taylor banks with ore from the Lake Superior region to increase the iron content. The PRR brought in the Lake ore and gave it to the CRR at the connection near the Morris limekilns in Armor Gap. The Central Railroad hauled this ore, plus limestone and coke, to Nittany Valley Junction. There it was given to the NVRR to take down to the furnace, where employees worked around the clock, seven days a week, to meet the steel industry's growing appetite for iron. By the fall of 1904, Nittany Furnace was averaging a daily output of 116 tons of iron, and in October it set its all-time daily record of 131 tons.[47] The

Nittany Valley Railroad carried 101,000 tons of freight in fiscal 1903 and nearly as much in each of the next few years.

Over on the Central Railroad of Pennsylvania, fully two-thirds of its annual tonnage in the early 1900s came from hauling material to or from Nittany and Bellefonte furnaces. Freight traffic of all kinds grew from 265,000 tons in 1900 to an all-time high of 462,000 tons in 1906. The CRR derived some of that tonnage from new sawmills opened at Snydertown and Mingoville by the McNitt brothers and E. M. Huyett, who would later log the Scotia area.[48] Additional tonnage came from the interchange the Central had established with the Bellefonte Central on the property of Bellefonte Furnace. That connection gave BFC customers an alternative to the PRR. State College consignees could receive carloads of merchandise, coal, brick, sand, and other materials that originated on the New York Central or its allied roads and had been interchanged to the CRR at Mill Hall—without ever burnishing PRR rails. Freight moving from the BFC to the CRR typically included seasonal fruit, wheat and other farm products, lime and limestone, and mine props and lumber.[49]

The Bellefonte Central also fed passengers to the CRR and vice versa, although the exact number is not a matter of record. The Central Railroad made special efforts to solicit Pennsylvania State College students headed to and from points on the New York Central, Philadelphia and Reading, Central Railroad of New Jersey, and Buffalo, Rochester and Pittsburgh lines. Unfortunately, no through-car service was available between the Bellefonte Central and the CRR. Ticket holders had to walk two blocks between Bellefonte stations to make connections. The Central Railroad's passenger business peaked in 1908, when slightly more than 100,000 tickets were sold.

The increase in both freight and passenger business masked the Central Railroad's underlying financial weakness. Even in years when operating income exceeded expenses, the company showed a net loss, as it struggled to pay down the indebtedness incurred during its construction—including interest on the $600,000 in bonds held by Drexel and Company. Its chronic problems took their toll on Wesley Gephart. He died of a stroke at his Bellefonte home on February 14, 1905. The *Democratic Watchman* observed, "There is no one living in Bellefonte today who could interest and command capital as Mr. Gephart did." The *Keystone Gazette*, ardently Republican in its leanings, eulogized the Democratic Gephart as "a citizen who for at least thirty-five years has been one of [the community's] most progressive spirits. . . . He was a promoter of more than ordinary tact and ability, his greatest ambition being to make Bellefonte a great manufacturing center."

Wallace Gephart succeeded his father as superintendent of the CRR and soon rose to its presidency. But the younger Gephart was largely a figurehead. Drexel and Company held the mortgage, and its chairman, Edward Stotesbury, decided the railroad had no future as an independent enterprise. Soon after Wallace Gephart took office, Stotesbury tried to sell the short line to the New York Central for $600,000. The NYC was not interested. It was already benefiting from the CRR's traffic; there was no need for a purchase. Bellefonte Central president Robert Frazer learned of the proposed sale. Desiring to preserve the BFC's connection to a carrier other than the Pennsylvania, Frazer offered Stotesbury $400,000 but refused to assume the road's debt. Stotesbury declined.[50]

A few years later, the New York Central revisited the possibility of acquiring not only the CRR but the Bellefonte Central. What prompted that interest is open to conjecture. The most likely reason is another attempt by Stotesbury to sell the property. In November 1912, a special train carrying officials from the NYC and both short lines made its way from Mill Hall through Bellefonte to State College. None of those aboard the special had any public comment on the purpose of their trip, other than BFC general manager Frank Thomas saying that the NYC officials were on a "tie-buying expedition," which in a sense was true enough. Newspapers speculated that the New York Central was considering a thrust into the Broad Top coal region, reviving an idea that Robert Frazer had raised in 1895 with the Pine Grove Mills extension.[51] There was logic to those suspicions: Drexel and Company controlled the CRR and owned the majority of Huntingdon and Broad Top Mountain stock. Drexel also was aligned with the NYC's banker, J. P. Morgan and Company—Stotesbury was a full-fledged Morgan partner. (There was enough logic so that immediately after the trip, as noted in chapter 4, the PRR's Sam Rea ordered a survey that could bring the L&T through State

College, potentially inflicting a mortal blow on the Bellefonte Central.) The speculation eventually trailed off in the absence of action by any of the roads involved.

Absent a buyer, the Central Railroad of Pennsylvania appeared doomed. Unlike the Bellefonte Central, it had few limestone and lime shippers to take up the slack when the bottom suddenly fell out of the local iron industry in 1910. Pig iron prices were then hovering around $15 per ton; conventional wisdom held that Centre County's iron makers could not operate profitably at anything less than $17 per ton.[52] With both furnaces out of blast at the beginning of 1911, ore mining ceased forever at Nigh and Taylor banks. Bellefonte and Nittany furnaces were sold for scrap and dismantled in 1914–15. The McCoy and Linn iron-works, which had never abandoned cold-blast technology, served a niche market in the manufacture of iron chain and remained in operation until 1919. However, it accounted for a small fraction of the CRR's total tonnage.

Stripped of their core business, the Central and the Nittany Valley railroads faced extinction. For the year ending June 30, 1913, the NVRR originated only 9,400 tons of freight, composed mostly of furnace slag, routed to the Bald Eagle Valley to be used as fill for the new Mount Eagle cutoff on the PRR's Bald Eagle Branch. The NVRR also transported Nittany Furnace's remaining inventory of pig iron. The company owned a single locomotive and no freight cars, and operated about one day a week. Later in 1913, still led by Jones Wister, the Nittany declared itself hopelessly insolvent and shut down. Bondholders took over its assets in 1915 and liquidated the property over the next several years.

At the Central, freight traffic was in steady decline, with no prospects for new customers. Passengers also were deserting the train as private automobiles and improved highways came to the area. The shift gained momentum after the passage of the landmark Sproul Road Act of 1911, which provided for a statewide network of publicly financed paved roads. Ticket sales plummeted from 92,400 in 1912 to 30,400 five years later. In 1917, the CRR reported a $33,000 deficit and still had not retired its $600,000 bond issue (which Stotesbury had refinanced for another fifteen years in 1908, after the New York Central turned down the chance to buy the road).

In July 1918 Drexel and Company petitioned the Philadelphia Court of Common Pleas to surrender the CRR's charter. The nation was engaged in a world war, and the bankers wanted to take advantage of high wartime scrap prices. Surrendering the charter would be a faster route to abandonment than the alternative means of petitioning the Pennsylvania Public Service Commission, successor to the state railroad commission. The court approved; and on September 28, the evening passenger train from Mill Hall to Bellefonte brought the curtain down on revenue operations. About fifty employees lost their jobs. The Pittsburgh-based salvage firm of Frank and Hirsh commenced removing rails, ties, and bridges, sparing only the 2-mile Mill Hall–Salona segment, which was purchased by the New York Central to serve limestone and sand quarries and the Mann Edge Tool factory. By spring 1919, the CRR's locomotives, cars, and most structures were sold or scrapped, including the great viaduct on the Furnace Branch. Many of the sandstone blocks from the viaduct's piers and abutments were used to build a retaining wall for the Roman Catholic cemetery along East Bishop Street in Bellefonte. The Chemical Lime Company bought the Bellefonte station for its headquarters.[53]

The reality was that the Central Railroad of Pennsylvania failed to attract a profitable level of business beyond the iron industry. Its portion of the quarry products trade—which became the mainstay of Bellefonte traffic for the PRR and the BFC after the demise of the furnaces—was far too small to sustain the company, and the CRR shared its largest lime and stone customer, A. G. Morris, with the Pennsylvania. Wesley Gephart overestimated the degree to which some customers were unhappy with the PRR and the willingness of that road to make adjustments to rates and services once it felt the sting of competition. Public proclamations of dissatisfaction with the Pennsylvania were relatively infrequent during the years the Central Railroad was active. The PRR also may have threatened to retaliate against shippers who left it for the Central. There is no direct evidence of such tactics, but the Philadelphia-based road was no stranger to bullying its shippers or adopting a no-holds-barred approach against competing carriers.[54] Finally, the CRR's experience suggests that even at high levels of patronage, short-haul passenger service offered an inadequate return on investment over the long term—confirming the beliefs of presidents Frazer of the Bellefonte Central and McCrea of the Pennsylvania.

The question can be raised as to whether the Central Railroad of Pennsylvania would have met the same dismal fate had its patron, the New York Central, adopted a more interventionist approach. As the CRR evolved, New York Central executives surely recognized the road's troubles, yet they chose to keep their distance from the company rather than throw it a life ring or even purchase it outright from Stotesbury. The conclusion must be, particularly after the collapse of the iron-making business, that the Bellefonte apple had lost its shine so far as the NYC was concerned; thus it was conceded to the PRR.

The rise and decline of the Central Railroad of Pennsylvania and the Nittany Valley Railroad coincides almost perfectly with the "golden age" of railroading in the state. When the CRR ran its first train in 1893, common carrier steam railroads were operating approximately 9,100 route-miles throughout Pennsylvania. The total peaked at 11,693 route-miles in 1915 and then gradually decreased for the remainder of the century. The CRR and the NVRR were among the first casualties of that contraction; there would be many more.

Notes

1. *Buffalo Run Railroad, a Prospectus Presented to Pennsylvania Railroad President George B. Roberts*, 12-page pamphlet, n.p., 1881; E. V. D'Invilliers, "The Brown Hematite (Limonite) Ores of Siluro-Cambrian Limestone, No. II, of Centre County, Pennsylvania." *Proceedings of the Engineers' Club of Philadelphia* (November 1884): 209–22.

2. Articles of Association of the Bellefonte and Buffalo Run Railroad Company, 16 September 1882, Subgroup A, Box 2, Bellefonte Central Railroad Records, HCLA 1434, Pennsylvania State University Special Collections Library.

3. *Centre Democrat* (Bellefonte), 17 April 1884.

4. "Merger and Consolidation of the Bellefonte and Buffalo Run R.R. and the Nittany Valley and Southwestern R. R.," n.d., Subgroup A, Box 2, Bellefonte Central Railroad Records, HCLA 1434, Pennsylvania State University Special Collections Library.

5. *Colliery Engineer and Metal Miner*, December 1895, 102.

6. BRB&BE rolling stock and motive power: *Philip Collins v. Bellefonte Central R. R. Co.*, Appellant's Paper-Book No. 509, Supreme Court for the Eastern District of Pennsylvania, January Term 1894. Collins contended, unsuccessfully, that some

of the equipment was his personal property and should have been excluded from the foreclosure proceedings.

7. *Altoona Mirror*, 27 April 1904; "John Reilly," in *Pennsylvania Biographical Dictionary* (Wilmington, DE: American Historical Publications, 1989), 322–23.

8. *Iron Age*, 7 March 1889.

9. William T. Hogan, *Economic History of the Iron and Steel Industry in the United States*, 5 vols. (Lexington, MA: D. C. Heath, 1971), 1:183–225; Richard Peters Jr., *Two Centuries of Iron Smelting in Pennsylvania* (Philadelphia: Pulaski Iron Co., 1921), 53, 73–77.

10. Fourth Annual Report to the Stockholders of the Bellefonte Central Railroad Company (for 1894). A complete set of the railroad's annual reports to the stockholders is in Subgroup G, Box 88, BFC Records. A history of the BFC and its predecessors is Michael Bezilla and Jack Rudnicki, *Rails to Penn State: The Story of the Bellefonte Central* (Mechanicsburg, Pa.: Stackpole Books, 2007).

11. Bellefonte Central Railroad Company, "Two Famous Resorts: Hunters Park and University Inn," 4-page pamphlet, c. 1898; *Keystone Gazette*, 29 April and 6 May 1892.

12. Michael Bezilla, *Penn State: An Illustrated History* (University Park: Pennsylvania State University Press, 1985), 47–48.

13. Michael Bezilla, *The College of Engineering at Penn State: A Century in the Land-Grant Tradition*, 2nd ed. (University Park: Pennsylvania State University Press, 1996), 55–56, 74, 103.

14. Jo Chesworth, *Story of the Century: The Borough of State College, Pennsylvania* (State College, PA: Borough in Cooperation with the Barash Group, 1995), 38, 40.

15. Frazer to BFC superintendent Frank Thomas, 20 October 1905, Subgroup A, Box 24, Frazer letterbooks, BFC Records. The letterbooks span the period 1892–1912.

16. Proposals for route extensions and a new Bellefonte station came before the BFC's board of directors periodically, 1893–1907. Board minute books, Subgroup A, Box 1, BFC Records.

17. BFC Annual Reports for 1901 and 1902.

18. The Frazer letterbooks are peppered with his complaints about the high costs of providing passenger service and rants against the state railroad commission.

19. *Centre Reporter* (Centre Hall), 24 November 1904.

20. *Centre Democrat*, 24 August 1905; Fred Warner, "Centre County Limestone," *Centre County Heritage* 9 (April 1973): 160–63.

21. *Centre Democrat*, 11 March 1897.

22. Frazer to Thomas, 4 January 1904, Frazer letterbooks.

23. "J. Wesley Gephart," in *Commemorative Biographical Record of Central Pennsylvania, Including Centre, Clinton, Union and Snyder Counties* (Chicago: J. H. Beers, 1898), 458–59; *Democratic Watchman* (Bellefonte), 17 February 1905; *Keystone Gazette*, 17 February 1905.

24. McLaughlin's offer to sell the NV&S to the P&R: unsigned, undated sales agreement between the two parties, Subgroup A, Box 2, BFC Records.

25. Michael Bezilla, "P&R in the Nittany Valley," *Bee Line* 23, no. 2 (2001): 19–23.

26. The untitled prospectus is included in the A. A. McLeod correspondence, Box 54, Folder 1, Reading Company Records, Hagley Museum and Library. See also *Williamsport Republican*, 7 March 1892.

27. *Centre Democrat*, 2 February 1888; *Democratic Watchman*, 13 January 1888; Nittany Valley Railroad report in *Annual Report of the Secretary of Internal Affairs on Railroads, Canals, Telegraphs, and Telephones* (Harrisburg: Pennsylvania Department of Internal Affairs, 1888), 623–27.

28. *Democratic Watchman*, 31 March 1893.

29. *Democratic Watchman*, 8 November 1895.

30. Albert Churella, *The Pennsylvania Railroad: Building an Empire, 1846–1917* (Philadelphia: University of Pennsylvania Press, 2012), 621–22.

31. *Keystone Gazette*, 22 July 1892.

32. Michael Bezilla, "Proxy for the New York Central: The Central Railroad of Pennsylvania," *Milepost* 24 (October 2006): 14–19. *Milepost* is a publication of the Railroad Museum of Pennsylvania.

33. I. H. Mauser, *The Central Railroad of Pennsylvania; A Description of Its Route, etc.* (Milton, PA: Milton Printing Co., 1894); *Railway World*, 3 June 1893. All of the Bellefonte papers covered the CRR's construction and start-up in detail.

34. *Democratic Watchman*, 12 April 1912.

35. *Keystone Gazette*, 16 March 1906.

36. Shugert to McLeod, 20 January 1891, Box 66, Folder 2, A. A. McLeod correspondence, Reading Company Records, Hagley Museum and Library, Wilmington, DE.

37. Motive power: Central Railroad of Pennsylvania reports in *Annual Report of the Secretary of Internal Affairs on Railroads; Philipsburg Journal*, 8 December 1893; *Democratic Watchman*, 13 April 1900.

38. *Democratic Watchman*, 14 January 1898.

39. *Bald Eagle Valley Railroad et al. v. Nittany Valley Railroad et al.*, in *Pennsylvania State Reports: Cases Adjudged in the Supreme Court of Pennsylvania* 171 (New York: Banks and Bros., 1896): 284–301.

40. *Democratic Watchman*, 8 November 1895.

41. *Democratic Watchman*, 6 January 1899.

42. Mauser, *Central Railroad of Pennsylvania*; *Democratic Watchman*, 6 January 1899; *Keystone Gazette*, 29 August 1902 and 16 August 1907.

43. *Democratic Watchman*, 27 November 1896.

44. *Centre Democrat*, 27 July and 24 August 1899.

45. *Keystone Gazette*, 12 May 1899.

46. *Keystone Gazette*, 11 April 1902.

47. *Keystone Gazette*, 30 September, 7 October, 4 November 1904.

48. Benjamin F. G. Kline Jr., *Pitch Pine and Prop Timber* (Lancaster, PA: Self-published, 1971), 165–67.

49. Per diem books listing ownership, contents, origin and destination of freight cars going to and from the BFC 1907–1910 are in Subgroup D, BFC Records.

50. Stotesbury's attempts to sell the CRR are discussed in BFC board of directors minutes and in Frazer's correspondence, 1905–6.

51. *Philipsburg Daily Journal*, 23 May 1912; *Centre Democrat*, 14 November 1912; *Keystone Gazette*, 22 November 1912.

52. *Bellefonte Republican*, 17 June 1909.

53. Paul Dubbs, "Some Notes on an Old Railroad," *Centre Democrat*, 1 March 1984.

54. The PRR's aggressive tactics are illustrated in cases reported over a five-year span in *Annual Report of the Pennsylvania State Railroad Commission* (Harrisburg: State Printer, 1909–13).

EIGHT

Railroads at High Tide

BETWEEN 1900 AND AMERICA'S ENTRY INTO THE FIRST WORLD
War in 1917, the national rail network reached high tide, peaking at about
254,000 route-miles, including nearly 12,000 miles in Pennsylvania. Centre County and the Moshannon Valley reached an all-time high of approximately 200 miles of principal lines, with many more miles of lesser
branches. Railroads were the lifeblood of American commerce, as freight
traffic nationally topped 366 billion ton-miles in 1916. That same year railroads reported 35 billion passenger-miles.[1]

As business boomed, the technology of railroading achieved new
standards of productivity and safety, especially on large roads such as
the Pennsylvania and the New York Central. More powerful locomotives
evolved, steel superseded wood in freight and passenger car construction, and steel rails and bridges supplanted those made of wood or iron.
Refrigerator cars, insulated boxcars, heated tank cars, and covered hopper cars were just a few of the specialized types of rolling stock that were
introduced to meet changing customer needs. New signaling systems increased efficiency and reduced risks. The PRR and NYC also developed
sophisticated management organizations, reflected in the hierarchical
structures of the PRR's Tyrone Division and the NYC's Pennsylvania
Division and the military-like discipline with which their respective
work forces carried out their tasks.

Until early in the twentieth century, railroad companies operated largely according to the dictates of free enterprise. Competition among individual carriers was fierce. Giving select customers rebates and preferential treatment in car supply was common in order to gain an advantage over competing roads. Occasionally cooperation replaced competition—for example, when railroads divided competitive traffic among themselves according to mutually agreed-upon ratios or shares. Such pooling arrangements were intended to prevent ruinous rate wars. The Seaboard Agreement of 1887 was one of the first experiments in pooling Appalachian coal traffic. The PRR's Clearfield District was allocated 32.25 percent of total market tonnage, with the next highest being the B&O's Cumberland District with 28.25 percent. The Beech Creek got 10.50 percent among the seven railroads and seven districts involved.[2] This particular pool, and virtually all other pools, failed because at least one of the participating railroads could not resist the temptation to secretly cut rates in order to capture competitors' traffic. Nevertheless, the pool signaled an important step in the transition from competition to cooperation between the Pennsylvania Railroad and the New York Central in the Clearfield District.

From the perspective of many shippers, pooling was only one reason why the cost of railroad transportation was too high; they demanded government intervention to ensure (in their eyes) fair rates and better service. Congress responded by creating the Interstate Commerce Commission in 1887. For nearly twenty years the commission was mostly a fact-finding body. It investigated cases where a shipper claimed railroad rates were unfair, then referred its findings to a court in the event the shipper wanted to pursue legal action against the railroad. The legislation that created the ICC did outlaw pooling, however.

In the early 1900s, an inflationary national economy replaced decades of declining prices and wages. Freight and passenger rates increased sharply, triggering public alarm and making railroads a favorite target for the progressive wings of both major political parties. Such an environment of unrest gave birth to the Pennsylvania State Railroad Commission in 1907. The commission had authority to gather pertinent information in response to complaints about poor service, discriminatory rates, and similar issues; but it lacked enforcement powers and relied on moral suasion to see that its recommendations were carried out. Otherwise it turned disputes over to the courts for settlement.[3]

On the federal level, Congress responded more aggressively to the rising wave of shipper and public unhappiness with the railroads. It enacted a series of laws based on the principle that when private property is devoted to public use, it should be subject to public regulation. Overseeing and enforcing the regulation that Congress desired was a strengthened Interstate Commerce Commission. Legislation was enacted that prohibited rebates and long-haul versus short-haul rate discrimination, and generally made it more difficult for railroads to give special treatment to customers. Railroads were required to obtain ICC approval when setting rates, even in cases where shippers did not complain. By 1914, few other industries were subject to such intense federal scrutiny or had to justify so many of their actions to a public agency. This transformation of the business environment from free enterprise to government oversight occurred so quickly partly because the public and shippers demanded it and partly many railroad executives welcomed or at least accepted regulation after decades of trying unsuccessfully to find ways of their own to end ruinous competition. Pennsylvania Railroad president Alexander Cassatt, for instance, helped to draft the Elkins Act that made rebating illegal.[4]

As PRR historian Albert Churella has pointed out, in their quest for stability Cassatt and his industry peers helped to open the door for public sentiment, in the form of government regulation, to trump the forces of the free market. The era when railroads went head to head in no-holds-barred competition had, with few exceptions, come to an end. How the hand of federal regulation would weigh on railroads in Centre County and the Moshannon Valley, where the Pennsylvania and the New York Central networks had crested, remained to be seen.

On all parts of the Pennsylvania Railroad, traffic volumes soared in the early 1900s, keeping pace with the nation's ever-increasing industrial and agricultural output. The PRR's Lines East of Pittsburgh and Erie carried 165 million tons of freight in 1902, more than double the 71.9 million tons of 1892. Lines East also carried about 90 million passengers in 1902, compared with 47 million ten years earlier.[5] Surging traffic placed a huge strain the Middle Division main line—the heart of the Pennsylvania's east–west system—and prompted the railroad to undertake a variety of measures to add capacity. Along the main line between the Susquehanna River and Altoona, curves were eased, bridges rebuilt, and track upgraded to allow higher train speeds. Four main tracks replaced two, except for the rugged stretch through the Little Juniata Narrows between Spruce Creek and Tyrone Forge, where the line was expanded from two to three tracks. The railroad introduced new motive power, epitomized by the brawny class H6 2-8-0 freight engine and the class E 4-4-2 passenger engine, both of which could pull heavier trains at higher speeds than their predecessors. In 1904 the PRR opened the world's largest freight classification yard at Enola, on the Susquehanna's west shore above Harrisburg, as a staging yard to expedite the movement of freight cars between the Middle Division and various East Coast points. The railroad also sought to divert some freight traffic away from the main line. In 1905, it completed a double-track freight-only line between Petersburg in Huntingdon County and Gallitzin, at the summit of the Alleghenies. The route, intended for use primarily by slow-moving mineral trains, followed the course of the defunct Pennsylvania Canal much of the way, bypassing Altoona and climbing the Allegheny Front by way of the Muleshoe Curve, located a few miles south of the more famous four-track Horseshoe Curve.

The amount of coal originating in western Pennsylvania and moving east over the Middle Division main line was expected to reach such proportions that even with the Petersburg relief line, the PRR feared it would interfere with faster merchandise and passenger trains. To prevent this outcome, the railroad decided to use the Bald Eagle Valley line as yet another way to build capacity. Bituminous coal destined for upstate New York, New England, and Canada would leave the main line at Tyrone and be routed through the Bald Eagle Valley to Lock Haven, and then on to points north and east. Even some coal headed for points south and east of Harrisburg and Enola would be sent over the Bald Eagle Branch, then south along the Susquehanna through Sunbury. Anthracite coal from northeastern Pennsylvania, dwarfed in tonnage compared with bituminous, would be routed west over the BEV rather than over the Sunbury and Lewistown Branch to Lewistown. A Bald Eagle Valley routing kept both bituminous and anthracite coal trains off the main line entirely, except for the 14 miles between Altoona and Tyrone.

In addition, the PRR decided to make the Bald Eagle line a strategic link in a route for merchandise traffic moving between the Midwest, and New England and Canada. Cars using the Bald Eagle would not have to be floated on barges across New York harbor and could bypass busy terminals in the Harrisburg and Philadelphia areas. The selection of the Bald Eagle Branch instead of the S&L Branch as a new coal and fast freight route came about in part because the line had a forceful and persuasive advocate: 43-year-old John Kilgore Johnston, who in 1903 succeeded the retiring Samuel Blair as Tyrone Division superintendent. Johnston was a self-taught civil engineer who had joined the PRR in 1880 in his native Westmoreland County. On his way up the managerial ladder, he had held maintenance-of-way positions on a number of PRR divisions, including the Tyrone. In fact Johnston's Herculean efforts in procuring men and material in Bellefonte immediately following heavy rains of May 29–30, 1889 (the same deluge that caused the Johnstown Flood), enabled the Pennsylvania to open the badly damaged Bald Eagle Valley Railroad to traffic in only six days' time, when similar lines were out of service for several weeks.[6]

In order to accommodate heavy traffic, the Bald Eagle Valley Railroad had to be improved in ways that went beyond laying heavier rail and strengthening bridges; but it was still a leased property. At the outset of 1906, the Pennsylvania owned a little less than half of the BEV's 30,602 total shares. Much of the remainder was in the hands of the descendants of Edmund Blanchard, Andrew Curtin, Moses Thompson, and other pioneer railroad investors. Prudence dictated that the PRR take full ownership of its affiliate before spending large sums to rebuild it. The Pennsylvania offered three shares of its own stock, then worth about $60 per share, plus $50 cash in exchange for each BEV share. The liberal terms testified to the great value the leased line held for the parent road, and the sale was consummated by the end of 1907. As of March 31, 1908, the Bald Eagle Valley Railroad ceased to exist as a legal entity. Its property passed to the Pennsylvania Railroad, which soon renamed the line the Bald Eagle Branch.[7]

The PRR had already made one major improvement to the BEV when it was still a leased property. In 1905 general contractor H. S. Kerbaugh replaced the old iron bridge that spanned the Little Juniata River at Tyrone with two larger all-steel structures and constructed a lengthy new approach to the spans on the town side. The new bridges formed a wye, with the Tyrone station in the middle. One leg of the wye faced east and followed the Tyrone and Clearfield Railroad's original alignment out to the main line. The other leg faced west, allowing trains operating between Tyrone and Altoona to enter or leave the Bald Eagle Branch without having to make a reverse move—a requirement when there was only the T&C alignment.[8]

In 1907 the PRR completed installation of a manual block signal system of traffic control over the entire 54-mile length of the branch. The line was divided into seventeen segments, or blocks. In the simplest form of manual block operation, train movements from block to block were governed by semaphore signals at the entrance to each block. The signals were controlled by block operators located in existing stations or specially built block stations. Block operators communicated with each other and with the dispatcher's office in Tyrone by telegraph; each block station had a two-letter telegraph call for quick and easy identification— MD for Port Matilda, JN for Julian, HO for Howard, and so on down the line. The manual block signal system, first used on the PRR in the 1870s, allowed safer travel and the passage of a greater number of trains than the timetable-and-train-order method it replaced. In particular it improved protection against rear-end collisions, although in that respect the Tyrone Division had a commendable history. Manual block signals also were installed in 1907 on the branch from Milesburg to Bellefonte, and a year or two later on the Clearfield Branch.[9] (The former T&C main line was designated the Clearfield Branch following the PRR's dissolution of the Cambria and Clearfield Railway in 1913.)

In 1909, as part of the plan to route more traffic onto the Bald Eagle Branch, the PRR began construction of a large freight-car classification yard and engine terminal along the Susquehanna River at Northumberland, a few miles north of Sunbury. The two existing yards at Sunbury were handling a combined 2,000 cars a day in 1900; the Pennsylvania's decision to put more traffic on the Bald Eagle line would tax those two yards beyond their limit. The contract to build Northumberland yard went to the Eyre-Shoemaker Construction Company, co-owned and managed by Thomas Shoemaker, Phil and Tom Collins's nephew and former Bellefonte Central general manager, who still made his home in Bellefonte. To help supply the 600,000 cubic yards of fill needed to raise the new yard above the flood plain, Shoemaker acquired 400,000 tons of slag left by Bellefonte Furnace and brought in the largest steam shovel ever seen in the area to load rail cars for shipment east. The first phase of "Norry" yard was opened for service in August 1911. The PRR estimated that when fully built, it would stretch for 3 miles and contain more than a hundred miles of track, enough to accommodate 8,000 cars each day. Northumberland served as the eastern terminus for some of the Tyrone crews running Bald Eagle branch through-freights. Likewise it became the eastern terminus for freight trains running over the Lewisburg and Tyrone Railroad, while L&T passenger trains still originated or terminated at Sunbury.[10]

By mid-1912 the Bald Eagle Branch was averaging a million ton-miles each month, prompting the trade magazine *Railway Age Gazette* to proclaim that the line had a greater traffic density than any other single-track railroad in the United States.[11] On most days, four passenger trains and about twenty-five through-freights traveled over the branch in each direction. Including light engine moves, work trains, and locals that operated over only part of the line, some sections of the branch witnessed the passage of more than fifty trains daily.

Bituminous coal trains accounted for most of the tonnage. Some of the coal originated in the Moshannon Valley and Snow Shoe areas. Other carloads originated at mines in Cambria and southern Clearfield and Jefferson Counties and came east on the main line as far as Tyrone. Many coal trains went east as far as Williamsport, then headed north on the Elmira Branch to the PRR pier at Sodus Point, New York, on Lake Ontario. There coal was transloaded into boats for Canadian markets. By 1911, the Pennsylvania was shipping more than 5 million tons of bituminous coal annually through the Sodus Point gateway.[12] Coal trains using the Bald Eagle Branch and destined for New England went to Northumberland yard and then east over the Wilkes-Barre Branch to interchanges with the Delaware and Hudson and Central of New Jersey at Wilkes-Barre. Merchandise trains between Pittsburgh and New England used the Bald Eagle Branch and the Wilkes-Barre gateway as part of a route that bypassed the congestion at Harrisburg, Philadelphia, and New York. All of these new routings robbed the PRR's Sunbury and Lewistown Branch of its strategic importance.

After introducing a manual block system and building the wye bridges at Tyrone, the Pennsylvania was slow to make other improvements to the Bald Eagle Branch. The pause in making further upgrades gave traffic officials time to debate the wisdom of double-tracking the line. Finally, in June 1912 a $500,000 contract was awarded to A. L. Anderson and Company of Altoona to realign the existing track between Vail and the village of Bald Eagle in Blair County, and to add a second, more gently graded track between Mount Eagle and Howard in Centre County. Supervising the work for the Pennsylvania was civil engineer Fred Field, a Lock Haven native and protégé of the veteran engineer of branch line construction C. S. D'Invilliers.

When John McMinn had located the first 3 miles or so of the railroad east of Vail in the 1850s, he put it on the shoulder of Bald Eagle Ridge to avoid the Little Bald Eagle Creek flood plain. But to reach that high ground, the line turned sharply at Vail and ascended a 1.1 percent grade—a tough climb for coal trains, even with a pusher or two. Field's realignment, consisting of a main track and a passing siding, made a less restrictive curve at Vail and followed the creek instead of seeking elevation. In some places it was as much as 2,000 feet distant from the old route. Field had the creek channel diverted slightly from the railroad and walled with stone and more than 2,000 cubic yards of masonry to keep the waterway within its banks during flood times. Taking the right-of-way off Bald Eagle Ridge reduced the ruling grade to 0.8 percent—still pusher territory but more practical for heavy coal drags.

The other eastbound grade in the valley lay between the settlement of Mount Eagle and the town of Howard. There, trains faced a 5-mile, 0.9 percent ascent, again following McMinn's survey along the shoulder of Bald Eagle Ridge, away from the flood plain. Most trains surmounted it without helpers by building up speed as soon as they passed Milesburg. However, by the time heavy trains—3,000 gross tons was the upper limit—approached Howard, they had usually slowed to a walk, creating a potential bottleneck. If they lacked sufficient momentum, they stalled and corked the bottle. Relying on earthmoving machinery unavailable in McMinn's time, Field laid out a bypass of Howard that had no grade of any consequence. Anderson and Company used three steam shovels to move 300,000 cubic yards of earth in building a new 5-mile line that ran for much of its length atop a substantial earthen fill to avoid high water. When the contractors ran short of fill material, they purchased Bellefonte Furnace slag from Tom Shoemaker. The Mount Eagle cut-off opened for service in February 1913 and was used primarily by coal trains, whose limit was increased to about 4,500 gross tons. All passenger trains and lighter eastbound freights used the original line through Howard, as did westbound freights of almost any tonnage.[13]

More powerful locomotives also boosted the capacity of the Bald Eagle Branch. New class H6 2-8-0 freight haulers had debuted in 1901. The H6, a heavier, more powerful successor to the stalwart H3, "was *the* freight engine of all freight engines of her day," according to locomotive historian Bert Pennypacker. "So successful was this bay that the railroad went whole hog with it during the booming traffic years of the early twentieth century. It was built in fantastic quantities [1,017 total] and used in every nook and cranny of the system."[14] It was not long before the H6 found its way in coal service on the Clearfield Branch, too.

The PRR introduced the H6 at a time when freight rolling stock was transitioning from wood to steel construction. The advent of the all-steel hopper car, beginning with the Pennsylvania's class GL twin-bay hopper of 1898, had particular implications for the Bald Eagle Branch. The GL cars could hold 50 tons of coal (a little more with a heap), compared with the 30–40 ton capacities of the wooden gondola hoppers it replaced. The GL was the PRR's first self-clearing hopper car; that is, the entire car floor sloped toward the hoppers, eliminating the need for hand-shoveling—the bane of partially flat-bottomed gondola hoppers such as the class GB. Steel cars also were more durable and required fewer repairs. By 1902, the PRR had 10,000 GL-class cars in use system-wide. The GL hopper cars and the subsequent class H21A—a 70-ton car that debuted in 1915—combined with the pulling power of the H6 locomotive to increase the capacity of the Bald Eagle Branch and influenced the Pennsylvania's decision not to double-track the line. (Berwind-White continued to use its wooden cars on the Clearfield Branch until the 1920s, when it finally closed its Osceola car shop. Those old-style cars would have found their way onto the Bald Eagle line, too, of course.)[15]

The Bald Eagle Branch in the early 1900s was proving its value to the PRR as a strategic link in long-distance routes for fast freight. By contrast, the Clearfield and the Snow Shoe branches, and the railroad in the immediate Bellefonte area, remained heavily dependent on the local extractive industries: coal and clay on the Allegheny Plateau, and lime and limestone in the Nittany Valley.

Coal still drove expansion of the Tyrone Division's total route-mileage, although the pace was nothing like the frenetic growth of the late nineteenth century. In the Snow Shoe area, the PRR extended the Sugar Camp Branch another 3.9 miles in 1914 to serve the new Lehigh Valley Coal Company No. 24 mine. In 1915 it built the 2.4-mile Big Sandy Branch—a Sugar Camp appendage named for Big Sandy Run, a tributary to the North Fork of Beech Creek—to reach newly opened No. 25. That mine was among the largest and most modern in central Pennsylvania's bituminous coalfields, with electricity powering all of its mining machinery, haulage equipment, pump, and ventilating fans.[16]

Having a dependable, low-cost source of bituminous coal, the LVCC began blending it with anthracite culm (the fine coal that washed out at the breaker while the anthracite was cleaned and sized for market) for use as fuel in the locomotives of its parent, the Lehigh Valley Railroad, which consumed 7,000 tons of coal daily. In the combustion process, the bituminous supplied most of the heat while the culm made a more uniform fuel bed, leading to more efficient combustion and less smoke. The coal company had plenty of culm; it erected a large blending plant near Hazleton, which became the destination for substantial quantities of Snow Shoe coal. The plant blended fuel for road locomotives at a rate of 2 tons of bituminous for each ton of culm; for yard engines, the blend was one-to-one.[17]

The Lehigh Valley Coal Company remained firmly entrenched as the Mountaintop's largest producer, with Kelly Brothers Coal Company second. The LVCC often vied with Osceola-based Moshannon Mining Company for the distinction of being Centre County's largest coal producer. In 1914, for example, Moshannon shipped 253,000 tons from its four Centre County mines, and Lehigh Valley shipped 237,000 tons from its seven Snow Shoe–area mines. Berwind-White was the Tyrone Division's largest bituminous shipper, but nearly all of its mines were

Figure 8.1. All-steel hopper cars are ready for loading under the tipple at the Brookwood Shaft mine, located near the terminus of the PRR's Moshannon and Clearfield Branch. *Author's collection.*

located on the Clearfield County side of the upper Moshannon Creek. In 1914 those mines sent 373,000 tons to market by rail.[18] All told, in the early 1900s the PRR was moving between 2 and 3 million tons of coal annually over the Clearfield Branch to Tyrone, less than the peak years of the 1880s but a prodigious amount nonetheless.[19]

New construction in Clearfield Branch territory in the early 1900s consisted mostly of extending existing spurs from the Moshannon Branch a little farther to reach new mines. Some consideration was given to extending the main stem of the Clearfield Branch north toward DuBois; a few miles were actually graded in that direction but never received track.[20] The topography was forbidding, and meanwhile other PRR lines had reached DuBois. With no good reason to go beyond Grampian, the T&C remained a dead-end railroad.

In the spring of 1913, the possibility of new construction in the Philipsburg area came to the fore, backed by Moshannon Valley coal magnate Charles H. Rowland. One of Philipsburg's wealthiest citizens, the 53-year-old Rowland headed the Moshannon Mining Company and the Pittsburgh and Susquehanna Railroad (formerly the Altoona and Philipsburg Connecting Railroad), and had numerous other business investments. He was a popular figure among his fellow townsmen—especially after he built the palatial Rowland Theatre in 1917 to replace a smaller structure destroyed by fire—and represented the area in Congress for two terms, beginning in 1915.

Rowland had acquired mineral rights to 10,000 acres surrounding the headwaters of Cold Stream and Forge Run (later renamed Six Mile Run), located a few miles southwest of Philipsburg. "The unusual coal and clay deposits in quantity and quality amaze geological experts," noted the *Centre Democrat* (Bellefonte), adding that Rowland was in the process of incorporating the Moshannon Central Railroad to serve mines that he intended to open, and surveyors were laying out the new route. Rowland projected his 5-mile railroad as a standard-gauge common carrier, making a connection with the PRR at the north end of Philipsburg near the town's coal-fired electric power plant, in which Rowland also had an interest. The surveyors had easy work, following a right-of-way that had been laid out years before by the Philipsburg Silica Sand

Company when that enterprise was seeking to develop silica deposits and a glass factory along Cold Stream near the latter-day hamlet of Glass City.[21]

Rowland's coal company was the PRR's second largest shipper locally, but he had at least an indirect allegiance to the New York Central through his leadership of the Alley Popper. Whether he planned to push the Moshannon Central beyond the PRR to reach the NYC near Loch Lomond Junction is unknown, because the MCRR fizzled just as the sand and glass venture had done previously. A segment of the right-of-way was graded, but rails were never laid. Exactly what caused the railroad's demise is not clear, since Rowland didn't discuss the matter publicly. He died in 1923, not long after the Alley Popper declared itself bankrupt.

The false start of the Moshannon Central in 1913 notwithstanding, the amount of coal mined in Centre County that year and its total market value hit record highs: 1,497,271 tons having a market value of $1,499,395, or about a dollar per ton. Centre ranked eleventh among the Commonwealth's sixty-seven counties in total bituminous production.[22]

The county's second most valuable mineral product at that time was found not on the Allegheny Plateau but in the Nittany Valley, where the lime industry was flourishing. In 1913 Centre County's total output of nearly 126,000 tons (with a market value of $390,000) ranked it second only to Chester County (by less than 6,000 tons) as the state's largest source of lime. Its quarrying and lime-making industries together gave employment to more than 900 persons directly, and thousands more indirectly.[23] The Bellefonte Central Railroad had established a solid economic footing in the lime trade in 1907 with the opening of Chemical Lime's quarry and lime plant on the Whitmer farm along Buffalo Run. By 1913 the BFC was originating almost a third of the county's total lime shipments. The Central Railroad of Pennsylvania served a more modest portion of the lime trade from plants in Armor Gap. The Pennsylvania Railroad put both short lines in the shade by receiving nearly all the BFC's lime cars and some of the CRR's output, and serving two of Centre County's "big three" lime makers directly.

The big three consisted of Chemical Lime, American Lime and Stone, and Whiterock Quarries. The American Lime and Stone Company dat-

Figure 8.2. American Lime and Stone Plant No. 1 in Bellefonte, as portrayed in a postcard image. Crushed limestone was dumped into the three shaft kilns from above and heated to 1,000 degrees Fahrenheit as part of the lime-making process. *Author's collection.*

ed from 1901, when seventeen quarrying and lime-making operations throughout the Nittany Valley combined their assets to form a single enterprise, headquartered in Tyrone at first and later in Bellefonte. Most of the components had already come under the control of either Alexander Morris or two other pioneers in the industry, Adie A. Stevens of Tyrone and J. King McLanahan of Hollidaysburg. American, with Morris as president, secured lime contracts from several Pittsburgh steelmakers and provided the Pennsylvania Railroad with ballast and bridge stone. The company also found a ready market for its lime among paper mills, glass factories, tanneries, chemical plants, and other manufacturing facilities from New England to the Midwest and the Deep South. By 1907, American Lime and Stone had fifty-seven kilns in service up and down the Nittany Valley. The heart of the company's production was a battery of kilns near the entrance to Armor Gap, on Bellefonte's northern outskirts, where William Shortlidge had first prospected for high-quality limestone in the 1860s. To reach that operation, the PRR built the Morris Branch starting at the west end of Sunnyside yard and crossing Spring Creek into the gap.[24]

Whiterock Quarries was incorporated in 1905. A group of Bellefonte investors led by William H. Noll and including banker W. Fred Reynolds and corporate lawyer John Blanchard (Edmund Blanchard's nephew) organized the company after Noll's prospecting confirmed the existence of commercial-grade limestone near the surface on farms near the village of Pleasant Gap. The outcropping lay at the base of Nittany Mountain and was of the same geologic mass—the Valentine Formation—as the stone on the opposite side of Nittany Valley. Whiterock acquired the land and opened a pit to reach a limestone vein that proved to be 70 feet thick where it rose upward against the base of the mountain. The Eyre-Shoemaker Construction Company won the contract to build a 1-mile spur, subsequently named the Whiterock Branch, from the existing PRR line about midway between Bellefonte and Lemont. Tom Shoemaker liked what he saw of the new quarry and offered to invest in the enterprise. As soon as Eyre-Shoemaker finished the Pennsylvania's Northumberland yard job, he withdrew from that firm to become Whiterock's president and general manager. By 1913, Whiterock controlled more than 350 acres, operated eighteen kilns, and was selling lime as fast as the PRR could haul it away.[25]

In contrast to the open-top hopper cars used in coal service, Nittany Valley lime shippers used boxcars almost exclusively. More than two-thirds of their output consisted of calcium oxide, or quicklime, in high demand as a flux in smelting various ores and for making cement. It was packed in barrels or bags that were supposed to be watertight. If a container leaked and the quicklime became wet, the resulting chemical reaction generated enough heat to start a fire in a wooden car; reports of lime-carrying boxcars ablaze in Sunnyside yard were not unusual. Lime companies also sold some of their output as hydrated lime, which had to be kept dry but did not give off heat when wet. Hydrated lime was made by adding a small amount of water to quicklime, turning calcium oxide into calcium hydrate. Hydrated lime was used in a broad range of applications, such as making paper, refining sugar, and tanning leather. Depending on the needs of the consignee, lime companies did not always bag hydrated lime, but sometimes used forced air to blow it into boxcars as a bulk powder.[26] The lime trade was a valuable part of the Tyrone Division's traffic mix. After the demise of the Central Railroad of Pennsylvania, the NYC's Pennsylvania Division had nothing comparable. It had no lime business worthy of the name; using track purchased at the CRR's quitting-business sale, it served only a small limestone quarry or two near Mill Hall.

When John K. Johnston became superintendent on the Tyrone Division, his counterpart on the New York Central's Pennsylvania Division was Patrick E. Crowley, a veteran of twenty-three years on the railroad, starting as a telegrapher at a small country station in upstate New York. From division offices at Corning, New York, Crowley presided over a territory that was away from the east–west mainstream of the NYC's traffic flow. The Beech Creek District in particular, with its endless procession of grimy coal trains creaking up one hill and down another, did not fit the New York Central's carefully cultivated image of sleek limiteds and time freights rushing over water-level routes between great cities. But Crowley's three years of service on the Pennsylvania Division (1901–4) did his career no harm. He rose through the executive ranks until 1924, when he began a seven-year tenure as the New York Central's president—the only superintendent on either the Pennsylvania Division or the PRR's Tyrone Division who eventually made it all the way to his company's top job.[27]

The Beech Creek District closely resembled the PRR's Clearfield Branch in that coal dominated, by tonnage, everything else on the rails, with clay and clay products ranking a distant though respectable second. The demand for firebrick, a refractory that could withstand the extremely high temperatures typically associated with making steel and glass, was practically insatiable. While the PRR served numerous brickyards along the Clearfield Branch beginning with the pioneer entry at Sandy Ridge in 1866, it was along the Beech Creek line where refractories traffic grew most rapidly after 1900.

Prospecting had revealed that the same belt of flint clay that gave rise to the Sandy Ridge brickyards extended eastward along the Allegheny Front into Clinton County. For about 10 miles Beech Creek (the waterway) forms the boundary between Clinton and Centre Counties, as it tumbles down the foothills in one of the least populated sections in all of Pennsylvania. On the ridgetops above the creek on the Clinton County side, flint clay deposits 7 feet thick were discovered, along with smaller amounts of silica or plastic clay. In 1899, the Clinton County Fire Brick Company opened a plant along the creek in Centre County's Liberty Township at what would soon become the town of Monument, a name derived from a large, monument-like rock formation along the stream bank. The company built a 3-mile narrow-gauge railroad to connect the plant with clay mines high on the ridge on the other side of the creek, using a series of switchbacks to negotiate the steep grade. (An inclined plane replaced the switchbacks in 1934, and the clay diggings became known as the Plane Hill mines.) In 1901 a second mining operation, Twin Run, opened less than a mile east of the original mines and likewise used a dinky line (without switchbacks) to reach the Monument plant.

The brickyard offered sufficient promise to attract the attention of Harbison-Walker, which purchased the Monument works in 1902 as part of a major thrust into the central Pennsylvania clay fields. The New York Central delivered coal to fire the Monument kilns; it shipped out brick to steel mills, railroads, and other industrial customers, along with raw clay from the Plane Hill and Twin Run mines for other Harbison-Walker plants. With several hundred residents, most of whom lived in company-owned dwellings, Monument also furnished the NYC with a modest passenger and express business.[28] The railroad was the only practical way in and out of the little town.

A similar story unfolded 3 miles upstream where Hayes Run flowed into Beech Creek from the Centre County side. There the Hayes Run Fire Brick Company, formed by a group of Centre and Clinton County investors, opened a fourteen-kiln plant in Curtin Township in 1904, using clay hauled by a narrow-gauge railroad from high atop the neighboring ridge in Clinton County. Bellefonte attorney Ellis L. Orvis was the company's president and principal shareholder, and the town that grew up around the brickyard was christened Orviston. He specialized in real estate law and also was a practicing land surveyor, both before and after he had prepared for the bar under James A. Beaver's tutelage. During a

Figure 8.3. Company houses add a neat uniformity to this view, looking east, of the community of Monument. The brickyard received clay from a narrow-gauge line that crossed Beech Creek on one of the bridges at far left. *Jim Davy collection.*

survey trip to Curtin Township years earlier, Orvis had learned of the extensive clay deposits there and resolved to exploit them as soon as the right opportunity presented itself.

Orviston prospered from the start. Eight more kilns went on line by 1907, boosting total daily production to 60,000 bricks. Needing 4 tons of raw clay and 1.5 tons of coal to produce 1,000 bricks, the plant consumed raw materials voraciously: 240 tons of clay and 90 tons of coal each day. The kilns typically operated seven days a week. Sold under the trade names of Hayes Run (or occasionally Hays Run), Kelso, Curtin, and Orvis, Orviston-made bricks were sought by customers as far away as Puerto Rico and the Philippines. The company had more than 200 employees, many of whom lived in Orviston's fifty or so company-owned houses, "neat brick buildings, with pure mountain water piped to each house," rented for about $6 a month.[29] The houses lacked sewer and electric service, although the town did have electric streetlights, lit by the brickyard's power plant. A church, school, company-owned store, and company-owned boarding house for single employees rounded out the community picture.

Orvis was elected to a ten-year term as Centre County's president judge in 1905 and consequently stepped away from active management of his business interests. Nevertheless, Hayes Run Fire Brick remained locally owned and operated at a time when larger firms from outside the area were swallowing up smaller brick-making operations throughout central and western Pennsylvania. Not until 1922 did Hayes Run sell out to General Refractories.

Orvis was an investor in a second Orviston-based enterprise, the Centre Brick and Clay Company, which lit its first kilns around 1908 and used a blend of flint and other clays to manufacture gray and cream-colored building brick. Its landholdings totaled about 600 acres, half the size of the Hayes Run company's tract; it had only about seventy-five employees, who at maximum production turned out 30,000 bricks daily. The plant was rebuilt after a devastating fire in 1912, but had a tough time competing with producers of higher-grade building brick and closed before General Refractories took over the Hayes Run operation.[30]

Concurrent with that takeover, General Refractories purchased the Pennsylvania Fire Brick Company, headquartered in the town of Beech Creek, 7 miles downstream from Monument. Brick making there had started in 1900, with a narrow-gauge line running up the Allegheny Front to clay mines on the mountaintops. Also in 1922, General Refractories moved its executive offices from West Virginia to Philadelphia and was rechartered as a Pennsylvania corporation. It owned plants in several states and sold to a national market; and thanks in part to its Centre, Clearfield, and Clinton County properties, it ranked second only to Harbison-Walker as the nation's largest manufacturer of refractory brick.[31] General Refractories continued its growth by leasing more than 2,000 acres of Clearfield Bituminous Coal Corporation clay lands near Peale, where two former Pennsylvania Fire Brick clay mines were still active and served by the railroad. Peale No. 1 was located between Peale station and Viaduct, and Peale No. 2 was within the actual Peale town site. To serve a third clay mine, the Pennsylvania Fire Brick Company in 1912 had incorporated a subsidiary, the Forge Run Railroad, to build 7 miles of standard-gauge track linking the mine in Rush Township to a tipple on the New York Central, at a point where Forge Run (later Six Mile Run) emptied into the Moshannon Creek. The track followed the right-of-way of a standard-gauge logging railroad formerly operated by the Ben Jones Lumber Company, which in the early 1890s had a sawmill at the confluence of the two streams. By 1925 clay-mining ceased and the track was removed.[32]

At the former lumber community of Clarence, near Snow Shoe, another brick manufacturer bucked the trend toward centralization in the refractories industry. Brick making began at Clarence in 1910 with the opening of the Snow Shoe Fire Brick Company, served by both the New York Central and the Pennsylvania. In 1924 the plant was purchased by the new J. H. France Refractories, headed by the company's namesake, James H. France of Philipsburg, who had served as general manager for General Refractories' Sandy Ridge plant. The Clarence works was to remain under France family ownership for many years to come.[33]

There were even more brickyards along the former Beech Creek line as it made its way deeper into Clearfield County. The rise of the clay and clay products industry compensated for the decline in forest-products traffic on the New York Central, just as it had on the PRR. The huge Byers-Hopkins mill at Clarence, successor to Hopkins and Weymouth, closed in 1895, its timber reserves exhausted. The Moshannon Lumber Company disbanded its sawmill and narrow-gauge railroad at Gorton about that same time. The last of the big NYC-served logging operations was the Lycoming Timber and Lumber Company. In the 1890s it had a large sawmill a few miles upstream from Orviston, where Eddy Lick Run met Beech Creek in an area so difficult to reach it was devoid of any permanent inhabitants. Lycoming harvested mostly hardwoods and hard pine, rather than the white pine and hemlock sought by most other loggers. The company also differentiated itself by using

a standard-gauge railroad rather than a dinky line to transport its logs
from forest to mill. The railroad's main track followed Eddy Lick Run
northwest before branching multiple times along the boundary between
Centre and Clinton Counties, aggregating about 31 miles of track. The
railroad hauled as much as 15,000 linear feet of logs daily down to the
mill until the timber played out in 1905. Three years later, Lycoming sold
nearly 15,000 acres to the state for $2.50 an acre.[34]

In spite of their value to the New York Central, clay and lumber remained sideshows to King Coal's main act. On the Beech Creek District
main line, the NYC entered the coalfields near the mouth of Panther
Run, in the wilds west of Orviston. The railroad in its early years had a
passing siding and a block limit station there, designated "Panther," and
by 1913 a small mine and tipple were in operation at the site.[35] Coal reserves became more abundant and accessible as rails proceeded 4 miles
farther west to Cato. Local newspapers made reference to the "Cato
coalfields" as early as the 1870s, but how that place derived its name is
unclear, since the territory was still uninhabited when the railroad came
through in the 1880s.

In 1890 the Cato Coal Company opened a drift into an outcropping
of the Lower Kittanning seam on a bluff overlooking the valley carved
by Beech Creek. Coal was brought down by inclined plane to a trackside
tipple. A few company houses were clustered around the tipple, but annual production remained below 10,000 tons into the early 1900s. The
Centre Democrat for April 11, 1911, observed that the operation was about
to expand in a big way: "The Cato Coal Company have decided to build
37 dwelling houses, a large boarding house and a new tipple . . . and the
company will open one or two more drifts." Two years later, the state's
district mine inspector reported that "a town has sprung up, with suitable houses for workmen, and a good, substantial store has been built,
which was greatly needed." The mine converted from mules to electric haulage in 1914, and production topped 100,000 tons the following
year.[36] By then the town was more commonly known as Kato—again,
the passage of years obscures the reason behind the name. However the
village spelled its name, it owed its existence to the railroad, an exemplar
of how all across the rugged Alleghenies, railroads, coal mining, and
community building went hand in hand.

British adventurer and writer Stephen Graham offered a firsthand account of this process in the early 1900s. He was trekking across the Mid-Atlantic states, tracing the path from New York to Chicago taken by thousands of Russian immigrants who were pouring into the country. His travelogue includes a unique glimpse of life along the Beech Creek Railroad.[37] Normally Graham preferred to walk the highways in the fashion of the immigrants, hitching only an occasional wagon ride. But as he made his way west from Scranton through Williamsport to Lock Haven, the rains of early June seemed endless and washed out many of the poorly engineered dirt roads. Starting from Jersey Shore, he decided to walk along the railroad track, at least as far as Snow Shoe and the summit of the Alleghenies, hoping to glimpse the culture and scenery along the way.

"By the time I came to Monument, it was dark but a great glowing kiln looked out into the dark, and there were houses with many lighted windows," he wrote. "I was directed to a workmen's boarding house and spent a night among miners, railway men, and brick-workers. . . . It turned out to be four in a room and two in a bed, sleeping in their clothes. You can imagine the state of sheets and quilts in a bed that brickmakers and soft-coal miners sleep in their clothes." One of the brick-makers told Graham there was plenty of work in Monument if he might be interested, and that two carloads of Italians were expected to arrive the next day for employment in the brickyard and clay mines. After daylight and a "disreputably bad breakfast," he resumed his westward journey.

> The track climbed higher and higher, and I learned that on the morrow, I should reach the top of the Allegheny Mountains—Snow Shoe. It was a fine walk to Orviston under a heavily clouded sky. The mountainsides were all a-leak with springs and trickling streams and cascades. There was the accompanying music of Beech Creek, but this would be swallowed up every now and then in the uproar of an oncoming freight train of coal; the appalling, hammering, affrighting freight train passing within two feet of me, taking my breath away with the thought of its power. . . . Orviston prides itself on its fire-bricks. The whole village is made of them, and the pavement as well, and every brick is stamped "Orviston" and is both a commodity and an advertisement.

Past Orviston, Graham encountered two track workers, both of whom identified themselves as Slovaks recently arrived in America. They struck up a conversation in broken English and agreed to pose for Graham's camera. "I photographed them as they stood—John Kresica and Paul Cipriela. They were unmarried men and living in a boarding house in Orviston."

Onward and upward went the Briton. "I tramped past homeless Panther and got to Cato at nightfall. Cato was a railway station of no pretension: a broken-down shed with no door, no ticket office, no porter. Passengers who wished to take a train had to wave a flag and trust to the eyesight of the engine-driver." Graham slept on a bench inside the station. After midnight he was awakened by a visitor—a German-born immigrant who claimed he had more or less been on the road in America for the past twenty-seven years. He was tramping east along the railroad, and like Graham, sought cover from the chill that nightfall brought to the mountains. At sunrise the two men built a fire, made coffee, and discussed where they might get handouts. Both agreed that local farmers seem unwilling to offer much.

"Say, you'll come to Snow Shoe," the German said, as the two men prepared to go their separate ways. "Don't go past it. You'll get something there. Rich miners." He pointed to a wad of chewing tobacco. "They gave me this at the company store." Graham nodded and set out on the track once more.

> It was pleasant climbing so high and feeling that Snow Shoe would be achieved. I had lived in the rumour of Snow Shoe for two days, and the name had come to correspond to something very beautiful in my mind. The sound of the name is pleasant to the ear. Every now and then, as I hurried along, I asked, 'Snow Shoe, Snow Shoe, what shall I find there? Then one after another eight freight trains, each about a quarter-mile long, came grinding past me, going up to the collieries to take their daily loads of carbon. Somehow I did not object; it was the new America, the America of today careering over the America of 1492 and it had to be accepted.

Alas, Snow Shoe proved to be a disappointment. The town "was the dreariest possible mining settlement," he avowed. "Its inhabitants slouched about its coaly ways and in and out of the saloons. Scarcely anyone could speak English; the mines were worked almost exclusively by Poles and Slovaks."

Places such as Snow Shoe, Monument, and Kato, where brickyards or mines were located adjacent to the main line, required only minimal

investment from the New York Central—a siding or two, perhaps a water tank, and at most a small wood-frame station. In other areas, such
as Grassflat and Winburne, the railroad built branches up to several
miles in length to reach new mines. The NYC's network of branches was
not as extensive as the numerous appendages that had sprung from the
PRR's Moshannon Branch, except in the Philipsburg area. Two spurs of
the Philipsburg Branch were especially productive and long-lived: the
2.1-mile Ophir Branch and the 2.5-mile Coaldale Siding, which despite
its name was in fact a branch line. The Ophir Branch took its name from
Hoyt and Ashman's Ophir mine, located at what originally was the end
of track. The Ophir left the Philipsburg Branch near Hawk Run and
crossed the Moshannon Creek, then headed south through the marshes
before gaining higher ground not far from the coal lands Charles Rowland had hoped to tap with his Moshannon Central. Coaldale Siding was
an Ophir Branch tributary, running parallel to the Moshannon Creek.
The Ophir and Coaldale trackage prior to 1917 served at least a half-
dozen mines belonging to such storied Philipsburg-area coal barons as
J. Edward Horn, John Barnes, David Atherton, James F. Stott, and the
Stratton brothers.[38] Other mines around Philipsburg were served by
lesser branches, including the Derby, Todd, and Hartley.

Near the end of 1900, as coal from dozens of mines along the former
Beech Creek Railroad flowed eastward in a seemingly endless parade
of trains, the New York Central announced plans for a new route to the
coalfields of northern Cambria and southeastern Clearfield counties
that would bypass the Beech Creek District. The former BCR main line
was better engineered than the PRR in making its way onto and through
the Allegheny Plateau, since it came decades later and benefited from
advances in construction technology; but it still included many troublesome grades and curves that resulted in slower train speeds and dimin-
ished the line's capacity to handle more traffic.

The New York Central's bypass of the Beech Creek took less than
eighteen months to complete. A few miles east of Lock Haven, a 1.2-
mile connecting track was installed from the original Beech Creek line
to the PRR's Philadelphia and Erie line. From that junction, the NYC
acquired 45 miles of trackage rights over the P&E to Keating. At Keating, the NYC purchased the PRR's 23-mile Susquehanna and Clearfield

Railroad up to Karthaus and then—in a style reminiscent of the PRR's legalistic terpsichore—incorporated the West Branch Valley Railroad (WBV) to build another 30 miles upriver to Clearfield. West of that community, 6 miles of trackage rights over the Buffalo, Rochester and Pittsburgh and an additional 16 miles of new construction brought the new railroad to a junction with the original Beech Creek Railroad near Curry Run. The NYC grouped these lines into a new organization called the Beech Creek Extension Railroad, kept separate from the corporate structure of the Beech Creek Railroad. Altogether, 102 miles of up, down, and around BCR main line between Browns and Curry Run were replaced by 125 miles of nearly water-level route. Four tunnels and three massive steel-bridge crossings of the serpentine course of the West Branch between Karthaus and Clearfield spoke to the NYC's earnestness in eliminating restrictive curvature.[39]

The Pennsylvania let go of the Susquehanna and Clearfield Railroad because it had not turned out to be the moneymaker its parent had anticipated. The S&C's largest (and practically only) customer, Berwind-White, encountered a host of unanticipated problems in its mines: deadly black damp, constant water seepage, and convoluted rock strata made coal recovery difficult and expensive. The portals were located so high on the ridge top that at least two inclined planes were needed to bring the coal down to the tipples. Total shipments from S&C-served mines fell from about 189,000 tons in 1890 to 57,000 tons in 1899. By then, Berwind-White was preparing to leave, and the Susquehanna and Clearfield was posting annual net operating losses.[40] There were no shippers at all on the Centre County side of the river, an area so remote that it was not even extensively logged until the 1920s, when Adam Gotshall—who had founded Poe Mills on the L&T Railroad many years earlier—established an operation based at Coleman Siding.[41] As already noted, had the PRR extended the S&C on up the Moshannon Creek to a connection with the Tyrone and Clearfield Railway and with the Snow Shoe coal basin as it originally intended, it would have eliminated the operational headaches associated with headlong assaults on the Allegheny Front. But the Pennsylvania, basing its plans partly on C. S. D'Invilliers's report, anticipated the imminent exhaustion of high-grade Lower Freeport coal in the Moshannon Valley and did not care to invest millions of additional dollars in serving coalfields considered past their prime or of inferior quality. So the S&C was deemed of little value as a connector, and it went to the New York Central.

Why the Pennsylvania granted trackage rights over the P&E to the New York Central is more difficult to explain; documentation about the deal is scant. This much is known: the NYC had acquired a right-of-way starting at or near Keating and extending eastward all the way along the West Branch to its own track east of Lock Haven. In fact, it still held some of property in the Lock Haven area as late as the 1950s.[42] The PRR may have reasoned that one way or another its rival was going to run its trains along the river, so income from trackage rights was better than no income at all. More likely, Pennsylvania and New York Central executives reached an understanding involving some kind of quid pro quo. What the PRR received in return for granting trackage rights is a matter for speculation; it would not necessarily have related to the central Pennsylvania coalfields. Sale of the Susquehanna and Clearfield Railroad may well have been part of the same. Regardless of the nature of the agreement, it illustrates how rivalry for raw materials in the late nineteenth century had evolved into at least tacit cooperation between the two roads in the early twentieth.

The New York Central officially opened the WBV—or River Line, as the entire segment between Keating and Clearfield was more commonly known—on July 1, 1902. As intended, the line saw heavy coal traffic. Almost immediately, however, the NYC weighed its value as a link in a projected long-distance routing of fast merchandise freights between Chicago and Philadelphia. The plan bore some similarity to how the Bald Eagle Branch fit into the PRR's strategic thinking at that very same time, except the Pennsylvania had its sights on New England rather than Philadelphia.

In the New York Central's plan, the connecting link west of Clearfield was its Jamestown, Franklin, and Clearfield Railroad subsidiary, opened over its full length in 1909. The JF&C was a costly, highly engineered line featuring massive steel bridges over the Allegheny and Clarion Rivers, three tunnels, and forgiving grades. Part of the NYC's Franklin Division, it connected the main line at Ashtabula, Ohio, on the west with Brookville on the east. Between Brookville and Clearfield,

NYC trains operated with trackage rights over the PRR and BR&P. On the east end of the would-be fast freight line, the Philadelphia and Reading Railway was to handle all trains between Newberry Junction —the interchange yard between the P&R and NYC on the western edge of Williamsport—and Philadelphia. The first train making the 183-mile trek between Ashtabula and Newberry operated on September 26, 1909. It consisted of twenty cars of automobile oil bound for export to Paris, France. At Clearfield it was filled out with sixty cars of coal for the trip down the River Line. In mid-October, William K. Vanderbilt and New York Central president William Carlos Brown personally inspected the line, beginning at Ashtabula and traveling by special train through Clearfield and over the Beech Creek District main line to Jersey Shore.[43]

The New York Central and the Reading planned to introduce through-passenger trains between Chicago and Philadelphia, according to the *Philipsburg Daily Journal;* but east of Clearfield they would operate over the Beech Creek rather than the River Line, since the trackage-rights agreement with the PRR did not provide for passenger service. Five days before the oil train ran, the newspaper predicted in a headline, "Passenger Trains from New York to Chicago to Stop Daily at Munson." The *Journal* went on to report that "towns all along the Beech Creek line are rejoicing that four vestibuled passenger trains each day, running between New York and Chicago" by way of Philadelphia, would give local residents direct access to long-distance travel. "Philipsburg will share in the benefits of this great convenience because of the N.Y.C. branch running to Munson, which will be one of the points at which the trains will stop."

However, the NYC hesitated to fully commit to using the JF&C and the River Line as a primary long-distance route. The railroad inaugurated no through-passenger service, vestibuled or otherwise. It continued to route most Chicago–Philadelphia merchandise trains via Buffalo and over the Fall Brook to Newberry, sending only a pair of regularly scheduled manifest freights via Clearfield: eastbound LS-7 and westbound CP-2. (The symbol "LS" denoted Lake Shore—derived from NYC component Lake Shore, Michigan, and Southern Railway—and "CP" denoted Chicago–Philadelphia.)[44]

The River Line saw plenty of coal trains that originated in former Beech Creek Railroad territory west of Viaduct. Cars loaded in the Philipsburg area, for example, were often taken to Clearfield and then down river to Keating, avoiding the more difficult operating conditions east of Viaduct. Grades were a less critical factor for trains of empty hoppers, so westbound trains over the Beech Creek typically outnumbered eastbounds. The BCR main line also proved to be a useful alternative route whenever there was a derailment or congestion on the River Line or in P&E trackage-rights territory, especially for the tightly scheduled LS-7 and CP-2.

Between 1903 and 1912, the New York Central made extensive infrastructure improvements that showed it still valued the Beech Creek route, even if the River Line got the bulk of the traffic. Passing sidings were lengthened and bridges rebuilt, including several bridges over Beech Creek plus those across Rock Run, Black Moshannon Creek, and Moshannon Creek. Steel replaced wood and iron, as most dramatically exemplified by the massive trestle at Viaduct. Its rebuilding included replacing the fifteen iron spans with steel plate deck-girders fabricated by the American Bridge Company, a job begun June 1, 1902, completed by July 11, 1903, and entailing 26,000 man-hours. Curiously, the project seems not to have included the replacement of the eight original iron towers.[45]

In conjunction with the purchase and construction of the River Line, the New York Central built a new classification yard and locomotive and freight-car shop complex in Clinton County at Oak Grove, soon renamed Avis. The shops replaced smaller, landlocked facilities at nearby Jersey Shore. Avis yard opened in phases beginning in 1902; it ultimately had a capacity of about 5,000 cars and could classify up to 1,100 cars in a twenty-four-hour period.[46]

With Avis yard as a hub to concentrate and dispatch coal trains, and the River Line as an expensive low-grade improvement to expedite the flow of traffic, the New York Central offered an interesting parallel to the Pennsylvania's own initiatives in improving the profile of the Bald Eagle Branch and building Northumberland yard.

The NYC also matched the PRR's innovations in rolling stock and motive power. The New York Central adopted all-steel self-clearing hopper cars in large numbers shortly after their introduction on the PRR. Larger and more powerful class G5 and G6 Consolidation-type locomotives replaced the Beech Creek Railroad's aging motive power. But even the new engines labored mightily to drag heavy coal trains across the Pennsylvania Division's multiple grades and tight curves; use of helper locomotives as pushers and ahead of the road power was common in many locations. Aiming to reduce the need for these helpers, the NYC in 1910 brought in a new one-of-a-kind Mallet compound locomotive for trials. (Mallet locomotives, a type named for their French inventor, had an articulated or hinged frame that enabled them to negotiate sharper curves without derailing. A compound engine uses steam twice, exhausting it first into high-pressure cylinders, and from there into low-pressure cylinders.)

A few railroads had already experimented with Mallets for high-tonnage, low-speed freight service. The New York Central's first was the 170-ton No. 1374, a 2-6-6-2 built by the Schenectady Works of the newly formed (1901) American Locomotive Company (ALCo). It could handle 4,000-ton trains (about seventy loaded hopper cars) at speeds of 10 to 14 miles per hour northward on the Fall Brook District main line without helper engines. The NYC was sufficiently pleased to order twenty-five additional 2-6-6-2s that incorporated improved designs based on 1374's experience. The new arrivals were designated class NE-2a, with the prototype remaining in service as class NE-1a.

The NYC chose not to include the Beech Creek District in 1374's trials, yet some of the new Mallets entered service in the district as soon as they were delivered in 1911. The big engines soon proved their mettle by pulling extraordinarily long trains over the relatively level track of the River Line. But they required helpers to surmount some of the grades on the route through Viaduct and Gorton and Kato, which prevented the railroad from obtaining the operating economies it desired. All the NE-class engines were gone from the Pennsylvania Division by the early 1930s, displaced by more modern 2-8-2 and 4-8-2 types made surplus as the Great Depression reduced traffic on the NYC's main routes.[47]

The Mallets also were the subject of a rare détente between bitter corporate rivals. The Pennsylvania Railroad wanted more powerful engines for main line service, especially for pusher work west of Altoona, and its mechanical engineers received permission to observe 1374's trials. The PRR in 1911 loaned the New York Central a class H8s 2-8-0—a more powerful version of the stalwart H6—to go head to head on the NYC's Pennsylvania Division with an NE class engine and a G6 2-8-0 for the purpose of gathering comparative data.

The PRR had previously borrowed a new Great Northern Railway 2-6-8-0 Mallet for similar trials on parts of its own system, including the Bald Eagle Branch. (The Mallet was en route from the Baldwin Locomotive Works to the Great Northern, a trip that conveniently routed it through Altoona.) The Great Northern engine replaced two H6's in pusher service from Tyrone up to Dix for a week in January 1909. It did not operate on the Clearfield Branch, where the Big Fill's extreme curvature posed a serious obstacle, even for an articulated engine. The Great Northern experiment obviously intrigued the PRR's engineers enough to pursue further trials with the New York Central's Mallets.

Those trials impressed the PRR's engineers in many respects but not enough to convince them to recommend similar locomotives. Measured by coal and water consumption per ton-mile produced, 1374's performance was superior to that of paired 2-8-0s in starting a train and moving it at speeds up to 20 miles per hour. At higher speeds, however, the Consolidations had the advantage. Test data showed that under some conditions, even a single H8s outperformed the Mallet. The PRR continued to show a modest interest in Mallet types; in 1911, it borrowed a Norfolk and Western Railway 0-8-8-0 for trials in pusher service that may have included the Clearfield Branch. However, the railroad never adopted articulateds in widespread numbers and stayed with more conservative designs.[48]

Before and after the advent of the NE class, Viaduct served as a base for helper locomotives. From that location, helpers assisted trains westbound to Van, near Wallaceton in Clearfield County. Eastbound trains received helpers at Viaduct for the ascent to Gillintown, where the grade topped out at 0.97 percent. Curves as sharp as 10 degrees also inhibited train speeds. Engine crews working heavy eastbound tonnage had to take care to avoid stalling their trains while heading upgrade through Peale tunnel.

"All crews had as a regular routine that if you stalled in that tunnel, you never put the air [brakes] on," recalled Percy "Buck" Hemsley, who began his railroad career as a Viaduct-based locomotive fireman in 1925. "You'd shut your stoker off, if you had a stoker, and you'd just let the train drift itself back out. You laid down on the deck, and when you saw daylight, that's when you put the air on." To prevent inhaling deadly coal gases while in the tunnel, crews used rags or gauze kept for that purpose. "You had the seatbox of your engine packed full of gauze, and you'd get a big armful of it, put the hose to it and soak it with water out of the tank [tender], and stick your face down in it and cover it up."[49]

From the apex of the grade at Gillintown, helper engines either returned tender-first to Viaduct or turned on the wye at Gorton first and then ran forward to Viaduct, depending on how soon they were needed to assist another train. Viaduct also served as a base for the area's local-freight motive power and boasted a coal dock, standpipes for watering the locomotives, an enginehouse, and other support facilities, including a bunkhouse and mess hall for crewmen and a half dozen railroad-owned houses.[50]

Helper engines to assist long trains of empty hoppers up the 0.99 percent westbound grade between Monument and Gillintown were added at the towns of Beech Creek or Monument. Even though the topography was not nearly as daunting as that confronting the PRR's Snow Shoe and Clearfield Branches, the NYC tended to run empty trains of prodigious length. Helpers might continue assisting their train beyond Viaduct all the way to Van, cut off at Viaduct to help an eastbound, or cut off at Gorton, turn on the wye, and return light downgrade to Beech Creek or Monument and await the next heavy westbound. A wye in the town of Beech Creek, at the entrance to the brickyard, enabled returning eastbound helpers to change directions for another westbound push.

In contrast to the PRR practice of dispatching most coal trains as non-scheduled extras, the New York Central initially preferred to run coal trains according to written timetable. When traffic required more trains, they ran as additional sections of trains already in the timetable. When fewer trains were needed, scheduled trains were annulled. Operating trains as separate sections figured in what was perhaps the most violent collision to occur in the Beech Creek District. In the predawn hours of February 8, 1900, engineer Oliver Bennett of Williamsport was at the throttle of eastbound train No. 4, waiting in the siding at Gorton with orders to proceed after the passage of the second section of westbound train No. 1. When No. 1 thundered past, Bennett eased his train onto the main track and headed east, assuming the block ahead was clear. It wasn't. The previous westbound train was the first section of No. 4; Bennett and his fireman, Michael Kane of Jersey Shore, had somehow mistaken it for the second section, which ran headlong into No. 1 near Gillintown at a combined speed of more than 40 miles per hour. Kane jumped in the nick of time and suffered minor injuries. Bennett and the engineer and fireman of second No. 1 were trapped in their respective cabs and killed. "In that terrible crash, coming so suddenly upon the crews of both trains," reported the *Centre Democrat*, "the engines were partly telescoped and 22 cars were smashed to smithereens. The wreckage was piled upon the track as high as a house, and under all this were the bodies of the dead."[51]

As the advantages of using the River Line became more apparent, the number of scheduled freight trains operating on the Beech Creek District main line was reduced. The October 25, 1908, edition of the Pennsylvania Division employee timetable listed four scheduled coal trains eastbound through Viaduct and a like number of empty return moves.

A few years later, all westbound freights—mostly empty hopper drags —were being run as unscheduled extras.[52] Operating a core of scheduled eastbounds made it easier for the Jersey Shore–based dispatchers to arrange meets with westbound extras, and gave them more flexibility in deciding when to send more empty hopper trains west over the Beech Creek in cases when eastbound traffic on the River Line was heavy.

Dispatchers also had to make sure passenger trains threaded their way safely and on time through the daily mix of freights. In the early 1900s, two passenger trains made daytime roundtrips between Williamsport and Patton; each train made nearly fifty scheduled station stops in each direction in the 150 miles separating the two towns. One of those stops was Munson, where a thrice-daily train from Philipsburg allowed passengers to make convenient connections. The River Line, traversing thinly populated territory, hosted only a single Clearfield–Keating daily roundtrip.[53] Throughout the Beech Creek District and on the River Line,

the NYC—like the Pennsylvania—limited its passenger-train aspirations to offering basic transportation: no-frills coach, mail, express, and
excursion service that met the needs of a population otherwise nearly
isolated from the outside world.

Notes

1. John F. Stover, *American Railroads*, 2nd ed. (Chicago: University of Chicago
Press, 1997), 133–66; Roger B. Saylor, *The Railroads of Pennsylvania*, Industrial Re-
search Report no. 4 (University Park: Pennsylvania State University College of
Business Administration, 1964), 6.

2. Joseph T. Lambie, *From Mine to Market: The History of Coal Transportation on
the Norfolk and Western Railway* (New York: New York University Press, 1954), 93;
Albert Churella, *The Pennsylvania Railroad: Building an Empire, 1846–1917* (Philadelphia: University of Pennsylvania Press, 2012), 672–73.

3. Commission history and operation: *Report of the Pennsylvania State Railroad
Commission for the Year Ending December 31, 1909* (Harrisburg: State Printer, 1910).

4. Churella, *PRR*, 664

5. Pennsylvania Railroad Company, *Annual Report of the Board of Directors
to the Stockholders* (Philadelphia: PRR, 1892 and 1902). At that time, Lines East
of Pittsburgh and Erie were those owned and operated directly by the Pennsylvania
Railroad. A subsidiary, the Pennsylvania Company, owned and operated the Lines
West system. The PRR reported most data separately for the two units.

6. *Tyrone Herald*, 2 November 1903; Jeffrey Adams, "J. K. Johnston: Industrialist
. . . and Friend," *Tyrone PastTimes* (Fall 2009): 3–9.

7. *Centre Democrat*, 18 July 1907; *Railroad Gazette*, 19 July 1907.

8. *Tyrone Herald*, 13 and 24 July, 21 December 1905; David W. Messer, *Triumph
IV: Harrisburg to Altoona, 1846–2001*. (Baltimore: Barnard, Roberts, 2001), 189.

9. Braman B. Adams, "The Telegraph Block System, Pennsylvania R.R.," in *The
Manual Block System of Signaling on American Railroads* (New York: *Railroad Ga-
zette*, 1901), 7–24; *Tyrone Herald*, 16 September 1907; Pennsylvania Railroad Tyrone
Division Employees Timetable No. 11, 31 May 1909.

10. *Railway Age Gazette*, 17 March 1911; "New Northumberland Yard Interlock-
ing," *Signal Engineer* (November 1911): 399–404; *Centre Democrat*, 13 May 1909.

11. *Railway Age Gazette*, 8 November and 13 December 1912.

12. Robert L. Gunnarson, *The Story of the Northern Central Railway* (Sykesville,
MD: Greenberg Publishing, 1993), 104–5.

13. *Tyrone Herald*, 13 June, 3 October, and 14 November 1912; *Democratic Watchman*, 14 June and 16 August 1912, 28 March 1913.

14. Alvin F. Staufer and Bert Pennypacker, *Pennsy Power* (Medina, OH: Alvin F.
Staufer, 1961), 33–34.

15. John H. White, *The American Railroad Freight Car: From the Wood-Car Era to
the Coming of Steel* (Baltimore: Johns Hopkins University Press, 1995), 580, 596–97;

Richard Burg, "The Berwind-White Coal Mining Co.: When Empty Return to Windber P.R.R.," *Keystone* (Autumn 1986): 8–9.

16. *Report of the Department of Mines for 1915* (Harrisburg: Department of Mines, 1916), 357; *Centre Democrat*, 25 June 1914; Christopher Baer, "1914," in *A General Chronology of the Pennsylvania Railroad Company, Predecessors and Successors, and Its Historical Context*, accessed 8 April 2016, http://www.prrths.com/newprr_files /Hagley/PRR1860.pdf.

17. *Coal Age*, 27 April 1918.

18. *Report of the Department of Mines for 1914* (1915), 319–65.

19. "Bituminous coal tonnage from the Cambria and Clearfield Railway, 1907–1911," two tables, Box 134, Pennsylvania Railroad Co., Executive Department, Record Group 5, Subgroup B, Officeof Vice President Samuel Rea, Hagley Museum and Library.

20. Tyrone and Clearfield Railroad board of directors minutes, 9 February and 23 March 1892, Pennsylvania Railroad Subsidiary Lines, Manuscript Group 286.1426, Pennsylvania State Archives; George A. Scott, *Clearfield Today and Tomorrow: Railroads of the Area* (Clearfield, PA: Progressive Publishing, 1968), 88, 130.

21. *Centre Democrat*, 13 March 1913; *Keystone Gazette*, 14 March 1913; and *Democratic Watchman*, 14 March 1913.

22. *The Mineral Production of Pennsylvania for the Year 1913*, Topographical and Geological Survey of Pennsylvania, Report no. 11 (Harrisburg: Topographic and Geological Survey, 1915), 27, 52–53, 64–65, 89.

23. *Second Industrial Directory of Pennsylvania* (Harrisburg: Department of Labor and Industry, 1916), 931–34.

24. Robert Frazer to A. G. Morris, 11 September 1901, Subgroup A, Box 24, Frazer letterbooks, Bellefonte Central Railroad Records, HCLA 1434, Pennsylvania State University Special Collections Library.

25. *Centre Democrat*, 3 August 1899 and 5 September 1907; Fred Warner, "Centre County Limestone," *Centre County Heritage* 9 (April 1973): 160–63; Myrtle Magargle, "History of Pleasant Gap," *Centre Daily Times*, 28–30 April 1936.

26. Raymond E. Murphy, *The Mineral Industries of Pennsylvania* (Harrisburg: Greater Pennsylvania Council, 1933), 133–39.

27. *Who's Who in Railroading in North America* (New York: Simmons-Boardman, 1930), 115.

28. Heinrich Ries and Henry Leighton, *History of the Clay-Working Industry in the United States* (New York: John Wiley & Sons, 1909), 209–13; Joseph B. Shaw, *Fire Clays of Pennsylvania*, Pennsylvania Geological Survey Fourth Series, no. 10 (Harrisburg: Pennsylvania Topographic and Geologic Survey, 1928), 35–38, 61–62. Jim Davy, *All Company Towns Ain't Bad* (State College, PA: Published by the author, 2011), includes an excellent description of the brick-making process.

29. *Keystone Gazette*, 12 July 1907.

30. *Centre Democrat*, 23 July 1908; *Democratic Watchman* (Bellefonte), 17 May 1912; *Keystone Gazette*, 21 July 1914.

31. *The Progress* (Clearfield), 9 January 1940; Corinne Azen Krause, *Refractories: The Hidden Industry; A History of Refractories in the United States, 1860 to 1985*

(Westerville, OH: American Ceramic Society, 1987), 50–51; *Clay-Worker,* September 1900, 218.

32. Benjamin F. G. Kline Jr., *Pitch Pine and Prop Timber* (Lancaster, PA: Self-published, 1971), 177; Thomas T. Taber III, *Railroads of Pennsylvania, Encyclopedia and Atlas* (Muncy, PA: T. T. Taber III, 1987), 77.

33. *The Progress,* 10 May 1954; Krause, *Refractories,* 197.

34. Kline, *Pitch Pine and Prop Timber,* 175–79; Taber, *Railroads,* 78.

35. E. V. D'Invilliers, *Geology of Centre County* (Harrisburg: Board of Commissioners for the Second Geological Survey, 1884), 8, 96–98.

36. *Keystone Gazette,* 17 January 1890; D'Invilliers, *Geology of Centre County,* 8, 96–98; *Report of the Department of Mines* for 1891, 1913, 1914, and 1915.

37. Stephen Graham, *With Poor Immigrants to America* (New York: Macmillan, 1914), 161–76.

38. S. B. Row and C. U. Hoffer, *Illustrated Souvenir History of Philipsburg* (Williamsport, PA: Grit Publishing, 1909), 29–21, 36.

39. *Thirty-seventh Annual Report of the New York Central and Hudson River Railroad to the Stockholders* (New York: Grand Central Station, 31 December 1905), 7; Scott, *Railroads of the Area,* 64–77.

40. S&C board minutes, 1879–1901, Pennsylvania Railroad and New York Central Railroad Collection, Pennsylvania State University Special Collections Library. The rise and decline of mining activity along the S&C can be traced in *Report of the Bureau of Mines* throughout the 1890s.

41. Kline, *Pitch Pine and Prop Timber,* 189–91, 194.

42. *Lock Haven Express,* 11 November and 13 November 1952.

43. "Recent Improvements on the Pennsylvania Division of the New York Central & Hudson River Railroad," *Railroad Men* (December 1902): 91–94; "Vanderbilt Operations in Pennsylvania," *Railway Age,* 20 March 1908, 376–79; F. N. Houser, "History of the Jamestown and Franklin Railroad," *Headlight* (2nd Quarter 2003): 27–31. The *Headlight* is the magazine of the New York Central System Historical Society.

44. LS-7 and CP-2: New York Central Pennsylvania Division employee timetables, e. g., 24 November 1912; Houser, "Jamestown and Franklin," 37–41.

45. Jeffrey Feldmeier email correspondence with Michael Cegelis of American Bridge Co., 8 and 15 February 2000.

46. "The Improvements of the Pennsylvania Division of the New York Central & Hudson River Railroad," *Railroad Gazette,* 14 March 1902; "Pennsylvania Division Shops of the NYC&HR RR," *Railway and Engineering Review,* 31 May 1902; "A Sketch of Avis and the Avis Shops," *Clinton County Times,* 1 May 1925.

47. "Economies Effected by Mallet Locomotives on the New York Central & Hudson River," *Railway Age Gazette,* 24 November 1911, 1054–57; Alvin F. Staufer and Edward L. May, *New York Central's Later Power, 1910–1968* (Medina, OH: A. F. Staufer, 1981), 46–47; Jeffrey Feldmeier, "The New York Central's Beech Creek District: The Not So Water Level Route," *Headlight* (2nd Quarter 2000): 12–32.

48. Richard D. Adams, "All Roads Lead to the I1s," *Keystone,* part 1 (Spring 2006): 7–17, part 2 (Summer 2006): 31–59.

49. Michael Bezilla and M. Scott Johnson interview with Percy "Buck" Hemsley, Woolrich, PA, 27 March 1993.

50. Jeffrey Feldmeier, "The Covered Bridge That Carried a Water Pipe," *Headlight* (2nd Quarter 2012): 11–15.

51. *Centre Democrat*, 15 February 1900.

52. NYC Pennsylvania Division Employees Timetable, 24 November 1912.

53. For example, NYC Pennsylvania Division Employees Timetable, 25 October 1908.

NINE

The Tide Recedes

Passenger Service

THE PENNSYLVANIA AND THE NEW YORK CENTRAL DID NOT actively compete for the passenger trade in Centre County and the Moshannon Valley; there was little to be gained, financially. Nonetheless, passenger trains had an impact in that area that was far out of proportion to the modest contributions they made to the financial ledgers of their respective companies. Passenger trains helped to build and sustain numerous communities throughout an area than had been mostly wilderness. They reduced the loneliness and geographic isolation of thousands of families who were otherwise cut off from the nation's social and cultural mainstream, and they gave middle-class families the opportunity to travel for pleasure. In the early 1890s, for example, the PRR advertised round-trip excursion tickets from Philipsburg to New Jersey shore points for only $8.35, to the nation's capital for $9.00, and to the Columbian Exposition in Chicago for $14.50. A two-week escorted tour to Watkins Glen, Niagara Falls, the Thousand Islands, and Montreal could be had for $90; the price included rail fare and lodging.

Passenger trains carried mail and—in the era before parcel post and private-sector package carriers—newspapers, packages, perishables, currency and other valuables, and just about anything else that depended on prompt shipment and could be loaded or unloaded by a station agent and his helper.

A decline in the railroads' important role in the nation's transportation network first became evident in branch-line passenger service. That service was most vulnerable to competition from other modes of transport, partly because of a cultural shift that placed a premium on automobile ownership. Most railroads were disinclined to put up a strong resistance to their rubber-tired competitors because they considered branch-line passenger operations unprofitable. So it was in Centre County and the Moshannon Valley: the number of passengers riding trains peaked between 1900 and 1915, and by the end of 1950 the area had no scheduled rail passenger service at all.

In 1890 the Pennsylvania reported carrying 373,000 passengers on Tyrone and Clearfield Railway trains, including excursions.[1] Impressive numbers do not necessarily indicate a golden age of train travel as measured by comfort, convenience, and safety. Almost without exception, riding the area's trains meant Spartan coach-only accommodations. In the early years, until supplanted by steam heat, potbellied coal stoves in each coach kept passengers warm. Open windows furnished the only air conditioning, and light often came from burning acetylene gas. On the whole, the cars were often too hot or too cold, odorous, uncomfortably dirty, and potentially dangerous. Although no passenger fatalities occurred in Centre County after the Miller's Spring trestle collapse of 1878, rail travelers across America were increasingly anxious about safety. The yearly number of collisions, derailments, or other train accidents nationally doubled between 1902 and 1907, to nearly 15,000. Put another way, Americans were ninety times more likely to die in a train wreck in 1907 than to die in a plane crash a century later.[2] Public and legislative voices called for mandatory use of all-steel passenger cars and block signaling, and government oversight to help ensure safe operating practices.

In Pennsylvania, ensuring safer rail travel was among the reasons why the legislature created the State Railroad Commission in 1907. In its first annual report, for 1908, the commission tallied 1,070 railroad-related deaths and 8,203 injuries. Twenty-three of those who lost their lives were passengers, and 736 passengers suffered injuries.[3] Six years later, the railroad commission was merged into the new Pennsylvania Public Service

Commission (PSC), which was given strengthened regulatory authority in safety and other matters over steam railroads, street railways, and such public utilities as gas, electric, and telephone companies.

Stations, too, were targets of public concern for the traveling public. If Centre Country reflected the national mood, then few towns that had ambitions to grow were satisfied with their passenger facilities. From Philipsburg to Bellefonte to Centre Hall, newspapers vented frustration with the small size or disrepair of their communities' stations and the vagrants, vandals, and other unsavory characters who frequented station locales during off-hours. The Bellefonte papers in particular seem to blame Tyrone Division superintendent Samuel Blair for their station's troubles. Instead of congratulating Blair upon his 1903 retirement, the *Keystone Gazette* chose to give him one last broadside. "Superintendent Blair has treated Bellefonte as though it were a flag station, in the face of the fact that it is one of the best-paying stations in his jurisdiction," thundered the paper, which claimed Blair had steadfastly refused to add a baggage room to the station, preferring to build "'hen coops' 20 feet away from the main structure that are not as good as some stable. . . . His prejudice was even so great against Bellefonte that he couldn't bear to see flowers blooming near the station, and turned the flower beds into a hay field."[4]

Most small-town stations throughout the state did in fact leave much to be desired, according to a 1912 report commissioned by the Pennsylvania Department of Internal Affairs.[5] "If there is any modern invention which is specifically designed for the purpose of bringing about a sullen hatred toward a railroad company, it is the average small town station waiting room," the report stated. "The annoyances of a poorly lighted, poorly heated, poorly ventilated waiting room, presided over by an uncivil agent, are known to all." The report singled out inadequate sanitary facilities for particular criticism. "There is probably no more difficult task which confronts a railroad superintendent than the proper policing of toilet rooms or water-closets in connection with passenger stations. . . . It is a delicate and unpleasant subject, but the disgraceful conditions which exist at innumerable stations should bring to our attention sharply that the traveling public expects to see that those conditions are mitigated."

In addition to substandard or unsafe stations and rolling stock, poor service was another target for a verbal hammering by the public. As far back as the 1880s, the PRR's Tyrone and Clearfield Railway was regularly criticized for such annoyances as its trains' plodding schedules, sooty interiors, surly employees, and inconvenient connections with other trains at Tyrone. In a typical attack, the editor of the *Philipsburg Journal* railed that the final train leaving Tyrone for Clearfield one August evening in 1884 had only one coach and one combine, offering not nearly enough seats for the number of tickets sold—despite the fact that extra cars appeared to be available.

> The train was so filled with passengers that a dozen or so were obliged to stand on the open platform, being unable to get inside to the seats for which they had paid the fare demanded. Thus it is that the traveler is forced to submit to the will of this gigantic monopoly. "Pay our price and we will condescend to let you hang on to the railing of the rear platform." . . . Courtesy and good treatment are not known to the men who make up the passenger trains that cross the mountains between Tyrone and Clearfield.[6]

Unsatisfactory stations and inadequate rolling stock could be attributed in part to a lack of financial incentives for railroads to invest in branch line passenger service. The Bellefonte Central's experience illustrated the situation. In 1914, when the BFC carried a record-high 74,086 passengers (including Hunters Park excursionists), passenger revenue accounted for barely 25 percent of the road's total gross income. Bellefonte Central president Robert Frazer, who had long complained that his company's passenger service was a money-loser, ordered a study to determine the exact dollars-and-cents cost. The study found that for the last six months of 1906, each one-way trip between Bellefonte and State College cost $15.00 in out-of-pocket expenses, principally for fuel and labor, while gross passenger revenue per trip averaged only $7.74.[7] The BFC's trains were heavily patronized during the beginning and end of each semester at Penn State, and during academic vacation times; otherwise they carried so few patrons that a single coach more than met the demand. It is reasonable to conclude that the area's Pennsylvania and New York Central passenger operations, which had similar fare structures and higher labor costs, also were incurring deficits.

Mail and express subsidized passenger losses, but not all trains carried mail and express; even those that did could still be unprofitable. The Bellefonte Central had a contract with the post office department to deliver mail to Pine Grove Mills—beyond State College at the very end of the line—twice daily, Monday through Saturday. The railroad gave up the contract in 1909 when it decided to cut back passenger service to a single trip three days a week in order to avoid losses that even a mail subsidy couldn't erase.[8] Reliance on express became more problematic beginning in 1913, with the introduction of parcel post. Sending parcels by mail proved to a great boon to American consumers, especially those living in rural areas, by allowing them to purchase many goods from catalogs and have them shipped at relatively modest expense by mail. Private companies such as Adams Express and American Express had previously handled much of this package traffic and paid the railroads more than the post office did. One result of parcel post was to reduce the income railroads had been receiving for carrying the very same items as express shipments, in effect reducing subsidies for passenger operations.

As already noted, the adverse economics of local passenger service underlay the Pennsylvania Railroad's reluctance to complete the midsection of the Lewisburg and Tyrone Railroad, when all it had to gain was passenger traffic to and from State College. And the Central Railroad of Pennsylvania's increased dependence on passenger revenues after the iron business collapsed ultimately led to that company's dissolution.

The introduction in 1908 of the Ford Model T—the first relatively inexpensive, mass-produced automobile—also tilted the economics against the passenger train. The Model T quickly became a best seller at Keichline's Big Spring Garage in Bellefonte, where the five-passenger version carried a list price of $490, within reach of many middle-class families.[9] In 1911, largely in response to the growing number of Pennsylvanians who owned automobiles, the state legislature passed a bill sponsored by Senator William C. Sproul that established a system of paved highways to be built and maintained exclusively with state funds. In Centre County and the Moshannon Valley, the proposed state road network bore an unmistakable resemblance to the existing railroad map. Among the highways the Sproul Road Act identified for construction were routes from Bellefonte through the Nittany Valley to Lock Haven via Mill Hall (CRR of PA); from Bellefonte to Lewisburg via Centre Hall (L&T); from Pleasant Gap to Tyrone via Lemont and Warriors Mark (L&T); and from Lock Haven to Tyrone via the Bald Eagle Valley (BEV). The valley highway was to have northern extensions from Milesburg via Snow Shoe to Clearfield (B&SS); from Port Matilda to Philipsburg; and from Tyrone to Philipsburg via Sandy Ridge and Osceola Mills (T&C).[10]

The first railroad in the area to make a serious attempt to shed passenger train losses and counter highway competition was the little Bellefonte Central. President Frazer, micromanaging his company from his Philadelphia office, had a well-deserved reputation for pinching pennies; but his abhorrence of waste also made him an innovator, unafraid to upset the status quo if it meant making operations more efficient. Deeming thrice-daily train service between Bellefonte and State College "excessive," he had the BFC temporarily eliminate the lightly patronized pair of midday trains, only to back away from making the cut permanent after it provoked strong opposition from local residents and Penn State officials. Searching for an alternative solution, the BFC early in 1908 acquired secondhand a self-propelled coach that carried its own coal-fired boiler, engine, and four-wheel power truck; seated sixty passengers; and had room left over for baggage, mail, and express.

"My idea is that with such a car employing only two men as a crew, we could make hourly trips between Bellefonte and State College entirely independent of the freight service," Frazer told his general manager, Francis Thomas. "The cost of fuel and wages would be less per mile and we might be able to reduce the fares."[11] Unfortunately, the steam car proved too heavy for the railroad's spindly 55-lb. rail and had trouble negotiating sharp curves. Never having entered scheduled service on the BFC, the car was sold to an Oregon short line in 1911.

After the Bellefonte Central dropped its contract to carry the mail to Pine Grove Mills and introduced thrice weekly service to that community, Frazer was still unhappy with losses his trains posted. In 1915 the railroad purchased a twenty-seat gasoline-powered motor car that, like the steam car, required only a conductor and an engineer. Resembling a small streetcar, it was kept in a shed at State College except when it was shuttling to and from Pine Grove Mills on Tuesdays, Thursdays, and Saturdays, carrying a handful of riders and occasionally pushing or pulling a freight car. The car failed to stop the flow of red ink across the railroad's passenger ledgers. Frazer ordered it taken out of service in 1916, and the BFC ended passenger service to Pine Grove Mills altogether.

In April 1917, America entered the First World War. In July, the Bellefonte Central reduced Bellefonte–State College operations from three round-trips a day to a single mixed train Monday through Saturday. It made the change under the guise of complying with a government request for railroads to reduce coal consumption in the interest of national defense; in truth, it neatly fulfilled Frazer's long-held desire to rein in passenger-train losses. There was no public outcry; putting up with wartime inconveniences was a patriotic duty. Rolling stock consisted of a single combination car—a coach modified to carry baggage, mail, express, and a few passengers. The combine also served as the caboose as the crew worked freight customers on the way to and from State College. Published schedules varied slightly over the years, but adherence to the advertised timetable was irregular at best because of the need to perform freight switching en route. All that riders could realistically expect was for the train to leave the PRR's Bellefonte station in late morning and return in late afternoon.

If the Bellefonte Central had given up on the passenger train, it had not quite conceded the battle for passengers. In October 1916, the railroad began carrying patrons between Bellefonte and State College in a motor car, running over public roads on a schedule coordinated with the arrival and departure of PRR trains in the county seat. Bellefonte-based Emerick Motor Bus Lines, which had just commenced motor bus service using state roads to link Bellefonte with Philipsburg, Lock Haven, and State College, protested to the Public Service Commission, arguing that the railroad had not secured the commission's authorization to introduce motorized service. The commission ruled that the railroad could operate as a motor carrier only if it incorporated a separate subsidiary to handle the service, a decision that led to the creation of the Bellefonte Central Transportation Company in 1917. Bus company owner William Emerick need not have feared. His new buses were far superior in comfort and reliability to the railroad's secondhand seven-passenger touring car, which often fell victim to mechanical troubles. The BFC conceded defeat and dissolved the transportation company in January 1920, after it had lost several thousand dollars.

Ridership aboard the Bellefonte Central's daily mixed train fell from 11,164 in 1918—the first full year of one-train-a-day service—to 4,626 in 1920. The decline occurred despite the growth of State College, which became the county's largest borough by 1920, with 5,603 residents (compared with 3,966 for second-ranked Bellefonte). The railroad exited the excursion business, having disposed of its aged fleet of wooden coaches and parlor cars during the war. By 1930 the mixed train was averaging two paying customers a week. At the same time, the competing bus trade was flourishing. Woolrich-based Johnston Bus Lines had bought out Emerick and was operating several Bellefonte–State College round-trips daily, along with service to more distant population centers. The BFC made one last attempt in 1938 to revive the Penn State community's interest in rail travel. A special train cosponsored by the PRR and using that company's rolling stock took students home for Christmas vacation, but the train failed to attract enough riders to make it an annual event. Competition from private automobiles and buses using the new state highway system was simply too much to overcome.[12]

The Bellefonte Central kept the mixed train in service through the Great Depression and then the Second World War. The railroad saw no need to go through a formal passenger-service abandonment process with state regulators so long as the old combine was fit to haul express and made a serviceable caboose, and few people bothered to buy tickets. Finally, in 1945 the decrepit old car gave up the ghost and had to be replaced by a conventional caboose. The change prompted a petition to the Public Utility Commission (formerly the Public Service Commission) to discontinue carrying passengers. The BFC stated that its mixed train had averaged $18 annually in fares over the previous twelve years, while the short line paid the PRR $576 per year for rights to use the Bellefonte station. Express shipments had once closed the gap between income and expense, but even that business had soured. The railroad planned to truck what little remained of express traffic between Bellefonte and State College. In the absence of public objection, the commission granted the BFC's request, effective March 20, 1946.[13]

The branch-line passenger service offered by the Pennsylvania and the New York Central was buffeted by the same forces with which the little Bellefonte Central struggled. In 1916 the federal government began allotting funds to states for construction of principal highways. Road building stimulated more automobile ownership, which enabled Ford and other manufacturers to ramp up production and take smaller profits on each car. By 1925, 8,500 Model Ts were coming off the assembly line each day and selling for about $250—offering truly independent mobility even to many blue-collar Americans. Across Pennsylvania, political pressure mounted for better roads. Good roads were notably lacking on the rugged Allegheny Plateau. Railroads had provided access to vast tracts on the plateau for the exploitation of mineral and forest resources, but only partially mitigated the area's isolation. Population was so dispersed among many small settlements that people not living near principal arteries of the Pennsylvania or the New York Central were unable to take full advantage of the mobility offered by rail travel.

One answer to the limitations of steam-railroad passenger service was the interurban electric railway. More than 15,000 miles of lightly built interurban lines once crisscrossed the nation's landscape. In Pennsylvania, interurbans often furnished mass transit for commuters, even in rural areas, where patrons were commonly miners and mill workers. Plans for several such rail lines surfaced in both the Nittany and Moshannon Valleys during the zenith of the interurban railroad's popularity—a few years on either side of 1900—but only one materialized. The 13-mile Centre and Clearfield Street Railway, financed by local investors, began service in 1903. It connected Philipsburg with a slew of mining patches as far down the Moshannon Creek as Winburne and carried slightly more than one million riders in its peak year of 1905.[14]

But transportation by steel wheel on steel rail was no match for its rubber-tired competition. Governors John S. Fisher (1927–31) and Gifford Pinchot (in his second term, 1931–35) won widespread popular approval for directing state and federal funds to build or pave many secondary routes that complemented the primary highway network established under the Sproul Act. (Ironically, Fisher was a former general counsel to the New York Central and had served seven years as president of the Beech Creek Railroad.[15]) More and better highways meant fewer

Figure 9.1. Near the end of PRR passenger service on the Snow Shoe Branch in 1929, the daily train from Bellefonte arrives at the Snow Shoe station behind an elderly H6 2-8-0. *Author's collection.*

people chose to ride the rails. Passenger trains serving Centre County's Mountaintop area were the among first to succumb to their rubber-tired competitors. The 1912 timetable showed two Snow Shoe–based passenger round trips over the switchbacks each day. The morning run, which seems to have been a dedicated passenger train, turned at Snow Shoe Intersection (Wingate), where travelers made connections with trains east and west on the Bald Eagle Branch, including trains to Bellefonte. The early afternoon mixed train went all the way into Bellefonte before heading back up the mountain. By 1927, in the face of declining patronage, the Snow Shoe Intersection station was closed and service was cut back to one mixed train originating Monday through Saturday mornings in Bellefonte. The train was usually powered by an elderly H6 2-8-0 pulling a coach and a combine equally long in the tooth, plus a few freight cars.

On Saturday, October 19, 1929, with the approval of the Public Service Commission, the mixed train made its last run. The following Monday, the Philipsburg Motor Bus Company began twice-daily runs between its namesake town and Bellefonte via Snow Shoe. The bus also carried mail that formerly had gone by train between Bellefonte and the Mountaintop settlements as "closed pouch" service; that is, it had been presorted and sealed at the Bellefonte post office. Few tears were shed when rail passenger service over the famed switchback route came to an end after seventy years of service. "The [bus] service will provide a great convenience to the residents of Philipsburg and vicinity who have occasion to visit the county seat," noted the *Centre Democrat* (Bellefonte).[16] True enough, because taking a PRR train from the Moshannon Valley to Bellefonte required a roundabout journey to Tyrone first, then changing to a Bald Eagle Branch train. Bus riders could make bus connections at Philipsburg's Hotel Philips for Clearfield and northward. At Bellefonte's Penn Belle Hotel, connections could be made for buses to State College and to Lock Haven and eastward.

Most car and truck owners soon showed that they and their families preferred neither the bus nor the train. The same week that passenger service ended on the Snow Shoe Branch, Bellefonte's Decker Chevrolet dealership advertised new Chevy coupes for $595, while across town Beatty Motor Company offered a used 1927 Ford roadster for $115 and a 1921 one-ton Ford truck for $30. With motor vehicle ownership becoming commonplace, few people seemed to notice that passenger trains no longer plied the Snow Shoe Branch. Nor did Mountaintop residents show much displeasure when the final New York Central train called at Clarence. Effective February 18, 1933, the NYC abolished trains 33 and 36 that operated over the old Beech Creek main line between Jersey Shore and Clearfield. The two trains were in reality a single round-trip that turned at Clearfield—a final, truncated version of trains that had once spanned the Beech Creek District, operating 149 miles each way between Williamsport and Patton.[17] The demise of trains 33 and 36 also spelled the end of New York Central passenger service in the Moshannon Valley, since they had been serving Philipsburg after the withdrawal of a separate pair of Philipsburg–Munson trains in 1923. The NYC's ally, the Pittsburgh & Susquehanna Railroad, or Alley Popper, had quit the passenger business in 1922.[18]

Passenger service in the Beech Creek District entered its death throes despite the New York Central's efforts to protect it by lowering operating costs. For decades, most passenger trains consisted of a small locomotive (almost always a 4-4-0), a combine, and a coach or two, overseen by a crew of four or five. Around 1930 the railroad replaced this traditional consist with a self-propelled gas-electric motor car—essentially a day coach powered by a gasoline engine connected to an electric transmission, reminiscent of the Bellefonte Central's ill-fated steam car. Built by the Standard Steel Car Company of Hammond, Indiana, the car contained passenger seating and separate compartments for baggage, express, and a railway post office (RPO), and required only an engineer and conductor (and a mail clerk supplied by the post office). The NYC was already operating similar cars elsewhere on the Pennsylvania Division. Railroads nationwide were finding these "doodlebugs," as they were popularly known, to be an economical alternative to locomotive-hauled trains on lightly trafficked branch lines.[19]

So steam gave way to a doodlebug on trains 33 and 36; but financial losses continued, as did the public's exodus from Beech Creek District rails. In its application to abolish the trains, the railroad pointed out that for the fifteen months ending July 31, 1932, it spent $42,800 to operate 33 and 36 and earned gross revenues of only $23,300. On January 3, 1933, the commission gave its approval, noting that not a single individual or organization had come forth to oppose the railroad's request. The ruling noted that "the territory served by this rail line was formerly a fairly prosperous mining country, but the coal mines have practically all been abandoned within the last two years and, while there may be some persons who will be inconvenienced by the withdrawal of the train service, the commission would not be justified in requiring the [railroad] company to continue to bear the loss of approximately $16,000 a year . . . ."[20] The doodlebug made its last run with engineer Link Dennis of Newberry at the throttle and conductor E. C. Sheasley of Jersey Shore punching tickets for a handful of riders. Postal clerk R. L. Struple of Williamsport affixed the Williamsport & Clearfield cancellation for the final times as

Figure 9.2. The New York Central passenger station in Philipsburg was actually a "union" station, hosting not only NYC trains, right, but those of the Pittsburgh and Susquehanna Railroad, or "Alley Popper," left, in this 1912 postcard view. *Author's collection.*

he handled the US mail. There was no interruption in mail deliveries: the post office department established "Star Routes" that used private motor carriers under contract to transport the mail to and from small communities previously served by rail.[21]

The *Clearfield Progress* lamented the disappearance of the NYC's passenger service. "While the discontinuance of the train makes little perceptible difference in the speed of handling the mails," said the newspaper, "it marks another severance of direct communication with small towns, which at one time were important in the life of Clearfield business interests. The discontinuance of a service so long and so efficiently conducted is regretted by the community generally and by all loyal New York Central men particularly."²²

After 1933, the Pennsylvania Railroad was the lone provider of rail passenger service in the Moshannon Valley and all of Centre County. Economic depression and the public's growing predilection for highway transport took their toll on Clearfield Branch trains. As late as 1925, the PRR was still operating three round-trips (two carrying mail and express) Monday through Saturday over the full length of the 52-mile branch between Tyrone and Grampian. The lone Sunday train, departing Tyrone in the morning, was especially anticipated because it carried the big-city Sunday newspapers, which were thrown off in bundles to waiting newsboys all along the route. In the pre-Depression years, the railroad operated occasional specials in addition to the scheduled trains. Advertisements from the summer of 1924 promoted weekend excursions to Atlantic City. Passengers could board at Philipsburg at 9:54 PM Saturday to arrive at their destination at 6 AM Sunday. A 3 PM seashore departure that day returned travelers to the Moshannon Valley around midnight. The round-trip fare: $4.25. For $3.50, one could take a day trip on select Sundays during the summer to Pittsburgh and visit the Phipps Conservatory, Carnegie Institute, and Highland Park Zoo.²³

The Great Depression wiped out the excursion business, along with two of the three Tyrone–Grampian round-trips. By contrast, Clearfield-based Fullington Auto Bus Company provided six trips each way daily from Clearfield via Philipsburg to Tyrone, using the new two-lane state highway that passed through Emigh's Gap, practically within shouting distance of the Big Fill. At Tyrone, travelers could make easy connections to numerous main line trains. "When you have a train to catch in Tyrone, take the bus," exhorted a Fullington newspaper ad. "And when you get off the train at Tyrone, you never have to wait long for a bus over the mountain. By bus—it's the way to travel these days."²⁴

Buses and autos also vanquished the PRR's short-haul passenger business up and down the Moshannon Valley. In the early 1900s, when the coal business was robust, local trains ran west from Philipsburg all the way to McCartney at the end of the Moshannon Branch, and east to Morrisdale at the end of the Philipsburg Branch. One pair of trains even carried a railway post office car offering same-day pickup and delivery for communities along the two branches. The PRR trains, together with their NYC counterparts and the C&C trolley line, helped to make Philipsburg the Moshannon Valley's commercial hub.

The 1920 census indicated Philipsburg borough had 3,900 residents—nearly equal to Bellefonte and more than four times the number who had lived in the borough at the dawn of the coal age in 1870. As the years passed, highway competition grew keener. The C&C trolley ceased operations in 1927, while the PRR steadily reduced the number of local trains. At the outset of the Great Depression, service consisted of a "rail-motor train" (the Pennsylvania's term for a doodlebug) that made two daily round-trips up the Moshannon Branch from Osceola Mills to Madera. There was no longer any service on the Philipsburg Branch to Morrisdale. The Public Service Commission allowed the Pennsylvania to discontinue Osceola–Madera service effective July 8, 1932, after the railroad showed it was losing nearly $50 in out-of-pocket costs each day the doodlebug ran. A bus line was already serving most towns along the Moshannon Branch, and Star Route contractors assured continuation of mail service.[25]

Philipsburg was left with a single Clearfield Branch passenger and express train, which after 1931 originated in Altoona instead of Tyrone, a move designed to make railway postal service more efficient, since Altoona was a major mail-sorting center. The railroad downgraded the train to mixed status and gave it a few cars of perishable and high-priority less-than-carload freight. Passenger rolling stock normally consisted of a single combination car that offered coach seating and compartments for a railway post office, express, and baggage. The train reached Philipsburg in midmorning, then headed north to Clearfield. Turning at the end of the line at Grampian, the southbound train arrived in Philipsburg in late afternoon. Motive power was usually a G5 4-6-0, the Pennsylvania's quintessential branch-line passenger engine, or a squat H9s 2-8-0 freight engine that was at ease with the 35-miles-per-hour speed limit applicable over much of the line.

Because of the large volume of mail handled by Clearfield Branch railway post office, a doodlebug with its closet-like space for a clerk and a few sacks of mail was not practical.[26] Nationwide, the number of trains carrying railway post offices declined markedly through the 1930s from a peak of around 4,100 in the mid-1920s, but RPOs still frequently made the difference between a profitable and an unprofitable passenger train. The decline in the number of railway post offices was not entirely coincidental with a decline in the number of passenger trains operated by the Pennsylvania Railroad. Passenger-train miles on the PRR peaked at 6.1 billion in 1929, then shrank by nearly one-third over the next ten years. Yet the railroad estimated in 1940 that 26 percent of its passenger-train miles still failed to earn the $1.00 per train-mile deemed sufficient to meet out-of-pocket operating costs.[27] The Clearfield Branch was included in the 26 percent despite the presence of a robust railway mail business. The PRR implemented such economy measures as discontinuing Sunday service (although the trains did run on holidays, even Christmas, Monday through Saturday) and cutting back the northern terminus from Grampian to Curwensville beginning in 1939. Nevertheless, with the trains usually carrying no more than six or seven riders, and parallel bus service available all along the route, there seemed to be no point in continuing the service. The Public Service Commission agreed. On October 20, 1942, trains 791 (north) and 790 (south) made their final runs. Ninety years of scheduled railroad passenger travel in the Moshannon Valley came to an end without a fanfare of bands and speeches, almost without notice of any kind.[28]

A similar story of retrenchment played out in the valleys of southwestern Centre County. On the Fairbrook Branch—the west end of the old Lewisburg and Tyrone Railroad—the Pennsylvania had operated mixed trains to Scotia since the line opened in 1881. Service lasted until April 28, 1923, when the track between Fairbrook and Scotia was formally abandoned following the exhaustion of commercial timberlands and the depopulation of Scotia until it was a ghost town.[29] After that date, twice-daily mixed trains from Tyrone turned on the wye near the Fairbrook station, and the 5-mile branch up to Scotia was torn out. In addition to passengers, outbound trains carried grain, fruit, and other farm products in season along with a few carloads of sand, clay, or timber that originated around Warriors Mark in Huntingdon County. Inbound traffic consisted mostly of livestock feed and farm machinery. Freight volume was so slim that the railroad closed the Warriors Mark station, leaving the agent at Pennsylvania Furnace to handle all business along the branch.

The PRR cut back service to a single daily round-trip effective June 22, 1925, asserting that many of its shippers were turning to newly built highways.[30] One train a day meant that residents of such hamlets as Fairbrook, Pennsylvania Furnace, Marengo, and Warriors Mark could no longer make a trip into Tyrone and return home later in the day. The number of riders using the mixed train fell from 5,519 in 1924 to 2,647 in 1926.

The Pennsylvania was far more concerned about freight traffic, which generated about $52,000 in operating income in 1926 compared with only $634 from passenger fares. Overall, the railroad said it suffered a net loss of nearly $25,000 on Fairbrook Branch operations that year. Early in 1927 the PRR filed applications with the Public Service Commission and the Interstate Commerce Commission to abandon the track beyond Stover, 2.2 miles east of Tyrone and the site of a large limestone quarry. The few remaining freight customers beyond Stover voiced opposition, but no one spoke on behalf of the passenger trade. Eventually, the ICC secured a compromise that allowed the Bellefonte Central Railroad to buy the track up for abandonment and build a 5-mile connection linking Fairbrook and State College. The BFC had stated in its proposal to the ICC that it had no interest in running passenger trains. The PRR's mixed train made its final run out to Fairbrook on October 28, 1928, just before the line went dormant until its new owner could assume operations.[31]

On the east end of the L&T—the Bellefonte Branch—the passenger station at Bellefonte was the busiest on the Tyrone Division after the Tyrone main line station. In the early 1900s, when there was still twice-daily service to and from Snow Shoe and when the Bellefonte Central was making three round-trips to State College, the Bellefonte station hosted twenty arrivals and departures Monday through Saturday. On Sundays, activity was limited to the arrival and departure of a pair of Bald Eagle Branch trains, east and west, that carried the mail. Sunday freight operations and passenger excursions had long been the norm. However, the PRR did not introduce scheduled Sunday passenger service on the Bald Eagle Branch until 1899 (and on the Clearfield Branch in 1900) in large measure to move the mails more efficiently. In fact, when the first mail arrived on a Sunday train, the Bellefonte postmaster announced that he would open the post office for a short time each Sunday evening so patrons could collect their mail.[32]

On many rural branch lines in Pennsylvania, dairy traffic—in addition to mail and express—subsidized passenger train operations. Such was the case on the Bellefonte Branch, which had long hosted two trains that ran the length of the branch, Monday through Saturday. Each morning one originated at Bellefonte and the other at Sunbury, and each made a round-trip over the line. On October 1, 1928, in response to declining patronage, the PRR discontinued the train originating at Bellefonte. Operation of the Sunbury-based train was extended to Sundays, but otherwise it maintained its previous schedule.[33] Most often powered by a class E 4-4-2 or a class G5 4-6-0, this train arrived in Bellefonte around 9 AM and typically consisted of a railway post office–baggage combine, a coach, and except on Sundays, one or two milk cars bound to or from the town's Sheffield Farms dairy. Sheffield Farms was one the largest dairies serving metropolitan New York and owned or controlled more than a hundred dairies in Pennsylvania, New Jersey, and Vermont. It had a major presence in Centre County, operating PRR-served plants in Bellefonte; at Centre Hall, Spring Mills, and Coburn, all on the Bellefonte Branch; and at Howard on the Bald Eagle Branch. Sheffield's distinctive rectangular tank cars, painted dark gray with yellow lettering, were glass-lined and insulated but not refrigerated, hence the need to get the product to market on expedited, passenger-train schedules. At Lemont, the eastbound train picked up butter from the Penn State creamery, as well as cream shipped the old-fashioned way—in ten-gallon cans that were loaded into the baggage portion of the combine. The college also shipped bottled milk packed in ice in boxes. More milk or other perishables might be gathered further along the line, then handed off to a fast train at Sunbury and forwarded east via Harrisburg.[34]

Occasionally the trains included extra coaches. In the 1920s, with the Bellefonte Central for all practical purposes out of the passenger business, the start of Christmas vacation at Penn State meant a hundred or more students boarded at Lemont, destined for either Sunbury or Bellefonte and connections to other trains. At such times, "every student had a trunk to check," recalled Lemont station agent J. Andrew Dale. "The freight had to be kept in boxcars [at the station] to free the warehouse for trunks, and it was piled full, with a lot on the platform. We had a special baggage master from Sunbury to check all the baggage, because tickets were sold all over and on other roads like the DL&W, D&H, LV, and P&R."[35] Additional coaches also were warranted at the start of deer season in the fall. In 1924, more than 200 "red-capped and brown-coated" hunters took the Saturday afternoon train from Bellefonte to such isolated locales as Ingleby and Cherry Run, from which they made their way to mountain cabins in preparation for the opening of the season on Monday.[36]

The PRR sometimes put on an extra coach to accommodate throngs of travelers headed to the annual Grange Fair encampment in late August at Centre Hall. Prior to the First World War, before automobile ownership was common, the railroad operated special trains to the fair. Special trains also carried Penn State students and other fans to away football games when the Nittany Lions faced major rivals. The last such trains operated in 1929, with two departures from Lemont: on November 8 for Philadelphia and the University of Pennsylvania game, and on November 27 for the annual Thanksgiving Day clash with the University of Pittsburgh.[37]

At some point, the PRR used a gas-electric car—a doodlebug—over the Bellefonte Branch, but details are scarce. According to the *Centre Democrat* for June 4, 1925, "a trial trip was made over the Lewisburg railroad using the new gasoline-propelled train. . . . The train replaced the regular passenger train due here [Bellefonte] at 4:35 P M. It is understood the railroad company is considering the replacement of a coal-driven train over this branch in the near future with this latest mode of travel." Even the most powerful of the PRR's gas-electrics, twin-engine cars introduced in 1927, were designed to pull no more than one other car— specifically, an ordinary coach—on level track.[38] Thus it is unlikely a doodlebug plied the Bellefonte Branch regularly after 1928, when the PRR reduced passenger service to a single daily round-trip and there was always a railway post office car or milk car in the consist.

Mail and milk ultimately deserted the rails. The postal service discontinued the Sunbury–Bellefonte RPO on April 25, 1948, turning first to a private motor carrier and then in July 1949 introducing a highway post office (HPO). Clerks on the red-white-and-blue HPO, a kind of modified bus, sorted mail by hand as they made their way east and west on state route 45, paralleling the railroad most of the way.[39] About that same time, in a general restructuring of its operations, Sheffield Farms dropped many of its rail transportation contracts and even closed some of its dairies, although it continued to operate the Bellefonte plant using trucks to haul milk until 1956.[40] Absent milk and mail, passenger service on the Bellefonte Branch was doomed. Effective January 3, 1949, a mixed train departed Sunbury on Mondays, Wednesdays, and Fridays, laid over in Bellefonte, and made the return trip eastbound on Tuesdays, Thursdays, and Saturdays. On Sundays a round-trip was made. Passenger service ceased entirely with the departure of train 586 from Bellefonte on Saturday, September 24, 1949. (Train 587 was the westbound counterpart the previous day.)[41] The service had become so insignificant that its discontinuance did not merit notice by the local newspapers.

The situation was equally grim on the Bald Eagle Branch, where trains 510 and 511 were the last survivors, operating as the nameless remnants of the once-plush *Pennsylvania-Lehigh Express*. The *Penn-Lehigh* had made its inaugural run on Sunday, June 25, 1916, on a route between Phillipsburg, New Jersey, and Pittsburgh via Bethlehem, Sunbury, and Williamsport, a distance of nearly 400 miles. The train used the Lehigh Valley Railroad between Phillipsburg and Mount Carmel; otherwise it was on PRR rails. The two railroads established the train at least in part upon the recommendation of the Pennsylvania's president, Samuel Rea, who in turn was responding to a suggestion from Bethlehem Steel Corporation executives. Early in 1916, Bethlehem had purchased the Steelton-based Pennsylvania Steel Company. The latter had extensive holdings of coal reserves in western Pennsylvania that necessitated an increased amount of travel for Bethlehem executives, yet there was no through-car service from corporate headquarters in Bethlehem to the western part of the state, including to the nation's steel-making capital of Pittsburgh. The *Penn-Lehigh* filled that need. Train 510 departed Pittsburgh at 9 A M daily, arrived in Bellefonte—its only stop between Tyrone and Lock Haven—in the early afternoon, and reached Phillipsburg around 9 P M. Train 511 left Easton at 8:30 A M, made a late-afternoon stop in Bellefonte, and terminated at Pittsburgh by 8 P M. Motive power normally was one of the PRR's high-stepping E-class 4-4-2s, and the consist included a combination baggage-coach car, a coach or two, parlor car, and dining car. The cars were of steel construction, distinguishing the *Penn-Lehigh* as the first passenger train in scheduled operation over what were then Tyrone Division rails using all-steel equipment. (The Pennsylvania led the railroad industry in introducing all-steel passenger cars in main line service in 1907.) Besides catering to business travelers, the *Penn-Lehigh* became popular with Pittsburgh's social elite, who used the train to gain convenient access to the "wilds" of central Pennsylvania for outdoor leisure activities. The trains had been running only a week when the *Democratic Watchman* (Bellefonte) identified a passenger on No. 511 as Harry K. Thaw. A household name after a sensational jury trial in 1906, the flamboyant Thaw had been acquitted by reason of insanity in the killing of prominent architect Stanford White. The *Watchman* reported Thaw was returning to his Pittsburgh home from a fishing vacation on Pine Creek in Lycoming County.[42] As a first-class train, the *Penn-Lehigh* was a fitting addition to the newly upgraded Bald Eagle Branch, with its improved alignment, a new block-signal system, and heavy-duty track structure that equaled main line standards.

The *Penn-Lehigh* was one of three passenger trains running in each direction over the Bald Eagle Branch during the 1920s. The other two were accommodations that made as many as twenty-five stops in the 54 miles between Tyrone and Lock Haven and whose ridership was bolstered by children traveling to or from the public schools.[43] At the outset of the 1930s, rail passenger service face twin challenges: fewer people could afford to travel during the hard times of the Depression, and a greater share of the people who did travel preferred the highways. Thanks to government-initiated public works programs, 70 percent of Pennsylvania's highways were paved by 1935. Good roads boosted car and truck ownership, which grew from 1.8 million in 1935 to 2.2 million in 1940.[44] It was in the context of those difficult years that the PRR abolished one of the Bald Eagle Branch accommodations and added scheduled stops for the *Penn-Lehigh* at Howard and Snow Shoe Intersection, and flag stops at Unionville and Port Matilda. Then, effective January 9, 1932, the Lehigh Valley Railroad substituted a lowly doodlebug on its portion of the train's route and eliminated the *Penn-Lehigh* banner. The Pennsylvania renamed its portion of the train the *Pittsburgh Wilkes-Barre Ex-*

press and ran it between those two cities, using the PRR's Wilkes-Barre
Branch east of Sunbury. The train's schedule through the Bald Eagle
Valley stayed about the same, and the dining and parlor car amenities remained. In 1935, the PRR rerouted its Pittsburgh–Wilkes-Barre through-
car service via Harrisburg. Trains 510 and 511, stripped of their names,
continued on the Bald Eagle Valley route as daylight, coach-only runs
between Pittsburgh and Sunbury.

Mere shadows of the old *Penn-Lehigh*, 510 and 511 became the only
passenger trains on the Bald Eagle Branch after May 24, 1942, when the
PRR discontinued a Sunbury–Altoona accommodation. Not only were
passenger trains disappearing; so were many agency stations up and
down the valley. Stations were abandoned at Beech Creek and Curtin by
1935, Howard and Eagleville no later than 1938, Vail by 1939, and Julian,
Unionville, and Milesburg by 1940.[45] The PRR progressively truncated
the routes of 510 and 511 until by the late 1940s, they ran only between
Altoona and Williamsport and no longer carried through cars for connecting trains. By contrast, those Centre County and Moshannon Valley
travelers who wished to take the bus enjoyed the convenience of direct
Greyhound Lines service to Harrisburg or Pittsburgh, or Edwards Motor Transit Company service to New York City, Buffalo, and Cleveland.
Many of the buses traveled on the new Lakes-to-Sea Highway, US route
322, intended to link Cleveland and Atlantic City. It bisected Centre
County northeast to southwest, running from Clearfield through Philipsburg and State College to Lewistown. A second main highway, US
route 220, ran the length of the Bald Eagle Valley, paralleling the railroad. Both arteries were built with a combination of state and federal
funds.

For the dwindling number of patrons who still chose to ride trains
510 and 511, a single coach was more than adequate. That car was usually accompanied by a railway post office-express combine, a baggage or
baggage-express combine, and a milk car or two for dairies in Howard
or Mill Hall. Heading the train was one of the railroad's signature K4s
4-6-2 passenger engines or the older and lesser-known class K2s. The
eastbound train arrived in Bellefonte in the late morning, and switched
out the RPO combine for loading and unloading mail and express. Westbound 511 arrived in the early evening and picked up the car for return

to Altoona. After the eastern terminus was moved from Williamsport to Lock Haven, 511 made the Bellefonte stop early in the afternoon.

In 1949 the PRR petitioned to discontinue the trains, telling the Public Utilities Commission that in the previous twelve months, they cost $82,000 to operate against gross revenues of only $30,000. Their six-man crews often outnumbered the passengers, and their milk and express traffic was plummeting. Among the few opponents of the petition was the Bellefonte Chamber of Commerce, which told the PUC the loss of the trains would "seriously impair" business in the town. That argument was short on specifics, however, and chamber president Tedd Colgrove found himself in an awkward position when he admitted to a newspaper reporter that he had never ridden the trains.[46]

The petition was approved, and trains 510 and 511 made their last runs on Wednesday, August 23, 1950. They drew attention beyond the usual impersonal termination notice in local papers and appropriately so, for those last runs represented the end of regularly scheduled railroad passenger service in the branch line empires of central Pennsylvania. In contrast to all the previous train-offs in the county, the PRR itself recognized the significance of the occasion: Middle Division superintendent P. M. Roeper and a few lesser officials rode the train that day. So did a group of PRR retirees that included 86-year old Mike Ammerman of Tyrone, who for thirty years had worked as a locomotive engineer, often at the throttle of the *Penn-Lehigh* since the train's 1916 inauguration. "I loved this train," he remarked with obvious sadness during a visit to the engine cab at the Bellefonte stop. "The Bald Eagle Valley will never be the same without her." Two *Lock Haven Express* reporters boarded the westbound run, planning to disembark at Bellefonte, take a cab to the State College Air Depot, and then fly back to Lock Haven on All American Airways DC-3 Flight 704. The story they subsequently filed highlighted the dramatic change in transportation modes. All American (soon to become Allegheny Airlines) had been serving the State College area with three daily flights east and west since June 1949.

Altogether about thirty passengers rode the coach as train 511 departed Lock Haven for the last time. A few more entrained en route, mostly older folks out for a last ride, some with children for whom the day marked their very first—and possibly last—train ride. It was an

ordinary work day for 511's crew—engineer Jim Conner and fireman
Albert Hymes of Altoona, conductor Fred Miller of Lock Haven, train-
man Harry Stuck of Northumberland, baggage master Merrill Fisher
of Sunbury, and postal clerk Earl Clouser of Altoona—and for K4s 5379
on the head end. At Howard, postmaster Don Gardner ceremonially
tossed the final mail pouch aboard the RPO. At the train's Bellefonte
stop, Mayor Charles Herr, Postmaster James Dennehy and a small crowd
of other townspeople turned out to say farewell. "People are going to
miss this train," remarked one of the onlookers. He was only half right.
They would miss seeing it on its daily trek through the valley, or hearing it chuffing and whistling its way in and out of the county seat; but
judging by all the years of anemic ticket sales, almost no one would miss
riding it. The train left Bellefonte at approximately 1:45 PM, heading for
Altoona and a passage into history.[47]

The absence of scheduled service did not spell the extinction of passenger trains in Centre County or the Moshannon Valley. Railroads
continued to run occasional specials, such as the three excursions over
Bellefonte Central rails to Penn State home football games. The first, on
October 19, 1955, consisted of two trains, one running an hour behind the
other and both using PRR power and rolling stock. The trains originated
in Pittsburgh and carried University of Pittsburgh alumni, students, the
marching band, and other fans—more than a thousand people in all.
On October 14, 1961, a twenty-car train came to State College from the
US Military Academy at West Point with 1,100 cadets and officers for
the Army game. That train originated in New York Central territory
and used cars from that road. After another Pitt special ran in 1964, the
Bellefonte Central determined that its track, a casualty of deferred maintenance, could no longer safely accommodate passenger equipment.

Long before such deterioration set in, safety was uppermost in the
operation of a passenger train over the BFC that had nothing to do with
Penn State football. On Saturday May 9, 1953, President Dwight "Ike"
Eisenhower and his wife, Mamie, rode the rails to State College to visit
brother Milton Eisenhower and his family. Milton, president of Penn
State since 1950, had invited Ike and Mamie for a weekend retreat, a
brief respite from the unrelenting glare of the public spotlight that had
shone on them since Ike's inauguration the previous January.

Unlike President Benjamin Harrison's visit to the Moshannon Valley in 1890, the 1953 POTUS (president of the United States) train attracted relatively few trackside spectators, much to the relief of the Secret Service. Although the presidential visit had been rumored publicly for a couple of weeks, the White House and Penn State refused to confirm it. No official business was to be conducted in State College, and large crowds would compromise the trip's purpose as a private getaway. The presidential party intended to fly from Washington until bad weather late in the week forced a change in plans. On Friday, May 8, Bellefonte Central officials received word that the Eisenhowers would be coming the next day on a PRR-originated train that would use their railroad on its last leg into State College. They were directed to keep the news in strict confidence as they worked with security officials to implement preparations.

The seven-car special departed the nation's capital in the wee hours of Saturday morning, carrying the Eisenhowers, a few staff members, a security detail, railroad officials, and a small band of journalists. It headed north over PRR rails to Harrisburg, then west over the Middle Division main line to Tyrone, where it swung on to the Bald Eagle Branch, three shiny Tuscan red E8 diesel locomotives in the lead. Running on the branch in advance of the POTUS special was the Altoona wreck train, complete with derrick, just in case something went awry. The special arrived in Bellefonte about 6:15 AM in a faint drizzle that painted a featureless, silvery dawn. After stopping only long enough to pick up some Bellefonte Central crewmen, the train resumed its journey, reaching State College less than an hour later. It reversed direction on the wye past the golf course and backed into the station, with the presidential car—the heavily armored former Pullman *Ferdinand Magellan*—now in the lead. About 400 people had gathered to greet the train, which was quickly cordoned off by a bevy of police as Milton and Helen Eisenhower arrived to have breakfast aboard the *Magellan* with their guests. An hour or so later, both presidents and their wives emerged amid waves and smiles but made no public utterances. They headed for campus and relaxation, and for the most part the town and gown communities understood and respected their privacy. Ike flew back to Washington the next day, while Mamie stayed behind to take part in some campus social events before departing by automobile on Tuesday. The POTUS train, meanwhile, had gone to Altoona later Saturday for servicing and to stand by just in case it might be needed for the return trip. In later years, sitting presidents would often come to Penn State and Centre County—Eisenhower again, Richard Nixon, Jimmy Carter, Bill Clinton, George Bush (father and son) and more—but never again by train.[48]

In the sixty-three years between the Harrison and the Eisenhower visits, at least one other US president traveled through Centre County on the rails, although his train did not pause. Early in the afternoon of Saturday, October 23, 1948, Harry S Truman journeyed west over the Bald Eagle Branch on his way from Wilkes-Barre to Pittsburgh as part of the famous whistle-stop campaign that ultimately won him reelection. Truman had intended to fly but poor weather grounded his plane. Despite a stop in Lock Haven, where the president addressed a hastily gathered crowd from the observation platform of the *Ferdinand Magellan*, few Centre Countians knew his train was coming; it rolled through the valley largely unnoticed.[49]

Truman's trip earns more than a footnote in local history because it highlighted the important role played by the Bald Eagle Branch as an alternative when other routes or plans proved unworkable. The PRR turned to the Bald Eagle Branch most frequently when derailments temporarily closed the Middle Division main line. One of the earliest detours of major proportions came in April 1892, starting on a day when blasting some rock for a new railroad alignment in Huntingdon County went awry and destroyed a bridge carrying the existing track over the Little Juniata River. A Milesburg correspondent for the *Democratic Watchman* seemed in awe of the subsequent parade of trains through Centre County.

> The Bald Eagle Valley saw sights to which it has never before been treated. Scarce had the rumbling of one train died away when another followed in its wake, and long lines of smoke hung in sinuous waves over the track. Monster engines, steaming and puffing to keep up with the smoke trails of the ones ahead of them, rattled through the valley. A deep, long whistle, a clang of a bell, and a black streak on the landscape told the flight of some limited passenger or express train, and the shrill toot of a Jack [a class H1 2-8-0] would resound along the route and a monstrous line of freight cars would be seen swinging into a siding to make clear track for the passing of a more speedy follower.[50]

Detours brought to Centre County such luxurious passenger trains as the PRR's New York–Chicago flagship, the *Broadway Limited,* and the equally distinguished New York–St. Louis *Spirit of St. Louis,* along with the only slightly less elegant *Liberty Limited, Red Arrow, Cincinnati Limited, General, Penn Texas, Gotham Limited,* and numerous other trains that comprised the Pennsylvania's grand east–west fleet. (As late as 1950, more than thirty passenger trains passed through Altoona on the main line each day.) None of the detouring trains made passenger stops in the county, of course, and most passed through the Bald Eagle Valley in the dead of night, in keeping with their normally nocturnal schedules through central Pennsylvania.

A handful of passenger trains also ventured onto other PRR lines in the county following the end of scheduled service. After losing its mixed train in 1949, the Bellefonte Branch saw two public excursions. The first ran on Sunday, June 19, 1955, originating in Williamsport and sponsored by that community's Exchange Club, a service organization. Two diesel locomotives pulling eight coaches filled with some 350 passengers (including two registered nurses toting first-aid gear) traveled a circular route: south along Susquehanna River, west at Montandon over the Bellefonte Branch to Milesburg, then home via the Bald Eagle Branch and Lock Haven. The train made an early-afternoon stop at Centre Hall, where most of the passengers availed themselves of a turkey dinner prepared by the ladies of the local Grange. It stopped again at Pleasant Gap to allow patrons a tour of the state fish hatchery, and yet again at Bellefonte, to enable the locomotives to change ends and push the train out to the switch at Milesburg, thus positioning themselves on the front of the train for the homeward dash.[51]

The second excursion was part of Bellefonte's sesquicentennial celebration and operated on Sunday, August 5, 1956. It took the same route as the Exchange Club train but in the opposite direction, traveling east from Bellefonte to Montandon. The consist included a single 1,600-horsepower diesel locomotive and seven coaches carrying 530 riders, more than 100 of them children. Hundreds of spectators turned out in each of the ten communities where the train stopped to allow the sesquicentennial committee to present local dignitaries with symbolic keys to Bellefonte borough. High school bands added festive music at Centre Hall and Sunbury.[52] On the Bellefonte Branch, the excursion was reminiscent of the special trains that shuttled hundreds of passengers between Spring Mills and Lewisburg in the summer of 1877, celebrating the Lewisburg, Centre, and Spruce Creek Railroad's triumphant entry into Centre County.

The sesquicentennial special also evidenced a shift in many Centre Countians' attitudes toward train travel. In 1949, no one wanted to ride the train between Bellefonte and Sunbury; in 1956, it sold out. Riding the rails was transitioning from something to be avoided or even scorned, to an event guaranteed to evoke fond remembrance of the good old days, worthy of sharing with the grandchildren. More proof of this change came on the Clearfield Branch in 1957. On Sunday, October 13, the PRR ran a sold-out "Autumn Glory Special" from Altoona to Grampian and return sponsored by the Altoona Kiwanis Club, with ticket sales benefiting the organization's summer camp for underprivileged boys. Before the trip, club president Byron McDowell, a Curwensville native, told a reporter that "for many children of our area, it will be an ideal opportunity for the first train ride of their lives."[53]

Two Sundays later, the PRR operated an excursion on behalf of the Philipsburg Elks Club. The diesel-powered train originated at Philipsburg and also boarded passengers at Osceola and Sandy Ridge, their ultimate destination being the Horseshoe Curve west of Altoona. Elks members sold 1,277 tickets, which when combined with the 300 or so children under age 5 who rode for free, accounted for just about every seat in every car and then some. All sandwiches, soft drinks, and ice cream novelties offered by the Elks sold out long before the train's evening return to the Moshannon Valley. "A good many of the passengers on the train were young people, and many of them were actually experiencing their very first train ride," reported *The Progress* (Clearfield). "There were some young people just a few years out of high school, and there were older folks, too. But young or old, all seemed to have a good time."[54] Net proceeds from the trip went to the Elks college scholarship fund. The public had a final chance to ride the old T&C on June 18, 1963, when central Pennsylvania coal operators sponsored a "Save Our Daddy's Job Express." The train was part of a grassroots lobbying campaign against proposed state legislation that would tighten strip-mining regulations and thereby raise production costs, threatening the competitive position

of Pennsylvania-mined coal. The twenty-car special carrying 971 passengers—mostly wives and children of coal company employees—left
Clearfield at 7:30 AM for Harrisburg. There they shopped, paying for
their purchases with company-provided two-dollar bills to demonstrate
the economic impact of the coal industry's workforce.[55] The express consisted entirely of Pullmans—many of ancient vintage, running out their
last miles—because the PRR no longer had coaches to spare for special
moves. "The Pennsy was so strapped for extra coaches on a daily basis
that there simply were no extra coaches," recalled a veteran manager. "By
that I mean no extra coaches to put on the regular trains, and no extra
coaches for special trains."[56]

Another passenger train of sorts traveled regularly over the Clearfield
Branch but did not use Pennsylvania Railroad cars or offer public accommodations. Making its first appearance on the eve of the Second World
War, the James E. Strates Shows became the featured attraction at the
annual Clearfield County Fair, held in the county seat in late July or
early August. Billing itself as "America's Biggest and Brightest Midway,"
Strates was the nation's largest carnival on rails. It consisted of forty
to fifty Strates-owned rail cars, including four sleepers for some of the
300 employees who traveled with the show, a diner, and the Strates family's private car. Prior to its Clearfield engagement, the Strates Shows
usually played in upstate New York and arrived in Clearfield from the
north. After the week-long engagement at Clearfield, the train headed
south over the PRR's Clearfield Branch. Watching its Sunday afternoon
passage through Philipsburg, Osceola, and over the mountain to Tyrone
was an annual ritual for hundreds of local residents.[57]

The Strates Shows is not known to have traveled the Beech Creek District main line between Clearfield and Jersey Shore. In fact, Beech Creek
rails seem to have been totally bereft of passenger trains since the last
doodlebug run in 1933, with the exception of a few "office car specials"
carrying railroad officials on inspection trips. The most notable of those
was an eleven-car train operated for newly installed New York Central
president William White and other top executives that went from Jersey
Shore via Orviston, Viaduct, and Munson to Clearfield on October 10,
1952, then on to Youngstown, Ohio. So far as is known, it made no stops
in Centre County or the Moshannon Valley.[58]

In contrast to the widespread excitement and anticipation elicited by the passage of the Strates train or the public excursions, one kind of passenger special often evoked sadness and dread: the troop trains that carried several generations of young men off to military service. Operation of the first known dedicated troop train in Centre County occurred in 1877, in connection with the call-up of the Fifth Regiment, Pennsylvania National Guard, to help quell violence in Pittsburgh stemming from the great railroad strike that year. (The regiment got as far as Altoona before strikers blocked all westbound train service.)[59]

The first troop train to be dispatched during wartime was in response to the outbreak of the Spanish-American War in 1898. Again the Fifth Regiment was at the forefront. The train started on the PRR at Clearfield on April 27, carrying about sixty soldiers from Company E and their equipment. More troops from Company E were picked up at various locations along the line as the train made its way south on the Clearfield Branch toward a rendezvous at Tyrone with a similar train coming west on the Bald Eagle Branch with Company B from the Bellefonte area. "All along the route to Tyrone, people were out," noted a contemporary newspaper account. "Philipsburg sent at least 1,000 down to the station to say good-bye.... Osceola was out in great numbers with a band, and a sea of faces greeted the train at Sandy Ridge." The troops went to a camp at Mount Gretna in Lebanon County for mobilization but saw no combat in the three-month conflict with Spain.[60]

Another troop train figured prominently in an emotional departure from Bellefonte in 1916. Troop L and other components of the Pennsylvania National Guard's First Cavalry Regiment were called to federal service in the American Southwest. Hostilities with Mexican revolutionaries seemed imminent, and General John J. Pershing was assembling an army along the border. On Sunday, June 25, at 6 AM, Captain Hugh Laird Curtin marched some 120 Troop L men from the armory to the PRR station, where an estimated 1,200 people had gathered to see them off for El Paso, Texas. Their train, already carrying Troop K from Lock Haven, arrived at 6:45 AM. "It took a few minutes to shift the cars, and during that time the final goodbyes were said," observed the *Democratic Watchman*. "Women sobbed, and even some soldiers broke down and shed tears, but they were not tears of regret or cowardice but merely the surcharge of an overwrought heart for the sorrow of others." The train pulled out to the sound of the Runville Band playing the "Star-Spangled Banner."[61] Troop L's farewell set the stage for other heartfelt departures at the station during the First and Second World Wars and the Korean conflict. Similar scenes played out countless times in communities large and small nationwide.

Notes

1. Pennsylvania Railroad Company, *Annual Report of the Board of Directors to the Stockholders* (Philadelphia: PRR, 1890).

2. Mark Aldrich, "Public Relations and Technology: The 'Standard Railroad of the World' and the Crisis in Railroad Safety, 1897–1916," *Pennsylvania History* 74 (Winter 2007): 74–104.

3. *Pennsylvania State Railroad Commission Report for the Year Ending December 31, 1908* (Harrisburg: State Printer, 1909), 101–103.

4. *Keystone Gazette*, 25 September 1903.

5. *Annual Report of the Bureau of Railways, Pennsylvania Department of Internal Affairs, for the Year Ending June 30, 1912* (Harrisburg: State Printer, 1913), xv–xxii.

6. *Philipsburg Journal*, 27 August 1884.

7. BFC *Annual Report*, 1906, Bellefonte Central Railroad Records, HCLA 1434, Pennsylvania State University Special Collections Library.

8. BFC *Annual Report*, 1909.

9. Middle class income: *MeasuringWorth*.com, "Seven Ways to Compute the Relative Value of a U.S. Dollar Amount—1774 to Present," accessed May 14, 2015, http://www.measuringworth.com/uscompare. Household income in the Mid-Atlantic states: *New York Times*, 23 November 1903.

10. *Keystone Gazette*, 7 June 1912; George Swetnam, *Pennsylvania Transportation*, Pennsylvania History Studies no. 7, 2nd ed. (Gettysburg: Pennsylvania Historical Association, 1968), 84–87.

11. Frazer to Thomas, 16 October 1907, Subgroup A, Box 24, Frazer letterbooks, Bellefonte Central Railroad Records, HCLA 1434, Pennsylvania State University Special Collections Library.

12. Michael Bezilla and Jack Rudnicki, *Rails to Penn State: The Story of the Bellefonte Central* (Mechanicsburg, PA: Stackpole Books, 2007), 102–8, 117–21, 168–73, 301; *Centre Democrat* (Bellefonte), 1 May 1930, 18 December 1952.

13. Application Docket No. 65672, *Decisions of the Public Utility Commission*, vol. 24 (Harrisburg: Public Utility Commission, 1946), 556–60.

14. Richard C. Albert, *Trolleys from the Mines: Street Railways of Centre, Clearfield, Indiana, and Jefferson Counties* (Forty Fort, PA: Harold E. Cox, 1980), 75–88.

15. Biographical note in Governor John S. Fisher Collection, Manuscript Group 72, Indiana University of Pennsylvania Special Collections and Archives.

16. *Centre Democrat*, 6 January 1927 and quote from 24 October 1929.

17. *Clearfield Progress*, 18 February 1933.

18. Richard D. Adams, *The Alley Popper* (Victor, NY: R. D. Adams, 1980), 42, 46; NYC Pennsylvania Division employees timetable no. 33, 26 April 1931; *Clearfield Progress*, 21 April 1931.

19. *New York Central Lines Magazine*, April 1927; John L. Kay and Fred MacDonald, *Mail Travel Guide: Updated Agent and RPO Routes Listed by State and Railroad with Route Numbers, Directions, and Maps*. (N.p.: Mobile Post Office Society, published serially, 1991–99, 2003–07), 735–90.

20. "Application of New York Central Railroad," Docket No. 24825, *Decisions of the Public Service Commission* (Harrisburg: The Commission, 1933), 706–707; *Clearfield Progress*, 10 January 1933.

21. Undated clipping from the *Lock Haven Express*.

22. *Clearfield Progress*, 18 February 1933.

23. Excursion ads appeared in the *Clearfield Progress* in the summer and fall of 1924.

24. *Clearfield Progress*, 30 August 1930.

25. "Application of the Pennsylvania Railroad Company," Docket No. 24374, *Decisions of the Public Service Commission*, 556–60.

26. John R. Borchert, "History of the RPO System of the Pennsylvania Railroad," *Keystone* (Winter 1999): 16–28, 35–62. Train consists can be gleaned from the *Clearfield Progress*, 1 March 1921, 30 August 1930, 3 October 1942.

27. Gregory L. Thompson, "How Cost Ignorance Derailed the Pennsylvania Railroad's Efforts to Save Its Passenger Service, 1929–61," *Journal of Transport History* 16 (September 1995): 134–57; PRR *Annual Report* for 1929.

28. *Clearfield Progress*, 16 September 1941, 3 October and 23 October 1942.

29. *Keystone Gazette*, 27 April 1923; Christopher T. Baer, "Pennsylvania Railroad Company Discontinuance/Last Runs of Passenger Service," 30 June 2003, accessed 24 July 2016, http://www.prrths.com/newprr_files/Hagley/PRR%20PASS%20Jun%2005.pdf.

30. *Democratic Watchman*, 19 June 1925.

31. "Application of the Pennsylvania Railroad Company," ICC Finance Docket No. 6152, PSC Application Docket No. 16018–27, 30 September 1927.

32. *Bellefonte Republican*, 27 July 1899 and *Keystone Gazette*, 31 May 1900.

33. *Democratic Watchman*, 20 April and 5 October 1928; *Centre Reporter* (Centre Hall), 27 September 1928.

34. *Centre Reporter*, 2 July 1925; Bert Pennypacker, "Mooving Milk By Rail," *Milepost* (March 2005): 16–24; J. Andrew Dale, *Memories of the L&T Branch of the Penn Railroad at Lemont and Related Stations—the Way It Was, 1915 to 1928* (N.p.: Privately printed, 1980).

35. Dale, *Memories of the L&T Branch*, 3.

36. *Democratic Watchman*, 5 December 1924.

37. *Democratic Watchman*, 26 July 1929; *Penn State Collegian*, 29 October and 15 November 1929.

38. Alvin F. Staufer, *Pennsy Power III 1847–1968* (Medina, OH: Alvin F. Staufer, 1993), 278–79.

39. *Keystone Gazette*, 6 January and 14 July 1949; *Centre Daily Times*, 28 July 1949; Kay and MacDonald, *RPO Routes*, 735–790.

40. *Keystone Gazette*, 6 January 1949; *Bellefonte Industries: Western Maryland Dairy Company*, Pennsylvania Historic Resource Series (Bellefonte, PA: Bellefonte Borough, 2006).

41. Baer, "Last Runs."

42. *Democratic Watchman*, 9 June and 30 June 1916; *Tyrone Herald*, 22 June and 18 December 1916; Christopher Baer, "1916," in *A General Chronology of the Pennsylvania Railroad Company, Predecessors and Successors, and Its Historical Context*, accessed 8 April 2016, http://www.prrths.com/newprr_files/Hagley/PRR1860.pdf.

43. PRR Tyrone Division employees timetable no. 4, 29 April 1928; *Democratic Watchman*, 26 July 1929.

44. Swetnam, *Pennsylvania Transportation*, 88–89.

45. *Centre Democrat*, 5 March 1942. The evolution of trains 510 and 511 can be found in the various PRR public timetables for the years under discussion. Station abandonment dates are listed on the PRR valuation map for the Bald Eagle Branch.

46. *Centre Democrat*, 10 August 1950.

47. Both quotes from the *Lock Haven Express*, 24 August 1950. See also *Williamsport Gazette*, 22 August 1950; *Keystone Gazette*, 16 June 1949 and 24 August 1950; *Tyrone Daily Herald*, 23 August 1950.

48. Bezilla and Rudnicki, *Bellefonte Central*, 216–21, 228–30, 243–45.

49. *Keystone Gazette*, 28 October 1948.

50. *Democratic Watchman*, 15 April 1892.

51. *Keystone Gazette*, 22 June 1955.

52. *Centre Democrat*, 19 July and 2 August 1956; *Centre Daily Times* (State College), 4 and 6 August 1956.

53. *The Progress* (Clearfield), 11 October 1957.

54. *The Progress*, 28 October 1957.

55. *The Progress*, 19 June 1963.

56. William D. Volkmer, "The Pennsy Fantrip That Thawed the Freeze," *Keystone* (Spring 2009): 45–54.

57. In its coverage of the county fair each year, *The Progress* highlighted the Strates train.

58. *The Progress*, 10 October 1952.

59. *Democratic Watchman*, 27 July and 3 August 1877; *Philipsburg Journal*, 28 July and 4 August 1877.

60. *Clearfield Republican* quoted in *The Progress*, 3 February 1984.

61. *Democratic Watchman*, 30 June 1916; *Keystone Gazette*, 30 June 1916.

TEN

The Pennsylvania and the New York Central on the Plateau, 1918–68

AS THEIR PASSENGER AND MAIL BUSINESS DECLINED, RAILROADS were less frequently in the public eye and began to fade in the consciousness of most residents of the Allegheny Plateau. The Pennsylvania and the New York Central remained essential components of the region's economy but seldom regarded each other as competitors. They had years earlier staked out their respective fiefdoms in regard to Clearfield District coal and other natural resources, and had learned to coexist. By the end of the First World War, motor carriers were emerging as the chief threat to the rail freight business, at the very time that the heavy hand of government regulation was limiting the ability of all railroads to deal effectively with competing modes of transport.

Coal remained the principal source of income for the PRR and NYC on the plateau, although tonnage no longer matched the boom times of the late nineteenth and early twentieth centuries. Coal companies in central Pennsylvania faced rising production costs and shrinking profit margins, as most of the easily accessible reserves were exhausted. In West Virginia, coal companies worked seams as thick as 8 feet, paid nonunion wages, and paid the same rates as their central Pennsylvania competitors to ship their product by rail to East Coast ports. In 1927 Pennsylvania lost its long-held status as the nation's top bituminous-producing state, mining 131 million tons to West Virginia's 152 million tons.[1]

Coal companies nationwide saw many of their longtime customers turn to other fuels. Bituminous coal as a home-heating fuel began to decline in many urban areas after 1918, bumped aside by oil, natural gas, and electricity. Many industrial consumers likewise changed to those alternative fuels. Ocean vessels, for instance, whose bunkers once brimmed with the famous Moshannon coal, were converting to diesel engines or oil-fired steam turbines. Railroads themselves were once the nation's leading consumers of coal, but by the 1950s they had largely replaced coal-fired steam locomotives with diesel-electric power. In 1928, the Pennsylvania Railroad was America's largest buyer of bituminous coal, purchasing for its own use 3.5 percent of the country's total output.[2] Thirty years later, it did not have a single steam locomotive in service.

In the late nineteenth century, coal operators had flirted with overproduction, but by the end of the First World War—with abundant deposits being exploited in West Virginia, Kentucky, and other states, and some sectors of the market stagnant or shrinking—oversupply was a constant problem. It depressed prices, and marginally competitive mines worked only sporadically as they reacted to short-term fluctuations in demand. The pages of *Saward's Coal Trade Journal* during the 1920s overflowed with such headlines as "Bituminous Market Stagnant," "Retail Prices Low," "Demand Only Moderate," and "Prices Soft."

Despite these unfavorable trends, coal mining was far from extinct in the Moshannon Valley and surrounding area. A 1928 survey by state geologists indicated that 308 million tons of coal had been mined in Clearfield County; 2.2 billion tons of recoverable reserves remained in the ground. That total included 600 million tons in the upper Moshannon Valley, overlain by the existing thicket of PRR branch lines. In Centre County, mining had removed 79 million tons; 275 millions tons of recoverable reserves remained.[3] Coal operators who were able to weather the Great Depression benefited handsomely from record demand created by the Second World War and the new markets that emerged afterward. Foreign demand for US-mined coal soared in the 1950s as many nations revitalized their war-flattened economies. On the domestic front, a seemingly insatiable appetite for cheap electricity led to the construction of large, coal-fired generating stations and an interconnected distribution grid. Long esteemed as a superior steam coal, bituminous from central Pennsylvania was eagerly sought by power plants throughout the mid-Atlantic region. Surface mines, with much lower production costs, supplanted underground mines and helped bolster central Pennsylvania coal's position in the marketplace. In 1955 Clearfield and Centre County mines combined yielded about 7.2 million tons of coal, nearly a million tons above their 1925 output. The increase was made even more noteworthy by a drop in statewide bituminous production from 135 to 85 million tons during that same thirty-year span.[4]

Although oversupply was no longer a serious issue amid the postwar boom, the PRR and the NYC did not share fully in coal's rebound. By midcentury, trucks were carrying a significant amount of coal that had formerly gone by rail, primarily where hauls were short or customers preferred smaller shipments. Even greater was the loss of high-value merchandise and less-than-carload shipments that were staples of the boxcar trade. Trucks offered faster and more dependable delivery than the railroads, and often at less cost. They could haul shipments directly from factory or warehouse to the customer's door, eliminating the expensive and time-consuming transloading and drayage often required between railroad freight station or side track and consignee. State and federal policies also favored trucks, which traveled on publicly financed highways and operated under fewer regulatory constraints than railroads. Over the long term, the loss of boxcar traffic meant an erosion of the most profitable freight traffic for railroads on the Allegheny Plateau, and more reliance than ever on hauling coal and other less remunerative bulk materials.

There was still plenty of coal left on the Mountaintop when the Pennsylvania Railroad abandoned the Snow Shoe Branch in 1959, in its hundredth year of operation. The Lehigh Valley Coal Company, historically the branch's largest shipper, had ceased mining coal many years earlier. The company's demise actually began in the early 1900s, when President Theodore Roosevelt vowed to limit the monopolistic power and perceived abuses of big business. Railroads—among the nation's largest corporations—quickly became a target for his administration's wrath. The Roosevelt-backed Hepburn Act of 1906 prohibited rail carriers from hauling any freight they produced or mined (other than lumber) except for their own use—in effect requiring railroads to divest themselves of most of their coal properties. Beginning in 1911, the Lehigh Valley Railroad reluctantly moved to put some legal distance between itself and its LVCC affiliate, which still controlled 45,000 acres of bituminous lands around Snow Shoe. However, the federal government demanded a clean break in ownership. In 1924, following protracted litigation, the Lehigh Valley Railroad completely divorced itself of all direct and indirect holdings in the Lehigh Valley Coal Company, including both bituminous and anthracite properties.[5]

The reorganized coal company retained the Lehigh Valley name and continued to be the dominant shipper on the Snow Shoe Branch. But where there were six LVCC mines at the outset of the decade, the new owners scaled back the smaller operations until one mine, Lehigh Valley No. 22, accounted for nearly all production. In 1926, No. 22 sent more than 357,000 tons over PRR rails, most or all from the Lower Kittanning seam. Lesser Mountaintop coal operators, with their higher per-ton production costs, did not fare so well. Only two other coal companies loaded on the Snow Shoe Branch in 1926; their combined shipments barely reached 20,000 tons. The disappearance of the small mines triggered an exodus of miners and their families from the Mountaintop area. Between 1920 and 1930, Snow Shoe Township suffered the largest population loss of any township or borough in Centre County, plummeting from 2,895 residents to 2,050. Snow Shoe borough's population fell from 650 to 520.[6]

So far as the PRR's Tyrone Division was concerned, the Snow Shoe Branch became a backwater. Locomotives based at the Snow Shoe terminal consisted of several weary H6-class 2-8-0s, suffering from prolonged deferred maintenance. Their decrepit condition came to light in a public way in March 1926, when an inspector from the Interstate Commerce Commission paid a surprise visit to the terminal. "The inspector examined each of the three [freight] engines," according to the *Centre Democrat* (Bellefonte), "and placed his condemnation marks upon them, ordering them out of service until necessary repairs could be made. He then swooped down on the passenger engine operating on the branch and 'padlocked' that iron horse for similar reasons."[7] The PRR had to cease all Snow Shoe–based operations until replacement power could be

brought in from Tyrone the next day. Not long afterward, the Pennsylvania pulled the old H6's off the branch and placed operations in charge
of newer (circa 1913) and more powerful H9s locomotives.[8]

The embarrassed Pennsylvania soon launched a series of cutbacks
designed to reduce operating costs on the Snow Shore Branch. It closed
the Snow Shoe engine terminal at the end of 1926 and transferred the
motive power and train crews' home base to Bellefonte. On most days
a single daily mixed freight departed the county seat around 5 AM to
work the mines and the J. H. France Refractories Company, whose daily
output reached 50,000 bricks, mostly under the "France" and "Lehigh"
brands. A boxcar of miscellaneous freight might be set out at the Snow
Shoe station, where the passenger coach also was spotted while the locomotive worked the mine runs. (As noted in the previous chapter, passenger service ended in 1929.) The block operator at NO tower at Snow
Shoe Intersection controlled all trains on the branch until the tower was
closed in the early 1930s in another cost-cutting measure. Control then
shifted to the operator at Miles tower at Milesburg. The PRR closed its
Snow Shoe yard and scale house effective August 1, 1930, upon the retirement of veteran yardmaster W. Grant Kesling, who had started with
the railroad in 1883 as a brakeman on the branch. An agent continued
to staff the Snow Shoe station during daylight hours, but weighing and
classifying cars was moved to Bellefonte's Sunnyside yard.[9]

With the onset of the Great Depression in 1929, the demand for coal
nationwide slumped to levels not seen since the mid-1890s. Lehigh Valley mine No. 22 closed in 1934, its place taken by a scaled-down No. 28
nearby. Smaller deep mines under local ownership came and went during those troubled years. The only long-lived PRR shipper in addition to
the Lehigh operation was the Cherry Run Coal Mining Company. Its
Cherry Run mine gave the railroad about 46,000 tons of black diamonds
in 1936, its best year.

Cherry Run was significant in another historical context: it was the
first of the Mountaintop mines to ship significant quantities of coal
to market by truck. In 1932, a new twenty-two-wheel, 25-ton capacity
"monster truck" was placed in service by owner/operator Lloyd Wingert
of DuBois to haul coal from Cherry Run to American Lime and Stone
plants in the Bellefonte area. Use of such a ponderous vehicle would

have been impossible had it not been for the newly opened state road down the mountain from Snow Shoe. In 1938, fully one-third of Cherry Run's 48,000-ton output went to market by motor carrier, mostly to lime plants, house-coal dealers, and commercial establishments in Belle-fonte, State College, Lock Haven, and other nearby towns. The railroad, with its higher costs, was at a disadvantage in offering competitive pric-ing for such short hauls, particularly where the truckers could use fast, direct routing over newly paved public highways. Trucks accounted for 1.4 percent of the state's bituminous coal movements in 1932, and 11.2 percent by 1947.[10]

As the Great Depression tightened its grip, the PRR considered quit-ting the Snow Shoe area completely and yielding remaining traffic to trucks and the New York Central. The two railroads connected at J. H. France property in Clarence, so having the NYC serve former PRR cus-tomers would pose no serious customer hardships, while allowing the Pennsylvania to abandon 17 miles of the Snow Shoe Branch. Any Moun-taintop traffic originating on the New York Central and destined for locations on the Pennsylvania Railroad could be forwarded through the existing interchange with the PRR's Bald Eagle Branch at Bald Eagle Junction, near Mill Hall.[11] Whether the Pennsylvania actually delivered its proposal to the NYC is unknown, but the issue became irrelevant with America's entry into the Second World War in December 1941. The Mountaintop area was an important source of coal for the war effort. During years when gasoline and rubber tires were strictly rationed, the Pennsylvania regained ground previously lost to the truckers and even managed to retain the advantage for a few years in the postwar era.

Lehigh Valley Coal Mining Company closed No. 28 in 1942 and ex-ited Centre County after more than a half-century as one of the area's largest bituminous producers and railroad shippers. The company still controlled vast coal reserves and parceled out mineral rights to other operators. Cavalier Coal Company, for instance, mined nearly 160,000 tons from two former LV properties in 1945 and shipped it all by rail. Cavalier eschewed deep mines in favor of surface mining, using drag-lines and other excavators to strip away overburden to get at the coal. Surface or strip-mining, a novelty in central Pennsylvania prior to the Second World War, was generally less costly and labor-intensive than

deep mining and helped to reinvigorate the coal industry on the Allegheny Plateau. By 1947 strip mines accounted for about half the 1.5 million
tons of coal produced in Centre County.[12] The largest Mountaintop
strip-mine operator by 1948, R. S. Carlin Inc., another beneficiary of
Lehigh Valley Coal properties, shipped virtually its entire 187,000-ton
output by rail.

Unusually a single train from Bellefonte was sufficient to handle the
business, although the train's normal departure time was changed from
near sunrise to around midnight, five and sometimes six nights a week.
Working the branch overnight enabled the train to use one of the locomotives that spent the afternoon and evening shifting Bellefonte-area
industries and to make sure the J. H. France brickyard would receive
empty boxcars in time for loading by day-shift employees. Power was
usually a hand-fired H9s 2-8-0, with a four-wheel cabin car (PRR's term
for caboose) bringing up the rear. One H9s could handle no more than
the equivalent of seventeen empty 55-ton hopper cars up the grade. Getting the train up to Snow Shoe meant hand-shoveling 10 tons or more
of coal, taxing both the fireman's physical stamina and the engine's coal
supply to near-exhaustion. "By the time you got up there, you were always digging in the back of the tender," recalled fireman Paul Anderson.[13] After the train left Bellefonte, there was no place for the locomotive to take coal until it reached one of the mining company tipples
beyond Snow Shoe. Running out of fuel along the way was unthinkable
(and perhaps cause for unpaid time off), so the engine crew had to take
great care in maintaining an efficient fire.

Transiting the switchbacks was a challenge in itself. The switchbacks
consisted of four spring switches and four tail tracks, with the tails following the curve of the mountainside so that it was impossible to send
hand or lantern signals between the cabin car and the locomotive. When
the ascending train pulled by the first spring switch onto the tail track,
it stopped momentarily to allow the brakeman to drop from the cabin
and align the switch for a reverse move. The engineman then signaled
with three short pulls of the whistle cord and started shoving cabin-first
up the next incline. If the engineman failed to pull his train completely
past the first switch, he would inadvertently start the train back down
the hill, in which case the brakeman had to dump the air and set hand

brakes. With luck, the engineman quickly realized his mistake, more whistle signals would follow, and the train would again pull forward, this time making sure to clear the switch. On the second and fourth switches the train backed onto to the tail track, so the head brakeman, stationed on the locomotive, dropped off to throw the switches and keep in visual contact with the engineman. No wrecks are known to have occurred from this complex maneuvering, but it made for some interesting nights on the mountain. Summers were even more adventurous for the brakemen, who in the darkness had to be careful not to step onto a rattlesnake nestled against a rail still radiating daytime warmth.

The local's first stop on the Mountaintop was the Snow Shoe station, where the daytime agent left the nightly switching orders, specifying empty and loaded cars that were to be picked up or set out at the J. H. France brickyard and the coal tipples. The engine then took water and turned on the wye west of the station so that it could work the mine branches running tender-first but face forward to pull loaded coal cars back to Snow Shoe. The first customer to be served was the brickyard. The train then made the rounds of the various mine branches, taking on coal at one of the tipples. The PRR had ceased making serious investments in maintaining its Snow Shoe–area trackage when abandonment seemed a possibility in the 1930s. Conditions deteriorated until speed restrictions of 10 miles per hour became the norm; on most days the sun had risen by the time the crew finally assembled all the outbound cars at Snow Shoe for the return to Bellefonte.[14]

In January 1949, the first diesel locomotive made its appearance on the branch, and by 1951 internal combustion in the form of 1,000-horsepower Baldwin switchers had vanquished steam. About that same time, the Snow Shoe local began operating on an as-needed basis, usually two or three times a week, as a result of a sharp decline in the number of carloadings.[15] Mountaintop coal companies maintained a relatively steady level of production, but most local customers now preferred truck delivery. Costs were competitive, arrival times more dependable, and unloading simpler. The Bellefonte-area lime plants, the new (1950) West Penn Power Company electric generating station at Milesburg, and paper mills at Lock Haven and Tyrone all received most of their coal by motor carrier. The Mountaintop's largest coal producer, R. S. Carlin, shipped nearly

178,000 tons in 1952, and for the first time, not a single ton went by rail. Indeed, the PRR's Snow Shoe local hauled only 43,000 tons of coal that year, while six times that much went by truck.

By 1958 the train from Bellefonte was operating over the Snow Shoe Branch only two or three times a month, generating gross annual income that barely topped $40,000. The Interstate Commerce Commission approved the PRR's request to abandon the branch effective May 1, 1959, although a few trains ran after that date to help shippers fulfill contractual obligations. The Snow Shoe local made its last revenue run on October 18, 1959.[16] The New York Central assumed the Pennsylvania's share of traffic from the J. H. France brickyard at Clarence.

In the public mind, the abandonment of the Snow Shoe Branch was sometimes linked to the discontinuance of rail service to Penn State University's coal-fired steam and electric power plant. In truth, no cause-and-effect relationship existed. Penn State did source its coal from the Snow Shoe area for many years and took delivery via the PRR and the Bellefonte Central. However, in 1946, Penn State began purchasing coal from Moshannon Valley producers in an effort to secure higher quality, cleaner burning fuel. Within a few years, it stopped buying Snow Shoe coal altogether. Moshannon Valley coal continued to be transported by rail until May 1959, when President Eric Walker approved a change to truck delivery. He based his decision on a study showing that using trucks would reduce transportation costs by about $1.20 per ton. The university was then burning about 35,000 tons annually; campus expansion was expected to increase that amount to nearly 80,000 tons by the late 1970s. Even a modest saving per ton would pay big dividends.

The Pennsylvania and the Bellefonte Central protested the shift to highway transport and offered to consider lower rates for carrying the coal. A member of the university's board of trustees, Walter Patchell, who was also a PRR senior vice president and a Penn State alumnus, privately threatened legal action against the school, even hinting that Walker's job could be in jeopardy. But there was little substance on which to build a court case, and the sizable reduction in costs that trucking promised made most other trustees wary of supporting Patchell. In the end, Walker's decision stood.[17]

The coal Penn State had been receiving from the Moshannon Valley came from one or more of the Kittanning seams. The shallower Moshannon or Lower Freeport bed so highly prized by Berwind-White and the PRR had been exhausted by the end of the First World War. Coal in the Lower and Middle Kittanning seams was abundant, even downstream from Philipsburg where the New York Central–served mines had been feasting on the Kittanning for a generation. Based on production data contained in state mine reports, it is probable that the PRR hauled on average approximately 2.5 million tons of coal each year from the valley to Tyrone throughout the 1920s, before trucks began to capture a significant amount of the business. That amount was equivalent to 35,000 to 40,000 carloads, based on a mix of 55-ton and 70-ton capacity hopper cars, or more than a hundred cars a day. Add outbound carloads of brick, clay, pulpwood, and lumber; various outbound empty cars; two passenger trains each way; and two 75–100 car freight trains incoming from Tyrone, and the double track between Osceola and Summit witnessed the daily passage of at least a dozen trains, exclusive of light engine moves—sufficient to rank that section of the Clearfield Branch second only to the Bald Eagle Branch as the busiest piece of railroad on the Tyrone Division.

The Depression put a big dent in this traffic. On the Centre County side alone, total combined output from Moshannon Valley and Snow Shoe mines dropped to 434,000 tons in 1935, about two-thirds of the tonnage of peak year 1926. The slump in activity on the Clearfield Branch forced severe cutbacks in the workforce. The number of men repairing and maintaining locomotives and cars at Osceola, for example, declined from twenty-eight in 1930 to fifteen in 1933.[18] The PRR permanently closed smaller stations and abandoned several mine spurs, although most trackage remained intact and was simply placed out of service pending the return of better times. Fewer trains brought changes in how traffic was controlled. At the outset of the 1920s, trains running between Osceola and Tyrone came under the watchful eye of block operators at Mills (in the Osceola yard office), Powelton, Summit, Gardner (site of an 89-car passing siding and water stop), and Vail. By 1937, all were shuttered except Mills. On the Moshannon Branch, all three manned block stations—Goss Run Junction, Smoke Run, and Madera—were eliminated.[19]

As elsewhere around the nation's rail system, traffic did not come back until stimulated by the approach of another world war. The PRR began calling back furloughed employees and hiring new personnel to work Clearfield Branch trains. The job of locomotive fireman on the branch was not high on most job-seekers' lists, according to Osceola resident Paul Frank, who hired out to the PRR in 1941 as a fireman assigned to Altoona. One day he heard there was an opening for a fireman in his hometown and asked his foreman for a transfer. "You want to work at *Osceola*?" the incredulous foreman asked. Hoping not to miss a rare opportunity to send a volunteer to that outpost, the foreman quickly called the appropriate supervisor to arrange the transfer. "P. J. Frank's comin' to Osceola as a fireman!" he fairly shouted into the telephone. Frank soon found himself pouring scoop after scoop of coal into the searing firebox of an H9s as it clawed its way up to Summit.[20]

Frank and his fellow firemen had their burden lightened when a handful of class L1s 2-8-2 locomotives arrived in Osceola to supplement the smaller 2-8-0s near the end of the Second World War. The L1s engines, introduced in 1914 as main line freight power, had stokers and found favor among crews for their improved riding qualities. That the railroad would assign main line power to work the Clearfield Branch (and in limited service on the Moshannon Branch) underscored the brute force that was required to hoist coal tonnage over the Alleghenies. All told, Osceola rostered twenty to twenty-five train crews along with maintenance-of-way workers, car and engine inspectors, clerks, and other support personnel.[21] With so many men entering military service during the war, the PRR hired women and assigned them clerical tasks at the car scales and the freight station. These were likely among the first females to work for the railroad in former T&C territory, with the exception of a few engaged as passenger car cleaners and station custodians.[22]

The demand for coal remained strong immediately after the war. Industry turned to meeting pent-up commercial and consumer needs, and there was a flourishing overseas market. Most Osceola-based mine runs were made Monday through Friday to distribute empty cars and bring loads back to the yard to be weighed and classified. By the end of the workweek, the yard was almost full, prompting the dispatch of additional locomotives from Altoona on weekends to help clear the congestion.[23] Sometimes the assistance came in the form of monstrous class I1s 2-10-0 locomotives. Officially known as the Decapod type, they were aptly dubbed "Hippos" by their crews. They exerted 96,000 pounds of tractive force, half again as much as an L1s. Their rigid wheelbase was so long that when they rounded the sharp curve on the Big Fill, the center driving wheels (which were flangeless or "blind") hung in midair, unsupported by the rail beneath. The PRR capitalized on the Decapods' brawn to push loaded trains from Osceola to Summit, but the behemoths were handicapped by their need to proceed around the Fill at walking pace.[24]

Crews knew the trains from Osceola to Summit as "pull up" jobs. Trains with as few as twenty loaded hopper cars could be handled by a 2-8-0 fore and aft. Longer and heavier trains received as many as five engines. The pull-up crew usually made three runs to Summit, setting out their loads each time and returning to Osceola. A new crew, with a fresh engine or two, assembled all the cars at Summit and took them down the mountain in a single train. Braking with compressed air, common since the 1890s, was still an imperfect technology. Repeated application and release of the train's air brakes while going downgrade could deplete the system of pressure and invite a runaway before the engineer could stop the train in order to recharge the system. Railroads adopted retaining valves in the early 1900s as an extra measure of safety. Located next to a car's brake wheel, this manually controlled device allowed enough compressed air to be retained in the brake cylinder on the car to cause its brakes to be applied even if air pressure in the train line was depleted.

Heavy trains making the descent from Summit rated a third brakeman to help set up retainers on a prescribed numbers of cars (depending on train weight) and knock them down when the train reached Vail on the valley floor. When a downhill train received only one H9s or H10s—engines that were equipped with only one air compressor—the three brakemen stationed themselves along the car tops, ready to apply hand brakes in the old style upon the appropriate whistle signal from the engineman. In keeping with another time-honored practice, a pusher was attached to long, heavy trains during the descent to avoid stalling on the Big Fill.[25] All in all, moving coal from Osceola yard to Tyrone was a slow, risky, and labor-intensive proposition in the 1940s, much as it had been in the nineteenth century.

If coal traffic held steady, the PRR was losing its hold on many other kinds of freight. Philipsburg historically was the Moshannon Valley's hub for high-value merchandise shipments—"boxcar traffic," as it was often called. In the 1920s, many Philipsburg shippers or consignees had rail sidings for their own use, including the Atlantic Refining Company (petroleum products), Moshannon Mill and Lumber Company, Swift and Company (meats), J. O. Reed (animal feed), Philipsburg Brewing Company, and Centre County Lumber Company. "Public delivery" tracks served numerous additional customers, and a siding at the freight station enjoyed a brisk trade in less-than-carload merchandise.[26] By the 1950s, much of this trade had left the railroad. Some traffic dried up because the shippers went out of business—the Philipsburg brewery closed its doors in 1944, for instance. In other cases, the traffic went to the highways. A refrigerator car of raw meat that was usually set out at Tyrone by a main line train every Sunday night for delivery by a Clearfield Branch to the Swift packing plant in Philipsburg was lost to motor carriers by 1956. During a four-month period between October 11, 1955, and February 8, 1956, Philipsburg freight agent J. H. Branstetter reported his station originated ninety-two carloads: sixty-one cars of pulpwood for various regional paper mills; twenty-eight cars of scrap steel, most for Pittsburgh-area mills; and three cars of empty glass bottles from a local beer distributor being returned to the Anheuser-Busch brewery in St. Louis. The bottle shipments were the last of their kind, Branstetter noted; that business would henceforth be handled by truck to A-B's brewery in Newark, New Jersey.[27] Railway express business dropped so much that Osceola station agent Eugene Danko often transferred the few incoming parcels to his car and delivered them door to door instead of requiring the customers come to the station. (His extra effort went unreimbursed and unsanctioned by the railroad.) Both Osceola and Philipsburg lost their station agencies by the early 1960s.[28]

The refractories trade declined, too, in the face of a shrinking market for fire brick. In 1923, the Clearfield Branch and associated lines served approximately sixteen brickyards and eight clay or coal mines captive to those brickyards. In 1944, the total number had decreased to about twenty such customers, many of them concentrated in the Clearfield area. Harbison-Walker's Clearfield works alone generated more than 1,200 carloads annually, and the PRR based several train crews in Clearfield during the Second World War primarily to serve the brickyards. The Clearfield Branch counted no more than ten refractories as customers in 1956 and only five by 1968.[29]

Brickyards at Sandy Ridge and Retort, owned by General Refractories (Grefco) and Harbison-Walker, respectively, thrived during the war but afterward were handicapped by obsolete equipment, dwindling reserves of nearby high-quality clay, and slumping demand for firebrick. The Sandy Ridge works' closure soon after the war was scarcely noticed, even though the plant ranked among the area's pioneer brickyards and was the first entry into the area for industry giant General Refractories. The works also had a major community impact, with Grefco owning at least thirty-four employee homes, a general store, and 400 acres of land around Sandy Ridge. Harbison-Walker shut down the nearby Retort brickyard by 1958.[30] For the first time in almost a century, bereft of coal tipples and brickyards, the PRR had no customers between Osceola and Summit.

The coal industry in the Clearfield district contracted, too, but the decrease was most visible in the number of mines and tipples served by the PRR's Clearfield Branch and its tributaries—205 in 1923 compared with 24 in 1956—and in the number of people employed in the industry.[31] The district was undergoing a transformation from many small producers to fewer but larger ones without suffering a precipitous decline in production. The closure of smaller mines was especially evident among the Moshannon Branch's spur lines, some of which were abandoned and others simply left in place awaiting a resurgence in mining. The fate of one of those lines is noteworthy because of what it said about the mining industry. In 1907, the PRR purchased a 2.1-mile segment of track that had been built by coal companies, starting at the junction with the Moshannon Branch near Osceola. The track paralleled the mountain stream of Trout Run, passing near the site where the town's founding fathers had built their sawmill. The largest among several mines served by the Trout Run Branch, as the PRR christened the line, was Penn Col-

Figure 10.1. Low-cost surface mining helped to keep central Pennsylvania's coal industry competitive after the Second World War. This is the Rice Brothers' mine near Houtzdale in 1955. *Author's collection.*

lieries No. 5 at the end of track, and the hamlet that grew up around the big mine took the name Penn Five. Osceola-headquartered Du Shan Coal Mining Company acquired the mine at Penn Five in 1938 and worked it continuously until closing it in 1950, when it yielded a still-respectable 45,000 tons. Du Shan continued to load rail cars with coal dug from smaller nearby mines until the last one closed in 1954.[32] The closure of the mines served by the Trout Run Branch signaled the end of traditional large-scale (by local standards) deep-mining up and down the Moshannon Valley. Surface mining was emerging in full force. In fact, extensive coal stripping continued for many years on the high ground above Trout Run, but the coal was trucked to preparation plants and then sent on to market. And so it was elsewhere—the mines either closed or trucked their coal. One by one, tracks that once groaned under the weight of heavily laden hopper cars were either removed or left for nature to camouflage with saplings and wild flowers.

There was no better exemplar of how the coal industry was transforming itself than the Elliot Coal Mining Company. In 1949 Elliot, headed by the Stein family of Philipsburg, opened a new coal preparation plant in the Osceola rail yard. The half-million-dollar facility was unusual in that it received run-of-mine coal not only from trucks but also up to 500 tons daily from railroad cars that had been loaded at mines owned by Elliot and other companies throughout the Moshannon Valley. In the process of washing, crushing, sizing, blending, and loading the coal for shipment to market, the plant sustained jobs directly or indirectly for about 1,200 people, according to the coal company. The PRR installed three new tracks totaling about 2 miles in length to serve the facility, and a dozen high-ranking railroad executives made the trip to Osceola by special train for the plant's May 18 dedication ceremonies.[33] The Pennsylvania had good reason to cultivate close relations with Elliot, which was by far the valley's largest coal producer. In 1948 Elliot's eleven strip mines and one deep mine shipped nearly 550,000 tons to market, nearly all by rail. The company expected to attract additional tonnage from smaller mining enterprises that found it more cost-effective to have Elliot prepare and market their coal.

With Elliot's new preparation plant coming on line, PRR mechanical officers decided the Clearfield Branch was ideal for testing the capabilities of the new diesel-electric locomotives in heavy-duty service. In February 1949, a three-unit set of model F3 locomotives newly delivered from the Electro-Motive Division (EMD) of General Motors underwent a three-day trial between Osceola and Tyrone. Rated at a total of 4,500 horsepower and 120,000 pounds of tractive force, the new diesels took loaded trains from Osceola to Summit without reliance on pusher engines. On one return trip from Tyrone, the trio of diesels hoisted ninety-two empty hopper cars up the mountain from Vail to Summit without help—a task normally assigned to three L1s 2-8-2s.[34]

Descending the Allegheny Front, the diesels had the advantage of dynamic braking in addition to the standard air brakes. In dynamic braking, as the locomotive proceeds downgrade, its electric traction motors become generators. The resulting resistance slows the train, and the electric power produced by the generators is dissipated in the form of heat. Thanks to dynamic braking, there was usually no need for the time-consuming practice of turning up and knocking down retainers on individual cars; the use of downhill pushers to prevent stalling around the Big Fill was eliminated, even with trains of a hundred cars.

In June 1949 a three-unit F3 set returned to Osceola for more testing. Taking into account such expenses as labor, fuel, and supporting infrastructure, the PRR estimated that using only diesel power on the Clearfield Branch would cut operating costs in half. The F3 units' performance on the branch contributed measurably to the $27 million diesel locomotives had saved the Pennsylvania system-wide in 1949. By the end of that year, the PRR rostered nearly 800 diesels, compared with about 3,000 steam engines.[35]

An incident starkly illustrating the pulling ability of diesels compared with steam occurred below Gardner during the steam-to-diesel transition. Three Fairbanks-Morse diesels were leading a long cut of empties up the steep climb from Vail, assisted by an I1s tucked ahead of the cabin car on the rear, crewed by veteran engineman Paulie Kincaid and young fireman Paul Frank. As the Hippo passed the Alder Run Orchard on a sharp curve and 2.65 percent grade, it suddenly lost its footing. The driving wheels slipped wildly, blowing Frank's carefully tended fire out the stack in a massive gush. Kincaid backed off the throttle and applied sand in a vain effort to regain traction. The engineman in the diesel, unaware of trouble on the rear, kept his train moving steadily upgrade in mountain-goat fashion, stretching out the slack until it yanked out the drawbar from the front end of the old Hippo, which Kinkaid then brought to a halt. He and Frank watched in disbelief as the hoppers ahead rumbled out of sight, moving steadily up to Summit as if nothing untoward had happened.[36]

For all their inefficiencies, coal-burning locomotives were not ousted from Osceola until 1954.[37] The Pennsylvania's motive power needs were so vast that in spite of placing orders with five separate builders, the railroad required a decade (1947–57) and $400 million to acquire enough diesels to replace steam completely. With steam gone from the Clearfield Branch, the railroad was able to reduce the number of train crews it based in Osceola to about a half-dozen; it made corresponding cuts in maintenance personnel.

In the early years of dieselization, Osceola received a variety of diesels that included many misfit types that had disappointed the railroad in main line service—a harkening to the early days of the T&C and the Winans Camels. Most notable was a brief trial in pusher service of a Baldwin-built Centipede type, a two-unit, twenty-four-axle, 5,000-horsepower behemoth that had been downgraded from passenger service.[38] The situation began to stabilize in 1959 after the PRR brought in a half-dozen RS-11 road switchers, built by the American Locomotive Company (Alco). Those 1,800-horsepower units, only two years old, were well suited to the low-speed lugging chores that characterized coal-hauling. The RS-11s, joined occasionally by an additional unit or two as traffic warranted, became familiar sights on the Clearfield Branch and its tributaries for the next ten years. Typically three RS-11s worked the run to Tyrone, making two trips up to Summit with thirty to forty loads each time. After the second trip, the two sections were coupled into one train for the tortuous descent to Vail and Tyrone. The same crew made the return trip from Tyrone with empties, again usually without assistance from a pusher engine. On the Moshannon Branch, a single RS-11 usually sufficed for mine runs and the trip out to Clearfield and Grampian and return, and as a yard shifter at Osceola.[39]

Elliot's new coal preparation plant went into operation just as demand for coal by electric utilities began to skyrocket. Nationwide in 1947, utilities accounted for about 16 percent of US bituminous coal consumption; that share climbed to 42 percent over the next decade, propelled by a 10 percent annual growth in the demand for electricity during the 1950s. Nationally, bituminous consumption for electric power generation jumped from 92 million tons in 1950 to 177 million tons in 1960; by 1965 it topped 245 million tons.[40]

By the late 1950s, electric utilities had become the largest single market for coal shipped by the PRR from its yard at Osceola Mills. Among the most notable consumers of Moshannon Valley coal was the Pennsylvania Power and Light Company (PP&L), headquartered in Allentown and serving twenty-nine counties in the state's central and eastern regions. In the early 1960s, PP&L operated two large bituminous coal-fired generating stations: Brunner Island south of Harrisburg, and Martins Creek near Easton. In the planning stage was an even larger plant to be located at Strawberry Ridge in Montour County, alongside the PRR's Berwick Branch. The Montour Steam Electric Station would consume about 2 million tons of coal each year. With each of the other two plants burning only slightly less coal, PP&L took steps to ensure an adequate fuel supply at the lowest possible cost. In addition to buying coal on the open market, it decided to mine some of its own coal in western Pennsylvania through a wholly owned subsidiary, Pennsylvania Mines Corporation (PMC). Captive mines would help protect the utility from price fluctuations and lock in the extensive reserves needed for future expansion of generating capacity.

But PP&L, a customer of the Pennsylvania Railroad since the early 1950s, no longer had confidence in the PRR's ability to reliably deliver the enormous quantity of coal the three power plants required. Although the Pennsylvania moved more than 25 million tons of coal each year, more than half of its 73,000 hopper cars were at least thirty-five years old and near the end of their useful lives. Experience had shown that when the coal trade was robust, the railroad's fleet was stretched to its limit despite its vast size; transit times and car availability were unpredictable.[41] Consequently, PP&L began acquiring its own fleet of new hopper cars that would form "unit trains," operating as a single block of cars in captive service between mine and powerplant. Unit trains did not include cars from other customers, eliminating the need to make time-consuming stops en route to pick up or set out cars. Unit trains saved time and money for both the railroad and the customer.

A few railroads began experimenting with unit trains for coal service in the late 1950s. In April 1962 the New York Central tested one version of the concept in the Clearfield coal district. Using its own cars, the railroad ran what it called "shuttle trains" from its Cherry Tree yard in the southwest corner of Clearfield County through Clearfield and Newberry to New Jersey destinations.[42] Later in the year, the Pennsylvania operated a train of nearly 100 cars that were loaded at the Bradford Coal

Company's preparation plant in Bigler and routed in a solid block via Tyrone and the Bald Eagle Branch to an Allied Chemical plant in Solvay, New York. Dubbed the "Solvay Express," it was the first unit train loaded and shipped anywhere on the PRR. The Pennsylvania soon originated more such trains at Osceola, loaded at Elliot's and Bradford's plants.[43] It also introduced similar service in other parts of its coal territory, offering shippers lower rates in return for increased tonnage. At that time, the PRR loosely defined "unit coal train" rather as a train of 7,000 net tons originating at no more than two mines and destined for a single consignee at a discounted rate. The cars did not have to be in captive service, and in fact none were. As thus defined, the railroad operated hundreds of unit trains during the two years subsequent to the Solvay Express.[44]

True unit trains could reap all the economic rewards inherent in the concept only at mines that produced huge amounts of coal, could flood-load entire trains within a few hours, and had a train-length loading track. Those requirements disqualified all Centre County and Moshannon Valley mines. Many underground mines in western Pennsylvania did meet those criteria, but they already had long-term contracts to supply steel mills and other heavy industries. They were not interested in taking on PP&L as a customer—another reason the utility decided to go into the mining business. Pennsylvania Mines Corporation opened its first mine at Tunnelton in Indiana County and began flood-loading seventy-four-car trains there in June 1964. Pennsylvania Power and Light became the nation's first utility to place shipper-owned cars in unit coal train service; the idea would prove so successful that within a few years power companies nationwide adopted the practice.[45]

Even as the first trains were shuttling to and from Tunnelton, PMC was starting an opening for a high-capacity mine in Centre County. The new Rushton mine was located in Rush Township, adjacent to the Clearfield Branch, about midway between Philipsburg and Osceola. A 650-foot main shaft was sunk at a 16-degree angle beneath the Moshannon Creek to reach the Brookville seam, sometimes called the Moshannon Valley's "sleeping giant"—an immense coal bed so deep that most of it still lay untapped despite more than a century of relentless mining in the area. In the area of Rushton mine, the Brookville seam was about 55 inches thick and lay some 230 feet below the surface.[46] A conveyor running the length of the slope brought the coal to the surface, where it was prepared to meet the requirements of PP&L power plants and then loaded into rail cars at the rate of one car each minute. Projected to yield more than a half-million tons annually for thirty or more years, Rushton was mining coal on a scale the valley had never known before.

Unit trains first called at Rushton in November 1965. By the end of 1967, they had hauled nearly 750,000 tons of coal, most of it destined for Brunner Island. Each train set was able to make the 300-mile round trip in about three days, compared to "loose car" turnaround times of two weeks or more. At first, unit trains visited Rushton no more than once a week, since the mine's early output was not sufficient to support more frequent loadings. After discharging their coal at Brunner Island, Rushton cars might next go to Tunnelton to load a Martins Creek train before returning to Rushton. The PRR offered PP&L reduced rates on all unit trains, saving the utility as much as $1.80 per ton compared with conventional haulage.[47]

The opening of Rushton mine changed the operating routine on the Clearfield Branch as nothing had since the transition from steam to diesel. Each unit train consisted of about a hundred 100-ton capacity hopper cars, pulled by a quartet of nearly new 2,250-horsepower Electro-Motive GP30 locomotives. The trains—PP&L had acquired enough cars for three sets—presented a distinctive sight: the dark green GP30s with their unique roof profile followed by a seemingly endless string of rust-red cars, each featuring a perky image of Reddy Kilowatt on its flanks. The car sides were constructed with a high-tensile-strength steel alloy called Mayari-R that resisted corrosion caused by prolonged contact with coal. The Bethlehem Steel–developed alloy was self-weathering and did not require paint.[48] The locomotives pulled the hoppers under Rushton's flood loader at a continuous speed of one-eighth mile per hour and could finish their task in about four hours. However, they lacked the muscle to take the loads up to Summit without help. Pusher engines made their first appearance on the Clearfield Branch since the steam age. The PRR tried various operating plans; in the end, the tried-and-true method of taking the train up in two cuts seemed to work best, with the GP-30s leading and three or four Osceola-based RS-11s shoving hard on the rear.

As expected, the PP&L unit trains boosted operating efficiency and lowered costs. Unfortunately, the railroad had numerous unhappy experiences with the trains' hundred-ton-capacity cars, and with the nearly identical class H43 hundred-tonners that the Pennsylvania itself introduced about that same time. The H43 cars were outshopped early in 1964 and almost immediately exhibited a tendency to derail. The first incident on the Clearfield Branch occurred on May 2, 1964, when fifteen H43s loaded at a mine near Curwensville jumped the tracks just after rounding the Big Fill. None tumbled all the way down the steep cinder incline to Mount Pleasant Run, but the accident was bad enough to warrant calling in wreck equipment from Altoona and Cresson on the south end. The north end of the branch was isolated, forcing PRR officials to swallow hard and put out a call to the New York Central, which dispatched a Clearfield-based wreck train featuring a heavy-duty derrick to help clean up the mess.[49]

The PP&L cars experienced similar derailments, leading investigators to discover that the hundred-tonners displayed a rhythmic, side-to-side rocking when traveling over jointed rail at certain speeds. The side sway was attributed to a harmonic created when the wheels passing over joints coincided with a motion in the springs of the wheel assemblies or trucks. Most of the main track between Osceola and Vail had long consisted of 130- and 131-lb. (per yard) rail—the same heavy-duty weight that PRR used in main line applications. But the branch received far less maintenance than the main, and low joints were common—hence the frequent mishaps. While troubleshooting the big cars' difficulties was ongoing, so were the derailments. During the fall and winter of 1966–67, two major wrecks occurred near Osceola and two more near Sandy Ridge. Eventually modifications were made to the spring mechanisms of existing cars, and shock absorbers were installed on new cars; wrecks became less frequent. Just to be safe, hundred-ton cars were prohibited on the badly deteriorated Moshannon Branch.[50] The challenge of sending larger cars and heavier trains over bad track on steep grades caused more headaches for an operating department long burdened by the inefficiencies and dangers associated with the mountainous portion of the Clearfield Branch.

The New York Central faced the same economic issues on the Allegheny Plateau as the Pennsylvania: a shrinking market for coal, an erosion of refractories traffic, and increased competition from trucks for the boxcar trade. During the 1920s, the NYC was the nation's third-largest transporter of bituminous coal by rail, hauling more than 30 million revenue-tons annually plus millions more for its own use. Over its tracks flowed about two-thirds of all bituminous coal consumed in New England, and three-fourths in lower Canada. Coal shipped over its rails through Clearfield accounted for nearly 10 million tons of bituminous annually, including NYC-originated tonnage plus coal received from two short lines: the Pittsburgh & Susquehanna (Alley Popper) in the Moshannon Valley, and the Cambria and Indiana Railroad in Indiana County. On average, about one in every four tons of coal originated by the New York Central stayed on its own lines and was used for locomotive fuel and other company purposes.[51] Additionally, the NYC received coal from the Buffalo, Rochester and Pittsburgh Railway at Clearfield, most of which came from western Pennsylvania mines located beyond the district.

Since the early 1900s, the railroad routed most Clearfield District coal east over the River Line to Keating and down to Avis, where the cars were weighed and trains were made up for destinations further north or east. A much smaller amount went west from Clearfield via the line of the former Jamestown, Franklin and Clearfield Railroad, a New York Central subsidiary, to Ashtabula. The majority of coal trains regularly dispatched east over the old Beech Creek Railroad main line came from NYC-served mines in the lower Moshannon Valley.

In the early 1920s, the former BCR main line again came under scrutiny as a possible link in an east–west trunk line. New York Central executives proposed that the Central Railroad of New Jersey (CNJ) and the Reading Railroad (RDG) be merged into their own road. The trunk line was nearly identical to the early 1900s plan to make the Beech Creek part of a grand Chicago-Ashtabula-Clearfield-Newberry-Philadelphia route; the only difference was that the new plan substituted the New York metropolitan area for Philadelphia, taking advantage of a RDG-CNJ connection near Tamaqua in eastern Pennsylvania for a direct route over CNJ rails to Jersey City. As outlined by NYC vice president and Beech Creek veteran Patrick Crowley in 1923, the new trunk line would shorten his railroad's run between Chicago and New York to 939 miles,

40 miles less than the distance over the main line via Albany. It would also help relieve freight-train congestion on the main line across upstate New York.[52]

Crowley and his boss, president Alfred H. Smith, were reacting to a series of proposals made by the Interstate Commerce Commission to consolidate the nation's railroads into thirty or fewer systems. The commission aimed not so much to pare down the nation's overbuilt rail network by ending duplication as to find homes for financially weaker railroads by placing them under the wing of stronger companies—in effect, preserving duplication. Alarmed by where the ICC was going with its planning efforts, most large railroads put forth their own consolidation proposals, and so it was with the New York Central.

By the time Smith testified before the commission in November 1923, the NYC had reshaped its trunk line idea, once again denying the Beech Creek the chance to be more than a backwoods coal road. Smith stated that the New York Central would run its Chicago–New York traffic over the River Line east of Clearfield instead of the former BCR, even though the River Line routing was longer and depended on PRR trackage rights east of Keating. Those rights would eventually be given up, Smith explained, since his company anticipated building its own route between Keating and McElhattan, using its own right-of-way.[53]

President Daniel Willard of the Baltimore and Ohio objected. His vision of a new Chicago–New York trunk line was to consolidate the B&O with the Reading, Central of New Jersey, and Buffalo, Rochester and Pittsburgh Railway. And if Crowley and Smith didn't have strategic use for the Beech Creek, he said he'd take that line, too. The B&O's jumping-off point from Chicago would be near New Castle in western Pennsylvania. Trains would then travel over the BR&P to Clearfield, down the former BCR to Lock Haven, and somehow—Willard offered no specifics—a link would be established with the Reading at Newberry. The B&O would thus gain a route between Chicago and New York that was just shy of 900 miles in length, compared with its existing 999-mile line via Baltimore. Willard let it be known that if he couldn't get the Beech Creek, he would obtain rights over the little Buffalo & Susquehanna Railroad between DuBois and Driftwood, a point on the PRR's Philadelphia and Erie line. From Driftwood east to Lock Haven, the

B&O would secure rights over the PRR or build its own line, perhaps using the undeveloped right-of-way below Keating previously secured by the NYC.

This time Smith and Crowley objected, contending that Willard's plan would put their road at a competitive disadvantage. And so it went; disagreements on consolidation in central Pennsylvania, magnified on a national scale, helped to doom railroad consolidation in any form. After nearly a decade, neither the carriers themselves nor the ICC nor any outside experts could come up with a national consolidation plan that satisfied all the major players. The onset of the Great Depression in 1929 finally put an end to the squabbling, although the ICC did permit the B&O to buy the BR&P and the B&S effective January 1, 1932. Battered by the Depression, the B&O made no attempt to obtain a Driftwood–Lock Haven extension, and the entire notion of a new east–west trunk line evaporated. The Beech Creek remained primarily a line that lived on whatever traffic it could generate along its route.[54]

Refractories were an important part of that traffic. Brickyards at Orviston and Monument and the little communities they supported flourished during the 1920s in response to a strong industrial demand for firebrick. Harbison-Walker completely rebuilt its Monument plant in 1922, installing state-of-the-art extrusion and pressing machinery to boost efficiency and production. It used steel rather than wood framing in the plant, an innovation at the time, and built large steel trestles to facilitate unloading coal and clay at the plant and to carry the narrow-gauge railroad across Beech Creek to the clay mines above the town. It also increased the number of company-built-and-owned houses by about one-third.

Prosperity came to a sudden halt at the end of the decade, when the nation plunged into economic depression and the need for firebrick shrank drastically. At the Orviston operation, General Refractories pulled up the narrow-gauge railroad that since 1907 had linked the plant with mines situated on the hilltops above the town. The easily accessible deposits of flint clay on that high ground were exhausted; extracting additional reserves would be more costly. The company decided it was cheaper to have the NYC transport clay from around Peale, and from Morgan Run in Clearfield County, where the PRR originated it and handed it off to the New York Central at Loch Lomond Junction. Orviston was able to continue operating its kilns despite the need to transport clay over longer distances because it had a tapped a niche market. It was Grefco's only Centre County source of "high duty" fire brick (sold under the Hayes Run brand) that was made especially for blast furnaces, and Pennsylvania's only source of "intermediate duty" fire brick (the Orvis brand) for less severe industrial applications.[55]

The Second World War and the economic boom immediately following that conflict brought renewed activity to both Monument and Orviston. The arrival and departure of the daily Avis-based trains that serviced the plants introduced at least one youth to the railroad mystique. Jim Davy, who attended elementary school in Monument, recalled the trains with fond detail.

> Daily traffic [stopping at Monument] consisted of a morning westbound local, and a late afternoon eastbound local. The power assigned to these locals was almost always 2-8-2 Mikados of the H6a series. . . . The locals had their own chorus of those sounds, sights and smells: the screech of the brake shoes as the train came to a halt, the immediate ka-chunk, ka-chunk of the air pumps as they replenished the pressure in the brake line used for the stop, and the discharge of the air hose disconnect as the engine pulled away from the train to do the switching. I would cover my ears to protect them from the high pitch screech of the wheel flanges when the 2-8-2 entered and departed the partially rust coated rails of the siding. I'd watch with amazement the bending and flexing of the lighter rail like wet noodles, as the massive weight of each driving wheel rolled over the space between the ties. When the pick up and drop off of box cars and hoppers was completed, the final coupling jolt when she backed in to her 12- or 14-car consist said she was ready to head on out of town.[56]

In addition to the locals, Davy recollected, there were at least two longer trains in each direction, consisting mostly of hopper cars and having no need to pause at the brickyard towns. One of the westbounds passed through Monument around midnight. Young Davy's house was a scant 50 feet from the track, and he gratefully accepted all the drama the railroad offered.

> The midnight train was the one with the most magic for me. I would be lying in my bed on warm summer nights, with the window open, and could hear all those wonderful sounds echoing from the surrounding mountains up and down the hollows! The two locomotives assigned to this task were massive beasts, at least in the mind of this ten-year-old. They were class L2a 4-8-2 Mohawks, with oversized six-wheel truck tenders. In my mind's eye I can still see that big feed-water

heater mounted on the front eyebrow of her smokebox. It gave her a look of such
ominous power! As she approached town in the cool night air, I could hear her
blow for the lower crossing. Seconds later, she would pass my open window, the
sharp dry crack of her exhaust giving evidence of the ruling westbound grade.
Just as she was passing my window, she began blowing the two longs, a short,
and another long for the upper crossing located a few hundred yards beyond,
where she departed our little town.

The inflated postwar demand for firebrick did not last long. Harbison-
Walker shut down all eight kilns at Monument in 1950. To the last, the
company had sourced most of its clay locally and had kept Plane Hill
and Twin Run mines operating. In 1952 the plant sputtered back to life
as it began making silica brick using ganister trucked from Huntingdon
County. Silica brick was superior to firebrick in certain high-heat applications, although in this case high production costs due to an aging
plant and high transportation costs undercut Monument's attempt at a
comeback. The brickyard closed permanently in May 1953, followed by
closure of the NYC's freight station. The agent there had also handled
the Orviston business, which was now transferred to the Snow Shoe
agent at Clarence.

General Refractories closed its NYC-served Beech Creek works, in
the Bald Eagle Valley, in 1954 and concentrated production at Orviston,
which limped along until the fall of 1962, when it too closed for good.
Grefco cited declining sales, high production costs associated with the
facility's age, and rising transportation costs stemming from its remote
location.[57]

Monument and Orviston were not the first communities along the
route to suffer catastrophic economic blows. Further up the line, the
Kato Coal Company was for many years the largest coal shipper on the
railroad east of Viaduct. Annual production during the 1920s occasionally exceeded 30,000 tons (600 carloads) and gave employment to about
sixty miners. When the Great Depression struck, demand for Kato's
riches plummeted. By 1935 production barely exceeded 5,000 tons; the
mine was idle much of the year. The village that had grown up along
the swift waters of Beech Creek, at the foot of the inclined plane that
lowered coal from the mine to the railroad, began melting away. The
post office closed in 1937, and the mine shut down forever the following
year, after yielding a mere 3,500 tons.[58] The site reverted to its natural

state and within a few decades became virtually unrecognizable as a one-time bustling community. A nearby railroad siding and tipple used by companies that strip-mined the area into the early 1960s reminded visitors of Kato's bituminous heritage.

Further west, business at the J. H. France brickyard at Snow Shoe (Clarence) remained fairly robust. Using minerals brought in by rail in addition to local clays, France produced silica brick and as many as ninety specialty refractories for a variety of domestic and foreign niche markets. As late as 1960, it was still receiving or shipping some 300 carloads each year. Inbound traffic consisted mainly of clay, bauxite, and kyanite, as well as broken bricks, or "brick bats," to be crushed and reused in the brick molding process. Outbound cars were laden with newly made brick. France's business accounted for about 80 percent of the rail cars that the NYC handled through its Snow Shoe agency, which typically posted annual revenues in the neighborhood of $100,000.[59]

The coal trade was longer lasting for the railroad west of Snow Shoe. Near Gorton, after the Clearfield Bituminous Coal Corporation gave up the Tunnel mines, they were reopened by smaller companies. Underground mining gave way to extensive surface mining after the Second World War, dominated in the 1950s by the Morrisdale-based Robert Bailey Coal Company. In some years Bailey mine No. 5 loaded nearly 250,000 tons of bituminous coal at a tipple near Gorton. In 1959, strip mining shifted to the Clearfield County side, and Bailey abandoned the Gorton tipple in favor of loading on the Grassflat Branch, which connected to the main line at Viaduct.[60]

West of Viaduct, the railroad served another brickyard at Winburne. Established around 1900, the plant differed from its counterparts by specializing in building brick. Highland Clay Products operated the works until about 1933, when J. H. France began using the kilns to produce specialty brick for industrial boilers, relying on clay brought in by rail from outside the immediate area. Output was modest compared with the company's Snow Shoe works. France ceased large-scale brick-making at the Winburne plant in 1957 in favor of consolidating operations at Snow Shoe, where production was expanded and modernized. The Winburne plant came under new ownership but was no longer an important rail customer.[61]

At Munson, 2 miles west of Winburne, the Philipsburg Branch fun-
neled coal shipments to the main line for forwarding west to Clearfield
and down the River Line or east over the Beech Creek route. In either
case, the coal cars eventually passed through Avis yard, where they were
weighed and classified for further shipment. State mining reports show
that in 1926, nine deep mines located on the Philipsburg Branch or its
tributaries loaded 227,000 tons of coal on the New York Central. In the
late 1940s, deep mining gave way to strip or surface mining. The tiny
settlements of Coaldale on Coaldale Siding and Horn's Heights on the
Ophir Branch disappeared along with the shafts or drifts they once supported, as draglines and bulldozers remade the landscape. In years to
come, surface mining would produce countless similar outcomes elsewhere. Even Coaldale Siding was obliterated; the Ophir Branch was
spared, serving as a steel lifeline for Stott Coal Company's preparation
plant and nearby strip mines.

Philipsburg itself declined in importance to the New York Central
as the twentieth century wore on. The Pittsburgh and Susquehanna
Railroad—the Alley Popper, an interchange partner since the 1890s—
ceased all operations as of August 31, 1931. Plagued with financial misery
throughout its corporate life, the little road remained a distant also-ran
for the Moshannon Valley's lucrative coal trade. The NYC gladly accepted what business the P&S generated but did not prop up its partner
financially, correctly judging that the railroad would never be able to
emerge from the Pennsylvania's shadow. The short line was not even
the beneficiary of hand-me-down NYC locomotives and turned instead to the PRR for a handful of worn-out 2-8-0s. Ironically, a New
York Central subsidiary delivered the mortal blow to the Pittsburgh
and Susquehanna. The Boston and Albany Railroad in 1930 canceled
locomotive-coal contracts from several P&S-served mines, sending the
smaller road into bankruptcy. The property was formally abandoned in
1936, and track removal commenced the following year.[62]

After the NYC ceased running passenger trains into Philipsburg in
1933, it razed the passenger side of the station, sold the nearby roundhouse and several acres of land in the Meadows for non-railroad use, and
lifted a quarter-mile of track that extended beyond the freight station
to the defunct P&S connection at Wigton Junction. In the late 1940s,

privately owned track was reinstalled between the station and Wigton Junction in order to serve the Bailey and Bragonier (B.B.) Construction Company. The new track joined the NYC at one end and the PRR's Clearfield Branch at the other, thus enabling B.B.—whose specialties included supplying ready-mixed concrete and assembling and hauling draglines and other heavy strip-mining equipment—to receive shipments from either railroad. In 1960, in one of the larger shipments consigned to its private track, B.B. received a Marion 7400 walking dragline to assemble for Bradford Coal Company. The machine arrived in Philipsburg on twenty-three railroad flatcars.[63] The B.B. track was not an interchange between the two roads, however, since there was little need in the Philipsburg area for interline movements. The once-busy interchange at Spring Hill Junction, where both railroads' Derby branches intersected, served no purpose after the nearby mines gave out, and the connecting track was removed. Loch Lomond Junction, where both railroads' Philipsburg branches connected in the swamps along the Moshannon Creek, saw the passage of fire clay from PRR to NYC. When refractories' output declined in the 1950s, interchange traffic dried up; the PRR took most of its Philipsburg Branch out of service.

After the Second World War, the most tangible symbols of the New York Central's shrinking presence in Philipsburg were the two-story RG tower at the diamond where the NYC's Philipsburg Branch crossed the PRR's Clearfield Branch and the single-story freight station in the Meadows. The tower, once the object of a bitter litigation between the two roads, had not rated a signalman since the New York Central eliminated passenger trains. Pennsylvania Railroad trains had the right of way; in the absence of an operator, New York Central crews had to stop at the tower and telephone for permission from the PRR to cross. A half-mile beyond RG, the freight station was left standing to provide space for the agent and storage of a few less-than-carload shipments. As NYC-served mines in the area either closed or started trucking their coal, Philipsburg's business dwindled. In all of 1957, for example, the agent reported only 114 outbound carloads, 81 of which were pulpwood loads consigned to regional paper mills; most of the remaining cars were laden with fresh-hewn crossties for railroad use. The NYC delivered thirty-seven cars at Philipsburg that year, containing cement for

B.B. Construction, wallboard, semifinished lumber, livestock feed, and earthmoving equipment for local coal companies. With little hope that the downward spiral would ever reverse itself, the railroad in 1959–60 applied to the Public Utilities Commission for permission to convert Philipsburg to a non-agency station. The PUC readily granted the request.⁶⁴

Beech Creek District train operations adhered for many years to a fairly regular pattern. From the Second World War until the mid-1950s, a road freight (Jim Davy's "magical" midnight train) operated daily from Avis to set out empty hopper cars and pick up coal loads between Viaduct and Munson. The road freight either turned at Munson or continued west to Clearfield, where the crew took their required eight hours rest before departing with a train for Avis. A second train from Avis, the Viaduct Local, made a roundtrip daily except Sunday to work the coal tipples as far west as Viaduct, including the Grassflat Branch. From Newberry yard came the Beech Creek Local, which was tasked with handling refractory products and freight other than coal. It worked the interchange with the PRR's Bald Eagle Branch at Bald Eagle Junction and the brickyards as far west as Snow Shoe before returning to Newberry. A fourth regular train differed from the other three in that it originated at Clearfield and worked east. The Munson Local, also known as the Philipsburg Local, normally worked east to Munson and then up the branch to Philipsburg, before returning to Clearfield. It set out cars destined for Avis and Newberry at Munson. The routine of the four trains was subject to the vagaries of the market for coal, brick, and pulpwood. On some days trains were annulled for lack of work, and on other days extra trains might operate to meet customers' changing needs.⁶⁵

All trains came under the authority of the dispatchers, who remained at Jersey Shore after Pennsylvania Division headquarters was shifted in 1931 to Corning, New York, where Fall Brook District offices were based. The move consolidated offices having division-wide responsibilities that previously had been split between the two district offices. Coincidentally it occurred during the tenure of Philipsburg-born William A. Hamler, the only Beech Creek District native to hold the post of Pennsylvania Division superintendent.⁶⁶ Expenses were further trimmed by closing many block stations across the division. Employee timetables show that

Figure 10.2. Two NYC road switchers, most likely power for the Munson local, pose for the photographer at the west end of Viaduct circa 1962. *Author's collection.*

between 1930 and 1937, the railroad withdrew agents/operators from Orviston, Kato, Gillintown, Viaduct, Munson (reopened in 1941), and RG.[67] By far the most severe cutback was the closing of the Avis locomotive shop in 1931, resulting in the loss of 700 jobs. The car-repair shop remained open with a smaller workforce, and the yard continued to weigh and classify cars. With a 5,000-car capacity, Avis was still the Beech Creek District's largest classification yard, easily outranking yards at Clearfield (2,500 cars) and Newberry (2,000 cars.)[68]

The railroad continued to downsize its presence in the Beech Creek District after the Second World War. In the early 1950s, the Avis car shops were closed. In 1958 the Pennsylvania Division was merged into the Syracuse Division. Dispatching offices remained at Jersey Shore for two more years before moving to Syracuse Division headquarters in Rochester, New York. About that same time, the railroad eliminated Avis as an engine and crew terminal, except for a yard crew. It ceased regular operation of the Avis road freight to Munson and the Viaduct Local. All work fell to the Newberry-based Beech Creek Local, which could work as far west as Munson. In another operating change, the Clearfield-based Munson Local was permitted to work as far east as Kato. Where the two trains met on any given day depended on empties to be placed and loads to be picked up.[69]

As on the PRR, steam on the NYC gave way to diesel-electric motive power in the early 1950s. For the previous two decades, road power on the Beech Creek line consisted mostly of handsome class L-1 4-8-2 locomotives, which had debuted in main line freight duty in 1916–18. The 4-8-2 wheel arrangement was known as the Mountain type on nearly every railroad that owned them; but the New York Central, finding that name at odds with the company's water-level route brand, dubbed them Mohawks for the upstate New York river. Neither the L-1's relatively large 69-inch drivers nor its 51,400 pounds of tractive force made it ideal for the hilly Beech Creek District. They were much more at home on the River Line. In the 1940s, a handful of larger Mohawks of the L-2 class, also bumped from the main line, arrived in the district to share road-freight duties. Working in concert with the L class were H-6a 2-8-2 Mikado types. Their smaller driving wheels helped to give them slightly more tractive force than the Mohawks. Rounding out the Beech Creek motive power scene were a few class E-1 2-6-0 Moguls, which despite their advanced years proved ideal for running on mine branches and sidings where light rail would not hold the larger engines.

In spite of the advent of brawnier locomotives, getting a train safely down a mountain grade in Beech Creek country demanded that locomotive engineers have a thorough knowledge of train dynamics and more than a little nerve, just as on the PRR descent from Summit. In the steam era, employee timetables contained a special instruction for trains going downgrade east of Gillintown: "Before leaving Gillintown one-half of the pressure retaining valves must be turned up or as many as in the judgment of the engineman are necessary." Brakemen—regardless of snow or ice or other inclement weather—climbed up and down on the necessary cars, turning up retainers to prevent the brakes on those cars from being fully released. At the bottom of the grade, beyond Monument, brakemen again walked the car tops of the moving train, using wooden clubs to push the retaining valves back down.

Diesel locomotives first appeared on the Beech Creek in 1949, bringing new measures of safety and efficiency to train handling on grades and eliminating the routine use of retainers. Thanks to their brute strength, diesels made regular helper assignments unnecessary. With the new diesels and a proficiency in train handling that came from years of experience, "it wasn't any different coming down the Beech Creek than it was coming down the River Line from Clearfield," recalled veteran engineer Buck Hemsley. "I brought trains down the Beech Creek—loads—with diesels with no problems whatsoever. As high as 130 cars of coal."[70] Diesels and steam coexisted briefly, but the economic and technological advantages of diesel power were plain. By the spring of 1953 the New York Central had dieselized all freight operations on its system east of Cleveland except for the Beech Creek District, where a few steamers still labored almost unnoticed. By 1954, however, the railroad had taken delivery of enough new diesels to banish coal-burners forever.[71] That led to the dismantling of numerous support facilities such as coal docks, ash pits, and water tanks. When the labor-intensive technology of steam locomotion left the railroad, many jobs did, too. "The change to diesels was all right in a way," Buck Hemsley said. "The only thing you hated about it was, you knew you were going to lose a lot of friends."

The New York Central dieselized the Pennsylvania Division primarily with road-switcher and cab-unit models from the two largest builders, EMD and Alco. For a few years during the steam-to-diesel transition, practically any diesel that the NYC rostered was fair game for the division, so products from minor builders Baldwin and Fairbanks-Morse made at least cameo appearances, especially when Avis yard was still active. Eventually the rugged Alco FA cab units and RS-3 road switchers proved themselves to be the workhorses of the Beech Creek District, complemented by various models from EMD.

Diesels were still a novelty in Clearfield when the US Army Corps of Engineers made public its proposal for a flood-control project that would close part of the River Line and divert its traffic to a portion of the Beech Creek. The corps wanted to build five dams to help control waters on the upper reaches of the Susquehanna's West Branch: at Curwensville in Clearfield County; on Kettle Creek and on the First Fork of the Sinnemahoning Creek in Clinton County; on Bald Eagle Creek near Blanchard on the Centre-Clinton border; and just above Keating along the boundaries of Clinton, Centre, and Clearfield counties. Estimated cost of the five dams was $255 million, of which $192 million was targeted for Keating, by far the most ambitious of the undertakings.

The corps planned to make Keating Dam a hydroelectric station, selling power and earning income to help the federal government recoup its mammoth investment. It would back up the West Branch for 53 miles and inundate nearly 16,000 acres. Waters would cover the River Line all the way to Mowry, several miles upriver from Karthaus. As an alternative route for the New York Central, the corps projected a line that began at Mowry, then left the West Branch and follow the Moshannon Creek upstream, much like the PRR's survey for extending the Susquehanna and Clearfield Railroad in the 1880s. The projected line climbed away from the Moshannon Creek after a few miles and tunneled beneath the summit of the Alleghenies, emerging to connect with the Beech Creek main line somewhere between Snow Shoe and Kato.

Had such a scheme come to fruition, a portion of the Beech Creek line would have hosted its own traffic plus the 6 million tons of coal that was annually routed down the River Line—more than 100,000 cars in each direction. But local coal operators would have none of it. In a series of public hearings and open letters, the Central Pennsylvania Open Pit Mining Association claimed the Keating Dam would bring economic disaster to parts of Centre and Clearfield Counties. It would flood land containing at least 20 million tons of recoverable coal, the association said. Rerouting the railroad would make another 55 million tons inaccessible to rail service unless expensive new road or rail connections were made. The Pennsylvania Electric Company (Penelec) was then considering construction of a steam-electric generating station further up the West Branch at Shawville. The plant and its need for millions of tons of coal would likely never materialize if Keating Dam and its hydroelectric station were built, coal proponents argued. The New York Central was not so adamant in its public opposition but did point out that its own engineering studies showed the corps had underestimated the project's price tag by a whopping $80 million, mainly by underestimating the cost of relocating the railroad and driving the tunnel.[72]

The negative reaction to Keating Dam among coal companies and local residents was so intense that the corps dropped the idea. It did proceed with plans for the other four dams, none of which evoked such a uniformly unfavorable response; and eventually they were built. Penelec went ahead with its plans for a new power plant and in 1954 opened the Shawville generating station, which after several expansions consumed up to 1.3 million tons of coal each year, most of which was delivered by the New York Central from area mines.[73]

For the third and final time, the Beech Creek was denied a chance to reclaim some of its nineteenth-century prominence; instead, deferred maintenance and a lack of traffic would be its hallmarks. In the diesel era, the River Line seldom experienced the kind of congestion that made routing trains over the Beech Creek necessary. Trains were still occasionally detoured but for less ordinary reasons. For example, a 1950 strike by locomotive firemen against the Pennsylvania caused the New York Central to cease exercising its rights over PRR rails between Keating and McElhattan for several days until the labor dispute was resolved. A rockslide near Keating in 1953 and a major derailment near Frenchville in 1956 each resulted in River Line closures lasting several days.[74]

There were no steady customers along the Beech Creek line east of Snow Shoe after General Refractories closed its Orviston works in 1962. Coal companies, which intermittently loaded rail cars at Kato and Panther from nearby strip mines, had shifted entirely to trucks about that same time. The Beech Creek Local began running intermittently, mostly when a strong demand for coal meant large numbers of empty cars were needed in short order at tipples between Snow Shoe and Munson. The railroad applied to the Interstate Commerce Commission for permission to abandon a 30.5-mile segment from just east of the J. H. France brickyard to the PRR interchange at Bald Eagle Junction. "It was apparent from the record that the loss of the coal and clay products formerly handled over this line precluded any hope of profitable operations in the future," ICC hearing examiner Paul Albus subsequently noted, "and that the expenditure of the amount necessary to rehabilitate the line for future service would be improvident." The railroad's request provoked no shipper protests, not even from J. H. France, which was preparing to undertake its second major plant expansion in a decade. The abandonment was approved in December 1965, meaning that all the NYC's Centre County and Moshannon Valley shippers soon would be served from trains originating at Clearfield.[75]

Given the Beech Creek's historical significance, the process of abandonment and dismantling attracted curiously little public notice. The final Beech Creek Local operated on April 23, 1966. The blare of the locomotive's air horn, sounding continuously as the eastbound train passed for the last time through Orviston, Monument, and Beech Creek, was about the only acknowledgment of the historic occasion. New York Central forces began removing the track that summer, working east to west. They salvaged many of the rails for use in expanding the NYC's Selkirk Yard, near Albany, New York. The Kato–Snow Shoe segment remained serviceable as late as January 1968 to accommodate gondolas for a shipper, Melvin Reese, who was in the final stages of harvesting pulpwood in the Kato area. When Reese finished, the track came out. The railroad permanently closed the Snow Shoe station.[76] Legally speaking, by the time the last of the old Beech Creek rails were lifted, they belonged to the Penn Central Transportation Company. The newly formed PC, an amalgam of the PRR and the NYC, ushered in an era of railroad history the likes of which J. Edgar Thomson, George Roberts, and the Vanderbilts could scarcely have imagined.

Notes

1. *Saward's Coal Trade Journal*, 4 August 1928; John N. Hoffman, "Pennsylvania's Bituminous Coal Industry: An Industrial Review," *Pennsylvania History* (October 1978): 351–63; Joseph T. Lambie, *From Mine to Market: The History of Coal Transportation on the Norfolk and Western Railway* (New York: New York University Press, 1954), 177.

2. *Railway Age*, 4 August 1928, 232.

3. John F. Reese and James D. Sisler, *Coal Resources; Bituminous Coalfields of Pennsylvania*, Pennsylvania Geological Survey, 4th series (Harrisburg: Department of Forests and Waters, 1928.)

4. Unless otherwise noted, coal production and shipping figures are drawn from published annual reports of the Pennsylvania Department of Mines and its successors.

5. Robert F. Archer, *History of the Lehigh Valley Railroad* (Berkeley, CA: Howell-North Books, 1977), 218; *Coal Age* 18, no. 24, (1920): 1204.

6. *Centre Democrat* (Bellefonte), 16 June 1930.

7. *Centre Democrat*, 11 March 1926.

8. PRR, "Statement Showing Nature of Economy Changes in Shops, Enginehouses, etc., for the Year 1930," photocopy in author's collection.

9. *Centre Democrat*, 6 January 1927, 18 April 1928, 21 August 1930.

10. *Democratic Watchman* (Bellefonte), 24 June 1932; Hoffman, "Pennsylvania's Bituminous Coal Industry," 361.

11. Bellefonte Central traffic manager Thomas Geoghegan to general manager George McClellan, 25 September 1942, Bellefonte Central Railroad Records, HCLA 1434, Series 3, Box 17, Pennsylvania State University Special Collections Library.

12. William Jaffe, "Coal Industry Project," typescript, part 4, 1960. The project was a ten-part series of articles describing the "history, production, and economic importance of the bituminous coal industry in Centre and Clearfield Counties," sponsored by the Central Pennsylvania Open Pit Mining Association for distribution to newspapers in the two counties during the summer of 1960.

13. Michael Bezilla interviews with Paul Anderson, Boalsburg, PA, 26 June 2007 and 17 August 2007.

14. Luther Gette interviews with Leonard Shilling, 4 and 5 June 2002, Bellefonte, PA. Shilling started with the PRR in 1946 as a Snow Shoe Branch brakeman.

15. George McClellan noted in his daybook for 17 January 1949 that at the PRR's invitation, he rode a brand new diesel locomotive on the local to Snow Shoe, BFC Records, Subgroup A, Series 3; *Centre Daily Times* (State College), 30 April 1955.

16. *Centre Democrat*, 29 January and 3 December 1959; ICC Order, Finance Docket No. 20448, 3 April 1959, Pennsylvania Railroad Company, Abandonment of Snow Shoe Branch.

17. Michael Bezilla, "Battle for Coal," *Railroad History* (Spring–Summer 2006): 58–67.

18. PRR, "Economy Changes," and "Statement Showing Shops, Enginehouses, and other M. of E. Facilities as of December 31, 1933," photocopies in author's collection.

19. PRR Middle Division ETT, 27 April 1930 and 26 September 1937; Luther Gette interview with John Hughes, retired PRR conductor, Osceola Mills, PA, 16 August 1999.

20. Luther Gette interview with retired PRR engineman Paul Frank, Osceola Mills, PA, 31 August 1999.

21. PRR Middle Division ETT, 28 April 1946.

22. Luther Gette interview with Rose and Michael Danko, Osceola Mills, PA, 21 August 1999. Rose Danko worked for the PRR at Osceola 1943–48. Her husband worked his way up from clerk to yardmaster on the PRR.

23. Hughes and Frank interviews.

24. PRR Middle Division ETT, 28 April 1946 and 29 April 1951; Luther Gette interview with Jack Renwick, retired PRR conductor, Sandy Ridge, PA, 19 October 1999; Hughes interview.

25. Renwick and Hughes interviews.

26. PRR Form C.T. 1000, List of Stations and Sidings, 1 November 1923.

27. Weekly reports by Branstetter to PRR district freight agent F. T. Brown, 11 October 1955–8 February 1956, copies in author's collection.

28. Gette interview with Eugene Danko, retired PRR clerk and relief yardmaster, Osceola Mills, PA, 1 November 1999.

29. Form C.T. 1000 for 1 November 1923 and 1 May 1945; Memo from J. R. Davis, Clearfield station agent, to N. B. Fagan, district freight agent, 23 January 1941, copy uploaded to PRR-FAX list, freight operations file, at Yahoo.com on 22 June 2013.

30. *The Progress* (Clearfield), 8 August 1947, 10 May and 16 June 1954, 7 May 1959.

31. PRR Form CT1000E for 1923 and 1945; "Bituminous and Anthracite Coal Mines of the Pennsylvania Railroad and Lateral Lines," PRR Coal Traffic Sales and Rates Department directory, 16 July 1956, in author's collection.

32. "Bituminous and Anthracite Coal Mines of the PRR"; Pennsylvania Department of Mines, *Annual Reports* for the period under discussion.

33. *The Progress*, 19 May 1949, 12 June and 16 June 1948, 5 October 1949, 17 February 1950.

34. Eric Hirsimaki, *Black Gold, Black Diamonds: The Pennsylvania Railroad and Dieselization*, vol. 2 (North Olmsted, OH: Mileposts Publishing, 2000), 97–99; *The Progress*, 23 February 1949.

35. Hirsimaki, *Black Gold, Black Diamonds*, 109–11.

36. Frank interview.

37. Hughes interview.

38. Joe Kovalchick to Bezilla, 20 December 2003. Kovalchick witnessed the Centipedes in pusher service at Sandy Ridge.

39. The author as a youth in Osceola observed RS-11s in service many times. See also John D. Hahn Jr., *Pennsylvania Railroad Diesel Locomotive Pictorial*, vol. 1 (Halifax, PA: Withers Publishing, 1995), 37–38.

40. Jaffe, "Coal Industry," part 7; U.S. Energy Information Administration, *Annual Energy Review 2011*, DOE/EIA-0384, September 2012, 203, 233–34.

41. "Integral Train Key to New Coal Rates," *Railway Age*, 9 April 1962; "What's Ahead for Unit Trains?," *Railway Age*, 20 April 1964; "PP&L Unit Trains," *Rails Northeast*, November 1976, 29–32; Bill Beck, *PP&L: 75 Years of Powering the Future* (Allentown: Pennsylvania Power and Light Co., 1995), 289, 327–30, 336–37, 350–51, 379–82.

42. *The Progress*, 21 and 23 April 1962; George A. Scott, *Clearfield Today and Tomorrow: Railroads of the Area* (Clearfield, PA: Progressive Publishing, 1968), 134–35.

43. Luther Gette interview with Ray Walker, founder of Bradford Coal Co., Bigler, PA, 26 October 2003; *Altoona Mirror,* 7 August 1962.

44. Pennsylvania Railroad Company, "Coal and Ore Traffic," in *Annual Report of the Board of Directors to the Stockholders* (Philadelphia: PRR, 1966); Memo of 11 August 1965, Unit Train Service from Elliot, in Pennsylvania Railroad Co., Office of Vice President Operations, Record Group 10, Subgroup A, Hagley Museum and Library; Albert Brinkley, "Pennsy Initiates Unit Coal Train Service," *Modern Railroads,* August 1964, 48–51.

45. "Savings by the Trainload," *Railway Age,* 29 June 1964; *Railway Age,* 15 November 1965; Beck, *PP&L,* 350–51; Eric Neubauer, *Pennsylvania Power & Light Coal Cars* (N.p.: self-published, 2006), 3–15.

46. *The Progress,* 20 March 1967.

47. *Railway Age,* 6 May 1963; "Savings by the Trainload"; Beck, *PP&L,* 350–51.

48. "Savings by the Trainload."

49. *Tyrone Daily Herald,* 2 May 1964; *Philipsburg Daily Journal,* 4 May 1964; Ryan C. Kunkle, "The Evolution of a Revolution: The H43 and the Unit Train," part 1, *Milepost* 27 (November 2009): 11–27.

50. Luther Gette interview with Don Rice, retired PRR track supervisor, Tyrone, PA, 31 October 1999; *The Progress,* 10 January and 8 February 1967; Kunkle, "Evolution," 24–25.

51. *Saward's Coal Trade Journal,* 25 February 1928; *Industrial Directory and Shippers Guide* (New York: NYC System, 1921), 285.

52. P. E. Crowley, "The Proposed New Trunk Line, Chicago to New York," *Railway Review,* 13 October 1923, 527–28.

53. "Trunk Line Proposal Arouses Interest," *New York Central Lines Magazine,* September 1923, 23–25; *Lock Haven Express,* 11 and 13 November 1952.

54. "Interstate Commerce Commission Hears Arguments for New Trunk Line," *New York Central Lines Magazine,* December 1923, 33–36; *The Progress,* 9 August 1930; Herbert H. Harwood Jr., "Nothing at the End of the Rainbow: The B&O's Adventures in Western Pennsylvania," *Railroad History* 129 (1973): 56–70.

55. *Lock Haven Express,* 2 December 1939; *The Progress,* 9 January 1940 and 20 August 1964; General Refractories Co., *Refractories* (Philadelphia: General Refractories Co., 1949), 109, 114.

56. Jim Davy, *All Company Towns Ain't Bad* (State College, Pa.: Self-published, 2011), 35–42.

57. *Lock Haven Express,* 4 March 1954; *Centre Democrat,* 30 August 1962; Michael Bezilla interview with Jim Davy, Orviston, PA, 3 April 2012.

58. Pennsylvania Department of Mines, *Annual Report* for 1938, 486; *Centre Daily Times,* 18 June 2002.

59. Application Docket No. 86694 in *Decisions of the Public Utility Commission,* vol. 38 (Harrisburg: Public Utility Commission, 1962), 13–16; *Centre Democrat,* 7 April 1966.

60. Pennsylvania Department of Mines, *Annual Reports* for 1950–60, and New York Central System, "Coal Service Directory," 1959, in author's collection.

61. Jeffrey Feldmeier telephone interview with Bill France, former principal of J. H. France Co., 11 October 2006; *The Progress*, 10 May 1954.

62. Richard D. Adams, *The Alley Popper* (Victor, NY: R. D. Adams, 1980), 35–52.

63. Jaffe, "Coal Industry," part 6; *The Progress*, 6 August 1960.

64. The New York Central Railroad Co., *Eastern District Pennsylvania Division Information Brochure*, 1957, in author's collection. This 46-page booklet, published by the railroad for internal use, provides a snapshot of operations and customers in the Beech Creek and Fall Brook districts. NYC Syracuse Division employee timetable, 25 October 1959.

65. The New York Central Railroad Co., *Eastern District Pennsylvania Division Information Brochure*, 1957, in author's collection.

66. *Wellsboro Agitator*, 22 January 1930; *Wellsboro Observer*, 11 March 1931.

67. Station closings can be traced through employee timetables.

68. "New York Central Railroad Co. Including Leased Lines, List of Officers, Representatives, Stations, and Other Facilities," pamphlet, 1 March 1943.

69. *Lock Haven Express*, 4 March 1954; *New York Times*, 4 October 1958; Memorandum, New York Central operations, Clearfield, 23 June 1965, Box 3, Merger Studies, Manuscript Group 286.400, Pennsylvania State Archives.

70. Hemsley interview.

71. *Railroad Telegrapher*, March 1953; *Clearfield Progress*, 16 April 1953; *Lock Haven Express*, 27 January 1954.

72. *Pennsylvania Division Information Brochure*; *Lock Haven Express*, 14 September 1950; *The Progress*, 17 May 1951 and 4 June and 25 June 1951.

73. "Pennsylvania Electric Company's Shawville Generating Station," Penelec-produced brochure, n.d.

74. *Lock Haven Express*, 12 May 1950, 1 June 1953, and 26 January 1956.

75. Albus quoted in *Traffic World*, 8 January 1966, 50; *Centre Democrat*, 14 April 1966.

76. *Centre Daily Times*, 29 June 1967; Harry A. Lingle and Vera A. Lingle, *History of the Beech Creek Area of Clinton County, Pennsylvania* (N.p.: n.p., 1981), 53.

ELEVEN

Railroading in the Valleys, 1918–68

ON THE ALLEGHENY PLATEAU, THE PENNSYLVANIA AND THE New York Central were primarily mineral haulers. In the valleys of southern Centre County, the NYC was absent after its surrogate, the Central Railroad of Pennsylvania (CRR), folded in 1918. Meanwhile millions of tons of coal flowed eastward each year over the PRR's Bald Eagle Branch, and thousands of carloads of limestone and lime originated annually in the Nittany Valley. Further to the southeast, in Penns Valley, the Bellefonte Branch—a segment of the former Lewisburg and Tyrone Railroad—eked out a modest existence based on agricultural and merchandise traffic. That kind of business was vulnerable to trucks, and in consequence, the branch was slowly fading into irrelevance. It was by no means a local phenomenon. By the middle of the twentieth century, highway transport threatened to make a substantial portion of the nation's railroad network irrelevant.

Effective May 1, 1929, the Pennsylvania dissolved the Tyrone Division, merging the Clearfield Branch into the Middle Division, and the Bald Eagle, Bellefonte, and Snow Shoe branches into the Williamsport Division. Operational experience soon prompted further reorganization, with the Middle Division absorbing all of the former Tyrone Division except the Bellefonte Branch east of Bellefonte. The Tyrone Division's dissolution was part of an effort to simplify the PRR's far-flung managerial hierarchy and end costly duplication. A number of other small divisions met the same fate, including in central Pennsylvania the Bedford, Bellwood, Cresson, and Lewistown divisions. The stock market crash of October 1929 and onset of the Great Depression accelerated the railroad's plans to rationalize the Tyrone Division's infrastructure. In Tyrone itself, the roundhouse, turntable, coal wharf, and car-repair and other shops were taken out of service and eventually razed. Further east in the Bald Eagle Valley, nearly a dozen passenger or freight stations or shelters that once affirmed the existence of such old-time iron-era settlements as Hannah, Martha, Julian, Unionville, Milesburg, Curtin, and Mount Eagle were closed. Block stations at Hannah, Unionville, Snow Shoe Intersection, and Sand (the west end of the Mount Eagle cutoff) were removed, while others were open or closed as needed, depending on what meager traffic the Depression allowed on the rails.[1]

The Bald Eagle Branch still offered the best route for western Pennsylvania coal to reach upstate New York customers and the Sodus Point dock on Lake Ontario. The PRR enlarged the pier at Sodus Point and the adjoining yard in 1927 to handle 500,000 tons of coal (as many as 10,000 carloads) annually. Improvements made after the Depression further boosted capacity so that by 1950, the railroad was loading more than 2 million tons each year into lake boats and sending additional tonnage to upstate New York power plants. Most of this coal was shipped via the Bald Eagle Branch, and much of it originated in Centre and Clearfield Counties. Coal-train crews ran between East Tyrone yard and Ralston, a relay point north of Williamsport, until the Tyrone Division was abolished. Altoona and Southport yard, near Elmira, then became the crew terminals.[2]

Several high-priority merchandise freights operated over the Bald Eagle Branch and through the Wilkes-Barre gateway despite the hard times. They included PG-13 (designated *The Dividend* for marketing purposes by the PRR's traffic department), CSB-2 (*The New Englander*), CSB-7 (which apparently traffic managers chose not to name), and PG-16 (*The Champion*). At Altoona or Pitcairn yard near Pittsburgh, these trains made connections with others serving the western part of the PRR system.[3]

Although it was bookended by Tyrone and Lock Haven, where paper mills and other industries depended heavily on the railroad, the Bald

Eagle Branch between those two locations accounted for relatively few carloads. Among the largest customers was the McFeely Brick Company at Port Matilda. Brick making had begun there about 1918, when the Superior Brick Company began operations using ganister rock quarried high on the northwest flank of Bald Eagle ridge. The ganister pits, extending laterally near the ridge top for a half-mile, were linked to the brickyard below by a narrow-gauge railroad and inclined plane. Latrobe-based McFeely acquired the plant in 1925 and in good times fired eight beehive kilns, employed about 200 workers, and could turn out 60,000 bricks daily, enough to fill six boxcars. Inbound rail shipments consisted mostly of coal and sand.

The Port Matilda facility was the only rail-served brickyard in Centre County or the Moshannon Valley that used ganister exclusively. The hard flint clay that area plants commonly made into firebrick was absent east of the Allegheny Front. Ganister, or quartzite, could be made into silica brick well suited for the extremely high temperatures of open-hearth furnaces in the steel industry and in glass-making furnaces. It was lighter and less brittle than firebrick and less subject to breakage during shipping. Harbison-Walker undertook the first commercial exploitation of the Bald Eagle ganister deposit in the early 1900s. It opened a quarry above Hannah, near the Centre-Blair county line, and used an inclined plane to bring the rock down to the railroad. Harbison-Walker shipped it raw to the company's Pittsburgh-area works, perhaps doubting the quality or quantity of the ganister and thus choosing not to erect a brickyard on site. The Hannah quarry closed around the time Superior planted its flag at Port Matilda.[4]

East of Port Matilda, the PRR did not have another major customer until Mount Eagle, about 36 miles east of Tyrone, where the Lycoming Silica Sand Company operated a quarry. A bit further east, near Howard, a siding constructed in 1937 served limestone quarries in nearby Jacksonville operated by the Bellefonte-based Valley View Lime Company and Whiterock Quarries. A narrow-gauge line connected the quarries and siding. Howard was also the site of a Sheffield Farms dairy. At Mill Hall in Clinton County, the railroad served two additional dairies and a General Refractories brickyard (which also was served by the New York Central).[5]

The absence of restrictive curves on the Bald Eagle Branch and the line's proximity to the Altoona shops continued to make it a favorite test bed for new or rebuilt locomotives and rolling stock. One series of tests even captured the attention of railroads from coast to coast. The Association of American Railroads in 1939 funded a project aimed at improving the design of high-speed freight-car trucks. Average freight train speeds nationally had risen by 61 percent since 1920, but freight-car truck technology had not kept pace, increasing the risk of derailments. Under the supervision of AAR and PRR engineers, a test train made an Altoona–Lock Haven roundtrip on alternate days, beginning in mid-June. It consisted of a class E6 4-4-2 locomotive, two baggage cars (one carrying measuring instruments and the other refurbished as an office car), a coach, and two test cars. On intervening days, different types of trucks were installed under the test cars (ten designs from various manufacturers were used) and the car weights were increased or decreased. Throughout the summer, the train routinely raced up and down the valley at speeds up to 80 miles per hour, the upper limit of what the AAR deemed necessary for modern freight railroading (and 35 miles per hour above the line's maximum freight train speed).[6] Better designs based on the test results came just in time to help the railroads meet the unprecedented surge of traffic resulting from America's entry into the Second World War in 1941.

Traffic surged on the Bald Eagle Branch during the war, then remained strong after peace returned in 1945, thanks to a robust national economy. A typical day saw the passage of six or seven eastbound coal trains and a like number of westbound empties. Three or four merchandise trains operated daily each way, along with passenger trains 510 and 511 and a few local freights, bringing the daily average to approximately 25–30 trains. Saturdays and Sundays brought only a slight decline. For example, the railroad reported that 40 freight trains hauling 2,297 cars moved over the branch on the weekend of June 15–16, 1946. (By comparison, the four-track Middle Division main line that weekend hosted 167 freight trains and 13,950 cars.)[7]

The branch's traffic density tested the skills of the dispatchers and block operators who controlled the single-track main line and its passing sidings. Adding to the challenge of keeping the railroad fluid was the mix of trains: fast freights, lumbering coal drags, poky locals, light helpers running from Dix to Tyrone, and the tightly scheduled passenger trains, as well as track gangs that periodically had to shut down portions of the railroad for maintenance. Even before the war, the Pennsylvania's operating department recognized that capacity could be increased only by adding a second main track the entire length of the branch or by installing centralized traffic control (CTC). The new technology put management of train movements in the hands of one operator, who used a control board that was wired to switches and signals along the line. Using an array of small lights and levers on the board, the operator could align these switches and signals remotely and determine the location of trains, thus eliminating the need for block operators and written train orders. In some instances, according to trade magazines, centralized traffic control boosted capacity of a single track line to as much as 75 percent of a two-track, non-CTC line.

Railroads had been using CTC since 1927. The Pennsylvania's first installation came in Illinois on the St. Louis Division in 1929, but it applied the new technology sparingly, already having invested heavily in automatic block signaling in multiple-track zones. The PRR considered the best candidates for CTC to be busy single-track lines where manual block signals governed train movements, since that's where cost savings from more efficient operation would most likely outweigh CTC's high installation costs. As late as 1947, the Pennsylvania had fewer than 360 route-miles under CTC authority.[8]

That total included 53 miles of the Bald Eagle Branch—everything east of Park tower in Tyrone. Installation began in mid-1945 and was completed in January 1946. The PRR eliminated block operators at Eagle, Port Matilda (where a station agent remained), West Julian, Wood, Beech, and Mill Hall. Park tower remained open to protect trains entering and leaving the Clearfield Branch and to control trains on that branch when Mills block station in Osceola was closed. The CTC board was placed in a newly built tower at Milesburg, roughly midway along the branch. Miles "tower" was in reality a squat, single-story brick building with large glass windows—a marked departure from traditional railroad architecture. Above the operator's desk, the board was alive with tiny colored lights depicting signals on the main track and passing sidings at Eagle, Julian, Milesburg, and Beech Creek, along with the position of all switches.

In 1947 the Pennsylvania reported CTC decreased average transit times over the Bald Eagle Branch by thirty-six minutes eastbound and fifty-nine minutes westbound. The number of train stops declined significantly. A key element in the CTC system's success was the design of the sidings. They were long enough to enclose two trains of average length traveling in the same direction to await a meet with an oncoming train, and to improve the chances of making nonstop meets when only one train in each direction was involved. (In such cases, one train would be authorized to proceed on the main track while the other train entered the siding and continued moving.) The turnouts at the end of each siding were good for train speeds of 30 miles per hour, and trackside signals midway through each siding indicated the road ahead—all enhancing the likelihood that trains would move faster in and out of sidings than had been possible under the old manual block protocol.[9]

Further efficiency came to the Bald Eagle Branch in 1949 in the form of Trainphone, a new (perfected on the PRR 1942) technology using electromagnetic induction that permitted tower operators and crews on moving trains to communicate via telephone. Voice communication in the form of low-frequency current was passed from a transmitter through the track or adjacent telephone wires and induced a corresponding current in a receiving antenna. Telephone handsets were located in lineside block stations and in locomotives and cabin cars, which sported distinctive antennae made from long lengths of pipe mounted horizontally on rooftops. Trainphone lessened the need to hand up paper orders to train crews and increased efficient movement of trains.[10]

Paul Anderson, who learned to fire locomotives on the heaving decks of 2-10-0 and 2-8-2 behemoths on the Bald Eagle Branch, recalled an instance of how Trainphone proved its value. "The operator [at Miles] would communicate with our train and any others in the vicinity to ascertain our estimated time of arrival at a particular location, so that he could arrange meets around Howard, if possible," using the old main line and the newer Mount Eagle cutoff. Anderson noted that even a lowly coal train could frequently run the length of the valley without stopping to wait for an oncoming train, thanks to Trainphone and CTC. Under such favorable conditions, coal trains could easily complete the 168-mile run between Altoona and Southport before their crews reached their limit of sixteen consecutive hours on duty.[11]

Nonstop running often challenged firemen on eastbounds to keep up steam pressure. Although Tyrone-based pushers assisted on the grade up to Dix, and the big L1s and I1s engines were equipped with automatic stokers, some hand-firing was required to spread coal evenly on the fire bed for optimal combustion. Firemen had to pace themselves on the Bald Eagle because the portion of the trip over Elmira Branch included heavier grades and a lot of shoveling. "You were beat when you got to Southport," Anderson remembered. "It was hard work." Fortunately, some relief was at hand in the form of the head brakeman, who normally rode in a small shelter (a "doghouse") on top of the tender's water tank. "We always carried two scoops [shovels]," Anderson explained. "The brakeman was expected to help when we did a lot of hand-firing. Besides, when the water got low in the tender, it did a lot of sloshing around and made for a pretty rough ride in the doghouse. The brakeman was glad to get out of there."

Trainphone also made the time-honored practice of getting a push from Tyrone up to Dix more efficient. In the cabin car, the conductor used information relayed by Trainphone from the pusher and the road enginemen to help him determine the best location to uncouple the pusher at speed, that is, without having to slow or stop to make the cut off. The flagman, stationed on the cabin's rear platform, received a hand signal from the conductor to pull the coupler pin, releasing the thundering locomotive that was barely out of his reach. The conductor then advised the head engineman the deed was done and on they went, as the steadily receding pusher slowed to a stop and readied for its tender-first trip back to Tyrone.

The road engine's fireman then had a relatively easy time of it until reaching Julian, where the fire had to be reinvigorated. Anderson recollected what happened next:

> You had to watch the steam gauge. When it started to drop, you shook the grates to let in more air for combustion. There were four sets of grates, and four bars protruding up at a slight angle from the floor in the cab, about ten inches, one for each grate. To shake the grates, you took the stoker bar, about four or five feet

long and hollow, and you slipped it over the bar of the grate you wanted to shake and moved it back and forth, back and forth. It was real hard manual labor, and you'd have the smoke rolling out of her all the way to Milesburg. Past Milesburg, at that last grade crossing [Holter's Crossing], we'd have plenty of steam, and the engineman would open her up for the run up to Howard.[12]

The transition from steam to diesel was more gradual on the Bald Eagle Branch than on the Clearfield Branch, whose imposing grades gave immediate and hefty rewards to dieselization. Steam-powered road freights could be seen on the Bald Eagle as late as the summer of 1957, the result of the PRR's decision to make Northumberland and Altoona the last bastions of its dwindling fleet of coal-burning freight locomotives. But diesels did not eliminate the need for a push from Tyrone to Dix, even though they possessed superior low-speed lugging capabilities. Diesels often received more tonnage to pull, and the grade was a challenge regardless of motive power, since getting a running start from downtown Tyrone was impossible.

Steam or diesel locomotives hauled the coal trains to Sodus Point, where activity reached postwar peaks in 1951 and again in 1956: each of those years saw about 2.4 million tons of bituminous dumped into lake boats. The situation changed abruptly in 1959 with the opening of the publicly funded St. Lawrence Seaway. Including improvements to the Welland Canal, the seaway opened navigation to larger lake vessels, which could take on coal at Ohio's Lake Erie ports for Canadian destinations at lower rates than what could be offered at Sodus Point. The PRR closed the facility in 1967, a year in which it dumped only 123,000 tons.[13]

Fewer coal trains traveled the Bald Eagle Branch in the 1960s. Most were bound for power plants in upstate New York or the New England gateway at Wilkes-Barre. Boxcar traffic declined as well, a casualty of increased competition from trucks using the new publicly financed interstate highway system. Freight schedules of the mid-1960s showed a pair of daily through trains operating between Altoona and Wilkes-Barre. Another pair ran between Altoona and Northumberland and made set-outs and pickups on the siding at Milesburg for the Bellefonte-based local.

The Bald Eagle Branch lost one of its oldest customers when the brickyard at Port Matilda closed in 1959. General Refractories had purchased the plant from McFeely in 1956, leading to speculation that Grefco was mainly interested in idling it in order to reduce excess capacity in the refractories industry. The closing also spelled the end for the agency at the Port Matilda freight station, where billing hundreds of carloads of brick annually had once warranted a full-time clerk. The station was shuttered in the summer of 1959, leaving Howard as the only agency station on the branch.[14]

The Howard station in the early 1960s was living on borrowed time: the community it served was about to experience a wrenching upheaval. In 1954 Congress had authorized the Army Corps of Engineers to build three of the four dams (excluding the Keating) that it had proposed earlier to control flooding in the West Branch basin. The Blanchard Dam, as it was first named, was to be located near its namesake town and back up Bald Eagle Creek nearly 8 miles, creating a lake for seasonal recreation that would normally inundate 1,700 acres and twice that during maximum high water. Such a large flood plain meant relocating 9.9 miles of the Bald Eagle Branch, many more miles of highway and utility lines, and four cemeteries—all of which required the acquisition of approximately 13,000 acres of land. In Howard, a community of some 800 residents, twenty-one families would be displaced, along with dozens more up and down the valley. The plan aroused strong sentiments among area residents, and years passed as the project's merits were debated and details fine-tuned.

Finally, in mid-1964, the corps received authorization to proceed. Building a new railroad was part of the project's first phase; work began in April 1965. At flood tide, the reservoir would inundate much of the low-lying Mount Eagle cutoff and some of the original main line through downtown Howard. With traffic on the branch forecast to continue its decline, and given the efficiencies of diesel locomotives, planners believed that one new track could easily replace the two older lines. The PRR laid out its requirements, and the corps oversaw preliminary engineering and the acquisition of about forty separate properties traversed by the new right-of-way. The new alignment began near the village of Mount Eagle and continued east on higher ground past Howard until rejoining the original right-of-way near the hamlet of Eagleville. The two contractors building the railroad—No. 1 Contracting Corporation of

Figure 11.1. The PRR's Bellefonte local is westbound near Howard on a segment of the Bald Eagle Branch newly relocated to accommodate the construction of Sayers Dam. *Author's collection.*

Wilkes-Barre and James J. Skelly Inc. of Malvern—finished their jobs on schedule and opened the new line for service in April 1967.[15]

By then, work was underway on the breastwork of the dam, which had been renamed for PFC Foster Joseph Sayers, a Centre County native who posthumously received the Medal of Honor for bravery during World War II. The railroad played an important role in hauling in construction materials for the structure, an earth fill 100 feet high and 1.3 miles wide with a 600-foot-long concrete spillway and a 440-foot outlet tunnel. Work was officially completed in August 1969 at a cost of $30 million, and the process of filling the lake began. The Commonwealth of Pennsylvania subsequently leased nearly 6,000 acres around the lake for recreational purposes, forming Bald Eagle State Park.[16]

In the twentieth century, as in the nineteenth, the Bald Eagle Branch provided Bellefonte with its chief means of rail freight access to the larger system. In the 1920s, limestone and lime gained primacy; in 1925, the Bellefonte Central alone gave the PRR 383,000 tons of the stuff. But a variety of other freight typically associated with small-town enterprise was received or dispatched by rail—lumber and other building supplies, grain, livestock feed, dairy products, machinery, coal and petroleum products, brass and other industrial metals, and many cars laden with less-than-carload (LCL) merchandise. The rail yard at Sunnyside was active seven days a week, and the PRR based several H6 2-8-0 Consolidations in Bellefonte for switching and local freight service.[17] In addition to routine activity, the keen trackside observer might have occasionally observed special moves, such as a specially built "fish car" outbound from the state hatchery at Pleasant Gap, or an inbound coach with prisoners being transferred to the new state correctional institution that had opened upstream from the hatchery at Rockview. Bellefonte also was a favored destination for circus trains, including the famous Walter L. Main show, in even larger and gaudier form after its 1904 sale by Main. It often ran in two sections, and regularly played Bellefonte up to its final year of operation in 1937.[18]

In 1921, the area's limestone and lime industry consisted of about twenty-five quarries and twelve batteries of shaft kilns employing more than 900 workers.[19] The majority of those operations belonged to American Lime and Stone, the largest of Centre County's "big three" producers. American concentrated its quarrying where the Valentine Formation outcropped on either side of the gap in Bald Eagle Ridge carved by Spring Creek. Chemical Lime, operating several quarries and two lime plants along Buffalo Run, was served by the Bellefonte Central. Whiterock Quarries had quarries and kilns across the valley at Pleasant Gap, where the Valentine Formation outcropped at the base of Nittany Mountain. Chemical and Whiterock were headquartered in Bellefonte, while American—the only one to have operations outside Centre County—was headquartered in Tyrone, hometown of its chief executive and cofounder, Alexander Morris.

American upped the ante among the big three in 1922, when it opened the Bell mine, the Nittany Valley's first underground limestone mine, three years in development. American had recognized that as quarries drove deeper into the Valentine formation, surface excavation would become impractical. The Bell mine began as a 390-foot-long inclined shaft driven into the limestone from the floor of an existing quarry above Coleville. A narrow-gauge railroad hauled the stone from a conveyor at the mine portal across a steel trestle above the Bellefonte Central tracks to Plant 19, a new lime-making and storage facility near the site of the former Bellefonte Glass Works. The PRR served the plant from the east side.

In conjunction with the opening of the Bell mine, American installed a huge coal-fired rotary kiln at Plant 19, among the first of its kind anywhere in the United States and the first in central Pennsylvania. The new kiln could produce 150 tons of lime daily, a major increase in capacity over the smaller, less efficient shaft kilns. The Bell Mine and adjacent Plant 19 required an investment so large that Morris had to sell majority ownership in American Lime and Stone to the Philadelphia-based Warner Company, one of the nation's largest producers and processors of lime, stone, and sand. With Warner's financial backing, the Bell mine drove its main shaft deeper into the limestone and simultaneously tunneled laterally at various levels into the rich 70-foot-thick limestone deposits. Plant 19 soon received a second rotary kiln to handle the mine's growing limestone output. Warner fully absorbed American in 1944 and a third rotary kiln came on line, by which time the mine's depth surpassed 900 feet.[20]

The Chemical Lime Company followed American's lead by developing its own underground mine and a completely new Plant 3 along the side of Bald Eagle Ridge, west of the much older Plants 1 and 2. Acquisition of property and mineral rights, begun in the 1920s, took years; the Great Depression had struck by the time the process was completed. Private investment had dried up, so the company turned to the federal Reconstruction Finance Corporation for a loan. Plant 3's 400-foot coal-fired rotary kiln was the longest in the United States when it calcined its first batch of lime in March 1937. The kiln could produce 200 tons of crushed or pebble lime from 400 tons of stone every twenty-four hours. The stone reached Plant 3 on a conveyor belt from

Figure 11.2. Chemical Lime Company's Plant 3, served by the Bellefonte Central, once boasted the nation's longest rotary kiln, seen here under construction in 1936. *Author's collection.*

the new mine, which eventually plunged nearly a thousand feet into the Valentine Formation.

With many federal and state public works programs in full swing, Chemical had anticipated a modest upturn in the demand for lime and stone. When the boomlet failed to happen, the company could not meet its financial obligations and declared bankruptcy in December 1937. Finally, in 1940, the National Gypsum Company purchased Chemical Lime and proceeded to install a second kiln and more processing equipment. Headquartered in Buffalo, New York, National Gypsum got its start in 1925 as a producer of wallboard. Through the 1930s, it bought a number of failing companies at bargain prices and expanded into the manufacture of lime, plaster, metal lath, cement, and other building products, many marketed under the Gold Bond label. With the Plant 3's upgrades installed in the early 1940s as promised, National Gypsum became the nation's second largest lime producer, after the Warner Company.[21] Plant 3 itself soon became locally known, with a certain communal pride, as "the Gyp," and obsolete Plants 1 and 2 nearby were closed.

On the other side of the Nittany Valley, Whiterock Quarries followed a less ambitious business plan. As American and Chemical were adopting rotary-kiln technology and tunneling deep underground in search of high-quality stone, Whiterock stood pat with the eighteen shaft kilns it had erected on the eve of the First World War and continued surface mining, sourcing from pits more than a hundred feet deep on the outskirts of the village of Pleasant Gap. In the 1920s, the company invested in new hydrating and pulverizing equipment; but much of the limestone it quarried was "blue stone," unsuitable for calcining yet ideal as crushed stone for fluxing and construction purposes.[22]

In 1941 the Bellefonte-area lime plants operated by Warner, National Gypsum, and Whiterock were among eighty-nine lime plants in operation statewide, serving steel mills, electrochemical plants, glass factories, paper mills, tanneries, and many other industrial consumers. Pennsylvania had far more lime plants than any other state—about 30 percent of the national total—and led all other states in the production of lime and crushed limestone. Centre County was a leader in both commodities.[23]

For the Pennsylvania Railroad, the county's lime and limestone industry represented a bonanza. In 1934, for example, when virtually all lime and stone produced in the county except for local deliveries was shipped by rail, the big three producers, as noted below, had a total annual capacity of more than 1.8 million tons—and that was prior to the opening of Chemical's Plant 3.[24]

When combined with the modest output of crushed limestone from a few small producers, the PRR had the potential to ship enormous quantities of lime and limestone from Centre County each year. Precisely how much the railroad did ship depended on actual production, which in turn depended on the condition of the state and national economies.

TABLE 11.1. LIME AND LIMESTONE PRODUCTION CAPACITY
OF BELLEFONTE'S "BIG THREE," 1934

	Lime in tons	Limestone in tons
Chemical Lime	100,000	750,000
American Lime and Stone	145,000	300,000
Whiterock Quarries	60,000	475,000

Output lagged behind capacity during the Depression and then exploded during the war years and remained strong when peace returned. The PRR acquired a fleet of covered hopper cars for lime and stone service, and stenciled about 600 of them with the directive "WHEN EMPTY RETURN TO BELLEFONTE PA PRR" in an effort to boost car utilization. It was the railroad's—and probably the nation's—largest single pool of cars dedicated to the lime trade.[25]

After the war, rather than invest in new facilities to replace the outmoded shaft kilns, Whiterock decided to exit the lime business and focus on stone; an ever-increasing share of the company's output moved by truck.[26] Although Whiterock began a period of decline so far as the railroad was concerned, the Pennsylvania had reason to be optimistic about its overall Bellefonte-area lime and limestone traffic. Early in 1949, Baltimore-based Standard Lime and Cement Company quietly began purchasing a series of farms northeast of Pleasant Gap in the vicinity of the old Bellefonte airport. Earlier test borings had convinced Standard that abundant limestone underlay that site, comparable in purity to what National Gypsum and the Warner Company were obtaining. It intended to open an underground mine and a lime plant, shipping both limestone and lime.

Standard negotiated with the PRR to build a spur line to serve the plant. From a junction with the Whiterock Branch, a survey took the track in a northeastward direction for about 2.5 miles. A fill and a steel girder bridge carried the track above the busy state highway between Bellefonte and Pleasant Gap. Land acquisition was completed by the end of 1950, and construction of both the railroad and the new Standard Lime facility began. The railroad contractor was C. J. Langenfelder and Son of Baltimore, a large firm that frequently did business with the

Pennsylvania Railroad. Langenfelder hauled much of the 200,000-ton slag pile left by long-gone Nittany Furnace to use as fill and handled the entire job of building the new line, from erecting the bridge over the highway to laying the track. It was a project of modest proportions for the contractor—the firm's next job was to excavate 8 million cubic yards of earth for U.S. Steel's new Fairless Works on the Delaware River north of Philadelphia—but it was unusual simply because railroad construction in Pennsylvania, once an everyday enterprise, had become a rarity. It was important enough to warrant a daylong visit from PRR vice president for operations James Symes in June 1951. Symes arrived via the Bald Eagle Branch in his private railcar and traveled the length of the new line out to Standard before going east over the L&T to Centre Hall and return.[27]

Standard Lime and Cement (the company was soon to change its name to Standard Lime and Stone) was already an important PRR customer. A family-run operation founded in Maryland in the late nineteenth century, it had plants in West Virginia, Virginia, Ohio, and Michigan and produced lime and stone for many industrial purposes. At Pleasant Gap, it opened both an underground mine and a quarry. The surface mine helped ensure uninterrupted production during the spring, when snow melted on Nittany Mountain and seeped into the underground mine faster than the pumps could remove it. Standard began shipping product via its new rail spur, officially the Pleasant Gap Industrial Track, by April 1952. During that entire year, the Pennsylvania originated nearly 4,700 carloads from Standard and Whiterock combined.[28]

Standard quickly supplanted Whiterock as one of Centre County's big three lime producers. By the mid-1950s, the three were each mining on average more than 1.1 million tons of limestone each year, most of which they made into lime. At National Gypsum, for example, the ratio of lime carloads to limestone carloads was typically four or five to one. Standard marketed as little as 10,000–15,000 tons of crushed limestone in some years. Lack of comprehensive documentation makes it impossible to say precisely how much of their total output these companies shipped by rail, but close to 90 percent seems to be a good estimate.[29]

The steel industry was the largest single consumer of Bellefonte-area lime. Mills were located at all points of the compass from Centre County: Bethlehem, Coatesville, and Conshohocken to the east; Sparrows Point (Baltimore) to the south; Wheeling, Pittsburgh, and Youngstown to the west; and Lackawanna (Buffalo) on the north. The county's dependence on the steel industry was highlighted when a month-long strike idled most of the mills in the summer of 1952. Warner and National Gypsum each shut down two of their three rotary kilns, and Standard temporarily discontinued all lime production. The three companies furloughed nearly 300 employees for the duration of the fifty-three-day work stoppage. Meanwhile, brickyards at Port Matilda and Orviston ceased production of industrial brick and laid off more than a hundred employees.[30]

At that time—the early 1950s—the Pennsylvania was originating approximately forty carloads of lime daily in the Bellefonte area, based on shipments in 70-ton-capacity railcars.[31] Covered hoppers constituted the backbone of the car fleet, although boxcars still saw some use, mainly when customers desired bagged lime. The era of bulk lime being blown into boxcars had pretty much ended. For consignees who required smaller than carload lots, the PRR introduced steel containers that could be carried in gondola cars, as many as sixteen containers per car.

As in the coalfields on the Allegheny Plateau, prosperous economic times often brought shipper complaints of car shortages. The railroad tried to ease the problem in the Bellefonte area by establishing quotas for allocating empties among the lime companies. After Standard reached full production, the Pennsylvania's formula called for allocating 43 percent of covered hoppers to National Gypsum, 34 percent to Warner, and 23 percent to Standard. Of container gondolas, Standard received 55 percent, National Gypsum 27, and Warner 18 percent. The railroad based these figures on consignees' preferences and the type of products each shipper specialized in. There were no formulas for boxcars or open-top hoppers, which were less in demand. The PRR fine-tuned allocations as market conditions warranted, but grumbling among the lime companies continued. They complained more about the lack of absolute numbers of cars than about whatever formula happened to be in effect. For example, if Warner needed 100 covered hoppers to meet consignee orders during a certain week, and its quota of 34 percent of the available supply equated to only 70 such cars, the shipper's outcry would be long and loud. In addition, the Bellefonte Central claimed the PRR sometimes ignored quotas in favor of making sure Warner and Standard were adequately supplied, even if it meant National Gypsum came up short.[32]

Through the 1950s, the Pennsylvania's Bellefonte-based service operated around the clock Monday through Friday and usually part of the weekend. Although specific times for calling crews and dispatching trains varied, there was nonetheless a certain regularity to the ebb and flow of rail traffic.[33] Each weekday around 6 AM, a crew reported to the open-air engine terminal at the east end of Sunnyside yard. Diesel locomotives, in the form of several Baldwin end-cab switchers, by 1953 replaced H9s and H10s Consolidations. The crew used one of the locomotives to work the yard, pulling cars that had arrived overnight for delivery to Bellefonte-area customers later that day. Two train crews reported in midafternoon. Division of labor might vary, but one crew usually weighed outbound carloads of limestone and lime and began building "blocks" of cars headed for common destinations: the steel mills around Pittsburgh, for example, or the Wilkes-Barre gateway. The crew might also deliver coal to West Penn Power Company's steam electric-generating station at Milesburg. West Penn opened the 44-megawatt plant in 1950 to replace an outmoded hydroelectric station at McCoy Dam on Spring Creek. The utility sourced coal from local mines, but proximity to those areas tilted the economics of delivery toward trucks, and the PRR lost the business after just a few years.[34] The other afternoon crew typically set out and picked up cars at customers in Bellefonte area and also served Standard and Whiterock. Going out to Pleasant Gap, the train's consist often included a few cars of miscellaneous freight—perhaps a gondola for loading at a scrap yard on the Whiterock Branch, a car of livestock feed or fertilizer for a distributor on the Pleasant Gap Branch, or coal (before trucks got the business) for Standard's kilns, which burned up to 500 tons weekly. In late afternoon the Bellefonte Central arrived with loads from the Gyp and a few empties from State College. The local from Northumberland was another frequent late-afternoon visitor at Sunnyside, setting out westbound cars it had gathered during its journey over the former L&T. It picked up any cars slated for delivery to customers at Lemont and points east and departed.

For many years, a train operated nightly from Tyrone or Altoona to Bellefonte, powered by one of the PRR's workhorse L1s Mikados. Inbound, the train consisted mostly of empty cars from Pittsburgh-area steel mills. When it left Bellefonte soon after sunrise, it carried mostly loads for those same mills. The railroad eliminated that train in the name of cost savings by the mid-1950s and eventually settled on having a Bellefonte crew make one or more daily trips to the Bald Eagle Branch at Milesburg. There the crew set out Pittsburgh-and-west loads for train AN-3, and picked up empties from eastbound AN-16. Those trains ran daily between Altoona and Northumberland.

The PRR was more consistent in maintaining an overnight run from Bellefonte to Lock Haven and return. That train carried limestone and lime cars destined for such upstate New York customers as Bethlehem Steel's Lackawanna Works, various electrochemical companies around Niagara Falls, and Thatcher Glass's Elmira plant. Curtis Publishing Company's sprawling paper mill at Johnsonburg, Pennsylvania, also was an important lime customer. The local often worked the quarry siding at Howard, where it picked up as many as a dozen cars a day for various steel mills.[35] Reaching Lock Haven just before daylight, the local gathered Bellefonte-bound cars and arrived back at Sunnyside soon after the morning yard crew began its chores.

And so the routine went, five days a week, year round. A Saturday crew was usually called to work Sunnyside yard, the BFC interchange (that road operated most Saturdays), and Warner and Standard, both of which loaded cars through the weekend. Until the PRR abandoned the Snow Shoe Branch in 1959, a crew was called as needed to serve customers on the Mountaintop. Bellefonte operations were supported by a yardmaster and a clerical force of about a half-dozen employees based in the former passenger station in Bellefonte.[36]

Bellefonte-based train crews figured in Centre County's last fatal train accident. On the afternoon of June 22, 1948, the operator at Miles tower cleared H9s No. 1422 at Sunnyside yard to go east on the Bellefonte Branch with three boxcars for a cannery at Oak Hall. Passing a block limit at White, where a switch led to the Whiterock Branch, Extra 1422 would enter that segment of the Bellefonte Branch controlled by the operator at Montandon tower, 62 miles to the east. However, the train crew was not qualified east of White, since Oak Hall was normally served by the Northumberland local. Extra 1422 consequently stopped at the Bellefonte passenger station until it could embark a qualified pilot engineer. Before the train got underway again, both the pilot and the conductor spoke by phone with the Montandon operator, asking for permission to pass White and proceed to Oak Hall. Unfortunately the three-way conversation was garbled. The Montandon operator thought the train was already at White, and he cleared it for Oak Hall. Minutes later, acting on the false assumption that Extra 1422 was now east of White, he permitted a train that had finished working Whiterock Quarries to come down the branch to White and head for Bellefonte. That train consisted of H9s No. 1742 running tender first, followed by a cabin car and nine cars laden with limestone and lime.

The two trains collided head-on while rounding a blind curve near the village of Axemann. The conductor and flagman in the cabin behind No. 1742 were crushed to death. Five other crewmen were injured. An ICC investigation pointed to confusion caused by having the Montandon operator (rather than the operator at Miles) control the block limit at White as a contributing factor in the collision. The PRR subsequently gave Miles authority over White and reorganized the Bellefonte Branch into two separate entities: the Bellefonte Secondary Track from Miles to White, and the Montandon Secondary Track east of White to Montandon. Bellefonte-based trains were then able make the run to Whiterock and return under verbal orders from one office—Miles—with no need to get permission from Montandon.[37]

Beginning in the late 1940s, it was not unusual for the local from Northumberland to turn back before reaching Bellefonte if there were no cars to be set out or picked up at Sunnyside yard. In such cases the train worked only as far west as the last customer to be served.[38] Shippers along the first 12 miles of the Montandon Secondary Track, as far west as Mifflinburg, on average accounted for about 60 percent of the line's total annual revenues.[39] The remote 25-mile segment between Mifflinburg and Coburn had generated almost no traffic after lumbering died out.

On the 26 miles of line from Coburn to White block limit, customers offered the railroad a variety of freight. Inbound cars might be laden with cement, liquid chemicals, livestock feed, or kitchen appliances. Outbound cars might contain canned vegetables, limestone, or (at harvest time) grain. Unfortunately for the railroad, no customer was of such a large scale that it could ship or receive even a half-dozen cars at a time; and nearly all the traffic on the rails was vulnerable to trucks. By 1958, the Northumberland-based train was operating on a Monday-Wednesday-Friday schedule. The PRR withdrew its agent from the Coburn station in 1959 and closed the Spring Mills station at about that same time. The Centre Hall agent represented the railroad at all three locations. The Lemont agent handled all business from the Oak Hall cannery on the east to the state prison at Rockview on the west. That segment included Neidigh Quarries, which in 1962 and 1963 bustled with activity as it loaded as many as a hundred open-top hopper cars weekly with stone for Kinzua Dam, a large Corps of Engineers flood-control project in north-central Pennsylvania. A promising new shipper, Corning Glass Company, built a manufacturing plant near Dale Summit, between Lemont and the prison in 1967. Corning looked at a number of locations in the county and selected the Dale Summit site in part because of easy access to rail service and to an abundance of inexpensive, high-quality water, which it piped to the plant from Bellefonte's Big Spring. The plant, which made glass panels for television picture tubes, received sand and various dry bulk minerals by rail. The finished glass panels were shipped by truck.[40]

Among the sites Corning had considered for the new plant was one along the Bellefonte Central near Waddle, on the approach to State College. The PRR would have been required to share a modest portion of the Corning freight revenue with the short line, of course; but the larger road would ultimately have gotten all the traffic, since it was the BFC's only interchange partner. The question of whether or not the Bellefonte Central would be captive to the Pennsylvania had been settled decades earlier. In the early 1900s, the PRR kept a watchful eye on the Central Railroad of Pennsylvania and the Bellefonte Central Railroad, just in case they should be the instruments by which the New York Central might attempt another thrust into the Pennsylvania Railroad's exclusive territory. The demise of the CRR in 1918 seemingly put an end to such a possibility. In fact, however, it reappeared in the 1920s.

The Central Railroad had hardly run its last train when the PRR adopted a hard line toward the Bellefonte Central. Instead of allocating to the short line a portion of the revenue on shipments to or from BFC customers, the Pennsylvania charged only a Bellefonte rate, forcing the BFC to add its own charge for haulage on its part of the route. The PRR's Bellefonte rate was applicable anywhere within the Bellefonte zone, defined as that area served by its Bellefonte-based trains. Whiterock Quarries was in the Bellefonte zone and shipped limestone and lime to Pittsburgh for the identical rate that the PRR charged the Warner Company for the same service. Chemical Lime was at a competitive disadvantage: it had to pay the PRR's Bellefonte rate to Pittsburgh, plus whatever charge the Bellefonte Central levied. Higher transportation costs in effect made limestone and lime from Chemical more expensive than the same products from Warner and Whiterock. In a similar manner, a State College furniture dealer paid the PRR's Bellefonte rate for a carload of new chairs delivered to Lemont (by the eastbound train over the L&T), and paid the Bellefonte rate plus the Bellefonte Central's charge for the same carload of chairs delivered to State College. In most cases, the drayage cost from the Lemont station was about the same as that from the State College station; simply because the BFC had a station closer to the consignee offered no significant price advantage.

Robert Frazer, in his fourth decade as the Bellefonte Central's chief executive, believed that one solution to his railroad's problem was to secure an interchange with the New York Central. He initiated discussions with NYC management about relaying rails between Bellefonte and Mill Hall more or less on the CRR's old right-of-way. The larger road seemed to welcome the opportunity to regain influence in the Nittany Valley. It offered one of its senior civil engineers to survey the route and identify alternatives where the original CRR alignment was no longer feasable.[41]

Meanwhile, at the BFC's urging, Chemical Lime appealed to the Interstate Commerce Commission for relief from the PRR's rate-making policy. The commission announced its decision in January 1928, setting a favorable precedent for short lines everywhere. The ICC ordered the Pennsylvania to include all points on the Bellefonte Central in the

Bellefonte rate zone and to work with the BFC to establish joint rates and devise a formula for sharing the revenues. The roads reached a short-term agreement on rate divisions in February. "The result has been an increase in tonnage over your line," Frazer told his fellow shareholders, "and net earnings have increased by approximately $3,700 per month." The Bellefonte Central's total freight movement increased from 182,000 tons in 1927 to 341,000 tons in 1929.[42]

Emboldened by this victory over the Pennsylvania before the ICC, Frazer and his board of directors decided to try for another when they asked the commission to force the Pennsylvania to sell them the Fair-brook Branch (the west end of the old L&T), most of which the PRR was planning to abandon. The short line proposed to build 5 miles of track to link the Fairbrook with State College. The Bellefonte Central could then interchange Pittsburgh-bound lime and stone with the PRR at Tyrone instead of Bellefonte, increasing the BFC's line haul from about 3 miles to 44 miles and giving it a correspondingly larger share of the revenues. The short line was then originating more than 5,000 carloads of quarry traffic every year; approximately half of those cars were destined for consignees in western Pennsylvania and Ohio.

In rebuttal, the Pennsylvania told the ICC that Chemical Lime would be ill served because cars would actually take longer in transit (although not explaining why that would be the case). Privately PRR vice president Albert J. County admitted his company feared that after acquiring the Fairbrook Branch, the Bellefonte Central would reconstitute the CRR's route between Mill Hall and Bellefonte. The New York Central might then buy the newly expanded BFC in an effort "to finally get down into the inner regions of Pennsylvania, into the coal territory."[43] By "coal territory," County meant the Broad Top field in south-central Pennsylvania with its highly prized low-volatile "smokeless" coal. From there the NYC could dip below the Mason-Dixon Line to establish a friendly connection with the Western Maryland or B&O. The era of aggressive expansion in the railroad industry had long since passed, yet County's fears were not misplaced. Bellefonte Central traffic manager and board member Tom Geoghegan talked openly with his company's shareholders about the advantages of making some kind of deal with the New York Central. He confided to one director, "Our only hope of doing something for the Bellefonte Central stockholders is to . . . connect it with some large line other than the Pennsylvania Railroad."[44]

The ICC was not persuaded by the PRR's insistence that service to Chemical Lime would suffer if the BFC hauled its cars Tyrone. The commission therefore directed the Pennsylvania to sell the 18 miles of line up for abandonment for its $52,000 scrap value. The Pennsylvania complied, and the Bellefonte Central promptly brought in a contractor to build the 5-mile State College–Fairbrook connecting link. On October 1, 1930, trains officially began operating over the line. A few months earlier, the BFC had opened a new station in State College, giving back to Penn State its lot in the campus core in exchange for a larger site near the campus's western edge.

The Pennsylvania reacted as if it were sparring with a road its own size—the New York Central, to be precise. It refused to accept any cars from the BFC at Tyrone that came from points east of State College, meaning Chemical Lime. Likewise, the PRR continued to route Chemical-bound empties from Pittsburgh-area steel mills through Bellefonte, as if the Tyrone interchange did not exist. The Bellefonte Central again went before the ICC but this time came away empty-handed. After forcing the PRR to sell the Fairbrook to the BFC in the first place, the commission inexplicably refused to intervene to help make it an economically viable route. The Fairbrook venture quickly soured. The Bellefonte Central shipped a total of only 51 outbound carloads over the branch in 1931 and 1932, mostly clay, sand, forest products, and potatoes that originated in the rural area between State College and Warriors Mark. During those same two years, it sent 5,746 carloads—nearly all from Chemical Lime—through the Bellefonte interchange.

When the chance to acquire the Fairbrook Branch first arose, Centre County banks refused to loan the short line money to buy it or build the new connecting track. Bellefonte Central officials accused the PRR of pressuring the prospective lenders to withhold funds. The short line alternatively obtained the money by issuing $200,000 in 6 percent, twenty-year bonds. As the Depression worsened and traffic levels dipped, the short line found itself behind in its interest payments. In a completely legal transaction, the Pennsylvania Railroad had purchased 70 percent of the bond issue. Near the end of 1932, vice president County informed the BFC's board of directors that his railroad intended to foreclose on the little railroad and take it over lock, stock, and barrel unless the Fairbrook Branch was shut down. The board had no realistic choice but to comply. Effective February 1, 1933, the BFC embargoed all traffic over the line west of State College. The track lay unused until it was officially abandoned and track materials lifted for salvage in 1941.[45]

An uprising occurred among the twenty or so active Bellefonte Central shareholders, who purged the company of leaders considered to be responsible for the Fairbrook debacle. (The deal's chief advocate, Robert Frazer, had retired in 1929 due to infirmities of old age.) Ultimately a new president emerged who was less likely to antagonize the Pennsylvania Railroad. He was Charles Wesley, a Philadelphia attorney who was also serving as president of the Huntingdon and Broad Top Mountain Railroad. Wesley made clear to PRR executives that his railroad was closing the door on any notions of selling out to the New York Central or laying track to a Mill Hall interchange with the NYC. About that same time, perhaps not coincidentally, the Pennsylvania agreed to a long-term division of freight rates that gave the BFC a more favorable share.

In 1938 Wesley made a remarkable proposition to the Pennsylvania. He was well aware that the larger road was troubled that many of its branch lines throughout the state were being operated at a considerable financial loss. "I would like you to consider the following," he wrote in a letter to A. J. County, "which at first blush would seem to be the figment of an excited imagination."

> The Bellefonte Central is seriously disposed to consider operation of the Lewisburg and Tyrone, which as you know extends from Bellefonte to Montandon. The road could be operated by us under lease or some other form, and perhaps we could operate the whole yard [at Bellefonte], including the L&T, making deliveries to the Pennsylvania Railroad at Milesburg. Our operating expenses are lower, our taxes are lower, our incidental costs are lower, and at first blush it would seem that we would be able to do the job much more cheaply than the P.R.R.... As we know the circumstances to be, we believe that the Pennsylvania's greater interest is in through traffic up and down the Bald Eagle Valley and that its interest in local development around Bellefonte is not of so much moment. In addition to which a short line could perhaps gain more support from the local inhabitants than the Pennsylvania could.[46]

Wesley's proposal mirrored almost exactly what would occur a half-century later throughout the United States. Large railroads sold or leased many of their weaker branches to short lines or public authorities, which in most cases did operate them at less cost and often were able to develop new business by giving customers more personalized attention. Two instances of the kind of arrangement Wesley outlined would actually occur in Centre County and the Moshannon Valley—but not in 1938. Vice president County politely declined Wesley's offer, saying that the Pennsylvania had not yet decided what to do with the money-losing L&T.

Notes

1. PRR Middle Division and Williamsport Division employee timetables for the 1930s indicate the progressive rationalization along the Bald Eagle Branch.

2. Bill Caloroso, *Pennsylvania Railroad's Elmira Branch* (Andover, NJ: Andover Junction Publications, 1993), 81–85; John W. Orr, *Set Up Running: The Life of a Pennsylvania Railroad Engineman, 1904–1949* (University Park: Pennsylvania State University Press, 2001), 106–15.

3. PRR General Notice No. 234-B, Scheduled Freight Train Service, effective May 1, 1931, with revisions.

4. E. S. Moore and T.G. Taylor, *The Silica Refractories of Pennsylvania* (Harrisburg: Department of Forests and Waters, 1924), 39–48; Corinne Azen Krause, *Refractories: The Hidden Industry* (Westerville, OH: American Ceramic Society, 1987), 26; General Refractories Co., *Refractories* (Philadelphia: General Refractories Co., 1949), 24.

5. *Tyrone Herald*, 21 July 1937; PRR Form C.T. 1000E for 1923 and 1945.

6. *Railway Age*, 8 and 22 April 1939, 24 June 1939.

7. *Huntingdon Daily News*, 17 and 25 June 1946.

8. Edwin P. Alexander, *The Pennsylvania Railroad: A Pictorial History* (New York: Bonanza Books, 1947), 58–59.

9. "CTC Saves Time on the Pennsylvania," *Railway Signaling*, January 1947, 31–37, 41–42. This same article and slight abridgements appeared in other railroad trade publications in 1946–47.

10. Alexander, *Pennsylvania*, 60; *Railway Age*, 4 November 1944, 652–53, 688, 695.

11. Michael Bezilla interview with Paul Anderson, Boalsburg, PA, 17 August 2007; Orr, *Set Up Running*, 139–50.

12. Anderson interview, 17 August 2007.

13. Caloroso, *Elmira Branch*, 25, 84.

14. Kim E. Wallace, *Brickyard Towns* (Washington: America's Industrial Heritage Project, National Park Service, U.S. Department of the Interior, 1993), 8, 159; *The Progress* (Clearfield), 15 May 1959.

15. News release, U.S. Army Corps of Engineers Baltimore District, 13 August 1965, in Paul Dubbs Papers, PSUA 240, Pennsylvania State University Special Collections Library. Dubbs, a Centre County journalist, maintained a folder of newspaper clippings, Corps of Engineers memos, photos, handwritten notes, and other materials related to the building of Sayers Dam. See also "Interim Report on the Blanchard Reservoir," Intervalley Regional Planning Commission, September 1965, copy in the Dubbs Papers; *Centre Daily Times*, 1 September 1964.

16. *Foster Joseph Sayers Dam and Reservoir*, 8-page pamphlet, U.S. Army Corps of Engineers, July 1969, Dubbs Papers; *Lock Haven Express*, 8 and 12 July 1969.

17. Michael Bezilla and Jack Rudnicki, *Rails to Penn State: The Story of the Bellefonte Central* (Mechanicsburg, PA: Stackpole Books, 2007), 298; PRR Form C.T. 1000E, 1 November 1923, lists Bellefonte-area shippers.

18. Jay Osman and Tom Klinger, "'Susquehanna,' Pride of the Fish Commission," *Pennsylvania Angler & Boater* (September–October 1998): 35–36; *Democratic Watchman*, 23 June 1916; *Centre Reporter*, 11 June 1925; Circus Historical Society, "Walter L. Main Circus Routes," accessed 28 July 2016, http://www.circushistory.org/Routes/WalterMain1928.htm.

19. Bezilla and Rudnicki, *Bellefonte Central*, 125.

20. Fred Warner, "Centre County Limestone," *Centre County Heritage* 9 (April 1973): 160–63; George V. Massey II, *Of Gold, Ships and Sand: The History of the Warner Company, 1794–1929* (N.p.: Harold Bell Hancock, 1957); edited, redesigned, and reprinted by Fred Warner (Bellefonte: 1978), 77, 93–96.

21. Bezilla and Rudnicki, *Bellefonte Central*, 176–81.

22. Myrtle Magargel, "History of Pleasant Gap," *Centre Daily Times* (State College), 29 and 30 April 1936; Benjamin LeRoy Miller, *Limestones of Pennsylvania* (Harrisburg: Department of Internal Affairs, 1934), 285–288; *Keystone Gazette*, 25 August 1905.

23. S. K. Stevens, *Pennsylvania: Titan of Industry* (New York: Lewis Historical Publishing Co., 1948), 360.

24. Miller, "Limestones of Pennsylvania," 285–288.

25. *Centre Daily Times*, 13 September 1961.

26. *Centre Democrat* (Bellefonte), 23 September 1949.

27. *Keystone Gazette*, 12 and 26 October 1950, 18 February 1952; *Centre Democrat*, 22 February and 8 March 1951. Symes's visit: *Centre Democrat*, 6 June 1951.

28. Standard Lime and Stone: William D. Theriault, *History of Eastern Jefferson County, West Virginia* (Hagerstown, MD: Published by the author, 2009), 310, 357–59, 377, 406, 479. In interviews with author Theriault, several Standard employees who worked at the company's plant in Jefferson County, West Virginia, also commented on their experiences at the Pleasant Gap plant. Carloads: Application Docket No. 81242 in *Decisions of the Public Utility Commission*, vol. 33 (Harrisburg: Public Utility Commission, 1955), 3–6, wherein the PRR applied, unsuccessfully, to have its Pleasant Gap non-agency station designated for carload freight only.

29. Big Three production data 1956–61 are included in *Warner Co. v. US*, US Court of Appeals Third Circuit, argued 4 April 1974, decided 27 September 1974, accessed 28 July 2016, https://casetext.com/case/warner-company-v-united-states. See also Bezilla and Rudnicki, *Bellefonte Central*, 298–300.

30. *Keystone Gazette*, 3 and 31 July 1952.

31. Robert D. Thomson, *The Mineral Industry of Pennsylvania in 1955* (Harrisburg: Pennsylvania Topographic and Geologic Survey), 13, 23–24.

32. Bezilla and Rudnicki, *Bellefonte Central*, 233.

33. *Centre Daily Times*, 12 and 13 September 1961; Anderson interviews; Bezilla interview with Leonard Shilling, Bellefonte, PA, 27 June 2002; Michael Bezilla and Jack Rudnicki interview with retired BFC vice president and general manager Harold Ammerman, Bellefonte, PA, 12 April 1986; *Grit*, 10 June 1956.

34. *Keystone Gazette*, 17 August and 7 September 1950; *Lock Haven Express*, 27 February and 1 December 1951; C. F. Schlenke, "History of Electric Service Operations in the Bellefonte-State College Area," *Centre County Heritage* 15 (Summer 1979): 131–36.

35. *Keystone Gazette*, 5 April and 14 June 1951.

36. *Grit*, 10 June 1956.

37. Interstate Commerce Commission, Investigation No. 3190, The Pennsylvania Railroad Company Report in Re Accident Near Pleasant Gap, Pa., on June 22, 1948, U. S. Dept. of Transportation, National Transportation Library, Digital Special Collections, http://specialcollection.dotlibrary.dot.gov/Contents, accessed 23 April 2016; *Centre Daily Times*, 23 June 1948; Bezilla interview with Shilling, who was a brakeman on the train headed to the cannery.

38. Bezilla interview with Shilling; Michael Bezilla interview with William Volkmer, former PRR Northumberland motive power foreman, 30 April 2010, Camp Hill, PA.

39. PRR vice president of operations J. F. Deasey memo to President Martin W. Clement, 1 October 1942, photocopy in author's collection.

40. Bruce Teeple, ed., *Glimpses of the Past: A Selected History of Penn Township, Centre County, Pennsylvania, 1844–1994* (Aaronsburg, PA: Aaronsburg Historical Museum, 1994), 11–27; PRR Through Freight Train Schedules, Pittsburgh Region, Middle District, 22 January 1958; sampling freight waybills from Coburn, Spring Mills, Centre Hall, and Lemont stations, 1962–1969, in the author's collection; *Centre Daily Times*, 3 March 1970.

41. Subgroup A, Series 9, executive correspondence between Van Jodon and Robert Frazer for March and April 1928, Bellefonte Central Railroad Records, HCLA 1434, Pennsylvania State University Special Collections Library.

42. Frazer quoted in BFC *Annual Report* for 1928. See also BFC *Annual Reports* for 1927 and 1929.

43. County is quoted from his testimony at an ICC hearing requested by the BFC, which wanted the commission to order the PRR to honor its interchange at the Tyrone gateway. See "Reply of the Pennsylvania Railroad et. al," Docket 26052, *ICC Reports*, 1938.

44. Geoghegan to Kate Du Vae Pitts (a BFC shareholder), 25 April 1933, Subgroup A, Series 8, BFC Records.

45. Bezilla and Rudnicki, *Bellefonte Central*, 152–55.

46. Wesley to County, 25 October 1938, Subgroup A, BFC Records.

TWELVE

Empires Dismantled

Penn Central and Beyond

THE PENNSYLVANIA AND THE NEW YORK CENTRAL MERGED ON February 1, 1968, to form a new railroad, the Penn Central. The amalgam operated more than 19,000 route-miles, employed 104,000 people, and posted annual revenues exceeding $2 billion. At the time, it was the largest business merger in US history. And when Penn Central declared bankruptcy on June 21, 1970, it was the nation's largest corporate failure.

James Symes, who became the PRR's president in 1954, saw the merger as his company's only salvation. He dedicated most of his nine-year tenure as the railroad's top executive to laying its foundation. The Pennsylvania's financial condition had deteriorated steadily after the Second World War, weakened by an extensive money-losing passenger service, high terminal costs, truck competition, rigid government regulation, a shrinking industrial base in the Northeast, and a host of other problems. In the decade after 1948, the company had not earned a rate of return on investment above 3 percent, making the task of attracting funds for capital improvements and modernization nearly impossible.[1] The New York Central suffered from similar difficulties, but Symes was confident that the two railroads served so many of the same markets that eliminating duplicate facilities and parallel trackage would produce enough savings to make the combined companies profitable. New York Central executives were less sure. They accepted the PRR as a suitor only because their road was shut out from mergers involving other railroads that they had considered more favorable partners.

Penn Central began stumbling immediately, beset with clashing corporate cultures, turf battles among executives, computer systems that failed to mesh, overly generous job-protection agreements, and other internal and external complications. Its plight mirrored a railroad industry that was struggling for survival. Ironically, PC's troubles eventually set in motion fundamental changes that reinvigorated railroads from coast to coast.

The Pennsylvania and the New York Central had launched a formal study of the feasibility of merging the two roads in 1957. By 1962, the companies presented a fairly complete consolidation plan that included specific proposals for eliminating duplication and making the combined railroads more efficient. In Centre County and the Moshannon Valley, the plan recommended rationalizing the complex network of track and other infrastructure that was still in place decades after the PRR and NYC had ceased competing with each other for the area's natural resources, and when some of those resources were no longer in high demand.[2]

The merger plan proposed to abandon the PRR's tortuous route between Osceola and Vail via Summit and the Big Fill. Running trains up and down the Allegheny Front even in the diesel era remained risky and expensive. In November 1968, eighteen loaded hopper cars jumped the track near the fill, putting the line out of service for several days. The following month, five loaded cars derailed at Sandy Ridge.[3] A merger of the two roads would enable coal trains that originated on PRR rails in the Moshannon Valley to travel north through Philipsburg to Wallaceton, and from there take NYC rails to Clearfield and proceed east over the River Line to Keating and a junction with the main line between Harrisburg and Buffalo. The change was part of a larger proposal to make the New York Central's yard at Clearfield the hub for all branch line operations in the four-county Clearfield coal district.

Not everyone at the PRR saw the wisdom of closing the mountainous section of the Clearfield Branch. Ernest Clausing, who was then Pittsburgh Region industrial engineer and not a member of the merger team, undertook a study of his own. "I looked at moving Osceola coal by way of Clearfield," he wrote, "and I concluded it was a bad idea [because] unit train operations having fixed origins and destinations do not necessarily make a hub and spoke operation economically feasible." Clausing calculated that the new route nearly doubled the 132 miles between Rushton mine and its prime customer, Pennsylvania Power and Light's Brunner Island power plant, and was 51 miles longer for Rushton trains headed for PP&L's new generating station at Strawberry Ridge, scheduled to come on line in 1972. "Every round trip would require more train-miles, create more maintenance costs, and need more train crews," he contended. "My conclusion was that the extra costs to take trains off the mountain far outweighed the cost of maintaining the short link between Osceola and Vail." According to Clausing, his report never got beyond the Pittsburgh Region general manager's office. In the spring of 1969 Penn Central's president and chief operating officer, Alfred Perlman, high-railed the line in a motor car. He was aghast at its steep grades and decreed that it be closed at once, per the merger plan's recommendation.[4] Perlman, who had been president of the New York Central and was well known for his mercurial temper and management-by-intimidation style, got what he wanted. Regular train operations between Osceola Mills and Vail ceased by June 1969 in favor of the new route via Clearfield. The railroad officially took the historic line out of service on August 13, 1969. The ICC approved its abandonment three years later, and the track was lifted for salvage.[5]

Coincident with rerouting trains via Clearfield, Penn Central closed Osceola yard, razing all structures including the enginehouse. As quickly as union agreements could be amended, employees were transferred to Clearfield or elsewhere on the PC system, or furloughed. Clearfield yard was larger than its Osceola counterpart and more strategically positioned to serve PC coal lines that extended into parts of Indiana and Cambria counties. Lacking a direct connection with Tyrone put Osceola yard off the beaten path of coal movements headed to eastern utilities and export piers. The yard was wedged between the Moshannon Creek and a steep hillside, making expansion difficult should the need arise to increase capacity.

Figure 12.1. Locomotives idle at the Osceola enginehouse on May 11, 1969.
Penn Central would raze the historic structure before the end of the month.
Michael Bezilla photo.

Moreover, Osceola's largest shipper, Elliot Coal Mining Company,
faced an uncertain future. Railcar loadings at Elliot's preparation plant,
embedded in the PRR yard, held steady in the late 1960s at about
300,000 tons annually, sourced mostly from strip mines. Before Penn
Central was formed, Elliot had been acquired from the Stein family
by a Texas-based energy firm, which did little to modernize the coal
company's aging equipment or resolve a troubled relationship with its
workforce. Elliot's 150 or so employees voted to affiliate with the United

Mine Workers of America in 1967, despite management's warning that
unionization would lead to higher production costs and a weakened
ability to compete for coal orders. The company avoided signing a col-
lective bargaining agreement until 1970. Three years later, it ceased all
operations and permanently closed the Osceola plant.⁶

Meanwhile PC began the process of shedding dormant and duplicate feeder lines that had been served from either the Osceola or the
Clearfield terminal—the dismantling of the branch line empires that
the PRR and NYC had constructed in the late nineteenth century. The
network was vast, built up over many decades, and much of the territory
was impenetrable by public road. At times railroad officials not familiar
with the hills and hollows of central Pennsylvania seemed a bit unsure
of exactly what Penn Central owned. For example, an attempt by the
New York Central just prior to the merger to determine how efficiently
coal cars were used in the area caused one official from Syracuse Division headquarters to label the situation "a mess." His explanation was as
applicable to the PRR as it was to the NYC:

> I would estimate that for every mile of main track [from] Clearfield there is a
> half-mile of auxiliary track. Some tracks, of course, are ordinary sidings for
> meeting trains, but a great many of them are for used or unused tipples and
> places where tipples were, and in some cases for no apparent reason at all. Some
> of these tracks are used quite frequently, and some of them very infrequently,
> and every gradation in between. A great number of them are not visible from any
> road, public or private, and must be reached either by walking the main track for
> some distance, or sometimes by fording rivers and streams on foot. Any accurate
> inventory would be rather a tremendous job.⁷

In former New York Central territory in the lower Moshannon Valley,
Penn Central continued to take apart the old Beech Creek Railroad. It
removed from service about 3 miles of the Philipsburg Branch from a
point near Loch Lomond Junction to the end of track at the Philipsburg
freight station, effective October 18, 1969.⁸ Keeping the remainder of
the branch from Munson intact permitted access to the Ophir Branch,
which served Stott Coal Company's preparation plant on One Mile Run
east of Philipsburg. Precisely when the final train operated into Philipsburg over the old NYC line is unknown; Penn Central did not call
attention to last runs.

Penn Central also finished the job of taking up the Beech Creek main line between Kato and Clarence. But west of Clarence, what Penn Central called the Snow Shoe Secondary Track still offered sufficient coal traffic to warrant a daily "Munson local" from Clearfield yard and occasional extra runs. It served such coal companies as R. S. Carlin and Johnson and Morgan near Gillintown, K&J near Gorton, E. M. Brown on the Winburne Branch, Ringgold at Morrisdale, and Stott on the Ophir Branch. Those producers loaded unit trains, though none came close to matching the output from Rushton mine. Still, when combined with pulpwood loaders and traffic generated by the J. H. France brickyard at Clarence, they gave Penn Central steady business.[9]

In the upper Moshannon Valley, in former PRR territory, similar dismantling occurred. For example, the Coal Run Branch—which passed the site of the original Decatur mine in which J. Edgar Thomson and other PRR executives had made their pioneering investment in 1866— came off the books on May 22, 1972. The Trout Run Branch leading to the long-defunct mine at Penn Five was abandoned effective August 21, 1972.[10] The 21-mile Moshannon Secondary Track—the old Moshannon Branch—was stripped of most of its tributaries and successively truncated over the course of several years until it served a handful of relatively small load-outs along 11 route-miles. And so the process went, branch by branch, as PC attempted to pare down the network of coal lines that had smothered the valley since the late nineteenth century.

Overall, there were fewer mines, miners, railroad employees, and coal trains in the Moshannon Valley than in previous generations; but the existing mines were much larger and the trains longer and heavier. Rushton mine, designed to serve unit trains, proved to be a valuable asset for debt-ridden Penn Central, loading 496,000 tons of coal in 1969, increasing to 599,000 tons (about 60 trains) by 1975. Just across the Moshannon Creek was the portal of the new Kephart mine of Johnstown-based Associated Drilling. It tapped the Middle Kittanning seam, which lay above the Brookville seam that fed Rushton. Associated, which loaded on a stub of the old Mapleton Branch, shipped 283,000 tons by rail when it reached full production in 1967. For a few years on either side of 1970, Rushton, Associated, and Elliot combined shipped more than a million tons of coal annually by rail.[11] The story was the same elsewhere in Penn Central's Clearfield district, whose high-BTU coal was eagerly sought by Pennsylvania Power and Light, New York State Electric and Gas, Delmarva Power and Light, Potomac Edison, Potomac Electric Power, Virginia Electric Power, and other regional utilities. A typical day saw four or five trains move eastward through Clearfield yard and down the river, carrying 15 to 20 million tons of coal annually from mines throughout the Clearfield district.[12]

This was the era of the unit train, which operated in solid blocks between origin and destination and did not need to be broken apart and reclassified at intermediate points. In that context, Avis yard no longer served much purpose. Penn Central closed it and consigned what little switching work remained to Clearfield and Newberry yards. Newberry had since the nineteenth century witnessed a steady handoff of coal and other freight from the NYC to the Reading Company for forwarding to consignees in the New York metropolitan area and around Philadelphia. Even during the Depression years, more than 15,000 cars a month moved through the interchange in each direction (including Fall Brook traffic).[13] Traffic had gradually declined since the Second World War, however, and Penn Central had little need for the Reading as a partner. It turned off the Newberry spigot and rerouted shipments over its own rails, dealing the Reading a crippling blow that within a few years would help force it into bankruptcy.

Clearfield district coal bound for upstate New York and New England that had formerly gone from Osceola to Vail and then east over the Bald Eagle Branch was now rerouted through Clearfield over ex-NYC rails to Jersey Shore, then sent north over the Corning Branch (the former Fall Brook Railway). Penn Central also routed onto the ex-NYC main line across upstate New York most of the general freight that had used the Bald Eagle Branch as part of the route between the Midwest and New England. Those changes, combined with the closure of the antiquated coal pier at Sodus Point on Lake Ontario, left the Bald Eagle Branch with little traffic. The railroad's 1969 schedules showed only CSB-7 and CSB-8 operating between Conway yard (Pittsburgh) and Wilkes-Barre; SA-1 and AS-2 between Altoona and Southport yard (Elmira); and AN-3 and AN-16 between Altoona and Northumberland. The railroad discontin-

ued even those trains after flooding from the tropical remnants of Hurricane Agnes destroyed the Elmira Branch and severely damaged the
Wilkes-Barre Branch. Post-flood operations over the Bald Eagle Branch
consisted primarily of a daily train running between Hollidaysburg and
Newberry. The dearth of traffic led PC to close Miles tower, effective
January 19, 1973. (The tower had been partially inundated by the waters
of Bald Eagle Creek during the Agnes debacle.) The tower's CTC machine was relocated to Gray tower just west of Tyrone, where the branch
joined the main line.[14]

Penn Central implemented equally drastic changes on the Montandon Secondary, the old Lewisburg and Tyrone route. The 25-mile section between Mifflinburg and Coburn was taken out of service, with the
Northumberland-based local making its last run to Coburn on May 9,
1968.[15] From then on, customers from Coburn west were served by a
Bellefonte-based train; the Norry local continued to make a triweekly
turn over the Montandon Secondary as far as Mifflinburg. Early in 1970
the railroad petitioned the ICC for permission to abandon the middle
section. The request met no serious objections from shippers, and abandonment became effective July 14, 1970. By mid-1971 Chicago-based
Hyman-Michaels Company was lifting rail and other track materials
for salvage. Conventional practice would have ownership of the right-
of-way revert to adjacent land owners. There were rumors—not denied
by Penn Central—that Paddy Mountain and Beaver Dam (Coburn)
tunnels would be blown shut to prevent them from becoming attractive
nuisances.

Before the scrappers lit their torches, however, a grassroots movement began, aimed at preserving the right-of-way as a public corridor
for fishermen and other outdoor enthusiasts. Local members of Trout
Unlimited pointed out that the railroad offered the only practical access
to much of Penns Creek in the rugged territory where Centre, Union,
and Mifflin Counties intersected. Trout Unlimited brought the matter to
the attention of the Nature Conservancy, headquartered in Washington,
D.C.; and Penn Central agreed to a change in plans. The conservancy
acquired the central portion of the line, adjacent to state-owned lands,
for $10,500, and then immediately sold it to the Commonwealth of Penn-
sylvania for an identical amount. The Pennsylvania Fish Commission

took the lead in modifying the Poe Paddy tunnel and two of the three bridges across Penns Creek for hikers, bicyclists, and horseback riders. Where the east and west ends of the line did not border state lands, the right-of-way reverted to private ownership. Unfortunately, by the time all legal agreements were in place, Hyman-Michaels had scrapped the bridge immediately east of Ingleby. It was not replaced, despite the Fish Commission's publicly stated intention to do so.[16] Still, the conservation effort ranked among the first successful rails-to-trails initiatives in the state.

By contrast, when PC prepared to abandon a portion of the Bellefonte Secondary Track, as the line to Coburn was designated, preservation of a public corridor received little consideration. The tropical storm that had been Hurricane Agnes did several slow loops over the Middle Atlantic states, devastating much of the Susquehanna River basin. The Bellefonte area received nearly 9 inches of rain on June 22–23, 1972, with 2 more inches over two subsequent days. A raging Penns Creek washed out parts of the railroad between Centre Hall and Coburn. No trains operated east of Lemont after June 23. Penn Central subsequently filed to abandon the 22 miles from that point to Coburn, arguing that repairs would cost nearly a half-million dollars. It could not justify such an expenditure for a line that had produced fewer than 150 carloads during each of the three previous years and offered no prospects for substantial growth. Using the ICC standard of thirty-four carloads per mile per year as a branch line's breakeven point, the line between Lemont and Coburn would have to support at least 738 carloads annually.

In a perverse way, the massive flooding in the Northeast was a blessing for the beleaguered Penn Central. Railroad representative Paul Mainquist explained at a January 1973 abandonment hearing in Bellefonte that getting rid of the Bellefonte Secondary east of Lemont was part of the company's overall system-wide plan to pare mileage by at least 25 percent. The line "is definitely operating at a loss," he told the ICC examiner. "We must prune out of the system little-used branch lines, and the Bellefonte Secondary Track is clearly one of these."[17] Farm and feed distributors at Centre Hall and Coburn attended the hearing to oppose the abandonment, saying they would have to pay at least $5 per ton more to receive animal feed by truck. The Pennsylvania Department of Transportation also opposed the abandonment. Deputy Secretary Edward Tennyson said at the hearing that the ICC profitability formula was "arbitrary at best" and accused the railroad of inflating the cost of repairing flood damage, although he offered no definitive figures of his own.[18] The Interstate Commerce Commission sided with Penn Central and approved the abandonment on May 8, 1973. By September, PC was publicly advertising the right-of-way for sale "free of all encumbrances."[19]

The wisdom of the ICC's ruling should be considered in the overall context of the railroad's tenuous financial health. Soon after Penn Central declared bankruptcy in June 1970, it noted that 80 percent of its revenues came from only 11 percent of its route-miles. The large-scale reduction in trackage that Mainquist outlined as his company's overarching goal was difficult and tedious under normal regulatory restraints: prior to the Agnes pummeling, the ICC had approved only 480 miles of the 3,700 total miles PC has proposed to liquidate.[20] But the flood handed the company an unprecedented opportunity to expedite the abandonment of much redundant or unproductive mileage.

In the particular case of the Bellefonte Secondary, the bureaucratic wheels turned slowly, even after the ICC gave its consent for abandonment. In 1973 Congress created the United States Railway Association to assess what key segments of Penn Central and other bankrupt Northeastern railroads were economically viable and might be combined into a single new, revitalized rail enterprise. The USRA halted abandonment of the track east of Lemont pending further study of the line's traffic potential. Perhaps the most telling measure of that potential came in 1974 when PennDOT offered the Bellefonte Central Railroad a chance to operate the line, with the understanding that public funds would be used to repair flood damage and that Penn Central would grant the BFC trackage rights between Bellefonte and Lemont. The short line calculated that it could get no more than 300 carloads annually from the line and turned down the offer.[21] The USRA then decided not to include the Lemont–Coburn segment in the final system plan for the new railroad it envisioned for the Northeast, and the abandonment became effective.[22]

Track abandonments could not cure all that ailed Penn Central. Late and misrouted cars, equipment breakdowns, derailments, unpredictable transit times, and shortages of empty cars all combined to arouse a torrent of angry complaints among central Pennsylvania shippers. The schedules of the Bald Eagle Branch trains that set out and picked up Bellefonte-area cars at Milesburg became so erratic that even PC's own people couldn't say from one day to the next when the trains might arrive or what cars they might set out.

Penn Central's troubles undermined the Bellefonte Central's ability to maintain a high standard of customer service. The short line was powerless to resolve complaints from National Gypsum that covered hoppers in the lime trade took two or three weeks to make a single round trip over PC rails between Bellefonte and Pittsburgh-area steel mills. State College building supply dealer O. W. Houts questioned why boxcars loaded with wallboard shipped from Buffalo—barely 200 miles distant—were in transit on Penn Central for ten days or more. Bellefonte Central general manager George McClellan sprinkled his daybook with notations of how PC's failings had weakened his own road: "We have been short [of cars] every day for weeks." "Average turnaround has increased from 12 to 21 days for Lackawanna [Bethlehem Steel's big mill near Buffalo]." "We have lost the Sparrows Point [a Bethlehem mill at Baltimore] and Aliquippa [J&L Steel near Pittsburgh] business account car shortage."

Customer service suffered another blow in August 1969 when, in a cost-cutting measure, Penn Central reduced the number of locomotives it based in Bellefonte from two to one, and the number of train crews from four to two—a daylight crew to switch local industries and a night crew to make the Lock Haven turn. Weekend work became uncommon. A few years later, PC reduced the interchange of cars with the BFC from Monday through Friday to three days a week and eliminated the Bellefonte-based night crew.[23] "These changes had a very direct and unfavorable effect upon our operation," BFC president Claude Wagoner noted in his annual report to stockholders for 1972, "causing a reduction in revenues and increased costs."

Penn Central's service woes played into the hands of motor carrier competition and influenced the Bellefonte Central's decision to abandon its line to State College. Motor carriage was not always cheaper, but Penn State University and other State College customers were willing to pay more for fast, reliable service, and for deliveries that could be made to their doorstep instead of the rail terminal. In 1969 George McClellan noted that State College consignees received a mere 220 carloads, providing a paltry 5.5 percent of his railroad's total gross income. "It is economically illogical that we have been maintaining approximately 75 percent of our total track mileage to serve an area that produces this percentage of our total revenue," he told another member of the BFC's board of directors.[24] There was no shipper opposition when the short line asked the ICC for permission to abandon the 13.5-mile line to State College; the last train operated on July 12, 1974. The Bellefonte Central retained only about 5 miles of track, enough to serve its one and only remaining customer, the National Gypsum Company.

Simply put, the railroad situation in the Northeast in the early 1970s was a mess. Penn Central was crumbling physically and financially. The Lehigh Valley, Erie-Lackawanna, Reading, Central of New Jersey, and other smaller roads—buffeted by the many of the same forces that plagued PC—also were bankrupt or on the verge. The remnants of Hurricane Agnes delivered the knockout punch, sometimes obliterating entire rail lines and the industries that sustained them.

The United States Railway Association, representing a mix of public and private interests, proposed grouping some lines of the financially weak carriers into a single for-profit railroad. Other lines would be abandoned, or conveyed to competing freight railroads and to the nationalized passenger railroad, Amtrak. Congress approved the plan, and on April 1, 1976, the Consolidated Rail Corporation came into being. Philadelphia-based Conrail (CR) included Penn Central and six other bankrupts, concentrated in the Northeast but having routes spread through fourteen states. All active Penn Central lines in Centre County and the Moshannon Valley became part of the new company.

Congress appropriated $2 billion to get Conrail started, much of that amount destined for infrastructure and equipment renewal. Reacting to the Penn Central debacle, lawmakers also began deregulating railroads, allowing free-market forces to play a much greater role in shaping the destinies of individual carriers. The movement toward economic deregulation culminated in the Staggers Act of 1980. Staggers gave back to the railroads much of the authority to set rates that they had lost to the ICC in the early 1900s. Railroad companies were now permitted to negotiate private contracts with shippers and no longer had to go through the laborious and very public process of obtaining ICC approval. In deregulation, Congress belatedly recognized that in most instances, a railroad's primary competitors were not other railroads but rather motor carriers, barge and pipe lines, and other modes of transportation.

Deregulation helped Conrail turn the financial corner. As late as 1980, the railroad reported an annual net operating loss of $349 million, on par with Penn Central's million-dollar-a-day losses. But once CR was able to set rates that reflected the true costs of providing service and implement them quickly, without waiting for years while the ICC investigated and turned thumbs up or down, the situation began to improve. The Northeast Rail Service Act of 1981 made further improvement possible by allowing Conrail to turn over its commuter passenger business to state and municipal authorizes and renegotiate labor contracts to eliminate archaic work rules and reduce the size of its workforce. By 1986, CR reported an annual net operating income of $348 million.[25]

Conrail shed more trackage than Penn Central had ever contemplated. In Pennsylvania, the USRA's preliminary plan labeled about 1,400 route-miles, or 18 percent of the state's total rail network, as "potentially excess" and therefore ripe for abandonment or sale. The preliminary plan drew strong negative reactions from many political leaders, who feared a loss of jobs that might accompany a shrinking rail system. However, the USRA did not deem any trackage in Centre County or the Moshannon Valley excess (excluding the Lemont-to-Coburn line, whose fate had already been decided). In a few instances it recommended that Conrail retain out-of-service spurs as part of a "fossil-fuel land bank" pending resumption of large-scale coal mining in certain areas. (The concept was later termed "rail banking.") Conrail had about 125 route-miles active in Centre County and the Moshannon Valley on start-up day, April 1, 1976. During the first few years, CR followed Penn Central's operating plan. Perhaps the only difference noted by that segment of the public who gave railroads more than a passing glance was a change in the look of motive power, which sported a medium blue livery in place of PC's black. A closer look would show that many of those locomotives were new, and so were the cars they pulled and the track structure that supported them, thanks to massive federal investment.

Clearfield remained the hub for coal operations. Initially trains ran on a more or less daily basis on the 29-mile Snow Shoe Secondary Track (the old Beech Creek Railroad main line). But total annual coal shipments from the mines along that route had declined to barely 200,000 tons. Production costs increased as coal seams became less accessible, at the same time that the coal's high sulfur content made it less desirable among some customers. Some formerly large-scale rail shippers loaded trains as infrequently as two or three times a year. In 1985, for example, R. S. Carlin Inc., which had a tipple near Gillintown, and Stott Coal Company's Belfast No. 14 tipple at the end of the Ophir Branch near Philipsburg together loaded only 45,000 tons. Another once-reliable Gillintown shipper, the Johnson and Morgan Coal Company, shipped no coal at all by rail in 1985 (although J&M did ship 120,000 tons by truck that year).[26]

In October 1985, Conrail served public notice that it intended to abandon 19 miles of the Snow Shoe Secondary beyond a point just east of Winburne, where the line crossed the Moshannon Creek into Centre County. The railroad claimed that coal from the Centre County side could be trucked to existing tipples in Clearfield County and the J. H. France brickyard could truck its materials to and from a transload terminal at Clearfield. Shippers protested. France, for example, depended on bauxite and other bulk raw materials from distant states and even overseas for making high-performance refractories. Production manager Robert Lutz described rail service as "absolutely vital" to his company.[27] Conrail halted the abandonment process in the face of these objections.

Nevertheless, traffic on the Snow Shoe Secondary remained weak and, according to the railroad, unprofitable. Conrail pointed to the extraordinary expense of having to maintain the aging bridge at Viaduct and Peale tunnel. In November 1989, the railroad renewed its abandonment effort by filing a formal request with the Interstate Commerce Commission. Johnson and Morgan loaded a train in December, probably the last coal loaded on the track to be abandoned.[28] The ICC approved CR's request in February 1990. For reasons that remain unclear, Conrail did not immediately consummate the abandonment. Although it no longer hauled coal on the line, the railroad continued to serve the France brickyard until April 1993.[29] At that time, the Headwaters Charitable Trust, an affiliate of Headwaters Conservation and Development Council, announced it had purchased of the right-of-way from Conrail with financial support from a private donation. The nonprofit, quasi-public council was formed in 1978 to promote the quality of life and economic sustainability of natural resources and communities across a multi-county region in north-central Pennsylvania. As Utah-based A&K Railroad Materials began pulling up the track, the council initiated efforts to repurpose the former rail bed as a recreational trail and improve access to public lands in the area, but with the ICC-stipulated provision that the right-of-way was "rail-banked" and could revert to use as a railroad line at some future date. The last segment of former New York Central trackage in the Moshannon Valley to be operated by Conrail was the Ophir Branch. Stott Coal Company's successor Northern Counties Coal loaded the final train at the Stott tipple in November 1993, and the ICC approved abandonment of the track in 1995.[30]

Further up the valley on former PRR lines near Osceola Mills, three large mines had long-term contracts with buyers and were thus shielded from spot market fluctuations. In 1983, Rushton mine loaded 630,000 tons for its parent, Pennsylvania Power and Light; Associated Drilling loaded 137,000 tons for various utilities; and Power Operating Inc., a relative newcomer, loaded 883,000 tons.[31] Power had emerged as an important rail shipper in the late 1970s. It and its contractors operated numerous strip mines on both side of the Moshannon Creek and handled coal preparation and loading at a new facility, Leslie tipple, located on a mile-long stub of the old Moshannon and Clearfield Branch above Coal Run Junction. To accommodate the heavy tonnage coming from Leslie, Conrail installed 5 miles of welded rail from Rushton all the way through Osceola and beyond to the tipple.[32]

Several smaller producers loaded at points further up the Moshannon Secondary Track (the old Moshannon Branch). They were not equipped to flood-load trains and could not even load hundred-ton hopper cars, which CR prohibited beyond the junction because of poor track conditions. By the late 1980s, combined annual shipments from these producers fell below 100,000 tons, and Conrail was ridding its hopper fleet of the older, smaller cars. The railroad consequently abandoned the Moshan-

Figure 12.2. Pausing at Coal Run Junction in October 1986, the conductor of a
Conrail light engine move uses a lineside telephone to call the train order office
at Clearfield before his train proceeds to retrieve loaded coal cars further up the
Moshannon Branch. *Steve Bezilla photo; author's collection.*

non Secondary beyond Coal Run Junction as of April 21, 1991.[33] Leslie
tipple became the end of the line for the Clearfield-based train crews.

Conrail's Moshannon Valley traffic suffered far more serious blows
with the closure of two of the "big three" producers it served. Associated
Drilling ceased production in the mid-1980s. Rushton mine closed in
June 1991. Plenty of coal remained underground; but Rushton's parent,
Pennsylvania Mines Corporation, said costs to obtain it had climbed to
about $43 per ton, at a time when spot market prices for coal of the same
quality hovered around $30 per ton. Pennsylvania Mines closed its two
other captive mines in western Pennsylvania at about that same time and

for the same reason. Since Rushton had loaded its first train in the fall of 1965, it had shipped more than 13 million tons of coal, all by rail. Its closure idled about 250 miners.[34] Thereafter, trains came to the Moshannon Valley only once or twice a week to serve Power's Leslie tipple. Thanks in large part to the lower production costs associated with strip mining and a nonunion workforce, Power was able to remain competitive for a few more years. In fact, for several years after Rushton closed, Power's annual shipments topped a million tons.

In 1990 Congress passed a major amendment to the Clean Air Act, dimming the long-term outlook for Clearfield-district coal. The amendment addressed acid rain issues and certain toxins emitted from fossil-fuel-burning power plants. The law's mandate for phased-in reductions of sulfur dioxide emissions made Clearfield coal, with its high sulfur content, unattractive to many utilities. They preferred to source low-sulfur coal found in other parts of the state, as well as in West Virginia, Kentucky, and even the distant Powder River Basin in Wyoming, rather than install expensive equipment to remove unwanted emissions. In addition, the coal export market sagged badly, as lower-cost producers from Australia, South Africa, and other nations made US-mined coal less competitive.

In the early 1990s, rail shipments from mines in the entire Clearfield district declined to a little more than 3 million tons annually, the equivalent of loading one train a day district-wide. Effective December 29, 1995, CR sold its so-called Clearfield cluster, about 225 miles of active lines in Centre, Clearfield, Cambria, and Indiana Counties, to R. J. Corman Railroad Company. Headquartered in Nicholasville, Kentucky, and founded in 1973 by Rick Corman as a railroad construction company, the privately held R. J. Corman firm had become by the mid-1990s a holding company that offered a variety of railroad-related services, including short line operations in at least four states. With lower labor and overhead costs and more operational and work-rules flexibility than Conrail, R. J. Corman Pennsylvania Lines (RJCP) figured to turn a profit even in a shrinking coal market. Because many coal-fired power plants were in close proximity to Clearfield district coal—which meant low transportation costs—some utilities found that blending high- and low-sulfur coals met federal emissions standards. In particular Pennsylvania Power and Light, with its large coal-fired generating stations at Strawberry Ridge and Brunner Island, remained a steady customer. Conrail and Corman developed a close working relationship, since the big road was the smaller one's only interchange partner—at Keating on the east and Cresson on the west.[35]

Locomotives in a handsome red and silver livery replaced Conrail blue in making the trip from Clearfield out to Leslie tipple. Those trains were the only railroad activity in the Moshannon Valley, where once three railroads hustled for not only coal but all sorts of freight, and passengers too. Three years into the Corman era, Power Operating filed for bankruptcy, citing cash flow problems; the company liquidated its assets at the end of 1999.[36] Leslie tipple stood idle, a prime candidate for demolition. In 2001 RJCP initiated proceedings to abandon the 23-mile line from Wallaceton through Philipsburg and Osceola to Leslie.[37] Sadly, local residents seemed to take little note that more than 140 years of rail service in the Moshannon Valley was on the verge of extinction.

Corman put the abandonment process on hold when a new shipper came forward. Philipsburg-based Junior Coal Company made arrangements to resume loading unit trains at Leslie tipple. The first train, for Strawberry Ridge, was loaded in June 2003. Subsequent loadings were sporadic as Junior sold coal by rail only in the spot market.[38] Rail shipments ceased in 2013, as increasingly restrictive federal emissions standards and a preference for burning inexpensive natural gas softened utilities' demand for coal, then resumed on a sporadic basis in 2016 in response to a more favorable international market for metallurgical coal.

Throughout its Clearfield cluster, Corman management was alive to prospects for developing non-coal traffic. One such possibility involved restoring rail service on the former Beech Creek main line between Wallaceton and Gorton. The track had been lifted from most of that section, but it was rail-banked (the right-of-way had not been abandoned) and thus eligible for re-lay if economic conditions warranted. In 2008, RJCP requested approval from the Surface Transportation Board (successor to the Interstate Commerce Commission, dissolved in 1995 as part of the deregulation process) to reactivate service to Gorton in order to serve a proposed landfill, biofuels plant, and sandstone quarry, all of which were backed by parties independent of the railroad. The railroad company estimated that if all those enterprises came to fruition, it could haul as many as 17,000 carloads a year to and from the Gorton area.

The request sparked a public outcry. There was already strong grassroots opposition to the landfill: the once strip mine–ravaged landscape around Gorton was steadily returning to a natural condition, and the idea of dumping urban trash there was anathema to many local residents and to conservationists everywhere. Rail-trail enthusiasts were unhappy with the prospect of being denied the use of the bridge at Viaduct and the Peale tunnel. The rail line had been absent for such a long time that some local residents were no longer comfortable with the notion of trains in their backyards—perhaps the most significant objection to the rail-banking concept. The railroad tried to mollify public opposition by proposing to bypass the populated area along the right-of-way from Wallaceton east to Munson. An alternative line would leave the active former PRR line north of Philipsburg, then follow the mostly unpopulated right-of-way of the long-abandoned NYC Philipsburg Branch along the Moshannon Creek to Munson. From Munson to Gorton, it would follow the Beech Creek main line as originally proposed. In 2012, the Surface Transportation Board approved RJCP's request to re-lay the track—the first time that the STB had approved reactivating a railbanked line in Pennsylvania. In spite of the board's unprecedented action, however, the company aiming to develop the landfill withdrew its application for a state permit in the face of determined opposition; the likelihood of reactivating the rail line seemed remote.[39]

Conrail retreated from the southern half of Centre County even before it exited the coalfields on the plateau, but the circumstances and outcome were decidedly different. The Bald Eagle Branch did not fit Conrail's strategic network of through routes any more than it had fit Penn Central's. There were no steady shippers on the line except at each end, where paper mills at Tyrone and Lock Haven continued in their longtime roles as traffic anchors. Neither mill had much need for rail service that ran the length of the branch. A single CR train made a daily run between Altoona and Newberry, sharing the line with a Monday-Wednesday-Friday local that operated from Bellefonte to Lock Haven and return, and an occasional coal train. Rumors circulated that the branch was slated for abandonment.[40]

In fact, it was. Another provision of the Northeast Rail Service Act of 1981 made the process of eliminating unwanted trackage much easier. The principal test for abandonment was not whether a given line was profitable, but whether it was profitable *enough*—that is, whether it produced a return on investment that exceeded the cost of capital. The goal was to allow Conrail to slim down even further and make the company more attractive to private investors. Following passage of the act, Conrail took the Bald Eagle Branch out of service as a through route, sometimes using the western half to store surplus cars. The train crew based in Bellefonte continued to make triweekly runs from Milesburg east to connect with the rest of the Conrail system at Lock Haven. The choice of Lock Haven as a gateway was a curious one, given that the Bellefonte area's principal rail commodity (about 75 percent by tonnage) was lime, most of it destined for steel mills in Pittsburgh and the upper Ohio River valley. From Lock Haven, Conrail routed Pittsburgh-bound cars south on the Buffalo line to Enola, then west on the main line through Altoona. The cars had already traveled more than 280 miles by the time they passed through Tyrone—only 31 rail-miles from Milesburg via the Bald Eagle Branch.[41]

Marblehead Lime Company, which had purchased the Standard Lime and Cement Company's operation at Pleasant Gap, was the single largest rail shipper in the Bellefonte area in 1981 with 520 carloads, mostly lime. The National Gypsum plant had been acquired by Canada-based Domtar, and the number of rail cars it shipped had slumped to about 350, roughly equal to the Warner Company's output. The Corning works near Dale Summit ranked as the top non–limestone and lime customer, typically receiving about 200 carloads of year of soda ash, feldspar, potassium nitrate, and other minerals used in glass manufacture. Including smaller customers, Conrail originated or terminated approximately 1,600 carloads in the Bellefonte market in 1981, compared with 5,400 carloads reported by Penn Central a decade earlier.[42]

The following year found the national economy mired in its deepest recession since the 1930s. Conditions in the steel industry were so bad that Domtar ceased production at the end of June 1982, effectively putting the Bellefonte Central Railroad out of business. Conrail's projections for a rebound by the steelmakers—the recipients of more than half of Bellefonte's rail traffic—were gloomy. Lime traffic alone was expected to plunge to as few as 300 carloads before leveling out.[43] With the process of shedding unwanted track now facilitated by the Northeast Rail Service Act, CR announced plans to abandon or sell the Bald Eagle Branch, the Bellefonte Secondary Track between Milesburg and Lemont, and the Pleasant Gap Industrial Track, about 70 route-miles in all.

Statewide, Conrail targeted about 725 route-miles for abandonment. Political and business leaders expressed grave concern, contending that more than 6,000 private-sector jobs were at stake. The Pennsylvania Department of Transportation undertook its own study of rail viability, which concluded that most of those jobs would be protected if only about 175 miles of track slated for elimination could be preserved. Rather than oppose abandonment of that modest amount of mileage, PennDOT announced that it would make available grants for maintenance and subsidies for operating losses if other operators, such as short line railroads, public authorities, or shippers themselves came forward to take over the service, or in some cases resume service that CR had already terminated.[44]

Shippers and public officials in affected counties throughout central Pennsylvania discussed possible next steps. Leading the drive to maintain rail service in Centre County was SEDA-COG—the Susquehanna Economic Development Authority-Council of Governments. Created by county governments to encourage regional economic growth, SEDA-COG had been monitoring railroad transportation since Penn Central days. Anticipating a wave of Conrail track abandonments in the counties it served (Centre, Union, Montour, Columbia, and Northumberland), SEDA-COG in 1983 established the SEDA-COG Joint Rail Authority (separate and distinct from SEDA-COG itself) to make sure the area's transportation needs continued to be met. Backed by a mix of governmental and shipper funding, the JRA's board of directors consisted of two representatives from each of the five counties—ideally, one representing a rail shipper and the other from the public sector. Following negotiations with Conrail, the rail authority agreed to purchase a total of 82 miles of track, effective August 1, 1984, for $2.13 million. The sale included the Bellefonte-area trackage, the Bald Eagle Branch between Milesburg and Vail (enabling an interchange with CR at the latter loca-

tion instead of Lock Haven), and the former Erie-Lackawanna Blooms-
burg Branch between Northumberland and Berwick in Northumberland, Montour, and Columbia Counties.[45]

The rail authority would own the lines but contract with one or more
private entities for professional services to operate them. From the eight
prospective operators who submitted service proposals for all or parts
of the lines, the JRA selected Richard Robey of Bethel Park, suburban
Pittsburgh. The 44-year-old Robey had management experience with
several large railroads and had helped to revitalize a short line in Chester County.[46] For operating purposes, he formed separate companies.
The Nittany and Bald Eagle Railroad (NBER) served the Bellefonte
area, while the North Shore Railroad served customers on the Blooms-
burg Branch. General offices for both railroads were located in Northumberland. Nittany and Bald Eagle operations, encompassing nearly
40 route-miles, came under the day-to-day supervision of general manager Jim Miller, who was serving in that same post for the Bellefonte
Central when the Domtar closure sounded the short line's death knell.
For motive power, Robey acquired three former Santa Fe Railway CF-7
road switcher locomotives and assigned one to Bellefonte. With Miller
at the throttle, it typically operated three days a week, including runs
to the Conrail interchange at Vail. When not in service, the locomotive
was stabled outdoors at the former PRR engine pit at Coleville. The JRA
began a ten-month physical rehabilitation of its Bellefonte-area lines—
much neglected by years of deferred maintenance—in December 1984.
Crews replaced rotted crossties and switch timbers, added ballast and
leveled track, cut brush, and repaired grade crossings. Those improvements made operations safer and permitted higher train speeds.

The rail authority's consultants estimated that the NBER would have
to handle a thousand carloads annually simply to break even. The railroad surpassed that minimum in 1987, when it originated or terminated
1,207 carloads. Three years later, it exceeded the 2,000-carload thresh-
old.[47] Much of growth came from the Corning plant at Dale Summit,
the lime and limestone companies, and Sonoco Products, a plastic bag
manufacturer newly established at Milesburg.

Richard Robey attributed the revitalization of the railroad business in
the Bellefonte area to the lower operating costs and personalized service

Figure 12.3. One of the Nittany and Bald Eagle's CF-7 locomotives has three cars of lime in tow as it heads timetable west on the Pleasant Gap Branch in 1989. *Michael Bezilla photo.*

associated with short line railroads. For example, two-person train crews were the norm on short lines, compared with three-to-five-person crews on large railroads. And relaxed work rules allowed short line crews to work in the shop or perform track maintenance on days when they were not operating trains. According to Robey, short line railroad managers also could develop close relationships even with their smallest customers to fine-tune the quality of service, a luxury big railroads did not have. "Conrail doesn't have time to mess with that. I do," he told a *Centre Daily Times* reporter. "What we're creating is a retail railroad operation—a pick up and delivery operation. Our customers are everything to us, and we're going to pay attention to them."[48]

For example, Conrail switched the Corning plant at Dale Summit on Tuesdays and Thursdays. If the glassmaker had an urgent need for cars that arrived at Bellefonte on Monday, Wednesday, or Friday, CR typically waited until the next regular service day to deliver them rather than incur the higher cost associated with making an immediate delivery. By contrast, the NBER with its lower costs delivered cars in a timeframe more satisfactory to the consignee—sometimes even offering what Robey styled "one-hour service." Customers liked that approach to doing business. In Corning's case alone, inbound carloads of sand and other bulk minerals increased from 174 in 1983 to 660 in 1988. The railroad's improved service also was a factor in Corning's 1988 decision to increase its plant capacity by 50 percent, bringing its total workforce to about 900 people.[49]

Railroad revitalization was not confined to increasing carload numbers. The Joint Rail Authority intended to acquire the eastern half of the Bald Eagle Branch (which Conrail had not included in the original sale and had placed out of service) in order to give the NBER an interchange with CR at both ends of the branch. The Clinton County commissioners backed the idea, and Clinton became the sixth county to join the JRA. In 1988 the rail authority bought the branch as far as Mill Hall and obtained trackage rights over the remaining 2.7 miles into Lock Haven. As with previous track acquisitions, the funds for the purchase came mostly from capital funds appropriated by the state legislature and released by the governor.[50] With more counties joining SEDA-COG and the rail authority, the JRA began negotiating with Conrail to take over the big road's operations in the Williamsport and Lewistown areas. In 1996 Conrail agreed to sell the two operations for one dollar each. They subsequently became the Lycoming Valley Railroad and the Juniata Valley Railroad respectively, operated by Robey under contract to the authority. Conrail also agreed to the sale of terminal trackage at Tyrone and Lock Haven, which enabled the NBER to switch the paper mills at those locations and placed the entire Bald Eagle Branch under the JRA's purview. In return, CR received rights to operate through trains over the branch (compensating the rail authority and the designated operator), along with the authority's commitment to rehabilitate the line to permit speeds up to 40 miles per hour.

Conrail's newfound interest in a branch that only a few years earlier it sought to abandon stemmed from PP&L's need for cleaner coal at its Strawberry Ridge power plant in Montour County. To meet stricter clean-air standards, the utility wanted to blend the high-sulfur coal that it received from the Clearfield district with cleaner-burning coal from southwest Pennsylvania. Sending "Ridge" trains via the Bald Eagle Branch shaved at least 80 miles off the former route that went by way of Enola. The JRA completed rehabilitation of the Bald Eagle Branch during the winter of 1996–97, replacing some 50,000 crossties, adding 35,000 tons of ballast, and refurbishing grade crossings. The first Conrail coal train operated over the line on February 12, 1997; soon the line was averaging fifteen to twenty coal trains each month, plus a like number of westbound empties. Conrail dispatched all train movements over the branch.[51]

In June 1999, the Norfolk Southern Railway acquired nearly 60 percent of the Conrail system, including the majority of CR's trackage within Pennsylvania. Most of the remainder of Conrail went to NS competitor CSX. The trackage rights agreement over the Bald Eagle Branch remained essentially unchanged under Norfolk Southern. Immediately following the Conrail takeover, NS even reinstated general-freight service over the branch, in the form of one daily Pittsburgh–Buffalo train in each direction. The routing was circuitous and fraught with operating inconveniences, however, and the trains were discontinued after a few months. General through-freight service returned to the branch in 2014, when Norfolk Southern inaugurated a daily train in each direction between Northumberland and Conway (and later Bellevue, Ohio) via Altoona. After fifteen months, NS rerouted this traffic over its own rails as part of a system-wide quest to improve efficiency and reduce operating costs. The Nittany and Bald Eagle continued to operate local freights from Bellefonte to the Tyrone and Lock Haven interchanges. Some weekdays found three train crews at work—more than at any time since the PRR era of the early 1960s. The rail authority acquired the former Bellefonte Central enginehouse and shop in Coleville for the NBER to use as an operating base.[52]

Limestone and lime, which had shaped the destiny of railroading in the Nittany Valley since the early 1900s, contributed in an important way to the Nittany and Bald Eagle's bottom line. In 1986—the second full year of NBER operations—the Warner Company completed sale of its Bell mine and Plant 19 lime-making operation to the Bellefonte Lime Company, headed by former Warner managers. Bellefonte Lime closed the mine in 1987, citing high production costs associated with its great depth. Using alternative local sources of limestone, the company continued to produce and ship pebble lime and a smaller quantity of hydrated lime at Plant 19. Graymont, headquartered in Canada and North America's second largest lime producer, acquired Bellefonte Lime in 1998. Graymont phased out calcining activities at Plant 19 in favor of upgrading and expanding lime production at the former Marblehead (Standard) facility at Pleasant Gap, which it had also acquired.[53]

Another element in the evolving lime and limestone picture was Glenn O. Hawbaker Inc., which was quarrying limestone on part of the old Whiterock site. Hawbaker, whose core business was road construction, was trucking limestone consigned for rail shipment to the nearby Graymont plant for loading into rail cars. But Hawbaker wanted to be able to load rail cars on its own property. The former PRR Whiterock Branch was still in place but had not been used in decades and was no longer feasible for operation. The state then allocated $4.1 million to support construction of a completely new Whiterock Quarry track. Hawbaker, the railroad, and the JRA contributed additional funds totaling $1.7 million. The 1.65-mile spur, completed in 2008, crossed undeveloped land and dipped under busy state route 26 on its final approach to a multitrack transload facility near the quarry. Hawbaker used the yard for outbound shipments of limestone and incoming bulk shipments—chiefly coal, asphalt, and road salt—that were transferred to trucks for delivery to individual consignees.[54] Among the earliest transload shipments was a trainload of low-sulfur West Virginia and Kentucky coal received in January 2010 for Penn State's west-campus steam plant—the first coal the university had ordered for transportation by rail since 1959. (More coal trains followed until the plant was converted to burn natural gas in 2015.) The Whiterock Quarry track was the first rail-line construction in Centre County in nearly six decades and boosted NBER-operated trackage to about 70 route-miles.

The Nittany and Bald Eagle Railroad knew adversity as well as success. In 2001 the paper mills at either end of the Bald Eagle Branch closed. Two years later, Corning closed its plant, which by then was owned in partnership with Asahi Video Products of Japan. New video technology has pushed television picture tubes into obsolescence. All was not lost: the Tyrone mill resumed production in 2003 under local ownership. Specializing in recycled papers, it found new markets and prospered, and once again became a rail-served customer. At Lock Haven, the International Paper mill was demolished; but First Quality, a diversified consumer-paper products company serving private-label markets, opened a large manufacturing facility near the old mill and turned to the NBER for service. There was no happy ending for Corning. A consortium of local business leaders purchased the plant and razed part of it. Spur tracks were removed, some internal machinery was shipped to China, and efforts focused on repurposing the remainder of the property. So successful was the Nittany and Bald Eagle Railroad in meeting the challenge of losing three major shippers and securing new business that the trade magazine *Railway Age* named it Short Line Railroad of the Year in 2004. "How did NBER deal with the unexpected shortfall of nearly 8,000 carloads or 50 percent of its business?" the magazine's editors asked. By aggressively marketing its services and expanding operations in the new era of deregulation was the answer.[55]

The Nittany and Bald Eagle also gained a measure of popular attention, especially among rail enthusiasts. The railroad hosted passenger excursions in 1987 that were powered by rehabilitated Pennsylvania Railroad steam locomotive No. 1361, a K4s class 4-6-2 that for thirty years had been on static display at the Horseshoe Curve near Altoona. The K4s trips were in addition to seasonal service provided by the Bellefonte Historical Railroad, an all-volunteer organization of rail enthusiasts that was formed in 1984. The historical railroad acquired the use of two Budd Rail Diesel Cars to offer seasonal excursion trips over portions of JRA trackage operated by the NBER. And in 1999 and continuing at regular intervals, the Nittany and Bald Eagle hosted fifty-car Ringling Brothers Barnum and Bailey circus trains—a rare event for any short line railroad. The circus played the Bryce Jordan Center on the Penn State campus. The elephant cars were staged near the Corning plant, while the passenger cars laid over for the week in Bellefonte's Sunnyside yard.

In 2010, Richard Robey withdrew from day-to-day participation in the Nittany and Bald Eagle and the four other railroads that he operated under contract to the Joint Rail Authority. He retired altogether two years later, when the sale of those companies to members of his management team was finalized.

By freeing railroads from the heavy hand of government economic regulation (as distinguished from safety and environmental regulation), the Staggers Act led many trunk lines to conclude that it often made good sense to sell to short line and regional railroads trackage that in an earlier era would have been abandoned. The congressional mandate for Conrail to become profitable added urgency to CR's spin-off of marginal lines. At the same time, unprecedented levels of public funds became available for the new short lines and regionals, usually done in the name preserving or creating jobs, and fostering the public welfare—keeping more trucks off crowded highways, to cite only one benefit. The number of short line and regional railroads increased from about 220 in 1980 to nearly 600 in 2015, when those smaller roads accounted for about 30 percent of the nation's rail route-miles.[56]

As localized responses to forces that were reshaping American railroads, the Joint Rail Authority, the Nittany and Bald Eagle Railroad, and R. J. Corman Pennsylvania Lines demonstrated the continuing viability of parts of the branch line empires created generations earlier by the Pennsylvania and the New York Central. Those three entities also were concluding testimony in the case of how a relatively small patch of territory in central Pennsylvania, over the course of 150 years, served as a remarkable microcosm of the rise, decline, and limited resurgence of the railroad industry at large.

Notes

1. Pennsylvania Railroad Company, *Annual Report of the Board of Directors to the Stockholders* (Philadelphia: PRR, 1957).

2. *The Progress* (Clearfield), 19 July 1962.

3. *The Progress*, 6 November 1968; *Tyrone Daily Herald*, 4 November and 27 December 1968.

4. Ernest L. Clausing, "Perlman Encounters," *Keystone Chronicles* (Spring 2010): 15–19. *Chronicles* is an "occasional" publication of the Pennsylvania Railroad Technical & Historical Society Philadelphia chapter.

5. Penn Central Railroad Central Region General Order No. 316, effective 13 August 1969, Central Region G.O. No. 446, eff. 21 August 1972.

6. *The Progress*, 4 February 1960, 25 August 1967, 22 and 26 May 1970, 26 and 27 July 1971.

7. C. L. Marsh Jr. to H. J. Slavin, 29 October 1964, Merger Studies, Box 3, Manuscript Group 286.400, Pennsylvania State Archives.

8. PC Cen. Reg. G.O. No. 321, eff. 18 October 1969.

9. Penn Central Coal and Coke Department, Clearfield, PA, Mine Index, November 1975, typescript, 25, in author's collection.

10. PC Cen. Reg. G.O. No. 442 and 446, respectively.

11. Tonnages are documented in Pennsylvania Department of Mines and Minerals *Annual Reports*. See also coal executive Alan Walker's two-part feature, "Despite Problems and Changes . . . Coal Industry Future Is Bright," *The Progress*, 1 October and 8 October 1966.

12. *Rail Service in the Midwest and Northeast Region: A Report*, vol. 2, part 1, Zone 74 (Washington, DC: Department of Transportation, 1974).

13. P. S. Lewis, "The Transportation Department's Most Important Responsibility," *Reading–Jersey Central Magazine*, May 1937, 3, 5–6; Bert Pennypacker, "Newberry Fast Freight," *Bee Line*, no. 4 (2006): 15–23.

14. PC Central Region employees timetable No. 1, 28 April 1968; PC Through-Freight Schedules, 15 March 1969 and 1 June 1974; *Penn Central Post*, August–September 1972; PC Cen. Reg. G.O. No. 536, 1 February 1973.

15. Longtime Mifflinburg resident Eugene Hoffman, in a 9 May 2010 email to Michael Bezilla, stated that he witnessed the last train operated between Mifflinburg and Coburn on 9 May 1968. PC Cen. Reg. G.O. No. 106 indicates the Mifflinburg–Coburn section was officially taken out of service effective 1 July 1968.

16. *Centre Daily Times* (State College), 22 August 1968, 3 March 1970, 6 June 1972; *Sunbury Daily Item*, 25 February 1970, 3 June 1971; *Union County Journal* (Lewisburg), 2 May 1971.

17. Mainquist quoted in *Centre Democrat* (Bellefonte), 1 February 1973. See also *Altoona Mirror*, 16 January and 7 September 1973.

18. Tennyson quoted in *Centre Democrat*, 1 February 1973.

19. *Centre Daily Times*, 6 September 1973; *Altoona Mirror*, 7 September 1973.

20. *Traffic World*, 14 May 1973; *Trains*, August 1972, 16–17.

21. Michael Bezilla and Jack Rudnicki interview with retired BFC vice president and general manager Harold Ammerman, Bellefonte, PA, 12 April 1986; *Centre Daily Times*, 26 August 1974.

22. *Final System Plan for Restructuring Railroads in the Northeast and Midwest Region*, vol. 2 (Washington: United States Railway Association, 26 July 1975).

23. Ammerman interview; Bezilla telephone interview with former BFC general manager Jim Miller, 18 August 2005. See also George McClellan daybooks for the Penn Central years in Subgroup A, Series 3, Bellefonte Central Railroad Records, HCLA 1434, Pennsylvania State University Special Collections Library, for details of PC reductions in service.

24. McClellan to Robert Walker, 3 April 1970, Subgroup A, Series 3, BFC Records.

25. L. Stanley Crane, *Rise from the Wreckage: A Brief History of Conrail* (New York: Newcomen Society of the United States, 1988) is an address Crane gave as he neared the end of his eight years as Conrail's chairman and CEO.

26. Jeffrey Feldmeier interview with Bill Morgan, partner in Johnson and Morgan Coal Company, Snow Shoe, PA, 20 October 2005; Pennsylvania Department of Environmental Resources, *Annual Report on Mining Activities* (Harrisburg: Department of Environmental Resources, 1985), 228.

27. Lutz quoted in *Centre Daily Times*, 27 December 1985. See also *The Progress*, 27 and 28 December 1985 and 25 January 1986. In a move away from previous nomenclature, CR designated the Snow Shoe Secondary the Snow Shoe Industrial Track.

28. *Centre Daily Times*, 7 December 1989.

29. CR Harrisburg Division G.O. 401 eff. 21 April 1991; Jeffrey Feldmeier interview with Roger Mayhew, Clearfield, PA, 19 April 2011.

30. *Centre Daily Times*, 11 August 1993; *Traffic World*, 22 November 1993; Consolidated Rail Corporation, Abandonment Exemption, in Clearfield and Centre Counties, PA, ICC Docket No. AB-167 (Sub-No. 1146X), copy in author's collection.

31. Pennsylvania Department of Environmental Resources, *Annual Report on Mining Activities* (Harrisburg, Department of Environmental Resources, 1983), 95, 137, 187, 200.

32. Michael Bezilla interview with Tim Potts, general manager of R. J. Corman Pennsylvania Lines, Clearfield, PA, 12 December 2012.

33. CR Harrisburg Division G.O. 401, eff. 21 April 1991. CR Allegheny Division Bituminous Mines list and map, February 1989, copy in author's collection.

34. *The Progress*, 27 June 1991.

35. Jim Bacon, "The Clearfield Chronicles," *Railfan and Railroad* (March 2001): 42–49; Potts interview.

36. *Construction Equipment Guide*, 27 November 1999, contains a detailed inventory of Power's equipment to be liquidated at auction.

37. Surface Transportation Board, Decision and Notice of Interim Trail Use or Abandonment, STB Docket No. AB-491 (Sub-No. 1X), 3 April 2003, copy in author's collection.

38. Potts interview.

39. *The Progress*, 14 September 2012; Surface Transportation Board news release, 21 May 2012, "Surface Transportation Board Authorizes First of Its Kind Rail Line in Pa."

40. *New Castle News*, 14 June 1977, is an AP story that circulated statewide.

41. Booz-Allen & Hamilton Inc., "Bellefonte Secondary System Lines: Potential for Short Line Operation," a report prepared for the SEDA-Council of Governments, 1983, typescript, 2–5; Miller interview.

42. Booz-Allen & Hamilton Inc., "Bellefonte Secondary System Lines," 5–7.

43. *Centre Daily Times*, 17 April 1983; Booz-Allen & Hamilton Inc., "Bellefonte Secondary System Lines," 3.

44. *Centre Daily Times*, 17 April 1983.

45. Allen Bubb, *SEDA-COG Joint Rail Authority: Preserving Rail Freight in Central Pennsylvania for 30 Years, 1983–2013* (Lewisburg: SEDA-COG Joint Rail Authority, 2013). See also *Centre Daily Times*, 5 August 1984 and 20 November 1985.

46. *Centre Daily Times*, 11 May 1984.

47. *Centre Daily Times*, 5 June 2000.

48. *Centre Daily Times*, 5 August 1984.

49. *Centre Daily Times*, 7 November 1988; Michael Bezilla interview with Leonard Shilling, Bellefonte, PA, 27 June 2002; Dan Cupper, "Nurturing a Short Line Dick Robey's Way," *Modern Railroads*, Short Lines and Regionals edition (July–August 1990): 31–34.

50. *Lock Haven Express*, 21 August 1987; *Centre Daily Times*, 29 February, 26 October, and 1 December 1988.

51. Bubb, *Joint Rail Authority*, 8–9,14; "Short-Haul Moves Equal Long-Term Successes," *Railway Age*, April 2004, 23–25.

52. *Centre Daily Times*, 5 June 2000.

53. Randy Pletcher, vice president of marketing and sales, Graymont (PA) Inc., "30 Years of Mineral Shipments on the NBER," speech given at Northeast Association of Rail Shippers Fall Conference, State College, PA, 1 October 2014; *Centre Daily Times*, 22 February 1987, 5 June 1994, 15 October 2006; *Industrial Specialties News*, 21 May and 24 September 2001.

54. *Centre Daily Times*, 26 April 1999; Bubb, *Joint Rail Authority*, 10.

55. "Short-Haul Moves Equal Long-Term Successes," 23–25.

56. W. Bruce Allen, Michael Sussman, and Drew Miller, "Regional and Short Line Railroads in the United States," *Transportation Quarterly* (Fall 2002): 77–113. Up-to-date information is available at the American Short Line and Regional Railroad Association's website, www.aslrra.org.

Maps

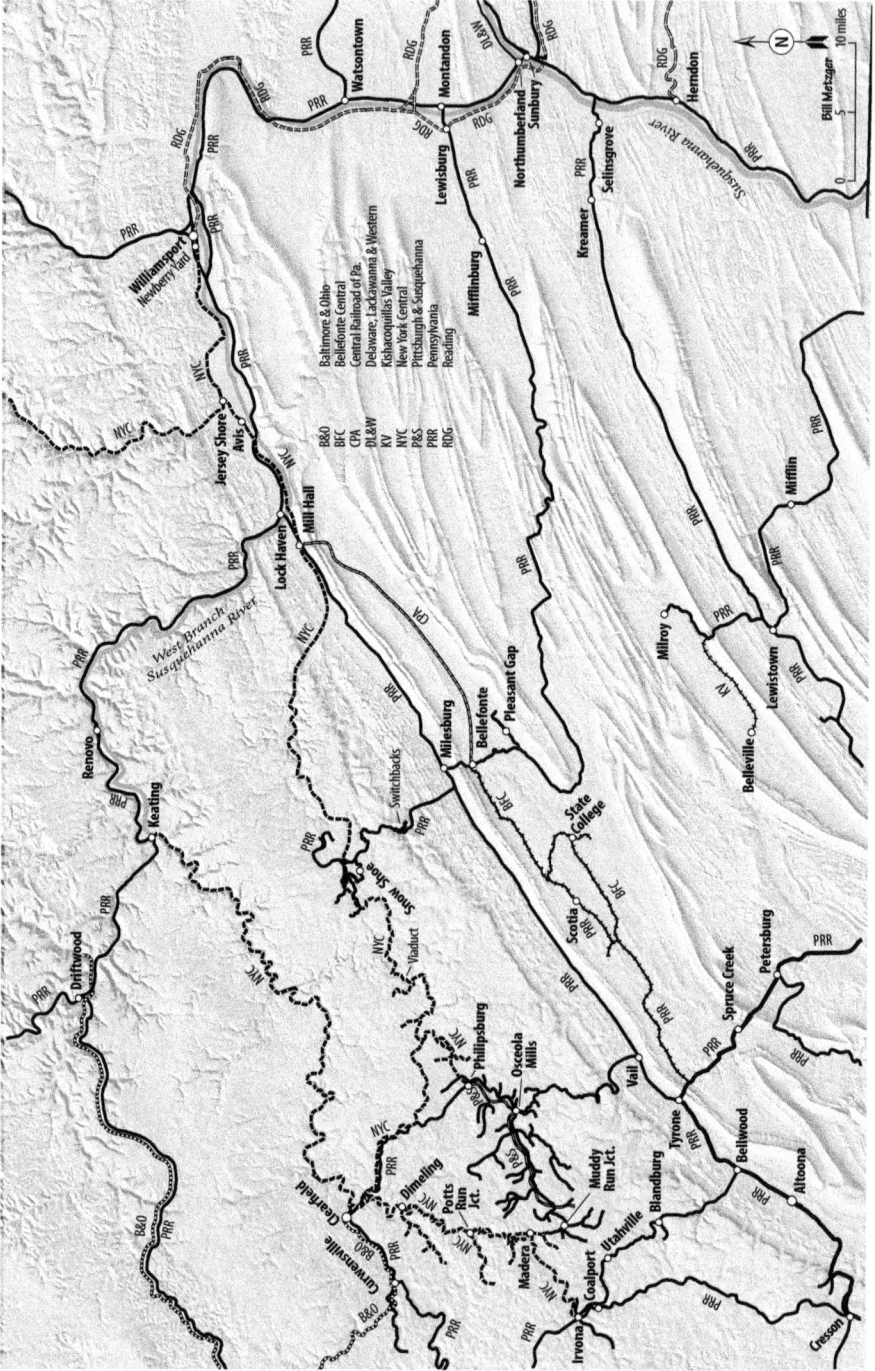

Central Pennsylvania Railroads (not all lines shown)

Upper Moshannon Valley (not all lines shown)

B&O   Baltimore & Ohio
BFC   Bellefonte Central
NYC   New York Central
P&S   Pittsburgh & Susquehanna
PRR   Pennsylvania

N

Bill Metzger

0   2   4 miles

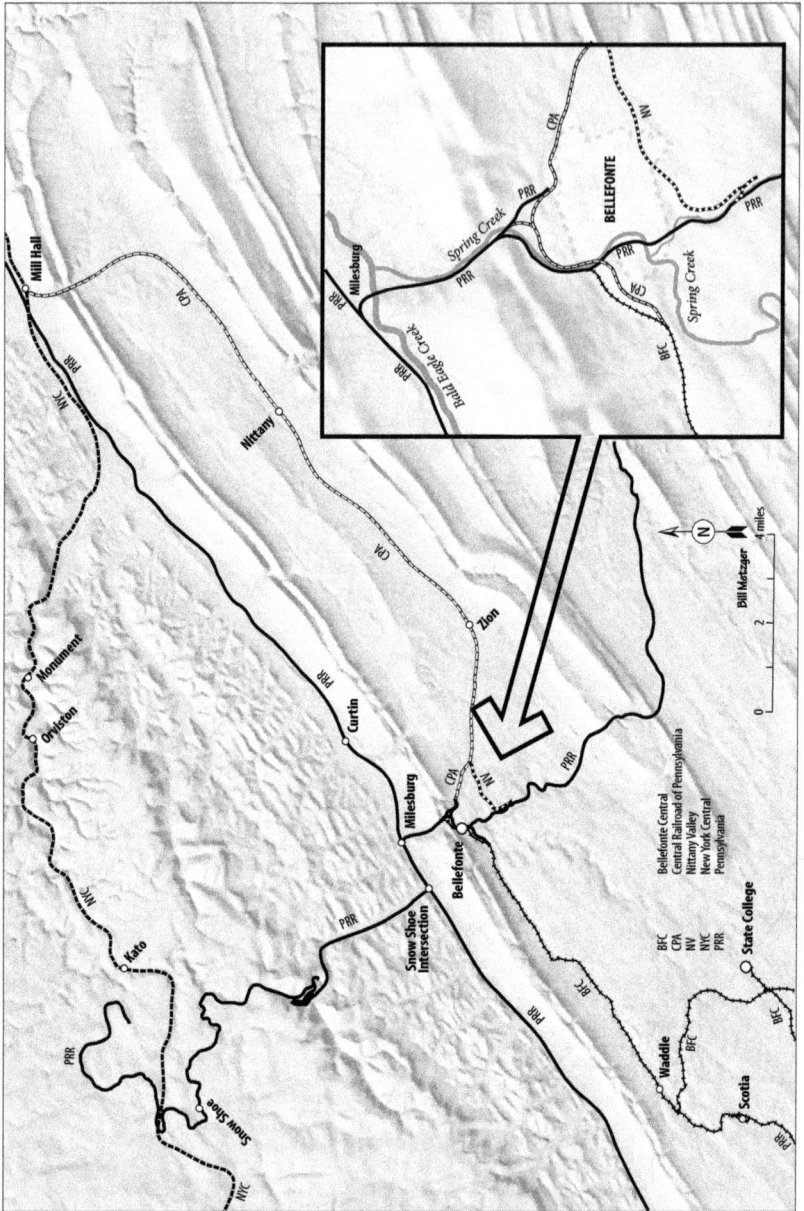

Bellefonte Area (not all lines shown)

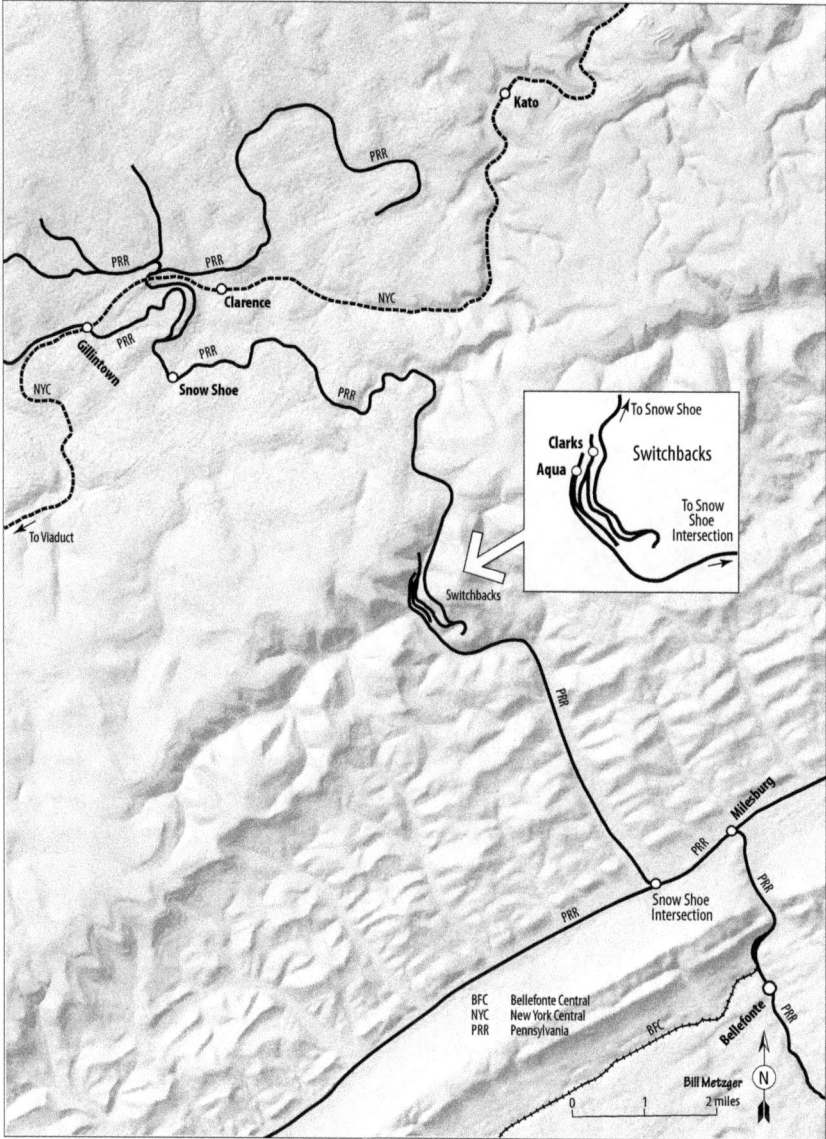

Snow Shoe Area (not all lines shown)

Index

Page numbers in *italics* refer to illustrations.

Miller's Spring trestle, 12–14, 99, 219
Mill Hall, PA, 166
Millheim, 62
mines. *See* coal mines; Bell mine; Nigh
Bank; Scotia; Taylor Bank
Monitor (locomotive), 9
Montandon, PA, 58, 69–70
Montandon Secondary Track, 311–12,
327, 348n15. *See also* Bellefonte Branch
Montandon tower, 311
Montgomery, James E., 21–22, 24–25, 94
Monument, 198–200, *199*, 203, 276–77
Morgan, Edwin D., 23
Morgan, Hale and Co., 23, 27
Morgan, J. Pierpont, 134. *See also* J. P.
Morgan and Co.
Morris, Alexander G., 158–59, 166–67,
169–70, 177, 195, 302
Morris, Wistar, 4, 6, 15, 63
Morris Branch, 167, 196
Morrisdale Coal Co., 32, 91, 133
Morrison, Bare, Cass and Co., 102
Moshannon (locomotive), 9
Moshannon and Clearfield Branch, 334
Moshannon Branch, 31–32, 85, 92, 127,
230–31, 260–61, 264, 268, 272, 325,
334–35
Moshannon Central Railroad, 193–94
Moshannon coal. *See* coal seams: Lower
Freeport
Moshannon Coal and Lumber Co., 9, 15
Moshannon Lumber Co., 201
Moshannon Mining Co., 193–94
Moshannon Railroad, 9, 13, 15
Mount Eagle cut-off, 176, 189–90, 293, 300
Murphy, Paddy, 81
Murphy & Allison, 12

National Gypsum Co., 304–9, 330–31, 339
Nature Conservancy, 327
Neidigh Quarries, 312
Newberry yard, 281, 326
New York, West Shore, and Buffalo Rail-
road, 133–34
New York Central Railroad: absorbs

Beech Creek Railroad as operating
company, 141–42; builds water-
level bypass of Beech Creek District,
205–7; declines purchase of Central
Railroad of Pennsylvania, 175; dis-
continues passenger service in Beech
Creek District, 228–31; leases Beech
Creek Railroad, 138; merger with
Pennsylvania Railroad, 320–21, 326;
operations in Beech Creek District,
279–84; organized, 114–15; possible
extension into Nittany Valley, 75–76,
313–14; studies Beech Creek Railroad
as part of Chicago-Philadelphia trunk
line, 139, 207–8, 273–75; willingness to
sell Beech Creek properties, 134–35
New York State Electric and Gas, 326
Nigh Bank, 166, 173, 176
Nittany and Bald Eagle Railroad
(NBER), 341, 342, 344–47
Nittany Furnace, 98, 173–74, *173*
Nittany Iron Works, 172, 176
Nittany Light, Heat, and Power Co., 154
Nittany Valley and Southwestern Rail-
road, 149
Nittany Valley Junction, 166
Nittany Valley Railroad, 107, 146, 163–
64, 166, 168, 170, 173–74, 176, 178
No. 1 Contracting Corp., 300–301
Nolan, Ed, 14
Nolan, Jerry, 104–5
Noll, William H., 196
Norfolk and Western Railway, 211
Norfolk Southern Railway, 344
Northeast Rail Service Act, 332, 339–40
Northern Central Railway, 55, 100
Northern Counties Coal Co., 334
North Shore Railroad, 341
Northumberland yard, 187–88, 209, 327
Nuttall, John, 27–28, 31–32
Nuttallville, 27–28
Nutting, James, 6

Ophir Branch, 205, 279, 324, 333–34
Orvis, Ellis L., 198–200

Thomas, William A., 4, 7, 10, 12, 15, 42
Thompson, Moses, 42, 44, 51, 61, 63–65, 68, 147
Thomson, J. Edgar, 3, 21–23, 28, 31, 34, 46–48, 61, 325
Todd Branch, 205
tonnage tax, 47
Tow Hill, 66
Trainphone, 297
Trout Run Branch, 264–65, 325
Trout Unlimited, 327
Truman, Harry S, 243
Twombly, Hamilton, 134–35
Tyrone, PA, 25, 30, 49, 50–51, 61, 65, 74, 82, 106
Tyrone and Clearfield Railroad: absorbed by Clearfield and Cambria Railway, 97; busiest branchline, 91; compared with Beech Creek Railroad, 132; construction, 21–30, 36; leader in bituminous coal traffic, 84; locomotive coal consumption, 93; operations on, 92–94; passenger service criticized, 221; Pennsylvania Railroad intervention in, 25, 28, 34–35, 51; revenue sources, 31–32, 35, 37; rights over Bald Eagle Valley Railroad, 48
Tyrone and Lock Haven Railroad, 5, 10, 25–26, 41–46
Tyrone Division, 79–80, 84, 93, 109, 186, 260, 292–93

Underwood, William H., 42, 45–46
Union Car Co., 141
Unionville, 42
unit coal trains, 269–72
United Collieries, 127–28
United Mine Workers of America, 323–24
University Inn, 152
University of Pennsylvania, 236
University of Pittsburgh, 236, 241
US Mail. See railway post office (RPO); highway post office (HPO)
US Military Academy, 241

US Railway Association (USRA), 329, 331–32

Vail, PA, 23, 25, 48, 81, 83, 189, 321–22
Valentine, Robert, 149, 163–65
Valentine Formation, 158–59, 196, 302
Valentine Iron Works, 163, 168–72
Valentines and Thomas, 4, 6, 52, 163
Valley View Lime Co., 294
Vanderbilt, Cornelius, 114–15
Vanderbilt, Cornelius, II, 121, 125
Vanderbilt, William H., 115–16, 121, 125, 133–34
Vanderbilt, William K., 125, 137, 208
Vandyke and Co., 62, 68
Viaduct, PA, 122–23, 129, 209, 211–12, 278, 281–82, 282, 333
Virginia Electric Power Co., 326

Wagoner, Claude, 330
Waite, Earl, 97
Walker, Eric, 259–60
Walker, John, 159
Walker, Scott, 105
Walker Brothers mill, 37
Wallace, William A., 34–36, 116–17, 121, 124, 131–32, 138, 149
Wallace Run Lumber Co., 102
Wallaceton (locomotive), 124
Wallaceton, PA, 321, 338
Warford, A. B. (civil engineer), 59, 62
Warner Co., 303–6, 308–10, 313, 339, 345
Warriors Mark, PA, 66, 233
Webb, Walter, 155
Welles, Gideon, 27, 30
Wesley, Charles, 316–17
West Branch and Susquehanna Canal, 10
West Branch Valley Railroad, 206. *See also* River Line
Westcott, Thomas, 23, 25
Western Maryland Railway, 76, 314
Western Union, 82, 104
Westinghouse, George, 93
West Penn Power Co., 258, 309

MICHAEL BEZILLA is the author or coauthor of seven books, four of them works of railroad history, and has contributed more than twenty-five articles about railroads to scholarly and rail enthusiast publications. He retired from Penn State University, where he received a doctorate in the history of technology, after a thirty-six-year career in institutional advancement.

LUTHER GETTE grew up in Philipsburg, Pennsylvania, a hotspot for both the Pennsylvania and the New York Central railroads. Fascinated early on with NYC and PRR steam power, he spent many years riding freight trains across the USA. Now living back in his hometown, he serves as curator of the Philipsburg Historical Foundation.

www.ingramcontent.com/pod-product-compliance
Lightning Source LLC
Chambersburg PA
CBHW071009140426
42814CB00004BA/169